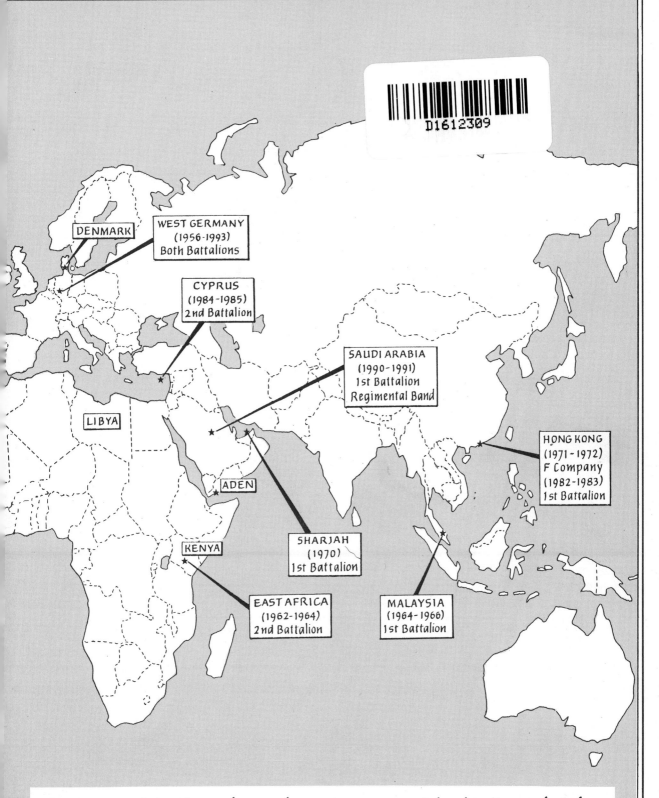

DENMARK

WEST GERMANY
(1956-1993)
Both Battalions

CYPRUS
(1984-1985)
2nd Battalion

SAUDI ARABIA
(1990-1991)
1st Battalion
Regimental Band

HONG KONG
(1971-1972)
F Company
(1982-1983)
1st Battalion

LIBYA

ADEN

SHARJAH
(1970)
1st Battalion

KENYA

EAST AFRICA
(1962-1964)
2nd Battalion

MALAYSIA
(1964-1966)
1st Battalion

Major Operational Deployments outside the British Isles
1956 to 1993

(also shown are those locations where battalions trained overseas or participated in major
exercises, for example WAINWRIGHT)

AMONG FRIENDS

The Queen's Guard, provided by the 2nd Battalion, leaves the Forecourt of Buckingham Palace in the summer of 1965. 2nd Lieutenant Peter Harvey is carrying the Regimental Colour and CSM Gifford is the Senior Sergeant of the St James's Palace Detachment.

AMONG FRIENDS
The Scots Guards 1956–1993

by

MURRAY NAYLOR

LEO COOPER

LONDON

First published in Great Britain in hardback in 1995 by
LEO COOPER
190 Shaftesbury Avenue, London WC2H 8JL
an imprint of
Pen & Sword Books Ltd,
47 Church Street,
Barnsley, South Yorkshire S70 2AS

© DM Naylor, 1995

A CIP record for this book is available from the British Library

ISBN 0 85052 455 5

Typeset by CentraCet Limited, Cambridge
Printed in England by
Redwood Books,
Trowbridge, Wiltshire

This History is dedicated
by Kind Permission,
to
Her Royal Highness
PRINCESS ALICE,
Duchess of Gloucester,
whose late husband
His Royal Highness
PRINCE HENRY,
served as 25th Colonel
Scots Guards 1937 to 1974.

CONTENTS

As Colonel of Her Majesty's Scots Guards, I am delighted to introduce this latest volume of the History of the Regiment, which covers the period from 1956 to 1993. Events of considerable significance have occurred during the 38 years since publication of the previous volume and the Regiment has undoubtedly seen as wide a range of operations and tasks as any in the British Army.

The demands placed upon the Regiment have been many and varied. Wherever they have served, Scots Guardsmen have always shown professionalism, courage and resilience, and the ability to adapt to new methods and tactics. I have no doubt that as the Army approaches the end of the century, fresh challenges will arise to test the Regiment both at home and abroad. I am equally certain that the Scots Guards will respond to such challenges as they always do, with determination, commonsense and good humour, thereby continuing to distinguish themselves as one of the Nation's foremost Regiments.

I congratulate General Murray Naylor on producing such an informative and readable account and I commend this book to all those who have an interest in the Scots Guards, whether serving or retired.

HRH The Duke of Kent, KG
Colonel, Scots Guards

FOREWORD

by

GENERAL SIR MICHAEL GOW, GCB DL

Three Histories of the Regiment have been officially commissioned: The first was published in 1925 by John Murray and entitled 'The Scots Guards in the Great War' and was the work of three successive authors; Wilfred Ewart was the initial writer but was accidentally killed in Mexico City on New Year's Eve 1922. Loraine Petre then took it on but died in May 1925, and it was left to Major General Sir Cecil Lowther to complete what should have been a book of historical interest and importance. The result, however, was sadly disappointing. In September 1934 'The History of the Scots Guards from the Creation of The Regiment to the Eve of the Great War' was published in two volumes by Chatto & Windus, written by Major General Sir Frederick Maurice. In his Foreword His Royal Highness the Duke of York, 24th Colonel, said that the story of our Regiment 'is now related for the first time'.

The story during the period 1919 to 1955 was published by William Clowes & Sons in 1956, and Captain Michael Trappes-Lomax originally undertook the task but handed the partly completed work to Major (now Major General Sir) John Swinton who, despite the fact that he was in Australia, continued it. Early in 1954 David Erskine completed this outstanding and most readable account. In this instance the change of authors in no way marred the book.

Major General Murray Naylor is the sole writer of this History of the Regiment from 1956 to 1993, and it covers, of course, the 350th Anniversary of our foundation. His material has been deeply researched, and the story of our operational and ceremonial commitments worldwide is presented in detail and in a very readable way. Unlike many military histories this author has not concentrated solely on our achievements but also on some of our failures and weaknesses, and this, in my judgement, adds greatly to the importance of the book not only for Guardsmen, and Scots Guardsmen in particular, but for a wider audience.

I have served in five battalions of the Regiment, and the changes that have taken place in the complexity and sophistication of weapons and equipment, and the professionalism of all ranks during those years and since have been remarkable. With altered concepts of defence further changes of even greater significance will undoubtedly take place and in the very near future. In order to match these, as General Naylor emphasises, it is imperative that the 'Ethos' of the Scots Guards which, together with that of the rest of the Household Division, is the envy of the British Army and many others, must be preserved. This book clearly explains this 'Ethos' in peace and war, in our twin ceremonial and operational roles in our Service to our Sovereign.

AUTHOR'S NOTE

Researching and writing this history has given me enormous pleasure. The task which was set me has been both rewarding and stimulating. Rewarding because it has brought me into contact with many old friends of whom I have seen all too little in recent years; stimulating because any study of an assembly of people such as a regiment which thrives or fades depending upon the skills and discernment of those responsible for its affairs at any given moment, must reward anyone who seeks to explore its history. In recording what the Regiment experienced and achieved during the years between 1956 and 1993 I have tried to balance factual reporting with a light touch in order to provide readers with an account which is both accurate and sensitive. In addition I hope that what I have written will allow all who served in the Scots Guards during the thirty-eight years in question to be able to relate to events and to identify with the successes and failures which have always been part of life in the Armed Services.

Many Scots Guardsmen, both serving and retired, have helped me in my work as have a number of other people who have had only passing contact with the Regiment. They are too numerous to thank individually but that in no way diminishes their contribution and I hope that they will all accept my gratitude for their assistance. However, the team at Regimental Headquarters most certainly deserve special mention since without their support and encouragement my work would not have been possible of fulfilment. I am indebted to Brigadier Kim Ross, the Regimental Lieutenant Colonel throughout the last two years, to the two Regimental Adjutants of the same period, Major Robin Whyte and Major Edward Woods, and all those who have worked for them at Wellington Barracks, for their tolerant good humour and unfailing willingness to help. I am also greatly indebted to Major Peter Le Marchand for all the work which he has undertaken in order to compile the various appendices to this book. His was an intricate and laborious task and errors, should there be any, will not have arisen through lack of endeavour on his account. However, two members of the Headquarters team deserve special mention for their loyal and generous support at all times: Sergeant Greenshields who will run the General office until April of this year and Mrs Jan Rawlings who has worked at Regimental Headquarters since 1979 and who typed the entire manuscript several times without complaint. Mrs Rawlings has arguably made the greatest contribution of all. Finally I wish to record the help which I received from Lieutenant Colonel Campbell Gordon and Mr Alan Shutt who read my draft before it was submitted to the publishers. Both offered relevant and constructive comments for which I am grateful.

I consider myself extremely fortunate to have been able to spend most of my professional life in a regiment such as the Scots Guards and I believe myself to have been doubly privileged to have been entrusted with the task of writing this History. Whenever I look back over all the years I have served within the Scots Guards family I always find myself treasuring countless happy memories of people and events. I also find myself silently thanking those alongside whom I served for their friendship, understanding and guidance. It may be invidious to name some but not others, but Campbell Graham, Sergeant Major when I was Adjutant of the 2nd Battalion in 1964, Jim Bunton, the Sergeant Major when I later commanded the same battalion in 1977 and David Torrance and Syd Carnegie, respectively the Company Sergeant Majors of Right Flank in the 1st Battalion in 1968 and of Right Flank in the 2nd Battalion in 1973 when I commanded those two companies, all occupy a special place in my affections. If any one group within the Regiment can claim to have helped lay the foundations for this book it must be them because they taught me most of what I know about Scots Guardsmen.

Murray Naylor
North Yorkshire
March 1995

ILLUSTRATIONS

ACKNOWLEDGEMENTS

The author is indebted to those who have given permission for photographs in their possession, to be reproduced in this book. Plates 7, 9, 10 and 33, are reproduced by kind permission of the Imperial War Museum; Plates 23, 24, 30, 31, 41 and 42 by kind permission of *Soldier Magazine*. Plate 54 was provided by Ciaran Donnelly. In addition a number of Scots Guardsmen have contributed photographs; principal among them are Lieutenant Colonel M. B. Scott, Lieutenant Colonel J. J. Cargill and Major E. A. Woods while Mr Dadley (formerly a Colour Sergeant in the Regiment) has undertaken considerable work reproducing photographs impossible of removal from books and magazines. I am most grateful to them all.

LIST OF MAPS

GLOSSARY OF ABBREVIATIONS
AND TERMS

A number of military abbreviations and terms have been used in this book and they are listed below or at the appropriate point in the text, or both. A wish to avoid tedious repetition has been the guiding principle in deciding what should or should not be abbreviated. No abbreviation should present the reader with any difficulty.

Military ranks and some appointments have been abbreviated using accepted military convention, for example: NCO for Non Commissioned Officer and CSM for Company Sergeant Major, etc. In accordance with regimental custom the senior Warrant Officer within a battalion, the Regimental Sergeant Major, is throughout referred to as the Sergeant Major. For those unfamiliar with terminology used in the Scots Guards, the flank companies of both battalions are referred to as Right Flank and Left Flank respectively, in accordance with regimental custom.

General abbreviations used throughout:

AMF(L) – Allied Command Europe Mobile Force (Land).

APC – Armoured Personnel Carrier.

BAOR – British Army of the Rhine.

BCR – Battle Casualty Replacement.

CPX – Command Post Exercise. (Involves formation, unit and sub-unit headquarters only).

FV 432 – Infantry APC.

GKN – Guest, Keen and Nettlefold (Manufacturers of the Warrior Infantry Fighting Vehicle).

GPMG – General Purpose Machine Gun.

GOC – General Officer Commanding.

LCU – Landing Craft (Utility). Used during the Falklands War.

LMG – Light Machine Gun.

R and R – Rest and Recuperation. A period of a few days granted to those undertaking an emergency, unaccompanied operational tour.
RCT – Royal Corps of Transport.
SBA – Sovereign Base Area (in Cyprus).
UKLF – United Kingdom Land Forces.
UN – United Nations.
UNFICYP – United Nations Force in Cyprus.

Abbreviations used in Chapter 3 – 'Malaysia and Borneo':

SEATO – South East Treaty Organization.
TAG – Tawau Assault Group (Sabah).

Abbreviations used in Chapter 5 – 'Sharjah':

SAF – Sultan of Muscat's Armed Forces.
OMEX – Oman Exercise (normally a patrol exercise in the *Jebel Akhdar*).

Abbreviations applicable to Northern Ireland and used in all relevant chapters.

RUC – Royal Ulster Constabulary.
IRA – Irish Republican Army.
TAOR – Tactical Area of Responsibility (applies only at battalion level).
ATO – Ammunition Technical Officer (usually an officer or senior NCO in the Royal Army Ordnance Corps).
UDR – Ulster Defence Regiment.
ASU – Active Service Unit of the IRA.
RVH – Royal Victoria Hospital, Belfast.
'aggro' – a term used to describe low level public aggravation and misbehaviour.
'roulement' – a term used to describe a short term unaccompanied tour of operational duty. Originally four months, more recently such tours have tended to last up to six months or longer.

CHAPTER ONE

THE EARLY YEARS

1st Battalion: London-Lydd-Windsor-Hubblerath-Gravesend
2nd Battalion: Hubblerath-London-Shorncliffe-Tidworth-London

Eleven years after the end of the Second World War both battalions of the *1956* Regiment found themselves stationed in Europe, the 1st Battalion at Wellington Barracks in London and the 2nd Battalion at Llanelli Barracks, Hubblerath in West Germany. Like numerous other units of the British Army both battalions had seen overseas service since the end of the war. In the case of the 1st Battalion during the last years of Britain's occupation of the Canal Zone which was eventually evacuated in 1955, while the 2nd Battalion had carried out a most successful tour in Malaya during that longest of all Internal Security campaigns, waged against a Communist-inspired insurgency between 1948 and 1960. Indeed the years since 1945 had seen little or no respite for the British Army which in a short space of time had been involved in the transfer of power in India, attempts to mediate between Arab and Jew in Palestine, a full scale war in Korea and the defeat of the Mau Mau rebellion in Kenya. Numerous other brushfire insurrections had flared up during the same period and one which began in 1955, an uprising by Greek Cypriot EOKA terrorists determined upon union with Greece, was destined to plague the British Army for many years to come. All these commitments, and a parallel requirement to maintain a sizeable standing force in West Germany, placed an army still recovering from nearly six years of global conflict under enormous pressure as the orders went out from Whitehall to begin the process of handing over power in the colonies to legitimate successors at a pace of Britain's choosing and in an ordered manner. Inevitably this led to many confrontations between the Nation's Security Forces and those thirsting to take control of their own destiny at the earliest opportunity. Meanwhile post-war National Service was still in force, not being discontinued until 1959.

The 1st Battalion had returned to London from Egypt in January 1955 under *1st Battalion* the command of Lieutenant Colonel Tommy Bulkeley. Relieved to be home after the tedium and frustration of life guarding military installations in the vicinity of the Suez Canal, the battalion soon settled into its first tour of public duties since 1940. High standards of drill and turnout were quickly achieved,

1

thanks mainly to the direction given by the Adjutant, Captain Neil Ramsay, and RSM Thomson, although a major disappointment occurred when the 1955 Queen's Birthday Parade was cancelled owing to a railway strike. It was not surprising that the battalion should so quickly pick up the theme of its new role since the standards of discipline and training so painstakingly inculcated in Egypt by successive Commanding Officers and which caused General Festing, a former Commander British Troops Egypt, to remark to a member of the Regiment that the battalion had been the best trained in the Middle East during his time in command, were easily transferable to the more restrictive yet equally demanding role of a ceremonial battalion in London.

1956 saw the battalion move from London to join Britain's Strategic Reserve. Before leaving the capital the battalion undertook a heavy round of public duties, taking part on the Queen's Birthday Parade with Numbers Three and Four Guards while in April Old Colours were laid up in St Mungo's Cathedral in Glasgow. On the latter occasion Major Nigel Bosville Macdonald commanded the battalion detachment while Major George Nickerson brought over a party of thirty volunteers from the 2nd Battalion in Germany. The Colours were handed over for safe keeping by Colonel Bulkeley to the Minister of St Mungo's, Dr Neville Davidson, in the presence of the Colonel, His Royal Highness The Duke of Gloucester, after which a Memorial Window, dedicated to the memory of all Scots Guardsmen who had given their lives to their country over the previous three hundred years, was unveiled. The battalion's final act before leaving London was to assist in organizing and running a parade for holders of the Victoria Cross in Hyde Park in the presence of Her Majesty The Queen; a Guard of Honour commanded by Major John Swinton and with the Queen's Colour carried by 2nd Lieutenant Michael Delmar-Morgan was mounted in Hyde Park. By all accounts it was a marvellous occasion with over three hundred holders of the decoration on parade, the battalion having played an important part in making the day a success.

Lydd

There could hardly be a greater contrast between Wellington Barracks and Lee-Metford Camp at Lydd in Kent. The latter remains to this day much as it was when the battalion moved there at the end of July, 1956: single storey huts of a rudimentary nature interspersed with some larger brick buildings standing only a short distance from the shingle beach a few miles to the north of Dungeness Point and close to the modern day nuclear power station of the same name. By 2 August the move was completed when Right Flank and C Company, both of which had opted to march from Maidstone, arrived in camp having spent two days on the road stopping overnight in farmers' barns and being well entertained by local villages. The battalion was now under command of 1st Guards Brigade in 3rd Division, the latter formation still commanded by Major General Jack Churcher whom the battalion had last seen in the Canal Zone when he had been its Divisional Commander. No sooner had the battalion unpacked and started to settle in than, along with other units in the Strategic Reserve, it was warned for possible deployment to the Middle East in support of

2

operations to re-occupy the Suez Canal recently nationalized by President Nasser of Egypt. The British Government, in concert with its French and Israeli allies, had declared its intention of wresting the canal from Nasser in order to hand it over to the United Nations to be run as an international waterway of strategic importance to the West. Thus began a process of military planning, preparation and deployment which led ultimately to the curtailment of the invasion operation before it had achieved its main objectives and the consequent humbling of Britain and France before the international community.

Meanwhile at Lydd the battalion was ordered to move to Higher Establishment and to absorb over 350 reservists, many of whom had served with the battalion in the Canal Zone. The process of assimilating the reservists went remarkably smoothly, thanks mainly to the way in which the battalion administrative team led by the Adjutant, Captain Lord Napier and Ettrick, the Quartermaster, Major Donald Fraser, and RSM Whyte, who had succeeded RSM Thomson in April, set about their task. Once men had been issued with their equipment they were allocated to companies, the battalion absorbing such a large influx by placing some reservists in a 'reserve' platoon in each of the three regular rifle companies and Support Company and by re-forming B Company, the latter comprised entirely of reservists and commanded by Major Nicholas Rivett-Carnac, himself recalled to the Colours. Right Flank's platoon was composed almost totally of Scottish policemen. In training the battalion for its role Colonel Bulkeley placed great emphasis upon shooting, night training and battle procedure with the hard shingle beaches around Lydd being used to practise a variety of assault landing and other operations. Standards achieved generally exceeded expectations and skills not exercised since the Canal Zone were once again perfected.

While the battalion trained for war, plans were also made to move its freight *Suez* and vehicles to the Middle East. A group comprising those essential vehicles and weapons required for the first forty-eight hours of an operation was allocated a Landing Ship (Tank) and at the duly appointed hour moved to Liverpool and embarked. After a short time at sea they were unloaded at Southampton and returned to Lydd. A few weeks later the group again embarked but never left port. A second group containing the battalion's follow-up heavy equipment was despatched to Barry Docks and, despite the best efforts of the dockers to pilfer vehicles and stores, finally set sail more or less intact in two merchant vessels. Lieutenant David Steuart-Menzies, the Assistant Transport Officer, sailed aboard the RMS *Paraguay*, eventually reaching Malta before being turned back, while the SS *Brookhurst*, being somewhat slower, only got as far as Gibraltar.

Within the battalion those recalled fitted in quickly and smoothly to a routine which the majority knew so well; most seemed glad of the chance to take part in an operation which they assumed was bound to take place, while a number of those who had served in Egypt relished any possible opportunity to settle scores with those who had in the past made life so miserable for them! However, after two months of hard training but with little firm information as to what

3

exactly the future might bring, a change in attitude took place and there were instances of some reservists refusing to obey orders. These were not isolated occurrences happening only within the Scots Guards but materialized throughout the Division and were probably orchestrated from outside the Army; firm handling within the battalion, including a warning from the Commanding Officer that the would-be mutineers were sailing close to the wind, ensured that the protest died as quickly as it arose. In any event the ill-fated operation to secure the Suez Canal was mounted soon afterwards without the participation of units based in Britain, only for the invasion forces to be withdrawn after a few days in the face of world-wide condemnation of the combined Anglo-French action. Following this it was only a matter of time before it was announced in late November that the demobilization of reservists was to begin immediately and after fifteen weeks at Lydd and, as a result of excellent organization by the Quartermaster and his staff, all those in the battalion were gone within forty-eight hours. Most left with few or no ill feelings towards the Regiment, although they were doubtless as frustrated as their regular counterparts by the indecision and muddle which characterized this particular operation and the length of time they were kept hanging around without knowing what was happening.

Nearly forty years after the event how will history judge the Suez operation? It is safe to assume that in Whitehall it will continue to be viewed as an episode in the life of the Nation which should best be forgotten. Among those serving in the 1st Battalion in 1956 it will be remembered for the way in which the reservists were welcomed and quickly absorbed into their companies and the will with which they tackled their unexpected return to military service. Some may have joked that 'they had only come for a weekend' but, despite the short-lived trouble of early October, most seemed to enjoy themselves and determined to pull their weight from the outset. Building upon foundations laid during the battalion's time in the Canal Zone and drawing upon a team of company commanders most of whom had had wartime or Malayan experience, Colonel Bulkeley was able to achieve high standards of training relatively quickly. However, in the Orderly Room there were different problems with which to grapple, the Suez Operation being characterized by lengthy signals and contradictory orders most of which did not go beyond the Adjutant and his staff. Captain Napier recorded in the Battalion Digest that over 800 signals were received, of which the prize went to an Headquarters Eastern District signal eight inches wide by thirty-four inches long! The system of placing units at notice to move also broke down and this produced real consequences on the ground with officers and soldiers often being recalled needlessly, the Transport Platoon holding the record by being summoned to return no fewer than four times.

However, reference to the landings at Suez would be incomplete without mention of the part played by Number 1 (Guards) Independent Parachute Company, a troop of which dropped with the French Airborne Forces at Port Fuad early on in the operation. Captain Murray de Klee commanded the troop involved which was later given the task of reconnoitring south along the causeway from Port Said, an operation successfully executed and for which he was subsequently awarded a Croix de Guerre. The troop which, in addition to Captain de Klee also included Lance Corporal Kent and Guardsmen Fletcher and Melville from the Regiment, was still engaged on its mission when the Anglo-French invasion was brought to a premature end. Thus ended the Suez 'crisis', a relatively short period in the life of the Regiment and the Nation, which fizzled out in anti-climax but which could so easily have ended very differently.

Lieutenant Colonel Michael Fitzalan Howard assumed command of the 2nd Battalion in January, 1956, on the departure of Lieutenant Colonel Digby Raeburn. Captain Blair Stewart-Wilson was his Adjutant and RSM Braid the Sergeant Major. The battalion worked hard in what was to be its last year in Germany and was regularly exercised across the North German Plain alongside or against other units of 4th Guards Brigade, at the time commanded by Brigadier George Burns. On one exercise the latter decided that he should contrive to 'sack' the Commanding Officer in order to allow the Second-in-Command to take over command for a period. While Colonel Fitzalan Howard was party to this ruse, others were not and matters got completely out of hand when the Major General telephoned Commander 2nd Infantry Division to remonstrate over the removal of a Household Brigade Commanding Officer without his permission. *2nd Battalion*

On 27 February, 1957, the battalion arrived at Chelsea Barracks, having crossed the North Sea and travelled by train to Victoria Station, whence it marched in sixes to Chelsea Barracks led by the Regimental Band and massed pipers and drummers of the Regiment. Preparations for public duties then ensued and the first Queen's Guard, commanded by Major George Nickerson, was mounted on 15 April. Thereafter there followed a continuous round of public duties when the battalion was to all intents given over to the Adjutant, Captain Tony Boam, and RSM Braid for regular drill practice and rehearsal and little time could be made available for any but the most basic military training. Colonel Fitzalan Howard left the battalion in February, 1958, his final act upon departure being to release all those held in detention in the battalion guardroom, much to the dismay of RSM Adams, the new Sergeant Major, who had expended so much energy to put them behind bars in the first place!

By Christmas, 1956, life in the 1st Battalion had returned to normal, the two freight vessels having returned from the Mediterranean with rather fewer of the battalion's stores than when they departed. Training for its role in the Strategic Reserve dominated life and companies travelled far and wide to use the best ranges and areas. Early in 1957 Left Flank undertook a trial of the Army's new combat equipment which, together with a new range of clothing, was to be introduced shortly; the principal advantage of the new equipment quickly appreciated by guardsmen was that the webbing could not be blancoed nor the brasses polished. RSM Whyte handed over to RSM Hughes in April and *1st Battalion*

5

thereafter went to the 2nd Battalion as the Transport Officer; he and RSM Tillotson, the Superintending Clerk at Regimental Headquarters, were both commissioned at the same time and became the first commissioned Warrant Officers to be appointed as Transport Officers in the Regiment.

Later in August command of the battalion changed when Colonel Tommy Bulkeley handed over to Lieutenant Colonel Earl Cathcart; a man of slight stature but great energy, Colonel Bulkeley contributed much during his three years in command, not least an ability to devise and put into practice imaginative training. He was a great enthusiast for everything that he did and was a notable steeplechaser and squash player in his time. He still skis in the Alps at the age of seventy! Following a major divisional exercise when it was flown by Beverley aircraft to deploy on Salisbury Plain, the battalion prepared to move from Lydd to Windsor in early November. The fifteen months in Kent had been busy and enjoyable but not without their frustrations most of which had their origins in the abortive Suez operation. Relationships between the battalion and the local population around Lydd were fostered from the outset and were developed in a special way, principally at Officers' and Sergeants' Mess level, something which was greatly to the battalion's advantage.

Guards Depot   Elsewhere within the Household Brigade major changes were taking place which would affect the lives of all guardsmen. Most notable was the decision to close the Guards Depot at Caterham and to move it to Pirbright to displace the Guards Training Battalion in early 1960. This decision was necessitated by the need to make economies, it having been decided that the Household Brigade could no longer justify two training establishments and it fell to Lieutenant Colonel Vernon Erskine Crum, the Scots Guards Commandant in 1958, to plan the move from Caterham where the Depot had been since 1877. For the Regiment these changes led to the disbandment of L Company at Pirbright and its replacement there by K Company which was to continue to train recruits for the Regiment. However, in future, basic fieldcraft and minor tactics were to be taught to guardsmen once they had joined their service battalions, something which could not always be easily achieved with battalions engaged upon public duties. Thirty-five years later the Guards Depot itself no longer exists, having been replaced at Pirbright by one of five Army Training Regiments designed by the Ministry of Defence to satisfy the training requirements of an Army, smaller in size and faced by a range of potential operational deployments vastly different from those envisaged in 1958.

2nd Battalion   On 3 February, 1958, Lieutenant Colonel Adrian Seymour took command of the 2nd Battalion at Chelsea Barracks. After a year of public duties the battalion was well settled in to what soon became a well established routine for any Brigade of Guards Regiment. Much of the routine associated with ceremonial duties is of a tiring and repetitive nature and allows little scope for innovation, other than when one of those rare opportunities arises by which a platoon commander suddenly finds his guardsmen free from duty and must therefore instantly devise something interesting and challenging for them to do at next to no notice. It was always thus and such challenges usually bring out the best in commanders who themselves can find the day-to-day routine of a battalion employed upon public duties to be rather stultifying despite all those other attractions which abound in a city such as London. Most Commanding Officers would admit to finding command of a battalion on public duties, while very different, to be every bit as challenging as command in an operational theatre and many would acknowledge that their sole aim under such circumstances is to keep their guardsmen going until a change of station and a more demanding military role offer something more stimulating. The 1958 ceremonial season found both battalions in close proximity with the 1st Battalion at Windsor and the 2nd Battalion sharing Chelsea Barracks with the 1st Battalion Grenadier Guards. On 12 June the Queen's Colour of the 1st Battalion was trooped on the Queen's Birthday Parade, the first time since 1934. Colonel Digby Raeburn, who had taken command of the Regiment from Colonel Henry Clowes the previous December, commanded the parade with the Escort and Number Two Guard found by the 1st Battalion and commanded by Majors Murray de Klee and John Denham respectively, while the 2nd Battalion furnished Numbers Three and Four Guards under the command of Majors David Scott-Barrett and George Nickerson. Unfortunately the day was wet but the parade went ahead nonetheless and without too great a toll in ruined tunics and bearskins. A week later a most successful Officers' Regimental Ball was held at Windsor attended by Her Majesty The Queen and several other members of the Royal Family. Following these events in the south a detachment from the 1st Battalion commanded by Major de Klee travelled to Scotland and paraded on a number of occasions before Her Majesty The Queen, including at Leith Docks at the start of her visit and when she later visited Falkland Palace.

On 21 June the 2nd Battalion also travelled north but only as far as Otterburn where it was scheduled to train for three weeks. The journey north was by special train but such was its weight that the locomotive could not manage the gradient up to West Woodburn Station and the train had to be divided in two. When the engine returned for the second half it was seen to be manned by the Commanding Officer and the Second-in-Command, Major Scott-Barrett, something which gave enormous confidence to those travelling behind them! Prior to its departure for Otterburn the battalion was joined by its first ever Paymaster; Major Andrew Cook, a former officer in the Royal Scots Fusiliers, was destined to stay with the battalion for eight years during which time he endeared himself to all who served with him. He certainly got off to a good start by insisting that everyone should claim the allowances due to them from the Army. On return from training Major Charles de Salis took a detachment of thirty from Left Flank to Belgium to participate in a ceremony at Waterloo when a plaque was unveiled at Hougoumont Farm to commemorate the part played by the Regiment in the defence of the area during the battle.

The late summer and autumn were taken up with a heavy round of ceremonial duties such as are the expected lot of a London battalion and, after turning out in force to welcome the President of West Germany in late October and providing eleven half companies for the State Opening of Parliament a week later, the battalion moved in mid-November to Shorncliffe in Kent to join 1st Guards Brigade generally glad to leave London after twenty months in Chelsea Barracks. After its departure the old barracks with its heavy Victorian architecture, gloomy barrack rooms capable of sleeping twenty or more soldiers and its tenement-like married quarters were handed over to the demolition contractors and builders who eventually replaced them with a modern version of what they had just demolished, albeit with rather more in the way of facilities for the living-in soldier. However, in its own way the demolition and rebuilding of a barracks so long associated with the Brigade of Guards marked the end of an era and life in Chelsea was never again to be quite the same.

Shorncliffe

Moore Barracks, Shorncliffe, situated atop the cliffs near Folkestone and therefore somewhat draughty when a gale blew up the English Channel, were destined to be the battalion's home for only five months before it moved along with other elements of 1st Guards Brigade to Tidworth in April, 1959. Just before Christmas the battalion was warned for possible deployment to Cyprus in the New Year to undertake internal security duties. Preparations were made, including a three-week reconnaissance party led by the Commanding Officer, but peace negotiations on the island achieved positive results and the battalion was eventually stood down whereupon it reverted to more traditional pastimes such as Spring Drills, that well known ritual of the barrack square so enjoyed by Regimental Sergeant Majors and their accomplices and so detested by those subjected to the torture involved. On this occasion a particular ploy devised by the Adjutant, Captain Tony Boam and Drill Sergeant Fowler was for the officers and any spare senior NCOs to drill for long periods in respirators at high speed with certain officers being selected to give the words of command! It was therefore with some relief that the battalion moved to Assaye Barracks in Tidworth to indulge in more normal training.

1st Battalion

No sooner had the main ceremonial events of the summer of 1958 been completed than the 1st Battalion at Windsor found itself warned to move to the Middle East under the command of Headquarters 2nd Infantry Brigade; in late July the battalion was placed at notice, which at one stage was reduced to as little as six hours, for an emergency move to Khartoum; all leave was cancelled, inoculations were given, khaki drill uniform was issued and air loading tables compiled, but all to no avail and, after a series of 'on-off' decisions, which necessitated the hurried posting in of Major Tony Harrison from the 2nd Battalion and Captain Lorne Campbell from the Guards Depot, the battalion was stood down. Despite the disappointment that it had prepared in vain, the battalion quickly got back into its stride and turned its attention to the forthcoming move to Germany where it was destined to become part of 4th Guards Brigade. The advance party left Windsor on 24 October, the main body of the battalion following three weeks later, sad to be leaving Victoria Barracks after a busy and enjoyable tour in what has always ranked as one of the best, if not the best, station to be regularly occupied by the Household Brigade. One member of the battalion who did not accompany it to Germany was Major Donald Fraser, the Quartermaster, who handed over his duties to Captain Roy Watts and departed to serve on the staff in the War Office. During his time as Quartermaster he had seen the battalion through two tours in London District and through two Middle East crises with commendable efficiency and good humour.

1959 also saw the lauding of another great Scots Guardsman when Sergeant George, the Police Sergeant at the Guards Depot, completed thirty-seven years' service. A man renowned for his experience and close study of human nature, he joined the Regiment in 1922, served in China and Palestine and moved to the Depot in 1938 where he became familiar to generations of guardsmen. There can be no more appropriate tribute to him than to quote a passage from the *Household Brigade Magazine* of the time: 'It is a source of wonderment to past members and one of admiration to present members of the Household Brigade that this splendid figure can still be seen moving with certainty and precision along the highways and byways of the Guards Depot. How often have those who have served there heard, "There has been a little bit of trouble, sir, but Sergeant George is investigating." For the majority his appearance at the Company Dance will always be familiar. The firm but dignified manner with which the uninvited or unsuitable is asked to leave; the admirable tact with which the Celtic group is dispersed, especially on those days when the saintless ones celebrate; the considerate "drawing of the covers" after the dance; these are some of the memories which hundreds hold of him.'

The move from Windsor complete, the 1st Battalion quickly adjusted to a *Hubblerath* very different routine from that demanded of a public duties battalion; Colonel Alan Cathcart described the battalion's transition from Windsor to becoming part of the ground force defence of Western Europe as being similar to 'being given a cold bath' and in the full glare of military light in which BAOR battalions so often found themselves then and since, everybody set to to discharge their new duties to the best of their abilities. People felt that they were soldiering for a serious purpose and the threat posed by the Soviet Union and her allies soon established itself in the minds of most members of the battalion. Gort Barracks in Hubblerath provided a good base from which to undertake low-level training and to familiarize the battalion with its new role.

Throughout the summer of 1959 companies trained hard and played equally hard, with the battalion quickly establishing a reputation with its football and cross-country running teams. However, the ceremonial side was not forgotten and it fell to the battalion to provide the Escort and Number Two Guard on the Queen's Birthday Parade held at the Rhine Centre in Düsseldorf; Majors de Klee and Mayfield commanded the two guards, while the Commanding Officer was in overall command of the parade with Captain Philip Erskine as his Adjutant. The new self-loading rifle, which had recently been brought into service, was carried for the first time and the 2nd Battalion Canadian Guards also provided a guard on parade. However, training dominated the life of the battalion and a period spent in camp at Sennelager when 'night was turned into day' with all training and administration conducted during the hours of darkness, and a series of formation exercises across the German countryside when the battalion worked for the first time with tanks and practised crossing water obstacles, all helped to inculcate the principles and mechanics of a form of warfare hitherto little known to many in the battalion. At the end of the training season and as BAOR went into hibernation for the winter, Colonel Alan Cathcart handed over command to Lieutenant Colonel Bill Lawson and a week later assumed command of the Regiment from Colonel Raeburn. During his time in the 1st Battalion Colonel Cathcart had led his guardsmen calmly and without fuss through a variety of stations and roles and had won the respect of all for his ability to guide and encourage his battalion, not least when under scrutiny in the 'goldfish bowl' of BAOR.

Tidworth   The 2nd Battalion completed its move to Tidworth by the middle of April, 1959. Although based alongside the two other infantry battalions in 1st Guards Brigade it is probably true to say that, while the battalion enjoyed itself at Tidworth, it never felt totally at home in what was by tradition a station more regularly occupied by the Cavalry or Horse Gunners. In particular the attitude of some Scots Guards officers to the conventions and pastimes held to be sacred by the Cavalry was not always appreciated by some others in the Garrison; the jocular advertising of a fox shoot to be held on the same day as a meet of the local hounds, instigated by Major Charles de Salis, went down badly while the use of the Polo Ground for purposes other than polo was definitely not approved of.

However the battalion had little time to indulge in such frivolities and was quickly involved in some intensive training. An exercise at Stanford to practise the battalion's airportable role in the Strategic Reserve was interspersed with training closer to home on Salisbury Plain, the 3rd Division Queen's Birthday Parade at Bulford and the divisional Tennis Championships when 2nd Lieutenant David Trimble and Lance Corporal Ferguson narrowly but no doubt wisely just failed to defeat the Divisional Commander, Major General Geordie Gordon Lennox and his partner in the Finals! In addition a Battalion At Home Day was held in Assaye Barracks on 25 July. While the day was arranged primarily for the parents and relatives of those serving in the battalion, a small tattoo in the afternoon attracted about 3,000 people and received excellent media coverage at both local and national level and, most importantly, in Scotland. The whole battalion was mobilized to deal with this enormous, largely unanticipated, influx of people who, besides viewing the tattoo which involved the use of helicopters, the firing of dummy mortar bombs and a jungle warfare engagement, all designed to portray the roles of a 3rd Division battalion, also visited a series of static displays, toured barracks, ate in the various messes, watched the pipers and drummers beating retreat and, if they were bold enough, descended down a parachute fan. Many contributed to the success of the day but probably none more so than Major Scott-Barrett, who in his inimitable style, a mixture of

10

inspiration and coercion, held it all together and 2nd Lieutenant Christopher Constable-Maxwell who volunteered to lie on the ground beneath a plank so that all the battalion's motorcyclists could drive over him!

At the end of August, 1959, the battalion was told that it had been selected to trial a new structure for infantry battalions under the auspices of an establishment termed the 774 Battalion, so named because that was to be the total of the manpower in the battalion. The trial required considerable internal reorganization and Support Company, commanded by Major Tony Harrison, with CSM Langlands as his Company Sergeant Major, was disbanded and the specialist platoons divided between the rifle companies in order to provide each with its own integral support platoon of 3 inch Mortars and MOBAT anti-tank weapons. The re-grouping, which led to a major increase in the size of Headquarter Company and the formation of a Reconnaissance Platoon, preceded a trial which lasted several months and was tested on Exercise RED BANNER in October when 1st Guards Brigade and 16th Parachute Brigade fought each other on Salisbury Plain. The exercise was not an unqualified success for the battalion since the unfortunate capture of a reconnaissance section early on led to the enemy discovering the battalion's orders and wireless codes. However, honour was later satisfied when, towards the end of the exercise, a party from the Guards Parachute Company led by Captain Anthony Hopkinson of the Regiment, attempted an attack on Battalion Headquarters only to be roundly defeated by the Corps of Drums! The exercise attracted a lot of high-level interest and Major Scott-Barrett spent much of his time impressing people with the need for the battalion to make its name, so much so that when one evening he announced 'there'll be no sleep tonight' Captain Peff Brown, the Medical Officer, took him literally and forced himself to remain awake! Prior to deploying for this major exercise the battalion had sent a small detachment north to Stirling to be present on 20 September when His Royal Highness The Duke of Gloucester, as Colonel of the Regiment, handed over for safe custody Old Colours of the 1st Battalion to the Minister of the Church of the Holy Rood thereby re-establishing the connections between the Scots Guards and the Royal Burgh of Stirling. The detachment was commanded by Major Harrison and Lieutenant John Gibb and 2nd Lieutenant Roddy Ingham Clark carried the Colours.

The battalion's second full year in Tidworth began with Exercise STARLIGHT in Libya. Directed by Major General Charles Harrington, the new Commander 3rd Division, 1st Guards Brigade was to fly to RAF El Adem south of Tobruk and was then to deploy against an enemy force occupying the hills and desert south of Derna and west of Tmimi, an area well known to anybody who had fought with 201st Guards Brigade in 1941, reminders of some of whose battles with the Germans were still to be seen in 1960. The Brigade, commanded by Brigadier Digby Raeburn, consisted of the Scots Guards, the 1st Battalion Grenadier Guards and the 1st Battalion The Duke of Edinburgh's Royal Regiment, each battalion reinforced by a company of Welsh Guardsmen. Shortly

Exercise STARLIGHT

11

before the battalion deployed Lieutenant Colonel George Burnett took over command from Colonel Seymour.

The flight to Libya in RAF Britannia aircraft proceeded smoothly, although few appreciated their stay in the transit camp at El Adem where the facilities were the minimum considered necessary to keep body and soul together; the move up country to Tmimi was an altogether more hazardous performance, principally because the old wartime runway broke up under the weight of the Beverley aircraft landing on it and aircraft therefore had to use parallel rough desert strips to put down on, almost invariably enveloped in an enormous cloud of dust. The first half of the training involved battalion exercises and these were followed by a brigade exercise against an enemy controlled by Divisional Headquarters. 1st Guards Brigade was to advance westwards parallel to the Mediterranean coastal road towards Derna.

On 23 March the brigade attacked Martuba, during which the battalion executed a long and most successful flanking march as a result of which Pipe Major Crabb wrote the pipe tune 'The 2nd Battalion's March from Martuba'. The battalion then went into reserve before carrying out a battalion attack of its own prior to taking part in the final assault on the enemy-held *Jebel* position. Throughout the exercise the brigade moved on light scales of transport which necessitated the battalion's landrovers being concentrated when and where they were required; the codeword for this was 'Go kart', while an instruction to one of the companies to take advantage of a lull in the battle in order to brew up before being committed again was given using the codeword 'Bertie Dawes'. The latter was the name of the Divisional Catering Adviser which Battalion Headquarters decided conveyed the order to have a quick brew precisely without risking compromise! Divisional Headquarters were less impressed when they discovered, and the use of Major Dawes' name had to be hurriedly discontinued. The exercise was a hard one with long marches, little rest, extreme heat and dust everywhere and the battalion did well to perform as it did after a very short period of acclimatization, mainly because of high standards of fitness. There was also an element of gamesmanship with the umpires which did not always endear the battalion to the directing staff. Despite this, at a higher level the exercise was deemed to have been well worthwhile since it demonstrated just how much could be achieved by airportable troops flown in on light scales and deployed into battle after a minimum of acclimatization and thereafter re-supplied only by air-drop or helicopter. The battalion certainly enjoyed itself and, after a period of recovery camped by the sea below the Roman ruins at Derna, returned to Tidworth by 3 April well pleased with its performance, and, as Colonel Burnett put it 'thinking like soldiers again'.

The summer of 1960 at Tidworth passed in much the same way as did that of the previous year, including the running of another tattoo, this time on a grander scale on the Tidworth Polo Ground, something which caused the Commanding Officer of the Royal Horse Artillery particular difficulty! Undeterred by criticism of his plans Major Scott-Barrett forged ahead and with the

1. "On 27 February, 1957, the 2nd Battalion arrived at Chelsea Barracks, having crossed the North Sea and travelled by train to Victoria Station, whence it marched in sixes to Chelsea Barracks." (Page 5). Lieutenant Colonel Michael Fitzalan Howard, followed by Captain Blair Stewart-Wilson, the Adjutant, and Major Mike Law, leads his battalion along Buckingham Palace Road. CSMs Graham and McKinder are the left and right guides. Lieutenant Tim Gosselin and 2nd Lieutenant Andrew Morritt are two of the officers marching behind Major Law.

2. "Relieved to be home after the tedium and frustration of life guarding military installations in the vicinity of the Suez Canal, the 1st Battalion soon settled into its first tour of public duties since 1940." (Page 1). Pipe Major J.S. 'Gabby' Roe and Piper Angus Macdonald (later Pipe Major of the 1st Battalion) prepare to mount duties at Wellington Barracks in the summer of 1956.

3. "The Scots Guards Association has been in existence since 1904." (Page 222). The 1959 Dinner of the London Branch was held at the Tavistock Rooms.

4. "An exercise at Stanford to practise the 2nd Battalion's airportable role in the Strategic Reserve was interspersed with training closer to home on Salisbury Plain." (Page 10). Gathered on Frog Hill at Stanford in 1959, awaiting orders from Colonel Adrian Seymour, are from left to right (in the foreground): Captains Donald Whyte and Peff Brown (the Battalion Doctor), Major Tony Harrison and Captain Tony Boam and (behind) Major George Nickerson, Lieutenants James Dunsmure and Thomas Boyd-Carpenter, Major David Trappes-Lomax, RSM Adams, CSM Melville and Major Bruce Bell.

aid of a loudhailer during rehearsals, demanded that everybody 'should get the flavour', which they most certainly did since 16,000 people, headed by the Secretary of State for War, attended on the night of 8 July and thoroughly enjoyed a spectacle of drill squads, bands, simulated nuclear warfare, company attacks, physical training displays and parachutists. Apart from the traffic congestion, it was all a resounding success and, as with all successes, everybody in the battalion was pleased to have been part of it. The opportunity to do it all again came sooner than many expected when the battalion moved to Scotland in early September for a month of training and recruiting and yet another mini-tattoo staged this time on the lower slopes of the Pentland Hills above Dreghorn Camp. Sadly 17 September was a damp and misty day but nonetheless 8,000 people turned out to see similar events to those performed two months earlier at Tidworth and few went home disappointed, despite some torrential rain.

The battalion's brief sojourn at Penicuik and the subsequent dispersal of each company to a different part of Scotland helped to remind people north of the Border, should they have needed such a reminder, that the Regiment was just as much part of the Scottish military family as any other and from that standpoint the visit was of enormous importance. Before returning south in early October the battalion reassembled at Penicuik, mounted the Edinburgh Castle Guard for a fortnight and on 10 October provided a Guard of Honour for Her Majesty The Queen at the Caledonian Railway Station. The occasion was not without its problems since when Major Michael Gow, the Captain of Right Flank, stepped the Guard off to leave the station, the top of the State Colour got caught up in bunting hanging down from the roof. 2nd Lieutenant David Saunders found himself unable to move with the guardsmen rapidly leaving him behind. Drill Sergeant Graham, exercising great presence of mind, drew his sword and slashed at the offending bunting in an attempt to cut the Colour free before the Guard disappeared completely, but failed to do so because he could not reach it. In the end the Ensign shook the Colour free and doubled forward to regain his position, no mean achievement with the State Colour! In the three months left before it moved to Wellington Barracks in mid-January 1961, the battalion ceased to be part of the Strategic Reserve and through a programme of Autumn Drills prepared once again for a period of public duties, the first of which was mounted on 17 November by a detachment by then based in London. At the same time 1st Guards Brigade was disbanded and for the final two months of its time in Tidworth the battalion was administered by 51st Gurkha Brigade commanded by Brigadier Raeburn.

One of the battalion's last duties before leaving Assaye Barracks exemplified the uneasy relationship which had existed between it and its more equestrian neighbours. It was described thus by the Adjutant, Captain Anthony Hopkinson: 'There now took place one of those events which bedevil the infantry battalion stationed at Tidworth. The Army Hunter Trials were held on the Tattoo Ground in almost continuous rain, and as usual the staff far outnumbered the competitors. The battalion erected a number of marquees and provided thirteen officers and the same number of sergeants as judges and fence watchers. At the end of the day a cavalry officer was heard to remark that "The Scots Guards were competent but bloody". This comment gave great satisfaction to those of us who took part as our impression was that the organizers of the event were not merely bloody themselves but also most incompetent.'

1960 was the 1st Battalion's last year in Germany and the pattern of events was not dissimilar to that of the previous year; shooting and athletics competitions, the Queen's Birthday Parade in Düsseldorf, battalion training and formation exercises all had to be dovetailed into a never-ending round of visitors, course requirements, leave and all the other duties that are invariably the lot of the infantry battalion in peacetime. In September the battalion enjoyed a period of brigade training in Schleswig-Holstein which culminated in Exercise HOLDFAST, a divisional exercise in which for the first time since the war German troops of the Bundeswehr took part. 4th Division played the role of the Soviet aggressor with the Lübeck to Hamburg autobahn being defended by a combined force of German and Danish units. The battalion had a thoroughly enjoyable exercise, being on the offensive for much of the time, and succeeded in out-manoeuvering the Germans deployed against them time and again, although for political reasons this success had to be somewhat played down. Colonel Lawson was at one stage congratulated on the battalion's performance against the Bundeswehr by the German Chief Umpire who said that he had not seen anything like it since his own battalion had done the same thing to the Russians in the last War. On another occasion the Commanding Officer encountered a guardsman wrestling with a German soldier as the latter desperately tried to swallow his orders before capture, while the guardsman equally desperately attempted to retrieve them by pushing his fingers down the man's throat! Luckily such incidents were not allowed to jeopardize the establishment of cordial military relationships between Britain and Germany, then in their infancy.

On return to Hubblerath the battalion prepared to hand over its role and barracks to the Welsh Guards and to move to Gravesend in Kent from where it was to undertake public duties. Because in 1960 the re-building of Chelsea Barracks had caused there to be a shortage of military accommodation in London District, the original plan had been for the battalion to return to Lydd but this was changed at the last moment, a move that was to make the regular mounting of duties at the Royal Palaces marginally less inconvenient than might otherwise have been the case. Colonel Bill Lawson was so horrified when he heard where the battalion was to move that he contemplated resigning in protest; luckily the Lieutenant Colonel dissuaded him from such drastic action!

By the end of January, 1961, both battalions were once again stationed in London District. The 1st Battalion was acclimatizing to a poorly heated and largely inadequate barracks some twenty miles east of London, while the 2nd Battalion finally concentrated in Wellington Barracks in the middle of the month. Both battalions quickly found themselves on the duty roster and, although every effort was made to ease the burden of public duties, it was not always possible to do so, especially since the Regiment was for the first time experiencing major recruiting problems. Some of these problems undoubtedly arose as a result of the decision to end National Service. Throughout 1961 the resultant difficulties were more or less contained although they were to manifest themselves with a vengeance in 1963 when the 2nd Battalion had moved to Kenya at full strength leaving the 1st Battalion to face a third year of unrelenting duty well short of the numbers it required and still commuting from outside London.

The planning and management of public duties is and always has been a matter for Adjutants, Regimental Sergeant Majors and their Drill Sergeants. Endless hours are spent co-ordinating conflicting demands for guardsmen's time and, although every effort is made to be fair, equity is not always achieved, sometimes because it just is not possible, but occasionally because the running of duty rosters is not undertaken in the most efficacious manner. In 1961 both battalions were fortunate to have Sergeant Majors of considerable calibre; RSM Adams had been with the 2nd Battalion since November, 1957, and knew his NCOs and guardsmen as well as anyone. He saw the battalion through its year in London and handed over shortly after arrival in Kenya when he was succeeded by RSM Graham, following which he was commissioned as a Quartermaster. He remains to this day a much liked and highly respected member of the Regiment. While based in London in February, 1961, he was the subject of ill-informed criticism when a Labour Member of Parliament complained about the manner in which he had conducted a battalion drill parade on the square at Wellington Barracks 'when the officers were walking about, quite at leisure while a big, fat regimental sergeant major with a big out-of-date moustache stood by, which I think is typical of the out-of-date methods still prevalent in the Army'. RSM Adams was strongly defended by Mr Profumo, the War Minister, in the Chamber of the House of Commons, and by Colonel Burnett, while the Peter Simple Column in the *Daily Telegraph* drily observed that '"Out-of-date" is, of course, the key word here. In an up-to-date Socialist Army there would be no big moustaches, no regimental sergeant major, no officers and no men, merely an undifferentiated collection of opinionated civilians'. The matter died as quickly as it arose, with, if anything, RSM Adams' reputation within the Regiment enhanced! Earlier RSM Hughes, a quiet rather avuncular figure but no less effective a Sergeant Major, had handed over the reins in the 1st Battalion before it left Germany and it therefore fell to RSM Rodger to prepare the battalion for public duties, something that he was well qualified to do since he had already been Sergeant Major of the Guards Depot.

During the last week of May, 1961, the Regiment planned a number of events to mark the twenty-fifth year of His Royal Highness The Duke of Gloucester's Colonelcy of the Scots Guards. Planning these events absorbed much of Regimental Headquarters' time over the preceding months and the main responsibility for implementing them fell to Major John Swinton, the Regimen-

1961 Royal Review

tal Adjutant. On the evening of 27 May 650 members of the Past and Present Association dined with the Colonel at Earls Court. During the Dinner In-Pensioner Everett of the Royal Hospital presented His Royal Highness with a picture of the Regiment on manoeuvres in the 1880s by Orlando Norie, on behalf of the Scots Guards Association, while Lieutenant Colonel Alec Greenwood, on behalf of the Regiment, presented him with a bound volume of watercolours by Mr Haswell Miller depicting orders of dress worn by the Regiment. The following day the 1st Battalion hosted an At Home Day for members of the Association at Gravesend which the Colonel attended, while on 29 May the Regiment paraded on Horse Guards to be reviewed by His Royal Highness. This parade was the principal event in the celebrations to mark the Colonel's twenty-five years with the Regiment and fifty-two officers and 1,067 soldiers were drawn up on Horse Guards in a hollow square; in addition to the two battalions there were detachments of Scots Guardsmen from all Household Brigade training establishments and Number 1 (Guards) Independent Parachute Company and 353 past members of the Regiment paraded under command of Major General Pat Bradshaw. Colonel Earl Cathcart commanded the parade and seven senior officers of the rank of colonel or above were mounted. Her Royal Highness The Duchess of Gloucester, accompanied by Prince William, was present, as was Her Majesty Queen Elizabeth The Queen Mother, who had requested that she might be allowed to attend in recognition of the fact that her late husband had been the 24th Colonel of the Regiment from 1932 to 1937. After the review on Horse Guards the Colonel placed himself at the head of the Regiment and, preceded by the massed pipers, led the way down the Mall to Stable Yard Gate where he took the salute as the Regiment marched past.

On 10 June the Queen's Colour of the 2nd Battalion was trooped on the Queen's Birthday Parade. The Lieutenant Colonel commanded the parade with Major Swinton as his Adjutant; the 2nd Battalion provided the Escort, commanded by Major Michael Gow, and Number Two Guard, while the 1st Battalion paraded with Numbers Three and Four Guards. Captain James Dunsmure was Subaltern of the Escort and 2nd Lieutenant David Saunders carried the Colour. Throughout the remainder of the year both battalions carried out a heavy programme of ceremonial duties interspersed with visits to Scotland and some low-level training. An event which gave the 1st Battalion particular pleasure occurred in July when the battalion team won the Lawson Cup at the London District Athletics Meeting, beating the Irish Guards by a short head; the cup had been presented by the Commanding Officer's grandfather in memory of Sir John Astley, a former Scots Guardsman and a great athlete.

At the Edinburgh Tattoo in August a detachment from the 1st Battalion under Major Douglas Prior performed a Guard Changing Ceremony demonstrating the changes that had taken place since 1661 when the Regiment first performed Garrison Duty at Edinburgh Castle. However, it was a special event in December which brought a year so full of regimental milestones to a most appropriate close. Lieutenant Colonel Alec Greenwood joined as a guardsman on 23 November, 1926. His early life in the Regiment was in the 1st Battalion but he served as both Regimental Sergeant Major and Quartermaster of the 2nd Battalion in the War seeing action in the Western Desert, Tunisia, North-West Europe and Italy. He later served in Malaya and ended an illustrious career with the appointment of Deputy Assistant Quartermaster General, Headquarters London District where he worked for the interests of countless guardsmen in his efforts to modernize military accommodation in and around the capital, his most notable success being the building, despite opposition, of the new Knightsbridge Barracks and the building of the new Guards Depot, Alexander Barracks, Pirbright where one of the streets is named 'Greenwood Road'. A dinner was held for him at the Café Royal on 5 December to mark his retirement after thirty-five years with the Regiment.

In February, 1962, the 2nd Battalion left Wellington Barracks for a tour in *1962* Kenya as part of East Africa Command, taking over from the 2nd Battalion Coldstream Guards. The 1st Battalion meanwhile remained at Gravesend until June when it moved to the newly built Elizabeth Barracks, Pirbright, next door to the Guards Depot. It continued to carry out public duties, but, despite low numbers and a heavy ceremonial programme, managed some training as well as making preparations for a dock strike that never materialized. Early in the year Lieutenant Colonel Charles Duffin took over command from Colonel Lawson, with Captain Michael Bowater as his Adjutant.

CHAPTER TWO

EAST AFRICA

2nd Battalion: Kahawa, Kenya

1962

When the 2nd Battalion arrived in Kenya at the end of February, 1962, it came under command of 24th Infantry Brigade which had been stationed in the colony since 1958. During the preceding four years units of the Brigade had on several occasions undertaken operational and humanitarian tasks both within Africa and elsewhere, the battalion's immediate predecessor, the 2nd Battalion Coldstream Guards, having been deployed during its time in Kenya to Kuwait and Zanzibar to augment local security arrangements at a time of potential unrest.

While in 1962 the main role of 24th Infantry Brigade remained the reinforcement of Kuwait, the presence of three infantry battalions and the Brigade's supporting units in Kenya provided some useful stability and allowed those responsible for moving the territories of East Africa from colonial rule to full independence to plan on doing so without undue interference. By the beginning of 1962, within East Africa, Tanganyika had already achieved her independence, while Uganda was to be granted hers in October, 1962, and Kenya and Zanzibar theirs twelve months later. The battalion's first home in Kenya was Muthaiga Camp on the outskirts of Nairobi; the camp was inherited from the departing Coldstream Guards and consisted of corrugated iron or 'Twyneham' huts, the latter because of their aluminium construction being very cool even in the hottest weather. However, the battalion remained at Muthaiga for only two months before moving to Templer Barracks at Kahawa, a purpose-built base for two battalions of 24th Infantry Brigade fourteen miles north of Nairobi. Built at a cost of seven million pounds, Kahawa Camp was laid out on a spacious scale with single-storey barrack blocks, sports fields, a shopping centre, a cinema and a swimming pool and with plenty of married quarters. Never fully completed, the camp was destined to be occupied by only three battalions before all British troops were withdrawn from Kenya at the end of 1964. In the intervening period it provided the 2nd Battalion with a pleasant base for what was to prove an exciting but enjoyable tour in a most beautiful part of Africa and at a time when events of considerable importance were to take place in the region.

18

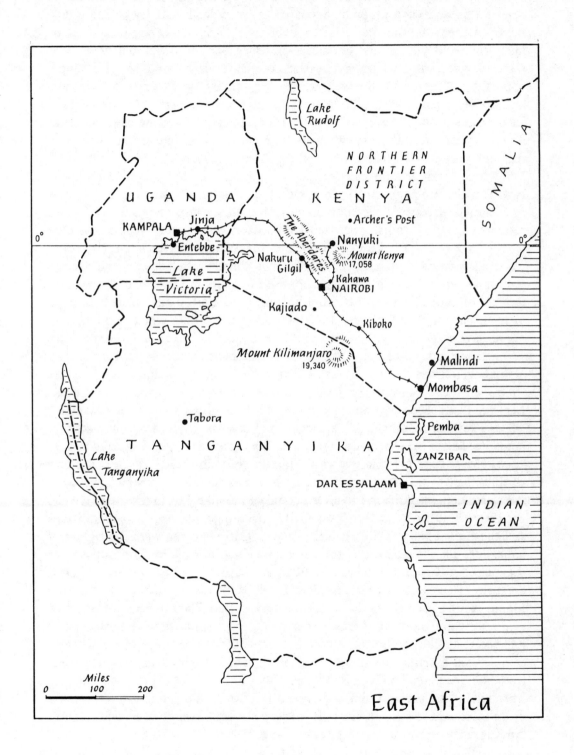

East Africa

Viewed through the pages of an atlas and set against the vast backcloth of the rest of Africa, Kenya probably appeared rather a small country to those who travelled there for the first time in February, 1962. However, maps can be misleading and soldiers and families soon learnt that, although distances could be deceptive, the topography of the country and its wildlife gave ample opportunity for travel and adventure. In fact the first adventurous activity was already in progress as the battalion flew to Kenya; a party of four officers, Lieutenants Robert Fellowes, Sam Vestey, Johnny Clavering and Nicholas Timpson, had set off from Wellington Barracks on 8 January to drive two Austin Gypsies to Muthaiga where they arrived on 11 March, only eight days late, having travelled through Turkey, Egypt and the Sudan. Meanwhile the battalion quickly adjusted to life astride the Equator and training for its new role started in earnest. Each battalion of 24th Infantry Brigade was given responsibility for familiarizing itself with an area of the country, that allocated to the 2nd Battalion being Nairobi and Masailand; this entailed visits and reconnaissances and on one occasion Colonel Burnett recalls meeting an African policeman who every night wrapped himself in a Union Jack for the protection that he assumed it would afford him! In June Left Flank visited Kajiado district, part of the Masai tribal territory and an area into which the battalion might have been required to deploy in the event of internal trouble. Major John Acland, accompanied by the retiring District Commissioner, arranged a series of demonstrations for the Masai which were intended to impress upon the tribesmen the importance of good behaviour and loyalty to the Government. Left Flank travelled 500 miles in and around the area of Mount Kilimanjaro, Africa's highest mountain, and soon got to know the traditionally warlike and nomadic Masai who usually appeared from nowhere carrying spears and knobkerries, their hair matted with a mixture of animal fat and red ochre and herding their cattle with them before vanishing as silently as they had arrived.

Earlier Left Flank had visited Dar-es-Salaam to take part in the final Queen's Birthday Parade to be held in Tanganyika, parading with the Tanganyika Rifles and the Indian Navy; CSM Armitage and CQMS Dalgarno were the right and left guides for the Guard and the parade was held at Government House with the outgoing Governor General, Sir Richard Turnbull, taking the salute. Drill Sergeant Grant accompanied the detachment and was instructed to bring the Indian Navy Guard up to the same standard as Left Flank but with little time to do so; throughout an intensive period of preparation he was continuously referred to as 'Jock Sahib, sir' by the Indians! At the same time Colonel Burnett commanded a similar parade in Nairobi for which Right Flank, a contingent from the 3rd Battalion King's African Rifles and the RAF provided Guards. Throughout the period training designed to practise the battalion's airportable procedures and deployment skills took place and nearly everybody found himself visiting some area of Kenya or Tanganyika.

In early June command of the battalion changed when Colonel George Burnett was relieved by Lieutenant Colonel George Ramsay; the fact that for a short time there were two 'Colonel Georges' in the battalion, while readily understood by Scots Guardsmen, caused some confusion amongst those Masai elders to whom they were introduced when they visited Left Flank at Kajiado! Also confused when he called upon the new Commanding Officer for the first time at Kahawa was the Brigade Major 24th Infantry Brigade, Major John Roden, who was caught unawares at finding Colonel George Ramsay, his Second-in-Command, Major Archie Fletcher, and the Adjutant, Captain Anthony Hopkinson, all sitting in the same open plan office in the Orderly Room, a regimental custom taken for granted by those in the Regiment but seldom understood by those who are not; Major Roden is alleged to have returned to Brigade Headquarters and to have likened his experience to being shown into the presence of 'Father, Son and Holy Ghost', a reference to all three officers being ardent Roman Catholics. However, subsequent jokes comparing the Orderly Room to the Vatican were not thought amusing.

Training in the Northern Frontier District, a semi-desert area of scrub and thorn bushes interspersed with large rocky outcrops north of the Equator, and an exercise on the coast near Mombasa in November, a substitute for another planned to take place in Aden but cancelled for political reasons, completed the battalion's initiation into the ways of East Africa Command. The first nine months of the battalion's tour had provided plenty of scope for people to enjoy some of the recreational opportunities that a country like Kenya had to offer: adventure training expeditions, safaris to game parks and holidays at the coast, usually at the leave centre at Malindi, were all fully subscribed and everybody took advantage of Kenya's fine climate. The temperature in the Nairobi area never fell much below that of a decent summer day in Britain and even in the rainy seasons of April and November storms were short-lived, being quickly replaced by blue sky. Some officers, including Captain Francis Spencer, learnt to fly during their first year in Kenya, while later in the tour 2nd Lieutenant Colin de Chair collected for himself a large number of extra 'picquets' for flying so low over the Staffordshire Regiment, on parade to commemorate Ferozeshah Day, as to cause everybody on the barrack square to duck!

Inevitably the Officers' and Sergeants' Messes tended to enjoy a more complete social life than more junior members of the battalion and there were a large number of European settler families to whom the officers in particular came to owe much. It was unavoidable that a country such as Kenya, with a largely African and Indian population and with only a relatively small proportion of Europeans mainly occupying the top positions in society, should have more to offer to officers than to guardsmen. That said, many guardsmen found plenty to interest them and even those who showed little display of initiative could rely upon enjoying themselves in the more lurid areas of Nairobi or Mombasa, even if such enjoyment usually led to a later encounter with a Military Police patrol.

During the autumn training and sporting activities continued apace with platoon test exercises, adventure training and a particularly strong showing by the battalion's cricketers, led by Majors Shuttleworth and Fletcher and the battalion football team which did so well as to prompt one Sunday newspaper to print the headline 'Why are the Guards so Good?'. In September the whole battalion was involved in either performing at or helping to administer the Royal Show in Nairobi, an event which meant much to the people of Kenya, particularly the farming and business communities, and which enabled the battalion to present itself in a very favourable light, apart from when a senior member of the organizing committee accused those operating the entry gates of purloining some of the takings, an accusation that was quickly proved to be without foundation. The show was a resounding success, with record-breaking crowds, an unexpected bonus being the hitherto undiscovered ability of Lieutenant Peter Johnson and a small team of assault pioneers who managed to floodlight the large central arena without a single interruption. October saw the granting of independence to Uganda, while in early December Left Flank under the command of Major Acland was dispatched to Zanzibar for a four-month tour of duty; the company relieved a company of Gordon Highlanders, its role being to provide stability on the island and on the neighbouring island of Pemba in the run-up to elections which were to be held in 1963 as a prelude to the granting of independence. Experience of the geography and politics of the Protectorate gained during the tour was to prove of enormous benefit when the battalion was called upon to deploy there in the summer of 1963. Meanwhile within 24th Infantry Brigade the battalion's neighbours at Kahawa, the 1st Battalion The Royal Inniskilling Fusiliers, had departed Kenya being replaced by the 1st Battalion The Staffordshire Regiment. The other major units in the Brigade were the 1st Battalion The Gordon Highlanders and the 3rd Regiment Royal Horse Artillery, both stationed at Gilgil. Major General Richard Goodwin was GOC East Africa Command and Brigadier David Lloyd Owen had recently taken command of 24th Infantry Brigade.

1963   The New Year heralded a number of changes in the battalion. RSM Graham arrived from Britain in January to take over from RSM Adams who was commissioned and went to the 1st Battalion; that was followed soon afterwards by a change of adjutants when Captain Hopkinson handed over to Captain Murray Naylor. The latter came from secondment with the Sultan of Muscat's Armed Forces in Oman, a secondment which, over a period of more than twenty years, was undertaken by a number of officers from the Regiment including Lieutenants Peter Harvey, Michael Whiteley and Tim Bell. At a more senior level in the colony Mr Malcolm MacDonald arrived as the Governor in succession to Sir Patrick Renison, a joint Guard of Honour with the King's African Rifles being provided for his arrival by Right Flank, commanded by Major Ossie Priaulx with Lieutenant Michael Scott as the Subaltern and with 2nd Lieutenant Andrew Clowes carrying the Regimental Colour. The months of January and February also saw the battalion deployed in the field for considerable periods, first on an exercise designed to test its ability to reinforce Left Flank in Zanzibar in an internal security situation, and subsequently on a much larger exercise in the Northern Frontier District when the battalion was

22

enemy to both 24th Infantry Brigade and 70th King's African Rifles Brigade, the latter commanded by Brigadier Miles Fitzalan Howard, a Grenadier Guardsman and brother of Michael, a former Commanding Officer of the 2nd Battalion. Exercise SHARP PANGA took place across miles of arid, dusty bush country north of Archer's Post and practised a wide range of conventional phases of war; the battalion was reinforced by an armoured car squadron of the 9th/12th Royal Lancers and a company of the King's Own Scottish Borderers, both from Aden. It was a tiring exercise involving numerous ascents of rocky hills anything up to 2,000 feet high but enjoyable nonetheless and one on which a number of ruses were attempted in an effort to disconcert the *askaris* of 70th Brigade, including deploying a psychological warfare unit to broadcast lion noises at them. The latter had absolutely no effect! Re-supply throughout was by Twin Pioneer aircraft of the RAF and two Cessnas belonging to the Kenya Police Airwing provided an aerial observation capability for the battalion.

In early March Left Flank returned from Zanzibar and Major Acland departed for Britain, having handed over his company to Major M.B. Scott, an old Kenya hand who had previously served on secondment with the King's African Rifles. Meanwhile Lieutenant Michael Scott set off with a party from Right Flank to climb Mount Kilimanjaro; this was one of a number of expeditions which attempted assaults upon Kenya's highest peaks during the battalion's tour in East Africa; Kilimanjaro at just over 19,300 feet and Point Lenana, the third peak of Mount Kenya at a height of 16,355 feet and only 700 feet below the twin peaks of the main summit, offered enormous scope for a challenging physical effort and rewarded those who reached the top with incomparable views and an enormous sense of achievement. Lieutenant Scott described the Right Flank climb of Kilimanjaro as follows: 'At last we reached Gillman's Point, the acknowledged summit of Kilimanjaro and the accepted highest point on the African Continent. We dropped exhausted in the snow, tears of triumph and tiredness running down our frozen cheeks .... It was now five o'clock in the morning and dawn was not due until six .... The dawn slowly came up, bathing the snow cap a rich red colour. The great ice crater glistened and sparkled, enormous blocks of ice heaped upon one another like a frozen sea. We could see far into the distance below us to the plains, hills and lakes of both Kenya and Tanganyika. We could even look down on the neighbouring peak of Mawenzi at a height of 17,000 feet. The view was quite out of this world.'

Zanzibar, an island off the coast of Tanganyika famous for being the world's largest producer of cloves, was to preoccupy the battalion throughout the summer months of 1963. In early April the battalion was placed at twelve hours' notice to move to the island to aid the civil power but was stood down two weeks later. This alert was confirmation that the battalion would be involved in July in helping to oversee the forthcoming elections in the Protectorate and contingency planning for the battalion's move and subsequent deployment was set in train. At Kahawa 'fly out' exercises designed to rehearse procedures for the quick recall, preparation and despatch by air of the battalion for an operational deployment were held on the barrack square with platoons and departments forming up in aircraft 'chalks'. Few would deny that these rehearsals for an air move, with all their attendant paperwork, but which either never left the barrack square or which culminated in a move by three-ton truck simulating an RAF transport aircraft, were extremely tedious. However, such training did pay dividends when in 1964 the battalion had to undertake a series of emergency moves with little or no warning. When the Staffordshire Regiment arrived at Kahawa the battalion was called upon to demonstrate these fly out procedures during which the Commanding Officer escorted his opposite number around each company. On coming to the Police Sergeant, Sergeant Mann, Colonel Ramsay ordered a particular box to be opened to show its contents, despite entreaties from Sergeant Mann that it might be wiser to look at an alternative. Embarrassingly, it was found to contain the Sergeants' Mess immediate re-supply of spirits!

Alongside these administrative preparations training continued and the Commanding Officer directed a company test exercise nicknamed Exercise STEEL BLADE which involved each company in turn advancing to contact, crossing a river, occupying a defensive position and finally withdrawing to the Kahawa training area. An unfortunate incident occurred when 2nd Lieutenant Andrew Clowes' platoon of Right Flank was deposited in the water while crossing the flooded Athi River; several rifles and a Bren gun were lost overboard never to be recovered, but happily no one was drowned. Much embarrassment and the longest ever Board of Enquiry ensued.

The scope for training in Kenya was almost unlimited and companies took full advantage of the wide range of options which vast tracts of bush and forest offered for dry exercises or live firing. The frequency with which European farmers made their estates available was remarkable, Sam Small who farmed near Nanyuki allowing most infantry weapons to be fired on his land seemingly without restriction other than that nobody should be shot.

Following the Queen's Birthday Parade on 8 June, the battalion turned its attention to the forthcoming move to Zanzibar to supervise pre-independence elections in the Protectorate. An advance party under the Second-in-Command, Brevet Lieutenant Colonel Peter Leng, left in the middle of the month, followed a week later by the main body which moved in two halves to Mombasa by rail and then crossed to Zanzibar in the SS *Seyid Khalifa*, a vessel displacing approximately 1,500 tons, owned and chartered by the Zanzibar Government, with a reputation for rolling atrociously in the heavy seas that are frequently encountered between the mainland coast and the islands. Right Flank was disembarked at Wete on the island of Pemba on the morning of 20 June and the *Seyid Khalifa* then sailed on to Zanzibar where the remainder went ashore. Left Flank arrived on the morning of 23 June. Once ashore, the battalion deployed with Battalion Headquarters and Left Flank at the Aga Khan Bungalow, G Company, now commanded by Major Tony Boam, at Chukwani Palace, all on

Zanzibar Island, and with Right Flank and the Drums based near Chake Chake on Pemba. The battalion had its own air support in the form of a Beaver fixed wing aircraft and an Alouette helicopter based at Zanzibar Airport and flown respectively by Captain Jeremy Hope, a Grenadier, and Captain Richard Nash, a 9th/12th Royal Lancer.

While the 2nd Battalion was preparing to deploy to Zanzibar, the Gordon Highlanders had been stood to for a possible move to Swaziland, a small British colony surrounded by South Africa, where demands were being made for accelerated progress towards independence. On 12 June troops were flown to Mbabane and within a period of ten days the Gordons had the situation firmly under control. That two battalions of 24th Infantry Brigade should be deployed out of Kenya at the same time gives some indication of the delicacy of the situation in many of Britain's dependent territories in the period immediately prior to their achievement of independence.

During 1961 and 1962 there had been outbreaks of racial violence in Zanzibar and troops and police had been sent from Kenya to restore order. Since 1962 a military garrison had been maintained on the island and when the 2nd Battalion Scots Guards travelled there in June, 1963, an uneasy peace existed between the Arab ruling elite and their former slaves who were generally of African descent. Four political parties contested the elections, of which only two carried any real influence: the Zanzibar National Party (ZNP) represented the Arabs on both islands, while the Afro-Shirazi Party attracted the support of most Africans. The battalion's role was to make a show of force among the local population, to familiarize itself with the geography of both islands and to effect maximum co-operation with the local police and to assist in arresting criminals, in particular those involved in the illicit brewing of *pombe*, a native liquor. In the days before the elections patrols from the battalion visited as many villages as possible to impress their presence on the local people and searches were made for illegal stills since it was calculated that the less alcohol in circulation the less chance of a riot.

Zanzibar Elections 1963

On 1 July Battalion Headquarters and G Company moved to Pemba aboard the *Seyid Khalifa* to reinforce Right Flank for the elections to be held there on 8 July. This move was not without its difficulties since the ship could only get to within three-quarters of a mile of the shore and all vehicles and stores had to be transferred by lighter, a time-consuming and, in view of the competence of some of the local dockers, a somewhat hazardous undertaking. An added complication occurred when, on the night of 30 June, the Sultan died following an operation on his leg; trouble might have been expected but did not materialize and his son succeeded him without incident, his Coronation being held on 5 July.

On Pemba voting took place over two days and G Company was deployed to man roadblocks to prevent unnecessary movement while Right Flank patrolled and held riot squads in reserve. Battalion Headquarters established a joint operations room with the police who had themselves been heavily reinforced

25

from Zanzibar. The election passed off peacefully, whereupon Battalion Head-quarters and G Company returned to Zanzibar Island where the whole process was repeated on 12 July, this time with Left Flank mounting an intensive patrol programme across the island. Again there were few incidents, although one woman, having voted, failed to have her thumb marked with indelible dye, was thought not to have voted by her villagers and was just stopped from trying to vote a second time – just the sort of occurrence potential trouble-makers would try to exploit – while a man being carried on a stretcher to the polling station died before he reached it! The counting of votes was arranged by the judiciary, although some officers were called upon to help while guardsmen guarded the ballot boxes until the results were announced on 15 July, when all three companies were deployed in strength to deter trouble. The result was a narrow win for the ZNP who missed achieving an overall majority over the other three parties by one seat; the Afro-Shirazi Party had a majority on Zanzibar Island and the Arabs a majority on Pemba which, after considerable horse-trading, led to the ZNP, under the leadership of Sheikh Mohammed Shamte, eventually forming a coalition government with the minority African Party. While at the time this appeared a pragmatic result from a potentially difficult election, it was an accommodation which could not endure as some officials of the British administration observed at the time. Sir George Mooring, the Resident in Zanzibar, and his advisers clearly foresaw potential trouble from the Afro-Shirazi Party who felt cheated of their rightful political inheritance on Zanzibar Island, and their forebodings of future trouble were amply borne out six months later when an African uprising took place.

Before leaving Zanzibar to return to Kenya the battalion, less Right Flank, paraded before the Resident and then marched past the Ruler who took the salute in front of his Palace on the waterfront in Zanzibar Town. The move back to Nairobi was executed by the same route as the move out and the whole battalion was back in barracks by 19 August. While the battalion was preparing to leave Zanzibar, reinforcements from Britain arrived at Kahawa in the form of 3 Company Irish Guards which was detached from its parent battalion in Germany to be part of the 2nd Battalion for the remainder of the Kenya tour.

Continuing recruiting problems and the deleterious effect that constant demands for manpower support were having on the 1st Battalion Scots Guards, had led to a change of policy and it had been decided that in future a complete subunit from another Foot Guards regiment would be used to reinforce an understrength battalion rather than to continue with a system of piecemeal transfer from within the regiment concerned; there was nothing new in this, such an arrangement having been ordered several times during the Second World War and indeed the 1st Battalion was also to be reinforced by the Irish Guards when it went to the Far East in 1964. 3 Company was commanded by Major Tony Plummer with CSM Shannon and CQMS Lynas as its senior ranks. The company soon settled into the ways of the Scots Guards and became well integrated although never quite losing that unique Irish Guards characteristic of easy informality which can cause those outside the magic circle who are unfamiliar with the ways of the 'Micks' to wonder sometimes if what was promised would be delivered! Invariably it was in Kenya. The Company made its mark in a variety of ways but shooting was a particular strength and Lieutenant Rory Brown swept the board at most rifle meetings. A consequence of 3 Company's arrival was that G Company disbanded as a rifle company and was re-designated G (Training) Company remaining under Major Boam's command with Lieutenant Ian McLaughlan being responsible for running tactical cadre courses.

At midnight on 11 December, 1963, Kenya became an independent country within the Commonwealth after sixty-nine years of British rule. His Royal Highness The Duke of Edinburgh came out from Britain to represent Her Majesty The Queen at independence ceremonies in both Zanzibar and Nairobi and on his arrival in the Kenyan capital was received at Government House by a Guard of Honour found from Right Flank and commanded by Major Douglas Prior who had earlier taken over from Major Priaulx. Later that same evening a ceremony was held at a specially built stadium near Nairobi when the Union Jack was hauled down for the last time and replaced by the standard of the new country; the Governor, Mr Malcolm MacDonald, stood with the Prime Minister, Mr Kenyatta, in the centre of the arena as three Guards of the King's African Rifles paraded opposite three Guards of the Kenya Army. The Colours were handed over to the new regiment and then trooped through the ranks symbolizing the farewell to the King's African Rifles and the birth of the new Army. Prior to this 1,200 tribesmen from the Kikuyu, Wakamba, Masai, Kalinjin and Samburu tribes had danced for nearly three hours before being replaced, not without some difficulty, in the arena by the massed bands, which included the battalion's own Corps of Drums and which were all under the direction of Drum Major Hickling. The latter's nerve was severely tested as he headed the massed bands into the arena since the dancers failed to understand the requirement to leave and had literally to be pushed out of the way. It was a happy occasion of enormous significance for the people of Kenya and the vast crowds behaved with enthusiasm and dignity, there being virtually no trouble. Mr MacDonald remained in the country for another nine months as Governor-General to assist the new nation to find its feet, while in due course Mr Kenyatta was to become Kenya's first President. Although few foresaw it at the time the first test of the new government was to come within a month.

In the early hours of 12 January, 1964, a *coup d'état* was mounted against the Arab dominated Government of Zanzibar starting a chain of events which were to threaten directly the political stability and future prosperity of the four newly independent nations of East Africa. In due course it fell to the units of 24th Infantry Brigade based in Kenya, with some assistance from others in Aden, to restore law and order in those countries where it had been lost, or to pre-empt its loss by timely deployment where a breakdown seemed imminent. Although at the time the events of January and early February, 1964, prompted headlines

Kenya Independence

Coup d'état in Zanzibar 1964

27

across the world few will now be able to recall what happened in those tense and uncertain days in East Africa nor in all probability did they really appreciate at the time the full part played by British troops in helping to restore peace to the democracies concerned.

On 12 January the battalion was due to fly to Aden to train as an all-arms battle group in the desert near Bir Fukum, the first aircraft from Nairobi being due away at 0700 hours and carrying, amongst others the Commanding Officer and the Adjutant. Alerted by a telephone call from Brigade Headquarters that there had been 'trouble in a place that the battalion had visited last summer', on arrival at the airport Colonel Ramsay was told by Major General Ian Freeland, the GOC British Land Forces Kenya (the successors to East Africa Command), to abandon plans to exercise in Aden and instead to prepare to invade Zanzibar in order to restore the legitimate government. The battalion was rapidly stood to, equipment repacked, live ammunition issued and plans for a landing against opposition at Zanzibar Airport made. In view of the company's extensive knowledge of the island Left Flank under Major M.B. Scott and CSM Louden was to lead the assault to secure the airport flying in by Beverley and Twin Pioneer aircraft, after which 3 Company and Right Flank would follow up and deploy into Zanzibar Town. By 1100 hours the leading elements of the battalion were assembled at the RAF Station at Eastleigh near Nairobi and were ready to go; the British Government gave early approval for intervention, but efforts to obtain agreement from the Kenyan Government for an operation to be mounted from Nairobi were rebuffed and as evening descended and no decision had been forthcoming it was decided to postpone the operation until the following day. In the event the Kenyan Government never gave its approval and the battalion was stood down and told to resurrect its plan to fly to Aden. It is not difficult to see why Prime Minister Kenyatta might have been reluctant to authorize the invasion of a neighbouring African state from his territory, particularly when a hated Arab régime was in the throes of being overthrown by Africans. With the benefit of hindsight, it is possible to appreciate that the chances of the battalion being deployed to Zanzibar were never very high. At the time it was all seen very differently and frustration and disappointment were keenly felt throughout the battalion as the day wore on and speculation became rife. Had Left Flank been launched to capture the airport the company would undoubtedly have had a difficult task, although subsequent intelligence showed that the rebels did not secure the airport and block the runway until mid-afternoon and that, had the leading elements of the battalion been dispatched as soon as ready, they would probably have been successful in their mission. Seizure of power by the rebels was followed by a bloodbath, retribution being visited upon the Arabs, resulting in the virtual sealing off of Zanzibar to the outside world until its incorporation into the United Republic of Tanzania in 1964 when some links to the mainland were restored.

Aden
13 January was a day of feverish activity as the battalion unravelled the plans made the previous day to invade Zanzibar and once again turned its attention to

28

exercising in Aden; flight manifestos had to be re-written and freight repacked and the RAF's strict rules on the carriage of hazardous cargo once again put into effect; with the exception of one Britannia aircraft which sustained acid damage to its floor owing to the incorrect packaging of a battery all went well and the battalion was complete in camp near Little Aden on 14 January.

Exercise SANDBIRD was designed to allow the battalion to train with its affiliated supporting arms and services, including tanks from 16th/5th The Queen's Royal Lancers based in Aden and an RAF Belvedere Helicopter. However, no sooner had this training started to develop a momentum of its own than news percolated to Little Aden that there was again trouble in East Africa and on 20 January it was confirmed that two battalions of the Tanganyika Rifles had mutinied at Dar-es-Salaam and Tabora. Headquarters Middle East Command made immediate plans to dispatch 45 Commando Royal Marines to position itself off Tanganyika aboard the aircraft carrier HMS *Centaur* and to return the 2nd Battalion Scots Guards to Kenya. The situation was extremely confused and the Commanding Officer was sent a signal which read 'Send 248 personnel including Tactical Headquarters to Khormaksar (the RAF airfield) soonest. Ring GSO 1 Ops'. This arrived at 1355 hours and, having summoned officers by the simple expedient of instructing the duty drummer to sound the Officers Call 'at the double', which incidentally very few recognized, Colonel Ramsay ordered training to cease forthwith and companies to prepare to fly back to Nairobi immediately. It was a tribute to all concerned that the first Beverley was ready to take off at 1655 hours, this being achieved not just by good work within the battalion and by the Unit Emplaning Officer, Major Tony Boam, but also because the RAF waived its own rules and simply stowed men and equipment on aircraft as they appeared; as with all emergencies the RAF was seen at its best. The move went more or less as planned, except that the lead Beverley with Colonel Ramsay on board burst two tyres on attempting to take off and had to be doused in foam, something that, much to his consternation Major Donald Whyte, the Quartermaster, witnessed from high up in the boom of the aircraft. By 1500 hours on 21 January the battalion was complete at Kahawa and being held at immediate notice for whatever might be ordered next. Again the Kenya Government refused permission for the mounting of an operation from its territory to restore the situation in Tanganyika and 45 Commando was eventually ordered to assault the Tanganyika Rifles barracks in Dar-es-Salaam and Tabora, which it duly accomplished. Before 45 Commando left Aden Captain Johnny Clavering, by then the Signal Officer, was attached to the Marines to act as a liaison officer with knowledge of the Dar-es-Salaam area and Zanzibar, invasion plans for which place were still being considered at that stage.

Back in Kenya, three units of 24th Infantry Brigade were being held at varying degrees of notice; the Staffords were in Kahawa with one company embarked on a frigate off Zanzibar; 3rd Regiment Royal Horse Artillery was complete at Gilgil as were the Gordons who were, however, deemed to be non-operational since their advance party had already returned to Edinburgh with a proportion of the battalion's key personnel. Completing the Brigade order of battle was the 2nd Battalion which was stood down to twelve hours' notice on 23 January when the Staffords took its place at immediate notice. As luck would have it, this was the day that the Uganda Rifles mutinied in their barracks at Jinja some fifty miles east of Kampala and the Prime Minister, Mr Milton Obote, requested immediate British assistance. This was quickly agreed to by the British and Kenya Governments and at 2030 hours the Staffords, with Right Flank under command to replace the company at sea, were despatched to help. The attachment of Right Flank to the Staffords to go to Uganda was some compensation for the alarms and excursions suffered by the battalion over the previous ten days; Major Douglas Prior recalls telephoning CSM F. Smith to tell him to get the company ready for an immediate move only to be told, 'Nae bother, we got everything done this afternoon!'

Uganda Mutiny   The genesis of the trouble which blew up in Uganda lay as much in inter-tribal rivalry as in a desire to seize power for power's sake. Well-trained by their British officers, the process of 'Africanisation' within the Uganda Rifles had proceeded at a faster pace than was probably wise and this, coupled with some inept internal planning and encouraged by the example of other African states, led to the Jinja mutiny. Lieutenant Colonel Dick Stuckey, who commanded the 1st Battalion The Staffordshire Regiment, planned that Right Flank should secure Entebbe Airport before the remainder of his battalion landed, something which was achieved in a text-book operation without incident, thereby allowing the Staffords to move directly to Jinja to disarm the mutineers. While this move was taking place intelligence suggesting that the dissident Ugandan soldiers were about to break out of barracks led to a change of plan and Major Prior was ordered to motor immediately to Jinja to join the rest of the battalion, leaving only a small group to secure Entebbe Airport. On arrival at Jinja, Right Flank found itself allocated the furthest area of the barracks to secure, an area that allegedly housed the 'intellectuals' in the battalion and the people responsible for the uprising. Having cordoned the area, the ring leaders were arrested and taken away without too much difficulty and Right Flank then turned its attention to removing the contents of the battalion armoury from Jinja to a more secure barracks near Kampala. This successfully accomplished, the company was called upon to execute one final duty when two platoons were deployed to Jinja to be present when the new Commanding Officer of the Uganda Rifles read a proclamation disbanding the battalion which had mutinied. Thus ended a highly successful operation to nip trouble in the bud before it could develop into something much more serious; not a single shot had been fired in anger during the whole operation, and as Major Prior wrote on Right Flank's return, 'A measure of our success was that we acted soon enough to prevent violence, yet not too soon to provoke it.'

Kenya Mutiny   At the same time as Right Flank flew to Entebbe with the Staffords the rest of the battalion was warned that similar trouble to that reported from Uganda could be expected within the Kenya Army. With this in mind, some pre-emptive deployment to protect British Army installations in Nairobi was ordered on 24 January, while reconnaissance parties from the battalion toured the city the same day to be briefed on security plans and to reassure the Nairobi Police that, in the event of trouble, the British Army would support them. In January, 1964, the Kenya Army was still led and trained by British officers and was very much a force to be respected, not least because it was well armed with modern weapons, while many of its soldiers came from the warrior tribes of Kenya and made good fighting men. Units were deployed throughout the country and some rifle companies were at the time engaged in operations against Somali *shifta* bands who had for some months been infiltrating the Northern Frontier District of Kenya in an attempt to promote a territorial claim to the area. However, peacetime deployment had not changed since Independence and the three infantry battalions were still based, one each at Langata near Nairobi, at Lanet in Nakuru and at Nanyuki, with a support battalion at Buller Barracks in Nairobi.

The mutiny within the Kenya Army began on the evening of 24 January when a small group in the 11th Battalion Kenya Rifles broke into the Armoury in Lanet Camp, Nakuru. This incident was subsequently dealt with by 3rd Regiment Royal Horse Artillery acting in the infantry role, the mutineers being finally disarmed on 25 January. Although there was no parallel action by dissident soldiers elsewhere within the Kenya Army, at 2100 hours on 24 January, the 2nd Battalion Scots Guards was ordered to secure certain key points in and around Nairobi with the intention of protecting vital installations and deterring any further attempted acts of mutiny. Left Flank was dispatched to watch the 3rd Battalion Kenya Rifles at Langata with orders to the Company Commander to use whatever force he felt might be necessary to disarm the *askaris* if they threatened trouble, a situation that could have posed Major M.B. Scott with something of a dilemma in view of his past service in that battalion. While this deployment was taking place the remainder of the battalion moved into Nairobi; Battalion Headquarters, 3 Company and A Company of The Gordon Highlanders, which had been placed under command on the departure of Right Flank, concentrated at Nairobi Area Police Headquarters while the Drums Platoon under Lieutenant Michael Scott secured the studios of the Kenya Broadcasting Corporation against an attempted seizure. Dick Angel, a former Scots Guards piper and the Superintendent in charge of the para-military Police General Service Unit throughout the battalion's time in Kenya, later told how at around 2200 hours an African waiter rushed into the police mess where a formal dinner was in progress, shouting, 'They've come! they've come!' as Battalion Headquarters drove in. Those in the know smiled with relief while those who were unaware of the action ordered by the Governor-General and who immediately envisaged an early demise at the hands of the mutineers turned ashen and reached for their pistols.

During the night 3 Company was ordered into Buller Barracks to take over the

Kenya Army armoury, while at 0200 hours the Drums were relieved at the Broadcasting Studios by the police. Further reinforcements arrived in the form of a company of Staffords from Mombasa which gave Colonel Ramsay command of a battalion of four companies, each from a different regiment. However at 1935 hours on 25 January, there having been no attempt to extend the mutiny within the Kenya Army and with the police remaining loyal to the Government, it was decided that Army deployment in Nairobi could be relaxed; 3 Company and A Company of the Gordons returned to barracks, followed forty-eight hours later by Battalion Headquarters and Left Flank, leaving only a small element at Police Headquarters. Thereafter until 11 March the battalion remained confined to barracks and at eight hours notice to repeat its deployment but was never called upon to do so. On 11 February Right Flank arrived back by train from Kampala and immediately took its place on the operational standby roster for Nairobi.

So ended a series of revolts throughout East Africa; with the exception of the Zanzibar coup against the Arab-dominated island Government, the uprisings on the mainland were inspired as much by soldiers dissatisfied with their pay and conditions and distrustful of promises, which, had they been allowed to go unchecked, would no doubt have been seized upon by darker political forces and been fanned into a major revolution intended to overthrow the legitimately elected governments concerned. That such a situation was not allowed to develop says much for the harmonious relationship which existed between Britain and her former territories in East Africa in the immediate aftermath of independence, and the speed and efficiency with which the British Army reacted to quell the mutinies when the call for help finally came.

The battalion's last six months in East Africa were marked by further training and a limited operation when the Reconnaissance Platoon deployed to escort 34 Field Squadron Royal Engineers building a road into the Northern Frontier District in support of Kenya Army units waging war on the Somali *shifta*; on one occasion Lance Corporal Tunstall fired over forty rounds from his Ferret Scout Car when caught in an ambush and thus became the first British soldier to engage the enemy in what became a long-drawn-out struggle between Kenya and Somalia but which attracted little attention outside East Africa. At one moment it looked as if the whole battalion might be deployed into the area and an exercise was held at Kiboko, a small staging post on the Mombasa road 100 miles south of Nairobi, to practise living and operating in semi-arid desert conditions. Endurance marches, night training exercises, the setting of ambushes and navigation were all practised and each company and Battalion Headquarters built *zariba* fortifications utilizing thorn bushes and scrub, interspersed with dannert wire, to protect their base camps. Exercise HOT ROD was to be Colonel Ramsay's last exercise and he handed over command to Lieutenant Colonel Michael Gow on 18 June, after an eventful two years during which the battalion travelled many thousands of miles to support the legitimate interests of the people of East Africa. Colonel Ramsay could leave well satisfied with the achievements of his battalion in that time.

While operations and training were rightly the battalion's priorities during its time in Kenya, most soldiers and their families were able to relax and enjoy the country, its magnificent game parks and the many chances to travel. Football was, as always with a Scottish regiment, a major preoccupation and the battalion won the East Africa Command Championships in 1964; RSM Graham and Orderly Room Sergeant Brown drove their teams relentlessly and with players of fine quality such as Sergeants Inglis and Howden and Lance Sergeant McRobb, swept the board on innumerable occasions. RSM Graham was also responsible for the Sergeants' Mess acquiring two lion cubs. Unita and Fortior were given to the Mess by a well-wisher in the summer of 1963 and were housed in a specially built compound at Kahawa; Sergeant Ryves, the Pioneer Sergeant, doubled up as the 'Lion Keeper' and the two cubs which quickly grew into formidable young adults attracted much publicity, not all of it to the good, as when the Sergeants' Mess of the Gordon Highlanders kidnapped them and demanded a ransom for their return. The Sergeant Major's plan to return them to Britain with the battalion and to parade them with the Queen's Guard collapsed in the face of an unenthusiastic response from Headquarters Household Brigade, and eventually it was agreed that both lions would join the cast of the film 'Born Free' in which Bill Travers and Virginia McKenna portrayed the work of George and Joy Adamson, a Kenya couple who for many years had been returning lions taken into captivity back into the wild. Following this George Adamson successfully returned Unita, the lioness, to the bush and she adapted well, later giving birth to two litters of cubs. Fortior, the lion, was less fortunate and, having had a steel rod inserted into his leg after attack by a buffalo, he killed an African and had to be shot.

Exercise LAST ROUNDUP in July was the final exercise to be held by 24th Infantry Brigade in Kenya and was conducted without transport support between Kiboko and Sultan Hamud under conditions of intense heat. A month later 9 Company Irish Guards, commanded by Major John Morrogh-Bernard, arrived at Kahawa for a two month stay prior to joining the 1st Battalion Scots Guards in Malaya; the company spent much of its time forest training on the lower slopes of Mount Kenya at a camp organized by Major M.B. Scott, valuable preparation for its forthcoming role in the Far East.

While 9 Company was allocated no operational role it was fully under the command of Colonel Gow and, for the two months of its stay in Kenya, the latter commanded almost as many Irish Guardsmen as Scots Guardsmen, Right and Left Flank having been amalgamated to form a single Flank Company. This was probably the only time in the history of the Regiment when there has been such a company. It was commanded by Major Prior and had CSM F. Smith and CQMS Watson as its senior ranks. Meanwhile 3 Company, by then commanded by Major Henry Blosse-Lynch, had after fifteen months become so well integrated into the ways of the Scots Guards as to be practically indistinguishable from the other rifle companies in the battalion. The way in which 3 Company was able to identify and work with the Scots Guards, without losing

33

any of its Irish Guards personality or spirit, reflected great credit upon it and its hosts and demonstrated once again the ease with which companies can be exchanged between Foot Guards battalions.

The final two months of the battalion's time in Kenya passed in a welter of packing up and preparations to hand over vehicles, weapons and stores to the 2nd Battalion Coldstream Guards which was to join 24th Infantry Brigade in Aden in late October. Elaborate plans were made to keep people occupied and interested during the last weeks in Kenya and parties dispersed to enjoy themselves all over the country as and when the operational situation permitted. 2nd Lieutenant Alastair Morrison's platoon of Right Flank marched the 300 miles from Nairobi to Mombasa in twelve and a half days, their reward being a bottle of Pilsner beer each from the Mayor on arrival! Back at Kahawa Lieutenant Andrew Clowes and Sergeant Davis, the Intelligence Sergeant, produced a battalion pantomine in which they sang a duet of unbelievable vulgarity; Sergeant Davis, a man of large girth and splendid voice, represented all that is best in the 'scouse' character. A fine soldier, he possessed a lovely sense of humour which was only matched by his keenly tuned awareness of the ridiculous; known wherever he went in the Regiment as the 'singing gut' Sergeant Davis could always be relied upon to find the remark to suit the moment and his early death in 1989 was a sad loss to all who knew him. On 11 October, 1964, the battalion paraded at St Andrew's Church in Nairobi for a service conducted by Padre John Deans when a pew made by Sergeant Ryves was dedicated by the Minister, the Reverend Robert Keltie, in the presence of the Governor-General, who together with the Commanding Officer, each read a lesson. A fortnight earlier a Beating of Retreat had been held at Kahawa as a farewell to all the battalion's many friends in Kenya and elsewhere. The retreat was preceded by a short speech by the Commanding Officer, the final words of which were, 'For nearly three years the 2nd Battalion Scots Guards, together with members of the Irish Guards has been stationed in Kenya, and during this time has served in Zanzibar, Uganda, Tanganyika and Aden, helping to maintain law and order. The Beating of Retreat this evening is the battalion's last ceremonial appearance here before we return to the United Kingdom. During the performance by the Drums and Pipes you will hear a tune which has never before been played in public. It is called the "Heights of Mount Kenya" and it is dedicated to the many people in this beautiful country who have opened their homes and their hearts to members of the battalion. This tune, and indeed the Beating of Retreat, is a token of our gratitude to you for your hospitality and kindness.' Pipe Major Kilgour composed the pipe tune. Three weeks later, amid emotional scenes at Embakasi Airport when the Caledonian Society of Kenya came to say farewell, the battalion departed Kenya for Caterham, being the penultimate battalion to leave the country and having played a not inconsiderable part in helping to ensure the stability of the region at a time of severe internal threat.

CHAPTER THREE

MALAYSIA AND BORNEO

1st Battalion: Pirbright-Terendak-Sarawak-Sabah

In the middle of June, 1962, the battalion moved from Milton Barracks, *1962* Gravesend, to the newly built but still unfinished Elizabeth Barracks at Pirbright. The move to a new barracks was necessitated by the requirement to locate another battalion at Gravesend and, in view of the contractor's estimate that work at Pirbright would be finished by late October, it was judged acceptable that the 1st Battalion should suffer some disruption upon its arrival in the new barracks. In the event the contractor encountered considerable labour problems and the last buildings, which included both messes and the Junior Ranks Club, were not finally handed over until the Spring of 1963. Despite the inconvenience of living in a partially completed barracks the battalion quickly settled in and took its place on the public duties roster, although when they set out to mount Queen's Guard guardsmen found themselves approaching London from the west rather than along the A2 from the east as had been the case from Gravesend.

The battalion had been destined to undertake a tour of duty as the Spearhead Battalion in the summer of 1962, but, in view of its low strength, that commitment, which involved a United Kingdom-based battalion being held at reduced notice to move anywhere in the world where British interests might be threatened, was passed instead to the 1st Battalion Coldstream Guards stationed at Windsor. As a result when the Coldstream Guards were subsequently deployed to deal with trouble in British Guiana in October, the 1st Battalion Scots Guards found itself undertaking ceremonial duties at Windsor in addition to being on the roster for London, despite suffering from a critical shortage of guardsmen. This shortage stemmed from two principal reasons: a failure on the part of the Regiment to recruit sufficient men at a time of intense competition for manpower nationally and because of the priority given to ensuring that the 2nd Battalion in Kenya was maintained at full strength. It was against this background that on 8 March, 1963, twenty-five guardsmen absented themselves from Pirbright claiming a number of grievances. This serious breach of discipline which, as might be expected, was widely reported in the media and in certain respects even encouraged by some reporters, had its origins in a variety of causes, some real and some contrived. While nothing can ever justify such action it is only right to record that the pressures on the battalion at that time were considerable and that with the benefit of hindsight it is possible to see why events took the course that they did. A breakdown in communication and in the battalion's internal procedures, an acute shortage of manpower, a programme of public duties and training which, when combined, was too heavy and a loss of respect and confidence between ranks were probably the main causes of the incident, although a lack of understanding of the battalion's problems on the part of the chain of command in London did little to assist the Commanding Officer who was at the time far from well supported by some of his officers and some senior members of the Sergeants' Mess. Whatever the spark that ignited the flare-up, the immediate incident was quickly dealt with by Colonel Charles Duffin, the culprits disciplined, changes in personnel and procedures made and a more durable system of communication set in place both within the battalion and London District. As one leader writer wrote at the time, 'That soldiers must accept sterner disciplines than civilians is self evident. The Brigade of Guards have had a proud tradition of demanding a discipline more rigid and unbending than any other establishment in the country – possibly the world. An indispensable element of this exacting regime is efficient administration. Unquestioning subjection to the fierce demands of the Regiment is tolerable only so long as the Regiment is equally fierce in its concern for its men.' In the aftermath of the humiliating events of 8 March, 1963, few in the Regiment or indeed in the Brigade needed to be reminded of that maxim.

1963   The summer of 1963 brought a continuing heavy load of duties, including participation in the Queen's Birthday Parade, but the battalion was able to train at Otterburn in October. Following the events of March it had been decided that the 1st Battalion would no longer be required to reinforce the 2nd Battalion in Kenya and, as the Regiment's poor recruiting situation started to show some signs of improvement, so the strength of the battalion slowly increased and in September it became possible to reform Left Flank as the battalion's second rifle company. Major David Walter was the Company Commander with CSM Cobham as his Company Sergeant Major. It was already known that the battalion was to move to the Far East in late 1964 for a tour of duty in 28th Commonwealth Brigade and Lieutenant Colonel Archie Fletcher, who had assumed command from Colonel Charles Duffin in April, made it clear to his battalion that while he could offer little but an unrelenting round of public duties in the short term, further ahead lay the prospect of a major exercise in Scotland in early 1964 and later the move to Malaysia. Such was the desire of the battalion to redeem itself that everybody buckled down, determined to show just what could be achieved; Major John Acland and Major Sir Gregor MacGregor returned to command Right Flank and Headquarter Company respectively, while RSM Forsyth came at short notice from Regimental Headquarters to take over from RSM Rodger who left at the end of his twenty-two years' service. History was also made on 10 June when CQMS Snuggs left the Regiment on the completion of his service; he was the last remaining member of a draft posted from the RAF Regiment in June, 1943. In late February, 1964, the battalion moved north by air and road to Kintyre as a prelude to a month's hard training which at various times took platoons to most parts of Argyll and Perthshire. Thanks to his contacts in the other two services the Commanding Officer was able to enlist the support of a submarine and a landing craft as well as transport aircraft and, during its time in Scotland, the battalion successfully 'captured' the Crinan Canal and each platoon in turn took part in an exercise which required them to sabotage a hydro-electric dam in Glen Shira before escaping by submarine at night down Loch Fyne. Positive leadership and imaginative planning helped to make the exercise a success, thereby further advancing the process of rehabilitation which Colonel Fletcher had set in train on arrival.

On 10 June, 1964, His Royal Highness The Duke of Gloucester, on behalf of *Presentation of* Her Majesty The Queen, presented New Colours to the battalion at Elizabeth *Colours* Barracks. It was a lovely day and history was made, not only because the parade took place away from one of the royal palaces where traditionally such events are held, but because it was the first time that a battalion of the Regiment was to receive new Colours at Pirbright, to the accompaniment of the sounds of trains across the Basingstoke Canal and rifle fire from the ranges!

Flanked by detachments from K Company and the Junior Guardsmen's Company and with a large contingent from the Scots Guards Association on parade, the battalion drilled with precision and dignity; the Old Colours, carried by 2nd Lieutenants Charles Gwyn and Anthony Leask, were marched off parade to the strains of 'Auld Lang Syne', after which the New Colours were consecrated by the Reverend David Henderson, Deputy Chaplain General and a former chaplain to the battalion, and were then presented by the Colonel to be carried on parade for the first time by Lieutenants Richard Fane-Gladwin and Kim Ross. Following the presentation the parade marched past the Colonel and advanced in review order, the Band playing amongst others such tunes as 'The Australian Ladies' and 'G Company's Welcome to Kuala Kubu Bahru' thereby drawing attention to the battalion's forthcoming move to the Commonwealth Brigade in Malaysia. In his address to the parade the Colonel too looked firmly to the future when he said 'I feel sure that your duties as the British Battalion in the Commonwealth Brigade in the Far East will be most exacting .... and that whatever duties you may be called upon to carry out you will, in the best traditions of the Regiment, add lustre to the Colours which I have now entrusted to your keeping.' Thus ended a resoundingly successful day when it could be fairly said that the ghosts which had haunted the battalion since March of the previous year were finally laid to rest, something which Colonel Fletcher had had in the forefront of his mind when he requested that the parade be held at Pirbright.

Elsewhere at Pirbright the Scots Guards were also fully in control of the *Guards Depot*

Household Brigade's destiny. Previously in March, 1963, Lieutenant Colonel David Scott-Barrett had taken command of the Guards Depot and initially had Captain John Arthur of the Regiment as his Adjutant. Colonel David, or 'Colonel Wobbly' as he will always be affectionately known to many Scots Guardsmen, soon made his presence felt. Whether through his policy of designating the more grimy areas of the Depot 'black spots' to be cleaned up instantly, or by visiting the sentries in the early hours by ambushing them in their sentry boxes, Colonel David imposed new targets of conduct and achievement upon recruits and permanent staff alike. No soldier at the Depot could be under any illusions as to what the Commandant expected of him or the part he was required to play in promoting the cause of his regiment and the Brigade. His tour in command was exemplified by an overriding wish that people entrusted to his care at the Depot should be given every opportunity to realize their natural talents to the benefit of themselves and their fellow men. He departed in July, 1965, being given a heartfelt send off by the Sergeants' Mess, much of which CSM Gifford of K Company helped to organize. The high point of the evening came when the company sergeant majors of the five regimental companies marched past the departing Commandant with motor mowers on the lawn in front of the Sergeants' Mess; the scene was later described in the *Household Brigade Magazine* as follows: 'To the collector of rare and exotic drill displays this must have been a unique prize for the Company Sergeant Majors, under the command of CSM Grindley, Coldstream Guards, "trooped" with motorized lawn mowers, the colours being a scythe wielded by CSM Grindley. The drill movements were of course expertly performed although there was for a time dispute, some favouring "Line Astern" and "Line Abreast" in preference to "Advance in Review Order".'

During part of Colonel Scott-Barrett's time at the Depot the Junior Guardsmen's Company was commanded by another Scots Guardsman, Major Tony Philipson, coincidentally a close friend of the Commandant. Major Philipson served the Regiment and the Household Brigade in a wide variety of roles during his long service but will be remembered chiefly for his generosity of spirit, his deep knowledge of people in the Regiment, be they a newly joined recruit, a parent, a senior officer, a wife or a girlfriend, his affection for everything connected with the Scots Guards and the enormous personal effort that he contributed to improving the Regiment's poor recruiting situation in the 1970s. When he handed over command of his junior guardsmen he bequeathed to his successor a company well established and rich in achievement, most of which had been brought about by his tremendous enthusiasm and pioneering work.

Malaysia

Following the presentation of New Colours by the Colonel on 10 June, 1964, the 1st Battalion turned its attention towards its forthcoming tour in the Far East. On 15 July the Old Colours were laid up in the Guards Chapel while the battalion's last public duty was mounted on 23 August. In early September a party of officers and NCOs left to attend courses in Malaya and the remainder

38

of the battalion flew out with its families to Kuala Lumpur at the end of that month, most flights being delayed for technical reasons. From Kuala Lumpur it was only ninety miles to Malacca and Terendak Camp, a cantonment of 1,500 acres holding the entire Commonwealth Brigade and, although described by one observer as 'looking in places like a tropical Welwyn Garden City', it proved to be an agreeably designed and well equipped base and an especially good home for the battalion's families when their husbands departed on operational tours in 1965 and 1966.

28th Commonwealth Brigade, composed of units from Australia and New Zealand as well as Britain, including the 3rd Battalion The Royal Australian Regiment, the Scots Guards' affiliated regiment, was commanded by Brigadier Terence McMeekin, a former Royal Artilleryman who was to prove a good friend to the battalion during its time in Terendak. The battalion order of battle was completed in mid October when 9 Company Irish Guards, commanded by Major John Morrogh-Bernard, arrived to provide the third rifle company, further evidence of the Scots Guards' inability to recruit sufficient soldiers to man two battalions at that time while at the same time demonstrating the flexibility by which regiments of the Brigade of Guards were able to reinforce one another without any loss of efficiency and without a lengthy period of assimilation. 9 Company arrived in Malaya having spent two months in Kenya with the 2nd Battalion under whose auspices it had undergone an intensive programme of forest training on the slopes of Mount Kenya.

The primary role of 28th Commonwealth Brigade was to prevent a Communist incursion developing against Malaya and Singapore from the north, such a threat being considered a real possibility in view of the war in Vietnam; as will be seen later the brigade was to be called upon to assist in Borneo during the latter part of 'Confrontation' with Indonesia, but this was always a secondary role and required rather different training and tactics from those which would have been employed to defeat an incursion from the direction of Thailand. However, the battalion's first priority was to learn its new business by practising living and operating in the jungle, by learning to work with helicopters and by mastering all those other skills so essential if an enemy who is normally only fleetingly seen in dense undergrowth is to be brought to battle and defeated with the minimum of effort. It was fortunate that a number of senior members of the battalion had seen service with the 2nd Battalion during the Malayan Emergency of fifteen years previously and the Commanding Officer, together with his Second-in-Command, Major MacGregor, two of his company commanders, Majors de Klee and Stewart-Wilson and RSM Forsyth had all been in the battalion at that time. They knew the importance of meticulously observing the smaller points of operational detail and doubtless had recollections of lives endangered through a momentary lapse of attention or negligence with a weapon.

Companies each deployed to the Jungle Warfare School at Johore Bahru for five days in late October and it was during this time that an Indonesian landing

39

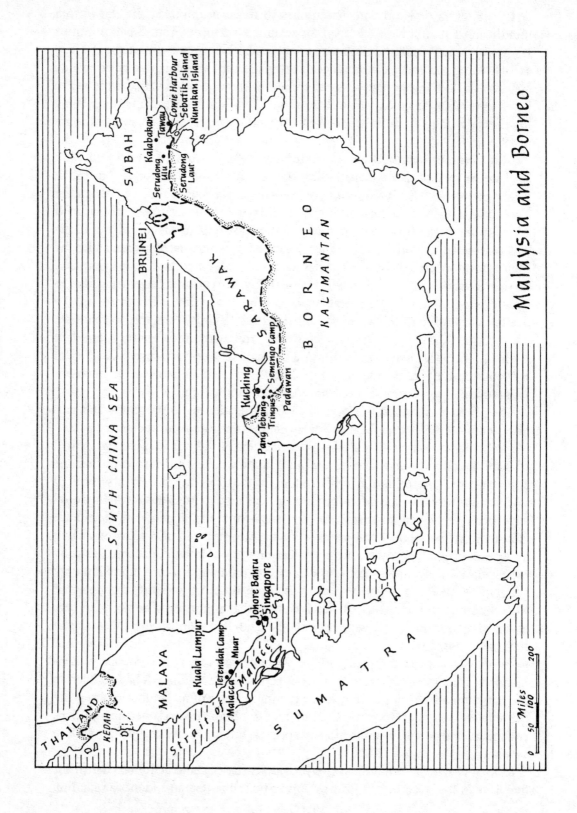

Malaysia and Borneo

took place at Muar, thirty miles south-east of Malacca. The battalion was placed at notice but was held in reserve and not involved in the immediate mopping-up operations, although, following a further alarm, a platoon of Left Flank was deployed to cover a possible riverline approach. On this occasion the invading Indonesians had shown themselves to be most incompetent but the fact that an enemy landing had taken place at all helped to put the battalion on its toes.

In late November Right Flank, commanded by Major Blair Stewart-Wilson, deployed for operations on the Thai-Malay border, followed a week later by the remainder of the battalion. Battalion Headquarters was situated at Sik in Kedah with all three rifle companies deployed up to forty-five miles away along the border. Operations were continually carried out against hardcore Communist Terrorists who lived astride the border and the operational pattern was for each company to establish a suitable jungle base with its platoons at close quarters and patrolling the area; little occurred during this initial deployment but the training achieved, sometimes in the company of tigers and elephants, was invaluable and provided useful experience for what was to come later in Borneo.

On 11 December intelligence from the Thai Police indicated the existence near the border of a sizeable terrorist camp thought to have been recently occupied by up to 250 men; Left Flank and 9 Company were re-deployed to cover possible routes from the camp, while Right Flank, who had returned to Terendak, was flown back into the area and once again deployed. Although some signs of a camp and possible food caches were found no contact was made with the suspected terrorists and a week before Christmas the battalion was relieved by the 1st Battalion Malaysian Rangers and returned to barracks.

No sooner had the battalion sorted itself out after this excursion to Northern Malaya than on 24 December it received an order warning it to be ready to move to Sarawak for a four month tour early in the New Year. In the light of intelligence which indicated a possible Indonesian attack on Kuching, it had been decided that the battalion's planned deployment should be brought forward. Preparations were hurriedly made over Christmas and the advance party departed on 1 January, 1965, to be followed twenty-four hours later by the main body of the battalion, half of which flew direct to Kuching while the remainder travelled by rail to Singapore and embarked on HMT *Auby*, a converted cargo steamer used for ferrying units across the South China Sea to Sarawak during 'Confrontation'.

Before describing the 1st Battalion's deployment in Sarawak it is first necessary to explain the origins of 'Confrontation'. The vast island of Borneo was in 1962 shared between Britain and Indonesia. Along the northern coast lay three British dependencies; the colonies of North Borneo and Sarawak and the Sultanate of Brunei, the latter rich in oil and natural gas. To the south lay Kalimantan, an integral part of the state of Indonesia and ruled by President Sukarno, a man ambitious for himself and his country with expansionist plans which were only likely to be satisfied by the acquisition of territory belonging to

41

a neighbour. In December, 1962, open revolt encouraged by Indonesia erupted in Brunei, although there had already been earlier stirrings of trouble amongst the Chinese population in Sarawak and North Borneo. Under the terms of the South-East Asia Treaty Organization (SEATO) military assistance from Britain was immediately made available and the revolt was quickly suppressed although not without loss of life.

However, no sooner had peace been restored in Brunei than Jakarta Radio warned that volunteers were standing by to liberate 'British North Borneo' and the first attacks came on 12 April, 1963, in Sarawak. Thereafter guerrilla forces, trained and equipped by Indonesia, infiltrated across the border and waged war on the inhabitants of Sarawak and North Borneo. On 16 September, 1963, Sarawak and North Borneo, the latter now renamed Sabah, gained their independence from Britain and joined the new Federation of Malaysia linking them with Malaya and Singapore. This infuriated Sukarno who resolved to break up the fledgling federation by whatever means he could and in March, 1964, the 2nd/10th Gurkha Rifles fought the first engagement of the campaign with Indonesian regulars whom Sukarno had by now committed to his offensive against Malaysia. To counter this threat British and Commonwealth troops had been deployed in increasing numbers since early in 1964, initially under the direction of Major General Walter Walker, although by the time the 1st Battalion Scots Guards was deployed to the First Division of Sarawak in January, 1965, Major General George Lea had become Director of Operations. It was against this background that the battalion arrived in Kuching and moved out into the jungle to occupy bases that were to be its home for the next four months.

Sarawak   Battalion Headquarters was located at Semengo Camp near Kuching Airport with Left Flank, commanded by Major Michael Bowater, initially based there as the reserve for both West Brigade and the battalion. Right Flank, commanded by Major Blair Stewart-Wilson, was deployed to Kampong Pang Tebang just to the north of the border with Indonesia in the western part of the battalion area, while 9 Company under Major John Morrogh-Bernard was deployed in the eastern part of the area at Padawan, again short of the border and at the end of a motorable road from Kuching. The battalion was under command of Brigadier Bill Cheyne whose 99th Gurkha Brigade provided Headquarters West Brigade and was responsible for co-ordinating operations in Sarawak.

A description of Right Flank's deployment and routine in the Pang Tebang area will probably best provide the reader with a feel for how the battalion established itself and began to operate in the jungle. A typical jungle base of the sort that Company Headquarters inherited from its predecessor would have a heavily defended perimeter, wired with dannert or coiled barbed wire with likely enemy approaches cleared of foliage and covered by light machine guns. Possible approach routes would also be interdicted with Claymore anti-personnel mines and trip flares, while bamboo *panjis*, a form of sharpened stake, were driven into the ground in such a way as to skewer anyone unfortunate enough to fall against them. Inside a base sandbagged tents and marquees or *atap* huts housed stores and sleeping accommodation and there were washing facilities and latrines constructed on a semi-permanent basis. The defences of a position like that at Pang Tebang were continually worked upon and had been developed over a long period in order to incorporate heavy weapons like an 81mm Mortar or a field gun, both of which could provide immediate close support to patrols which made contact with the enemy. It was from this base that Major Stewart-Wilson controlled his platoons which were deployed anything up to two miles away and which only returned to Company Headquarters for briefing or re-supply. Replenishment was planned at Company Headquarters but executed by the Quartermaster, Major Joe Hughes, and his staff in conjunction with CQMSs direct to jungle bases and invariably by air. Movement through the jungle in the battalion area was slow and tiring with patrols usually achieving little more than two to three miles a day. Patrols might occasionally use tracks made by local traders who moved to and fro across the border to barter with their Indonesian neighbours to the south although regular use of such tracks invited the risk of ambush.

Much of Sarawak consists of flat coastal plains from which rise craggy outcrops of limestone rock anything up to 4,000 feet high with sheer cliffs on each side. These plains and hills are covered either by uncut primary jungle or rain forest which was relatively easy to move through, or by secondary jungle which had been cut and then cultivated by the local people before falling into disuse and reverting to nature. Secondary jungle formed a tangled mass of thick scrub which was often quite impenetrable and slowed patrol movement to a snail's pace. Sarawak abounds with rivers, great and small, and, although the larger ones were often difficult or impossible to cross, they sometimes provided patrols with an excellent route along which to move. As was to be expected in a tropical environment rain storms were frequent and intense, their effects felt long after they had passed as powerful drops fell from the jungle canopy. It was into such country and under conditions of steamy heat and rotting vegetation that the three platoons of Right Flank were dropped by helicopter as the company took possession of its area in early January. 1 Platoon under 2nd Lieutenant Anthony Leask deployed to a semi-permanent base at Tringus, taken over from a previous platoon, while 2 and 3 Platoons led by 2nd Lieutenant Jeremy Warren and Lieutenant Kim Ross, pitched camp on a rocky ridge near the border, nicknamed Bukit Scrunch; these temporary bases became home for the platoons for the two months that they were deployed in the jungle. Within each base soldiers would build *bashas* utilizing their poncho capes and *atap*, a palm leaf which, when interleaved, provided a more or less waterproof covering under which to sleep. A perimeter would be established, fields of fire prepared and covered with GPMGs or LMGs and Claymore mines and booby traps set up. This quickly became the pattern when any base, whether permanent or temporary, was established in the jungle.

Movement through the jungle was slow and debilitating not only because of the nature of the going but because each soldier had to carry all the ammunition and rations needed for a patrol, which could last for a considerable period. Jungle operations entailed many sweaty hours clambering up and slithering down vertical hills and wading rivers, frequently in drenching rain. Map reading was very difficult and few could identify with any real accuracy where they were at a given moment; the need to avoid crossing steep ridges led to patrols normally contouring around a feature, resulting in their often completing a circle and ending up where they had started from after many hours of exhausting effort. Leeches and scorpions added to the discomfort of life, while flies abounded and could only be kept at bay by a good growth of beard! The forward companies had as their mission the domination of their areas in order to prevent Indonesian patrols moving across the border to attack targets in Sarawak. The usual pattern was for platoons to be allocated areas into which they would patrol with the aim of establishing ambushes on routes likely to be used by the Indonesians; these platoon-level operations were of variable duration and whenever possible were planned on intelligence of probable enemy activity. Jungle operations stopped at night when, unless a platoon was deployed into an ambush position, a temporary base would be established and soldiers would get what rest they could under their *bashas* before resuming patrol at first light. Although some cross-border operations comprised up to ninety men and were led at company level, both Borneo tours were primarily a platoon commander's war with company commanders cast more in the role of directing and co-ordinating activity on the ground rather than leading it.

During the first two months of the Sarawak tour Right Flank and 9 Company patrolled their areas continuously. Indications of an enemy presence in the battalion area were few, although 9 Company made contact with a group of six terrorists on 18 February. One terrorist was killed and another wounded in the ensuing fire-fight. Meanwhile Left Flank in reserve at Semengo Camp carried out what training it could and practised riot control measures against the contingency of Muslim unrest in Kuching, something which, although predicted, never materialized.

12 Platoon was detached to 9 Company in February to relieve an Irish Guards platoon; Lieutenant Campbell Gordon described the deployment in the following terms: 'Attached to 9 Company at Padawan, forty-three miles from Kuching. Road a morass after torrential rain. Company Camp inside the Kampong and two guns in emplacements. Very steep patrol country with soaked and slippery vertiginous bamboo "bridges" to cross often at some height from the ground. The assault pioneers had cut helicopter landing zones for penetration patrols into the border area.'

The Assault Pioneer Platoon, commanded by Lieutenant Anthony Forbes with Sergeant Rosie as the Platoon Sergeant was much in demand and used large quantities of explosives to clear trees and level ground to allow the construction of landing zones in the forward areas close to the border; these tasks were always carried out with great enthusiasm although not every site was

5. "Before leaving Zanzibar the 2nd Battalion, less Right Flank, paraded before the Resident and then marched past the Ruler who took the salute in front of his Palace on the waterfront in Zanzibar Town." (Page 26). (left to right) Lieutenant Peter Johnson carrying the Queen's Colour, CQMS Morcom (G Company), RSM Graham, Lieutenant David Saunders carrying the Regimental Colour and CSM Louden (Left Flank).

6. "At midnight on 11 December, 1963, Kenya became an independent country within the Commonwealth after sixty-nine years of British rule." (Page 27). Colonel George Ramsay explains the finer points of a 3.5 inch Rocket Launcher to the Country's new leaders, among them Mr Jomo Kenyatta and Mr Tom Mboya (behind and to the Commanding Officer's right).

7. "RSM Graham was also responsible for the Sergeants' Mess acquiring two lion cubs." (Page 33).

8. "By 1100 hours on 12 January, 1964, the leading elements of the battalion were assembled at the RAF Station near Nairobi and were ready to go." (Page 28). 10 Platoon Left Flank commanded by 2nd Lieutenant Lachlan Maclean stand by to fly to Zanzibar to restore order on the island. Sergeant Little (with binoculars) is the Platoon Sergeant.

9. "In late November, 1964, Right Flank deployed for operations on the Thai-Malay border, followed a week later by the remainder of the battalion." (Page 41). A patrol of Left Flank of the 1st Battalion crosses a river in Kedah Province during the three weeks of operations against terrorists still believed to be living astride the border.

10. Colonel Archie Fletcher and his Second-in-Command, Major Sir Gregor MacGregor, plan anti-terrorist operations during the same deployment.

11. "Observation Posts and patrols on land and water were able to maintain a watch on any Indonesian movement along the border and on Sebatik and Nanukan Islands." (Page 51). During the 1st Battalion's deployment to Sabah in 1965, the Tawau Assault Group had orders to prevent the enemy using the many waterways that converged upon Cowie Harbour. Here Sergeant Stephenson and Guardsmen Rough and Cruickshank of an 11 Platoon patrol are using an assault boat powered by a Johnson outboard motor. Note that members of the patrol are carrying US Armalite rifles which were issued for jungle operations.

12. "On 13 January, 1966, Their Royal Highnesses The Duke and Duchess of Gloucester visited Kalabakan." (Page 52). Flanking their Royal Highnesses on the steps of the Sergeants' Mess are from left to right: Drum Major Wrisberg, CQMS Torrance, RSM Grant, CSM Roberts, CSM Irvine (IG), Sergeant Pask (REME), Staff Sergeant Beatson (REME), CQMS Mack, CSM Evans, ORQMS New and CSM F. Lawrie.

13. "After being received with a Royal Salute, she inspected the parade." (Page 57). Her Majesty The Queen, accompanied by Colonel Michael Gow and followed by His Royal Highness The Duke of Gloucester and Colonel George Ramsay, inspects the 2nd Battalion prior to presenting new Colours in the gardens of the Palace of Holyroodhouse on 30 June, 1965. CQMS Mann is the left guide.

14. "Apart from the list at Appendix G of those who, since 1956, have reached the rank of major general or above, several former members of the Regiment have gone on to achieve high positions in public life outside the Armed Forces." (Page 211). Four of those whose names are included at Appendix G feature in this photograph of the staff of Headquarters 4th Guards Brigade Group taken at Iserlohn in 1966. From left to right: Captain Murray Naylor, Captain Henry Hugh Smith (RHG/D), Major John Acland, Brigadier Vernon Erskine Crum, Major Tony Boam, Major Ian Donnelly (RHF) and Captain Fane Gaffney (WG).

15. "From 4 August to 10 October, 1967, the 1st Battalion had, for the first time ever, the privilege of finding the Royal Guard at Balmoral." (Page 63). Major Philip Erskine escorts Her Majesty The Queen on her inspection of the Guard of Honour mounted on her arrival on Deeside. CSM Meade is the right guide of the Guard and Lord Plunket, The Queen's Equerry.

16. "Jamaica might seem a strange place for a public duties battalion based in Scotland to train but nevertheless it was the location for Exercise CALYPSO HOP." (Page 66). In August, 1968, Colonel Sir Gregor MacGregor watches some of the 1st Battalion navigating the Rio Grande on rafts improvised from bamboo. Few remained dry!

constructed precisely as directed by Battalion Headquarters. As a result aircraft sometimes found themselves approaching a landing zone from the direction of the enemy. While operations were rightly the companies' first priority, winning the support and confidence of people living in the battalion's area was accorded almost as much importance; provision of medical treatment, the building of power supplies and the furnishing of water purification systems all helped the soldier on the ground to demonstrate the Army's presence and its commitment to defending the area against Indonesian attack. Border *kampongs* were visited on a regular basis and medical orderlies held surgeries whenever needed, that at Padawan being attended by people living either side of the Border. Since the Second World War and despite the barriers imposed by language, the British Army has everywhere pursued a policy of 'hearts and minds' in an effort to win the backing of local people when engaged upon counter-insurgency operations and the campaign in Borneo was no exception.

In early March Left Flank relieved Right Flank at Pang Tebang with the latter going into reserve at Semengo Camp. A similar pattern of patrol activity to that of the first two months of the tour continued but with growing emphasis on deep penetration patrols into Kalimantan. Operations were conducted at platoon and company level, often for up to fifteen or sixteen days duration. The purpose of such patrolling was to ambush Indonesian patrols undertaking similar operations in the opposite direction. Major Michael Bowater wrote of one operation which he led as being 'lengthy, fairly exhausting despite the high state of physical fitness, and uncomfortable. I think to be wet either through heat or rain or a combination of both day and night for two weeks is a little taxing; notwithstanding morale was superb .... We had contacts and brought down gunner support on a few occasions, probably successfully although it was difficult to tell in thick jungle.'

All patrols were accompanied by Iban trackers, those lively and energetic people who came to Sarawak from Kalimantan over 200 years ago and who supported British battalions throughout 'Confrontation' with Indonesia. For those in the battalion who had served with the 2nd Battalion in Malaya it was, however, the helicopter which really revolutionized the way in which jungle operations could be conducted. In early March the 1st Battalion became the first battalion in Borneo to be allocated its own air platoon. Comprising two Sioux helicopters, the platoon, commanded by Captain Tony Drake, Coldstream Guards and later by Captain Simon Gordon Duff of the Regiment, was an invaluable asset. The platoon, along with other Army aircraft and helicopters and fixed wing aircraft of the RAF and the Royal Navy, supported the battalion throughout both tours in Borneo, both by flying troops forward to jungle landing zones and by re-supplying all bases around the clock either by winching down, dropping or landing supplies for those on the ground. Ownership of an air platoon meant that the Commanding Officer could reach any position in his area within minutes while the Wessex helicopter delivery service allowed all bases to enjoy a relatively civilized existence with refrigerators, fresh rations and cold drinks, comforts never dreamt of in Malaya fifteen years previously! The battalion owed the pilots and groundcrew of all three services a considerable debt of gratitude for the way in which they kept flying whatever the conditions. They certainly proved their worth on a number of occasions.

Early March, 1965, saw an increase in enemy activity along the border opposite the battalion but frustratingly for the forward companies there were few incidents in their areas. There was some activity in Left Flank's area in the middle of April when 2nd Lieutenant William Bull's 11 Platoon spotted an Observation Post and later opened fire on three enemy who approached the perimeter of the platoon base. Earlier in the previous month Colonel Archie Fletcher had had the misfortune to contract leptospirosis, a disease carried in rat's urine which is quickly disseminated by the many rivers and streams in the jungle. The Commanding Officer was taken ill on 16 March shortly after swimming a flooded river; following shrewd and careful diagnosis by the battalion's Medical Officer, Major Roland Williams, Colonel Fletcher was evacuated immediately to hospital in Singapore from where he later went to Terendak to convalesce before returning to the battalion in late April. Major Gregor MacGregor assumed command of the battalion in the Commanding Officer's absence and Major Murray de Klee came from commanding the rear party to be Second-in-Command. There is little doubt that Colonel Fletcher was fortunate to suffer only mild effects from his attack of leptospirosis and he and the battalion had much to be grateful to Major Williams for on this and other occasions. Earlier in the tour, after two guardsmen in Left Flank had become unconscious through dehydration, Major Williams, having been briefed in a whisper over the radio by Major Bowater, diagnosed their condition and detailed their treatment thereby undoubtedly saving their lives. Both men were subsequently able to walk out of the jungle.

On 7 May the 2nd Green Jackets arrived in Sarawak to relieve the battalion which returned to Terendak by sea via Singapore. That there had been few incidents of significance during the tour should not be allowed to diminish the battalion's success in keeping its sector of Sarawak quiet at a time when the battalions on either flank were experiencing a relatively high level of enemy activity. The tour gave the battalion confidence, sharpened its jungle skills and prepared it for whatever its next commitment in the Far Eastern theatre might be. Above all there had been no silly accidents and no active service casualties. Two quotes sum up the attitude of guardsmen on leaving after a hard and demanding tour. The first from Major Bowater: 'Five months is probably long enough in one haul. I personally enjoyed every bit of it although I don't suppose everyone did. Complaints were few and, if they did occur, completely justified. Comradeship amongst all ranks was a must and this we achieved. Returning to Terendak and our families was a wonderful occasion; R and R and then we readied ourselves for the "next round" and some European style exercises as part of 28 Brigade.' Another taken from a letter written by Lieutenant Gordon to his father towards the end of the tour shows that a guardsman can usually be relied upon to remember his sense of humour, however difficult or unpleasant the circumstances of the moment: 'Message received from Battalion Headquarters 9 March. "Court mourning ends 14 March reference Queen Louise of Sweden. No action need be taken in your location".' So ended a tour on active service when people grew up, became self-reliant and learnt to work with one another as a matter of course and to quote Colonel Fletcher 'behaved exactly as guardsmen should'.

Return to Terendak and its families was a welcome relief after nearly five months in the jungle. On both operational tours in Borneo the battalion's wives and families supported their menfolk superbly and their contribution to the way in which the battalion discharged its operational duties should not be underestimated. For a soldier in the depths of the jungle to know that his wife and children, although hundreds of miles away, are with him in spirit and anxious for his well-being provides enormous reassurance at a time when he himself may be under great pressure. Over a period when, global war apart, the Regiment has experienced a greater number of unaccompanied operational tours than at any other period in its long history, it is appropriate to acknowledge the loyal support that the families have always furnished. They are every bit as much members of the regimental family as their husbands or fathers and share in the successes and failures that life as a soldier invariably brings. *Return to Terendak*

Following a period of well deserved leave the battalion adjusted to the less frenetic routine of Terendak and 28th Commonwealth Brigade. Courses, some low-level training and the necessary administration to repair standards which had suffered as a consequence of a long period deployed in the jungle, were all undertaken. Personalities changed too. Captain Thomas Boyd-Carpenter handed over to Captain James Dunsmure as Adjutant while RSM Grant arrived from Britain to succeed RSM Forsyth who was commissioned and remained in the battalion as the Transport Officer. Jim Forsyth had played an important role in helping to pull the battalion together at Pirbright. RSM Grant or 'Froggy' as he came to be universally known throughout the Regiment, soon settled in and made it a particular point to build strong links to 9 Company. Command of the Irish Guards Company changed as well when Major Giles Allan took over from Major Morrogh-Bernard. On 12 June the battalion provided four Guards for the Queen's Birthday Parade at Terendak when Brigadier McMeekin took the salute in the presence of the Sultan of Johore. Less than a week later a Guard of Honour was mounted at Loeng Nok Tha when a military airfield built by Britain under the provisions of the SEATO treaty was handed over to the Thai Government; Major Blair Stewart-Wilson commanded the Guard, with 2nd Lieutenant Jeremy Warren carrying the Regimental Colour. In July the battalion trained near Malacca following which in early August the Commanding Officer led a reconnaissance party to Borneo in preparation for a second tour of operational duty there, this time in Sabah. Meanwhile on 9 August the State of Singapore seceded from Malaysia, leaving only Malaya and the former British territories and dependencies of North Borneo as remaining members of the Federation.

On 7 September, 1965, the main body of the battalion embarked in the aircraft carrier HMS *Albion* and set sail for Sabah. The ship's destination was Tawau, a small settlement on the shores of Cowie Harbour at the extreme south-eastern corner of Sabah and barely five miles from the border separating Indonesia from Malaysia. On arrival off Tawau companies were flown direct by Royal Navy Wessex helicopters to jungle bases destined to be their homes for the next four months, quickly relieving the 1st Battalion The Gordon Highlanders which was flown out to *Albion* the same day. The battalion deployed with its Headquarters and 9 Company at Kalabakan, a small logging camp run by The Wallace Bay Timber Company situated some twenty miles north-west of Tawau, while Right Flank and Left Flank, the latter by then commanded by Major M.B. Scott, were based respectively at Serudong Laut and Serudong Ulu both within a few miles of the border; Lieutenant Campbell Gordon's 12 Platoon of Left Flank was initially deployed to a position to the west of Serudong Ulu on the upper reaches of the Serudong River covering a possible Indonesian incursion route, but, after two months, the platoon was withdrawn and the base destroyed. The battalion also had responsibility for the command and co-ordination of the operations of the Tawau Assault Group (TAG); this joint service, multi-racial organization had its Headquarters at Grassy Point on the southern side of Cowie Harbour and was commanded by Major Blair Stewart-Wilson who had handed over Right Flank to Major Simon Turner before the tour began. The activities of TAG will be covered later in this chapter.

The 1st Battalion Scots Guards was the only British battalion in 5th Malaysian Infantry Brigade Group, the formation responsible for operations in Sabah. The battalion area covered 1,000 square miles varying from tidal mangrove swamps in the east to jungle-clad mountains up to 4,500 feet in height in the west. The central part of the area offered reasonable going away from the rivers; the rivers themselves had been used extensively for the extraction of timber and were bordered by secondary jungle where the forest had been cut. These areas and the land once cultivated around old *kampongs* or native villages where secondary jungle had again taken over, and the more extensive mangrove swamps, were all obstacles to movement. In addition all rivers were liable to flash flooding, sometimes rising anything up to sixteen feet; they were considered to be dangerous hazards and were rightly treated with respect by patrols. Nearer to the sea the waters of Cowie Harbour could be deceptively calm but when whipped up by a combination of a strong tidal race and squalls quickly became dangerous for small boats; another danger met by those whose operations took them along the miles of waterways surrounding the Harbour were 'sinkers' or large logs which had become detached from timber rafts and which, floating just below the surface of the water, could inflict considerable damage on smaller craft, especially at night.

The battalion's mission in Sabah was to dominate the border area and, when appropriate, to deploy across it to conduct offensive operations against Indonesian units located on the other side. Kalabakan had been the scene of a major raid in 1964 when the Indonesians had attacked the police post and village, following which the 10th Gurkha Rifles had been flown in to hunt down and destroy the raiding force. Since that time the Indonesians had tended to remain on their side of the border, showing little inclination to patrol aggressively against the British or Malaysian units in Sabah. Initially companies concentrated upon learning their areas, checking on all helicopter landing zones, improving their bases and getting all ranks used to operating in small section size patrols. During the previous tour in Sarawak patrols had tended to operate in platoon or greater strength because of the threat posed by the Indonesians, but this was considered less necessary in Sabah where the enemy were seemingly more on the defensive. Cross-border patrolling started on 25 September and the next day a patrol from Right Flank engaged two men clearing an area of jungle but without confirmation of success. October produced no contacts although a number of patrols crossed up to 3,000 yards over the border searching for traces of Indonesian activity as well as reconnoitring the many tributaries of the Siglayan River.

Maps of the area tended to be very uninformative showing little but rivers and streams and no hills or contours; patrols never became lost in the sense that they did not know how to get back to base but they seldom knew with any confidence which map square they were in; on occasions a patrol commander might have to call upon a supporting 105mm Howitzer in one of the bases to fire a couple of rounds to enable him to fix his position by taking a back bearing on the explosions. Wireless communications between bases in the battalion area usually worked well, mainly because the Signal Platoon had managed to deploy a rebroadcast station on Mount Tampilat which dominated the surrounding country, although foot patrols tended to lose contact as soon as they entered the jungle and kept moving. The frustration of not knowing where you are and not being able to make contact with base or another patrol has to be experienced to be fully understood.

November saw patrols penetrating over the border to a depth of up to 8,000 yards. On 1 November a patrol of Right Flank was conducting a reconnaissance south-east of Serudong Laut along the edge of a swamp when they encountered and engaged a small party of enemy, one of whom was thought to have been hit. Later in the month Major Turner carried out a company level reconnaissance of a known enemy camp opposite Serudong Laut just across the border, with a view to a full-scale attack at a later date. Accompanied by Captain Dann, the Royal Artillery Forward Observation Officer, and CSM Roberts, Major Turner took with him 1 Platoon commanded by Lieutenant Michael Nurton and an attached platoon of South Wales Borderers under Lieutenant Mike Harry. Supporting Right Flank in its operation, but at some distance, was 12 Platoon of Left Flank commanded by Lieutenant Campbell Gordon. On 25 November, the company having reached a position close to the enemy camp, a reconnaissance patrol led by Lieutenant Nurton, and including Captain Dann's Forward Observation Team, was despatched by Major Turner to pinpoint the camp and report details of the enemy. Lieutenant Nurton's patrol succeeded in finding the camp but were prevented by an outer ring of sentries from assessing its layout and strength. Captain Dann and a few of the patrol therefore remained in place to provide a firm base while Lieutenant Nurton took advantage of a sudden tropical rainstorm to move further into the camp, and with Guardsman Nicol, Guardsman Laden, and Naga, their Iban tracker, got far enough inside to establish that the enemy base was far larger than expected. At this critical stage the rain stopped, enemy sentries discovered and attacked Captain Dann's position and soon became alerted to Lieutenant Nurton's presence. There was then an extensive fire-fight during which Lieutenant Nurton managed to withdraw his forward group while Captain Dann's team, including Guardsman Whittle, the patrol radio operator, slipped back into some very thin cover, unable to move or use their radio for fear of further discovery from an increasing number of searching enemy. For Major Turner, himself under fire from what he correctly assumed to be an enemy mortar, out of radio contact with his patrol and unable to influence events, it was an anxious time and he despatched Lieutenant Harry's platoon to assist in extricating Lieutenant Nurton from his battle. It was fortunate that Lieutenant Nurton had used different entry and exit routes, as Lieutenant Harry, following his inbound tracks, came on the rear of an enemy ambush placed to cut off their withdrawal. This resulted in a further fire-fight, allowing Captain Dann to join up with Lieutenant Harry and direct the very welcome artillery support which Major Turner had now called for from the single 105mm Howitzer at Serudong Laut. It was not long before both patrols managed to disengage, miraculously with no casualties, and rejoin Company Headquarters. Major Turner then quickly re-organized his company and effected a rapid withdrawal under cover of further artillery support, directed on to his own recent position to ensure a clean break from an enemy who appeared to be forming up for a fresh assault. For this brave action in the face of a much larger force of enemy Lieutenant Nurton and Captain Dann were subsequently mentioned in dispatches. It is one of the frustrations of jungle operations that, unless an action can be followed up immediately and details of casualties confirmed, there is little or no way of verifying the claims of those who, in the heat of battle, believe that they have killed or wounded an enemy. To this day therefore the claims made by Lieutenant Nurton and his guardsmen must remain unconfirmed, although there is anecdotal evidence to suggest that their action and the subsequent shelling of the enemy position caused considerable Indonesian casualties. At the time Right Flank's action was the subject of a formal complaint by the Indonesian Government!

At the end of November 9 Company relieved Left Flank at Serudong Ulu and the latter became the battalion reserve company at Kalabakan from where it patrolled remote areas not covered by the forward companies and provided Lieutenant Charles Gwyn's 10 Platoon to reinforce TAG. Meanwhile Right

Flank and 9 Company continued to patrol forward of their bases, although Right Flank for a time kept clear of the area of the Indonesian camp attacked the previous month. Despite a high level of patrolling and some signs of enemy movement there were no further contacts with the Indonesians, whom it had been anticipated would try to mount a reprisal raid against the battalion, probably at Serudong Laut. However, elsewhere diplomatic moves were being made to bring 'Confrontation' to an end and at the end of December an embargo was imposed upon all offensive operations. This ban was extended into the New Year and for the last six weeks of the tour the battalion was restricted to carrying out only defensive patrolling.

While the three rifle companies were concentrating upon defeating any attempt by Indonesia to infiltrate across the land border, TAG's attention was focused on preventing any enemy move to use the myriad of waterways that converged upon Cowie Harbour, in order to threaten Tawau. The group had been established following an Indonesian raid on Kalabakan mounted along one of the waterways. An intricate network of land-based platoons and floating patrol bases, backed by fast naval patrol craft and a guard ship, usually a destroyer or frigate from one of the Commonwealth navies to provide heavy fire support, had been designed to ensure that no enemy could slip into the area unnoticed. Observation posts and patrols on land and water were able to maintain a watch on any Indonesian movement along the border and on Sebatik and Nunukan Islands and regularly provided useful intelligence, although the Indonesians doubtless took steps to deceive those observing them. Both Right and Left Flank provided platoons to reinforce TAG during the tour and, while these were based on land, they did most of their patrolling using assault boats powered by Johnson outboard motors or recorded enemy movement from static Boat Observation Posts. Apart from its military value as a deterrent to offensive enemy action along the coast, TAG provided the battalion with a totally different way of countering the Indonesian threat and one which was enjoyed by all who served within its organization. Excellent relationships developed between the seven different services and six separate nations which comprised the staff; so complete was the integration that one day a Malaysian gunner, reporting a shortage of water down at the jetty at TAG Headquarters, was heard to say in a broad Glaswegian accent, 'There's nae watter at the jetteh'.

In addition to Major Stewart-Wilson, who, as Senior Officer Tawau Assault Group (SOTAG) commanded the Group, Lieutenant Kim Ross and CSM Evans served at TAG Headquarters assisting with the co-ordination of operations across Cowie Harbour and the complex task of maintaining and replenishing a wide and diverse troop deployment. SOTAG had his own flagship, the KD *Petrel*, formerly the Governor of Sabah's yacht and naval customs were observed when visiting or being visited by ships coming on station for a tour of duty as the guard or picquet ship. Piper Swan, as SOTAG'S personal piper, was always sent in the assault boat to collect the captain of a newly arrived ship when he came to call upon SOTAG at TAG Headquarters and then piped him ashore,

Tawau Assault Group

51

invariably to the skirl of 'We're no' awa' to bide awa''! There may have been 'a touch of Somerset Maugham about life in TAG but it proved a valuable counter to a particular threat from Indonesia and in the process reinforced that oft-quoted rule that, whenever possible, soldiering should be fun.

On 13 January, 1966, Their Royal Highnesses The Duke and Duchess of Gloucester visited Kalabakan, a most successful visit which was appreciated by all who met them. The following day the advance party of the 2nd Battalion The Royal Green Jackets arrived to begin taking over the battalion's area and on 24 January companies were lifted out of their bases and on to HMS *Albion* which then set sail for Singapore. A second successful tour of operational duty completed, the battalion once more returned to its families and the relaxation of Terendak Camp. Borneo Two, as the tour was colloquially known had been every bit as successful as that undertaken in Sarawak in 1965 and the battalion returned justifiably well pleased with itself; it was true that, with the exception of Lieutenant Nurton's action in November, there had been no major incidents and no great acts of heroism, but the battalion had dominated its area with total success and in a most professional manner and, far more importantly, had lost no one to the enemy.

The End of
'Confrontation'

The battalion's last full year in Terendak was to be marked by success and sadness. While it had been expected that there would be a third tour in Borneo in the autumn of 1966 it was confirmed in June that this would not after all be the case; negotiations to end 'Confrontation' which had begun during the battalion's Sabah tour bore fruit when on 1 June an agreement was signed in Bangkok. Prior to this President Sukarno had been relegated to the role of a puppet president, his place as effective leader of Indonesia being taken by General Suharto, an avowed anti-communist who quickly set about discussing peace terms with Britain and the Malaysian Federation. As a result Britain undertook to withdraw from Malaysian Borneo by the end of September, 1966, something which was successfully achieved despite a brief resurgence of terrorist activity on the border in July. Within the battalion the news that there was to be no third tour was greeted with disappointment in some quarters but with relief by the families who had no desire to be parted from their husbands once again. After leave the battalion settled in to re-learning the intricacies of counter-revolutionary warfare and was subjected to a series of exercises set for it by 28th Commonwealth Brigade and designed to test it in its primary role, all of which it seemingly passed with flying colours. Meanwhile Lieutenant Richard Fane-Gladwin was killed in a flying accident at Middle Wallop where he was about to graduate as an Army pilot; Support Platoon Commander in Left Flank in Sarawak, he had always had an earnest desire to fly helicopters and would have in all probability returned to the Far East had he not died so tragically.

In bringing 'Confrontation' with Indonesia to a conclusion Britain and her allies had waged a highly successful campaign. What might have so easily degenerated into a long drawn-out and bitter war of attrition had been ended after little more than three years partly due to the professionalism of those sent to fight in the jungles of Borneo and partly because the confidence of the local people had been won and retained through the assiduous pursuit of a 'Hearts and Minds' policy. In reporting to the House of Commons at the end of the Borneo Campaign Mr Denis Healey, the Minister of Defence, predicted that, 'In the history books it will be recorded as one of the most efficient uses of military force in the history of the world'. The 1st Battalion Scots Guards could certainly claim a share of the credit which accrued to the British Army following the successful ending of 'Confrontation'. Life in the jungle encouraged improvisation, initiative, resourcefulness and involvement at all levels, the very qualities that were going to be needed in abundance less than five years after Borneo Two when the first Scots Guardsmen came to find themselves involved in the fight against terrorism in Northern Ireland. Many of those at middle and junior level who were to bear the brunt on the streets of the latter's cities learnt their military craft during the Regiment's tours of duty in Kenya and Malaysia, although few would have had any inkling of how soon they would face the next test.

Colonel Archie Fletcher left the battalion in April, 1966, after three highly successful years in command; from inheriting a depleted and dispirited battalion at Pirbright in April, 1963, he had built up its strength and self-confidence to such a pitch that it was able to undertake two demanding operational tours in Borneo without loss of life and without conceding anything to the enemy opposing it. He was succeeded by Lieutenant Colonel Sir Gregor MacGregor who commanded for the final months in Malaya, during which time the battalion was joined by a platoon of the Coldstream Guards commanded by 2nd Lieutenant Edward Crofton which came from Britain to replace 18 Platoon Irish Guards, which was itself required to reinforce its own 1st Battalion in Aden. A series of exercises took place all over Malaya, the final one in November, following which thoughts turned to home and in the case of Scots Guardsmen the prospect of the battalion being based in Scotland for the first time since 1707.

CHAPTER FOUR

SCOTLAND AND LONDON

1st Battalion: Edinburgh-London
2nd Battalion: Caterham-London

2nd Battalion Caterham 1965

When the Guards Depot moved to Pirbright in March, 1960, the barracks at Caterham became a station for a London District battalion engaged upon public duties. Twenty-five miles south of London on the edge of the North Downs, the 'barracks on the hill' had always been popular with guardsmen who took advantage of their isolation from other military camps to enjoy the good 'walking out' to be had in Croydon and Coulsdon. However, when the 2nd Battalion reassembled there on 2 December, 1964, following disembarkation leave, the immediate prospect was not so appealing; the weather was bitterly cold and raw, the barracks in none too clean a state and the business of learning all about public duties had to begin immediately, since the first Queen's Guard was scheduled for the middle of the month. Indeed there could hardly have been a greater contrast with military life in Kenya.

Undeterred by the difficulties, RSM Graham and his Drill Sergeants quickly concentrated minds on the intricacies of mounting London duties whilst a blitz on the barracks soon produced a more tolerable standard of living. On 16 December Right Flank mounted the first Queen's Guard, appropriately taking over from 3 Company Irish Guards in the forecourt. In preparing his battalion for what was likely to be a long stint of duty in London District, Colonel Gow was concerned not to repeat those errors which had caused problems for the 1st Battalion when, in 1963, it had been based outside the capital, was expected to discharge a heavy programme of duties and was short of guardsmen. Whenever possible officers always mounted duty with their own guardsmen and everybody was given time off after a guard, a rule rigorously enforced.

Sir Winston Churchill's Funeral

On 24 January, 1965, following a long illness during which the nation seemingly 'stood still', Sir Winston Churchill died at his home in London. Immediately Headquarters London District began the implementation of contingency plans already drawn up and codenamed Exercise HOPE NOT. The next week was taken up with conferences, covert reconnaissances and early morning rehearsals, and at Caterham those destined to be on parade learnt to

54

slow march with arms reversed. At 0915 hours on 26 January the body of the wartime Prime Minister was taken from his home in Hyde Park Gate to Westminster where, in the presence of Lady Churchill and the Earl Marshal, his coffin was placed upon a catafalque in Westminster Hall. At 2100 hours that night the first of a series of watches was mounted in the Hall; commanded by Colonel Gow, the first Watch included Lieutenant Colonel Lord Burnham and Majors Swinton, Denham, Harrison and Mayfield, along with officers from the Grenadier and Coldstream Guards. At a later stage in the four-day vigil the Lieutenant Colonels Commanding the five Regiments of Foot Guards also mounted a complete Watch.

At 0945 hours on 30 January the coffin was taken from Westminster Hall by a bearer party found by the 2nd Battalion Grenadier Guards and placed upon a gun carriage drawn by the Royal Navy. From there the coffin, draped with the Union Jack and surmounted by the insignia of the Order of the Garter, was taken in procession to St Paul's Cathedral by way of Whitehall, the Strand, Fleet Street and Ludgate Hill. A marching party of three officers and ninety-six soldiers from the 2nd Battalion under the command of Major M.B. Scott formed part of the procession which comprised 2,500 soldiers and civilians, while four half-companies from the battalion lined the route along the Strand. Following a Service in St Paul's Cathedral the gun carriage continued through the City of London to Tower Hill from where the bearer party, led by sixty pipers under Pipe Major Kilgour, carried the coffin down to Tower Pier. Here the coffin and bearer party were embarked in the Port of London Authority Launch *Havengore* for the short journey upstream to the Festival Hall Pier and Waterloo Station, following which a special train conveyed Sir Winston's body to Bladon in Oxfordshire for private burial. Several senior officers of the Regiment were closely involved in controlling and marshalling the procession. Lieutenant Colonel David Scott-Barrett was in command on Tower Hill whilst Colonel George Ramsay, the Lieutenant Colonel Commanding, had responsibility at Tower Pier and supervised the transfer to *Havengore*. The battalion, in addition to finding a marching party and streetliners, also provided the Queen's Guard under Major Philip Erskine. Virtually every man was on parade with the exception of the cooks and attached personnel; even so it was found necessary to use a corporal in the Royal Army Pay Corps as part of the Bank Picquet the night prior to the funeral. While the underlying mood was understandably one of great sadness, the day of the funeral was a far from gloomy one and all on parade took considerable pride in being involved in such a great event. Afterwards the Adjutant wrote in the Battalion Digest: 'Without a doubt the State Funeral on 30 January was the most moving parade that the majority of the Battalion had ever taken part in or observed. Perfect timing, detailed rehearsal and great dignity all combined to make it a proud and wonderful occasion.' Perhaps the most poignant moment of the day came as *Havengore* slipped her moorings at Tower Pier and proceeded up the Thames; whilst she was still opposite the pier and as sixteen RAF Lightning aircraft flew overhead, the cranes lining the south bank of the river dipped their jibs in unison in a final unrehearsed salute to a great leader.

Throughout the spring and early summer the battalion undertook a heavy programme of public duties including providing Number Seven Guard on the Queen's Birthday Parade. In June celebrations to mark the 150th anniversary of the Battle of Waterloo were held in London and Belgium. The Commanding Officer and Major Tony Harrison, accompanied by a detachment of Left Flank, were among those who paraded at Hougoumont Farm on 18 June; a wooden cross with the badges of the three regiments whose light companies had defended the farm carved on its base had been specially made by Sergeant Ryves. A silver plaque on the cross was inscribed with the words: 'Remember the men of the 1st Guards, Coldstream Guards and Third Guards who died defending this farm and the wounded who survived in this chapel.' The cross, which had been dedicated at morning service in the Guards Chapel on 13 June, remains to this day on the altar of the chapel at Hougoumont. Another important event took place at Caterham on 14 June when Drum Major 'Nick' Taylor retired from the Regiment after thirty-five years service, twenty of them as Drum Major of the 2nd Battalion. On his final day of duty the officers of the 2nd Battalion gave him a farewell lunch after which Colonel Gow escorted the Drum Major to the barrack gate where he was ceremonially 'drummed out' by his old Corps of Drums.

Edinburgh   On 20 June the battalion flew north to Edinburgh by Argosy aircraft from the RAF Station at Odiham to parade for the presentation of New Colours by Her Majesty The Queen on 30 June. Rehearsals were held on the Redford Barracks playing fields which were laid out to represent the gardens at Holyroodhouse; during one rehearsal the Commanding Officer was so dissatisfied with the drill of the two Quartermasters carrying the New Colours that he instructed the Adjutant to admonish them. Having delivered an appropriate rebuke, the Adjutant turned to resume his place on parade but inadvertently caught his foot in a pothole and fell to the ground, tearing his breeches in the process. After the rehearsal Captains Donald Whyte and Fred Adams remarked that they were surprised that their curse on the Adjutant had worked so quickly and to such good effect! A service of Dedication was held at St Giles' Cathedral on 27 June in the presence of the Lord Provost while the Minister, Doctor Whiteley, preached. The Colours, carried by Lieutenants Michael Smart and Andrew Clowes and escorted by CSM Gifford and Sergeants Hunter and Couper, were marched up the aisle before the service began and laid on the table. During the service the congregation sang the hymn 'Courage, brother, do not stumble', a refrain which, in the light of their brush with the Adjutant a few days previously, gave the two Quartermasters much pleasure. Besides rehearsing for the parade, the battalion managed to squeeze in a dance for the guardsmen, an Officers' Mess cocktail party in the Surgeons' Hall and a Beating of Retreat by the Band and Pipes and Drums on the Castle Esplanade.

Presentation of   After several days of brilliant sunshine 30 June was wet with a heavy storm
New Colours   breaking an hour before the parade. However, this did not mar the marvellous

spectacle of the battalion in tunic order drawn up in the gardens of the Palace of Holyroodhouse against the magnificent backcloth of Arthur's Seat. Watched by 3,600 spectators and with detachments of adult recruits, junior leaders and junior guardsmen and 280 members of the Scots Guards Association on parade, the Colonel was first received with a Royal Salute following which the Band and Pipes and Drums trooped and the Old Colours carried by Lieutenant Alastair Morrison and 2nd Lieutenant Jonathan Seddon-Brown were marched off parade. Her Majesty The Queen was then escorted on parade by a detachment of the Queen's Bodyguard for Scotland (Royal Company of Archers), formed from past officers of the Regiment under the command of Major Sir Charles Maclean and, after being received with a Royal Salute, she inspected the parade. After the inspection the New Colours were consecrated by the Reverend Gordon Bennett, Assistant Chaplain General Scottish Command and The Queen presented them. The Ensigns for the New Colours were 2nd Lieutenants Malcolm Ross and David Dalglish, escorted by Colour Sergeants Hessleden and Duncan and Sergeant Jamieson. The Queen then addressed the parade and Colonel Gow replied; in his reply the Commanding Officer included particular reference to the Association with the following words: 'This morning Your Majesty has inspected not only this battalion, but also representatives of the Scots Guards Association. Over fifty years of service in the Regiment is here. That some no longer serve with the Colours does not matter. What does matter is that we are all of us Scots Guardsmen bound together in the Queen's service until we die.' The New Colours were then marched to the centre of the battalion and received with a General Salute following which the battalion marched past The Queen and then advanced in review order. Despite the weather it had been an excellent parade.

A Gathering for the Association at Redford, a dance given by the officers at the Assembly Rooms in George Street and attended by The Queen and other members of the Royal Family, and a cocktail party held by the Sergeants' Mess in the Banqueting Hall in Edinburgh Castle and attended by Their Royal Highnesses The Duke and Duchess of Gloucester completed a busy fortnight in the Scottish capital and on 5 July companies dispersed to different parts of Scotland to train and show the Scots Guards flag. Perthshire, Argyll and the Borders were all visited and Battalion Headquarters made history by basing itself at Victoria Barracks, Ballater, the first time ever. On 14 July the battalion concentrated again at Dunstaffnage Castle just to the north of Oban.

Prior to leaving Caterham for Edinburgh Colonel Gow had assembled *Mull* everybody in the gymnasium and briefed them that, on the instructions of the Government, the battalion might be ordered to undertake a secret mission in Scotland for which purposes the move to Edinburgh to parade at Holyroodhouse was but a cover. A communist takeover of the island of Mull was feared and it was expected that King Charles 23rd (alias Major Sir Charles Maclean of Duart) would invoke a treaty of friendship with Britain and request military assistance. While most quickly spotted the subterfuge underlying the Commanding Officer's briefing, there were some in the battalion who believed what they had been told. The battalion was brought up to date in Edinburgh when the Commanding Officer produced Major George Nickerson, at the time serving on the staff of Headquarters Scottish Command, who, masquerading as a Police Inspector, painted a gloomy picture of a situation on Mull which was fast deteriorating. A fortnight later and once it was assembled at Dunstaffnage the battalion learnt that it was to be deployed to the island immediately to destroy a band of communist guerrillas led by one Hamish McPuke. These guerrillas were in fact the Drummers and Pipers commanded by the Adjutant, Captain Murray Naylor, and divided into patrols led by RSM Graham, Drum Major Hickling, 2nd Lieutenant Jonathan Seddon-Brown and QMSI Underwood, the battalion Physical Training Instructor. The battalion sailed from Dunstaffnage and after disembarking at dawn in Fishnish Bay, started to hunt down the guerrillas who had taken to the hills in the southern part of Mull; in glorious weather the enemy were chased across the island but always managed to escape final capture, although there were some narrow squeaks. On one occasion McPuke himself was nearly caught by Left Flank, being saved in the nick of time by RSM Graham who, realizing that one of Major Ian McKay's signallers had caught sight of the rebel leader fast disappearing over a skyline and was about to tell his Company Commander, popped a sticky sweet into the astonished guardsman's mouth with the words, 'Want a sweet, laddie!' On another occasion Major John Gibb and G Company captured the guerrillas' administrative base because Pipe Major Kilgour, who had charge of it, had got bored of the exercise and had decided to indulge in some chanter practice. Unfortunately G Company was at that moment passing the area of rhododendron bushes behind which the Pipe Major was concealed and it did not take Major Gibb, himself a piper, long to appreciate what he was hearing. The exercise culminated in a sea battle in the Firth of Lorn as the battalion and the guerrilla force both returned to Oban; firehoses were used as cannon with fishheads and flour bags as ammunition but the superior firepower of the Tank Landing Craft *Aachen* soon told over that of the two fishery protection trawlers in which McPuke's guerrillas were sailing. Before leaving Mull the battalion had camped in the open below the ramparts of Duart Castle, the home of the Macleans, the glorious weather holding that night and not breaking until the battalion was safely aboard its special train and on its way to Caterham when the heavens opened! Exercise JOCK SCOT was a fitting climax to a memorable month in Scotland and one unlikely to be quickly forgotten by those serving in the battalion at the time.

The autumn of 1965 found the battalion heavily engaged in public duties from Caterham with a move to Chelsea Barracks scheduled to take place early the following year. In December the battalion undertook a month of Spearhead duty when it came directly under command of Headquarters United Kingdom Land Forces (UKLF) at Wilton and had to be prepared to deploy anywhere

where British interests might be threatened. Joint Theatre Plans drawn up by the staff at Wilton covered a wide range of contingencies from rescuing British subjects assessed as being at risk in a foreign country, to helping a nation to recover after a natural disaster or to intervening to quell trouble in a British dependent territory. Deployment of a battalion alone might be sufficent to deal with a particular situation or it might be judged necessary to deploy a larger force of which the Spearhead battalion would be but the leading element; whatever the contingency to arise – and frequently none did – much detailed planning and preparation were necessary whenever a battalion undertook this important duty.

On 11 November Prime Minister Ian Smith of Southern Rhodesia illegally declared his country to be independent. During the weeks that followed this declaration intensive diplomatic negotiations between London and Salisbury failed to heal the rift between Britain and her colony and by the time the 2nd Battalion assumed Spearhead duty from the 1st Battalion The Royal Scots at the end of the month, the dispatch of a military force to Zambia was under active consideration by the Government. Following a successful St Andrew's Day Dance which later gave rise to light-hearted comparisons with the Duchess of Richmond's Ball held the night before the Battle of Waterloo, on 1 December the battalion found itself faced with the real possibility of being deployed to Southern Africa. The leading company was placed at twenty-four hours' notice to move to Zambia and the remainder of the battalion hastily issued with khaki drill clothing and maps of Zambia and Southern Rhodesia. Despite attempts by the Commanding Officer to obtain clear guidance as to what his battalion's role and *modus operandi* would be if deployed, none was forthcoming and at no stage was there a clear concept of how the battalion might be employed. At one moment a move to Lusaka was mooted, while later an operation to seize and hold the Kariba Dam was apparently contemplated. Throughout the three weeks that the battalion remained at notice to deploy the barracks at Caterham became a centre of unaccustomed operational activity and was besieged by the media for long periods. To the amazement of those who did not understand the Household Brigade or the manner in which it conducts its business, the battalion continued to mount London Duties throughout the period. The Press were a particular source of frustration, hanging around the barrack gate, touting for information that could not be given and posing delicate questions as to how guardsmen would react if called upon to fire upon white Rhodesians, to which the response had invariably to be that they 'would do their duty'. In the end the resolve and discipline of the battalion was never put to the test and shortly after Christmas it was stood down from any task in Southern Rhodesia. Apart from a second alert in late January after the battalion had moved to Chelsea Barracks and when all equipment for a Rhodesian deployment had been returned to Ordnance, there were to be no further alarms. The question of what should be done about Southern Rhodesia's illegal declaration of independence was to continue to be the subject of much debate and intermittent negotiation until

Standby for Rhodesia

1979 when a military monitoring force led by a Scots Guardsman, Major General John Acland, was established to assist in returning the country to legality and subsequent independence. Viewed from Caterham in December 1965, the prospect of deploying into a virtually unknown country with minimal support and at the end of a tenuous logistic supply line cannot have been very attractive. Had the battalion been sent to Zambia it is hard to see what would have been achieved, whilst any move into Southern Rhodesia would doubtless have had to be undertaken by a force considerably larger and better equipped than the Spearhead battalion group.

By 14 January, 1966, the battalion was firmly established in Chelsea Barracks and able to conduct public duties without the long journey by coach from Caterham. On 18 February the Transport Officer, Captain Ron Tillotson, collapsed and died as he was crossing the barrack square. 'Tilly', a man big in heart and stature, unflappable and self-effacing, was aptly described in his obituary as a 'tower of strength'. He spent most of his long service in the 2nd Battalion serving as CSM F Company at the Battle of Medenine, as a Drill Sergeant at Salerno and as RQMS in Malaya. He later became Superintending Clerk at Regimental Headquarters and on being commissioned was appointed Quartermaster of the 3rd Kenya Rifles, a posting which kept him in close contact with the battalion when it was serving in Kahawa in 1964. At the end of March Colonel Michael Gow relinquished command of the battalion and handed over to Lieutenant Colonel John Swinton who had been his Second-in-Command since the battalion's return from Kenya. The same day Their Royal Highnesses The Duke and Duchess of Gloucester visited Chelsea Barracks for the first time since the Colonel had laid the foundation stone for the new barracks on 27 June, 1960. It was also the Colonel's birthday and he and the Duchess left barracks to the strains of a specially composed pipe tune entitled 'Prince Henry, Duke of Gloucester'.

By 1966 the Director of Army Training and his staff in the Ministry of Defence had begun to compile a comprehensive portfolio of overseas training exercises which, with a degree of adaptation, could be undertaken by a unit of any arm or service. While the purpose of such exercises was primarily to provide the Army with fresh training opportunities, they also presented soldiers, increasingly denied the experience of serving overseas, with a chance to see something of the rest of the world. Exercises in Kenya, Cyprus, the United States, France and Portugal have all become commonplace, although today there are many other countries to which British Army units deploy to train on a regular basis. It was against this background that in June, 1966, the 2nd Battalion was allocated a six-week period of overseas training in Canada, an event which neatly broke up its second year of public duties and provided welcome relief from the ceremonial round.

With a mind to obtaining the maximum value from such training and as a preparation for moving to Germany in 1967, the Commanding Officer decided to re-form G Company as the battalion's third rifle company in late May under the command of Major John Whiteley; that this could happen was due in no small part to the efforts of the Regimental Recruiting Officer, Major Tony Philipson, and his team of Special Recruiters based across Scotland and the North of England. Working with teams of 'satisfied soldiers' from both battalions and with the support of recruits and junior guardsmen from the Guards Depot, Major Philipson's team worked assiduously to promote the Regiment and to win recruits against fierce competition from the rest of the Army and industry. That the Regiment's strength in 1966 was beginning to grow was some reward for their dedication, although everybody concerned with planning the use of manpower knew that there could be no grounds for complacency.

Base Gagetown, near Fredericton in New Brunswick, was the battalion's *Canada* temporary home for six weeks from the middle of June; assigned an area equivalent in size to the county of Bedfordshire the battalion was given almost unrestricted licence to train as it wished. Excellent range and field firing areas provided just what a public duties battalion required to allow it to dust off its ceremonial cobwebs and to start thinking and behaving the way soldiers in the field should. Prior to the arrival of the main body of the battalion the Second-in-Command, Major Tony Harrison, and the Quartermaster, Captain Donald Whyte, both assisted by Major Michael Bowater who, having done an attachment to the Canadian Guards 'knew the lingo', supervised the construction of Thistle Camp, a tented base from which companies deployed to train at platoon and company level. The hospitality and friendliness shown by the battalion's Canadian hosts was overwhelming, quite literally so for those unaccustomed to the tradition of the 'happy hour', and during the battalion's time at Base Gagetown most people saw something of the Canadian Maritime States and in some cases even managed to travel down to the United States. Guardsman Scott got to Salt Lake City while Lieutenant Malcolm Ross's platoon of Right Flank won the Platoon Test Exercise, thereby earning themselves a long weekend in New York. A platoon of Lancashire Fusiliers was attached for the exercise to enable it to travel to Ontario to attend the centenary parade of its affiliated regiment, the Lorne Scots of Canada. Neither was the Scots Guards' own historical association with New Brunswick forgotten and when appropriate the battalion's numerous Canadian well-wishers were reminded that a Guards Brigade had been dispatched to Canada at the time of the American Civil War and that the 2nd Battalion Scots Fusilier Guards had been part of that brigade from 1862 to 1864 when for a time it had been based at St John. After six weeks of relaxed but useful training, glorious weather, many opportunities to travel and, having experienced at first hand the generosity of the Canadian people, the battalion returned to London ready to complete its last six months of duty before moving to Germany. Most importantly the battalion returned from Canada with the same number of soldiers with which it had arrived, the first battalion never to leave anyone behind, something which the Canadians bet RSM Graham a crate of whisky he would not achieve.

61

Once re-established in Chelsea Barracks public duties quickly re-asserted themselves as the first priority, although some preparatory training for the battalion's mechanized role in BAOR also commenced. As if this was not sufficient, a platoon thirty-five strong commanded by Lieutenant Malcolm Ross with Sergeant Cameron as its Platoon Sergeant left on 18 October to reinforce the 1st Battalion Irish Guards on active service in Aden for six months. 29 October saw the laying up of the battalion's Old Colours in St Mary's Kirk in Dundee in the presence of the Colonel, while on 17 November the battalion mounted its last Guard of Honour in London at the Tate Gallery on the occasion of the State Visit of President Ayub Khan of Pakistan. The Captain of Right Flank, Major Iain Ferguson, commanded the Guard and Lieutenant Charles Gwyn carried the State Colour. By custom Guards of Honour mounted upon Commonwealth Heads of State are presented to the visitor in English rather than in the language of the latter's country, something which His Royal Highness The Duke of Edinburgh had evidently forgotten because he chided Major Ferguson for not reporting his Guard in Urdu, despite the latter's explanation that English was in fact correct for the occasion. Not to be left out of the exchange and doutless seeking to mollify both parties, President Ayub Khan put his arm around Major Ferguson's shoulders and said, 'Anyway, who in Scotland has ever heard of Urdu'. The battalion's final Queen's Guard was mounted on 11 December; prior to that on 7 December Guardsman Duffy of Left Flank whilst on duty at Buckingham Palace apprehended a man attempting to enter the palace and held him at bayonet point until relieved by the police. While attempts to break into the Royal Palaces have unfortunately become commonplace in recent years, such an occurrence was virtually unknown in 1966. If nothing else Duffy's action highlighted the importance of the role performed by the Queen's Guard in helping to maintain security at the Royal Palaces and it is to be hoped helped to disprove the misconception held by some that such guards were an anachronism.

1st Battalion Edinburgh 1967   On 24 April, 1967, the main body of the 1st Battalion re-assembled at Redford Barracks, Edinburgh, after disembarkation leave following its return from the Far East. Discounting previous temporary visits, this was the first time in 260 years that a battalion of the Scots Guards was to be stationed in Scotland's capital city and the Ministry of Defence 'Arms Plot' for infantry battalions specified that the battalion would remain in Edinburgh for eighteen months before moving to Chelsea Barracks in the New Year 1969. Prior to the Arms Plot being agreed the Major General, Major General Basil Eugster, had put two alternatives to the Lieutenant Colonel Commanding; either the 1st Battalion went to Chelsea on return from Malaya and trooped its Colour on the Queen's Birthday Parade in 1967 in its rightful turn or it went to Edinburgh and did not 'troop' until 1969 by which time it would be in London. With little hesitation Colonel Ramsay opted for the second of these two alternatives: a tour in Scotland for a battalion, for which Regimental Headquarters had been pressing for sometime, would provide the Regiment with an excellent opportunity to present itself as Scotland's own Regiment of Foot Guards and could help to win recruits who were still in far too short supply. Such a tour would also have the added advantage of basing the 1st Battalion's families in Scotland after two and a half years in the Far East.

Redford Barracks lie to the south-west of the city and have sufficient space to accommodate two battalions. Built at the time of the First World War the barracks were designed in the late Victorian/early Edwardian Imperial manner and at the time of construction were considered to be the most advanced in Britain. In April, 1967, they were still divided into two self-contained barrack units with the 1st Battalion occupying the Infantry Barracks while the 1st Battalion The Cameronians was in the former Cavalry Barracks. The 1st Battalion's role was that of general duties battalion with shared responsibility for finding public duties in Edinburgh and it came under command of Headquarters Edinburgh Area. For the first six months Colonel Gregor Mac-Gregor gave his priorities as public duties and training with companies encouraged to lose no opportunity to be seen around Scotland. Naturally public duties predominated and, in addition to mounting the Edinburgh Castle Guard on a regular basis, in May the battalion provided a Guard of Honour commanded by Major Simon Turner at the Opening of the General Assembly of the Church of Scotland by the Lord High Commissioner, Lord Reith of Stonehaven, while on 3 June 200 men paraded with the Regimental Band for the installation of the new Governor of Edinburgh Castle, Lieutenant General Sir Derek Lang.

From 4 August to 10 October the battalion had, for the first time ever, the *Royal Guard* privilege of finding the Royal Guard at Balmoral, a duty invariably undertaken by one of the three infantry battalions stationed in Scotland. Commanded by Major Philip Erskine, the Guard was based at Victoria Barracks in Ballater and was required to perform a range of duties whilst Her Majesty The Queen and other members of the Royal Family were in residence at the Castle. These duties ranged from providing a Guard of Honour on The Queen's arrival and departure, being on parade for church at Crathie each Sunday and providing parties of beaters, ghillies and ponymen whenever the Royal Family and their guests shot the moors at Balmoral.

For those who appreciate the open air, physical exercise and being in such marvellous surroundings as can only be found in the Highlands of Scotland, life as a member of the Royal Guard must have been idyllic. Those who went to Ballater were all volunteers and hand-picked from throughout the battalion and few returned having not enjoyed themselves, although it helped that the weather was excellent most of the time. The officers of the Guard who, in addition to Major Erskine, included Captain Andrew Parsons and Lieutenants Kim Fraser, Anthony Forbes and David Drummond Moray, had the best of the deal since when not beating with their guardsmen, they found themselves invited to shoot on neighbouring moors. The administration of the detachment fell primarily to Drill Sergeant Armitage and CSM Meade, although they too managed to get out 'on the hill' on occasions, especially during the stalking season when they were offered the chance to stalk at Balmoral. It would be surprising if a tour of duty so close to the Royal Family and of such interest to the media did not produce its fair share of 'incidents'. However, most could be laughed about as when Lance Corporal Brizzle, a well built, genial countryman who had charge of the deer ponies, chose to move them through a Royal picnic. One Sunday following his normal practice he went to water his ponies in Loch Muick oblivious of the fact that The Queen and her picnic party lay in his path. Undeterred, Brizzle pressed on allegedly scattering the picnic as he went to the loch and back by his accustomed route. Happily The Queen was reported as being 'amused' by the incident. Several members of the Guard attended one of the Ghillies' Balls held in the Castle and danced with members of the Royal Family as well as with other staff who were supporting them during their time at Balmoral; on one occasion one guardsman found himself dancing with The Queen Mother at the end of the first Paul Jones while the next time round he ended up in front of The Queen and danced with her. Later as he left the dance floor The Queen Mother passed him and, with a twinkle in her eye, whispered out of the corner of her mouth 'Snob!'

There were sporting successes as well and Lieutenant Anthony Forbes, running in army boots, did well to finish in seventh place in the Ballater Hill Race; the following year he returned to Deeside with eight guardsmen to compete again and won. When the Guard finally left Ballater Major Erskine received a letter from The Queen's Private Secretary: 'On her departure from Balmoral The Queen commanded me to write to you to let you know how satisfied she had been with the conduct of the Guard at Balmoral this year .... The Queen was impressed by their smartness on and off parade, and by the cheerfulness with which they carried out their tasks at Balmoral and on the hill.' It was beyond question that the Guard had been a great success; a determination that the job to be done should be done properly but that people should enjoy themselves when off duty ensured a happy detachment and further helped to promote the good name of the Regiment in Scotland.

During the absence of the Royal Guard at Ballater the remainder of the battalion were heavily involved in the Edinburgh Military Tattoo, an annual event organized by the Army but sponsored by the City Council. 1967 saw much of the tattoo programme made over to events involving the Regiment and it was most appropriate that it should also be Brigadier Jack Sanderson's first year as the Producer; a former Commanding Officer of the 2nd Battalion during the Malayan emergency, Brigadier Sanderson already knew the Tattoo well from his time as Area Commander and soon settled into his stride. As well as providing many of the participants, the battalion supplied most of the administrative support to the Tattoo, while a star performer each evening was Lance Sergeant Muir, the Sergeants' Mess cook, who sang 'If I ruled the World' and 'Abide with me' emulating if not quite surpassing Harry Secombe!

Apart from a Guard of Honour in Glasgow for the President of Turkey on 4 November which was commanded by Major Murray Naylor and found by Right

Flank with CSM Torrance and CQMS Miller as the right and left guides, little happened during the winter until late January, 1968, when a succession of violent gales swept across the Lowlands of Scotland ripping roofs off tenements in Glasgow and Edinburgh and rendering many buildings structurally unsound. Contingency plans whereby the Army could assist the civil community at times of disaster were quickly sanctioned and companies of the battalion were dispatched in rotation to help in making buildings safe or, where this was not possible, to evacuate families, and Right Flank operated for several days from a Territorial Army drill hall in Shettleston from where daily forays were made into the Gorbals to help with the problems there. The efforts of the battalion were greatly appreciated by those whose hardship the Army helped to alleviate, although it did not pass unnoticed at the time that this appreciation was more forthcoming from the people of Glasgow than from those in Edinburgh.

Some important changes in senior ranks took place in the battalion after a few months at Redford. Major Joe Hughes who had been with the battalion throughout its tour in the Far East left in October, 1967, to assume that most prestigious of Household Brigade appointments, Quartermaster at the Guards Depot; his place as Quartermaster of the 1st Battalion was taken by Major Gordon Mitchell who had started life in the Argyll and Sutherland Highlanders and subsequently served with considerable distinction not only with the Regiment but also with the Parachute Regiment, Number 1 (Guards) Independent Parachute Company and the Special Air Service Regiment; a man of quiet demeanour and shrewd judgement, 'Mitch' could always spare a moment for those seeking help or advice. Another important change occurred in the New Year when RSM Grant handed over to RSM F. Smith, also a former member of the Guards Parachute Company. RSM Smith's appointment to be the Sergeant Major reflected a growing move away from 'the old school' towards the selection of younger men who were often noticeably different from their predecessors in both style and temperament, for this most crucial of battalion appointments.

On 1 January, 1968, the Household Brigade was officially re-titled the Household Division, while the Brigade of Guards was in future to be called the Guards Division. These changes had been announced the previous May when the Army Board had decided that the existing grouping of infantry battalions within Brigades and Large Regiments was too small. As a result it had been proposed and agreed that in future battalions should be grouped into divisions of which the Guards Division containing eight battalions was to be one; the only exception was the Parachute Regiment which was to remain in its current form. In reaching its decision the Army Board rejected the possibility of forming a Corps of Infantry 'as being unwieldy and impersonal to a degree inimical to effective personnel and general management'. However, these changes hardly affected life at Redford Barracks where 1968 followed a not dissimilar pattern to 1967. A detachment paraded at Windsor on 4 May when the Guards Division received the Freedom of the Borough of Windsor, while on 8 June the battalion paraded at Redford Barracks in celebration of Her Majesty The Queen's

Birthday; Her Royal Highness The Duchess of Gloucester took the salute, deputizing for her husband, with 5,000 people watching. The Commanding Officer, Major Richard Mayfield, his Second-in-Command, and Captain Michael Campbell his Adjutant, were all mounted on horses of dubious disposition loaned by the police or the local Co-operative Society but managed to survive.

The local Edinburgh ceremonial scene was concluded on 2 July when a Review of Regiments and Corps of the Army in Scotland was held in the presence of Her Majesty The Queen and His Royal Highness The Duke of Edinburgh in Holyrood Park. Colonel MacGregor commanded the parade which was held in appalling weather which almost caused him to cancel it, not least because nobody else seemed able to decide whether or not it should go ahead.

Jamaica Jamaica might seem a strange place for a public duties battalion based in Scotland to train but nevertheless it was the location for Exercise CALYPSO HOP, an overseas training exercise which took Battalion Headquarters and Right and Left Flank to the island for a month in the middle of August. Base camp was established at Port Antonio on the north-east coast of the island and the two rifle companies trained in the adjacent jungle. This training was directed by Captain Michael Nurton and was designed to revise jungle skills last practised in Malaysia and to teach those new to the jungle how to operate and survive in it. This was probably as much as could be achieved in a month and Colonel MacGregor placed equal emphasis on people indulging in and enjoying the many opportunities for water ski-ing, deep sea fishing and exploring the island; he himself became one of the foremost of the battalion's anglers, while Captain Kim Ross, the Signal Officer, led a party which climbed Jamaica's Blue Mountain and Captain Mitchell walked alone through the Cockpit Country, an arid, inhospitable area of desert south of Montego Bay. The month away from Scotland did everybody good and many aspects of soldiering in the field were re-learnt the hard way; however, the exercise would not have been so successful nor would it have run so smoothly had it not been for RSM Jordan, a redoubtable Grenadier who by 1968 had served seven years with the Jamaican Defence Force and who used his not inconsiderable contacts within Jamaican 'society' to ensure that the battalion obtained maximum benefit from its stay on the island.

During the battalion's time in the Caribbean a party from the Jamaican Defence Force trained in Scotland and were looked after by the Second-in-Command and C Company commanded by Major Michael Whiteley. By the end of September all involved in this exchange training had returned home and the 1st Battalion started to prepare for its move to London in the New Year. On 4 October the battalion marched through Edinburgh and, after he had taken the salute, the Lord Provost entertained a number of officers and soldiers to lunch to mark the battalion's tour of duty in Scotland. This was a fitting climax to the battalion's time at Redford Barracks, a period during which no effort had been spared to show the Regiment to the people of Scotland and to emphasize that, while Scots Guards battalions might spend most of their time outside the country, they were in every way as much part of the Scottish family of regiments as any other. The decision to send the 1st Battalion to Edinburgh in April, 1967, had been more than vindicated.

When Major Murray de Klee left the 1st Battalion in Malaya in February, 1966, he went to Hereford to form and command G Squadron of 22 Special Air Service Regiment, many of whose soldiers were drawn from Foot Guards Battalions. Three years later, in April, 1969, he returned to the 1st Battalion to take command on the departure of Colonel MacGregor whose final act had been to move it to London. 1969 was to be the battalion's turn to troop its Queen's Colour on the Birthday Parade and throughout the early summer months all efforts were concentrated on preparing for the parade. Colonel de Klee was the Field Officer in Brigade Waiting, Major Murray Naylor commanded the Escort for the Colour and Major Philip Erskine Number Two Guard while 2nd Lieutenant Alec Ramsay carried the Queen's Colour. CSM Bone and CQMS H. Forrest were the right and left guides of the Escort. It was without doubt a good parade as one ex-Coldstream Guardsman made clear when he wrote to RSM Smith afterwards 'I thought the Escort easily the best since the War and were beyond criticism – the box misses nothing! .... Please allow me to congratulate you and thank you all for making me dash to the wardrobe, don my Brigade tie and stick my chest out again.' The day was also notable for the fact that the spectators broke into spontaneous applause as the Guards marched off Horse Guards and for 14 June being the first occasion when the Public were to see Concorde which flew over Buckingham Palace after the march down the Mall.

The battalion was told shortly after arriving in London that it was to deploy to Sharjah in February, 1970, for a nine-month unaccompanied tour after which it would return to Pirbright. In the meantime it was to provide the enemy force for an exercise to be held in Denmark in September, 1969, to test Allied Command Europe Mobile Force (Land) (AMF(L)) in its role defending the Baltic Approaches against Soviet attack. After eighteen months of public duties the battalion's standard of training hardly qualified it to play such an important part, a reality that Colonel de Klee openly acknowledged at the time; however, he placed his faith in the guardsmen's customary ability 'to cut about' when the situation demanded and his confidence was subsequently proved to be fully justified. On 8 September the battalion sailed to Wilhelmshaven in Northern Germany where it learnt to operate with the German *Kriegsmarine* who were to land the invading force in Denmark; thereafter the battalion moved to Neustadt on the Schleswig Holstein coast before embarking for a very rough and unpleasant sea voyage which landed it on the Danish islands of Mon and Falster. A number of contacts with the AMF(L) ensued during which the battalion covered many miles on its feet before it crossed the sea again, this time to Zealand where the final battle with the NATO forces took place. It was a thoroughly enjoyable exercise and, as with the 2nd Battalion's visit to Canada three years previously, just the sort of tonic that a battalion engaged on public

Chelsea Barracks

Denmark

duties needs from time to time. The whole exercise was conducted against the background of demonstrations for peace by the Danish equivalent of the Campaign for Nuclear Disarmament, although the worst the battalion suffered was when Battalion Headquarters was serenaded by the local town band before the crossing to Zealand and while the Commanding Officer was trying to give orders! Elsewhere Right Flank was allocated seven platoons of Danish Home Guard – 'loosely under command' – which, once they had consumed a large meal laid out on tables covered with white tablecloths, set out unassisted to attack the Canadian battalion defending the area to their front. The battalion returned to London on 28 September, having given a good account of itself and with the praises of General Walter Walker, Commander in Chief Allied Forces Northern Europe, ringing in its ears, to undertake once again London duties for the four months that remained before it was to move to Sharjah.

Earlier, in May, 1969, Major Dusty Smith had left Regimental Headquarters to become a Military Knight of Windsor, the first Scots Guardsman since 1871 to hold such a position. His knowledge of the Regiment was unsurpassed and during his nine years at Regimental Headquarters, where he first held the appointment of Assistant Regimental Adjutant and later that of Records Officer he filled the role of 'continuity man' so successfully that many a visitor would arrive in the Headquarters saying, 'Of course the only person I know here is Dusty Smith'. He joined the Regiment in 1920 and died at Windsor in 1990. Another event of the same period involved the transfer to the Regiment of two officers of the Cameronians which battalion had been disbanded in 1968; on having to leave their old regiment Captain Robin Buchanan-Dunlop and Captain Jeremy Cox both chose to join the Scots Guards and both were to serve with the 1st Battalion in Sharjah. Each contributed considerably during his time with the Regiment.

CHAPTER FIVE

GERMANY, SHARJAH AND WINDSOR

1st Battalion: Sharjah-Pirbright-Windsor
2nd Battalion: Iserlohn-Munster-Windsor

Iserlohn, a medium-sized Westphalian town situated on the edge of the *2nd Battalion* Sauerland a few miles to the south of the River Ruhr, is, despite its close *Iserlohn 1967* proximity to the coalmines and steelworks in one of the densest concentrations of industry in Western Europe, a remarkably pleasant place and one which in 1967 British troops had garrisoned since the end of the Second World War. However, by the time that the 2nd Battalion arrived there in January, 4th Guards Brigade, of which it was to be part, had only been in Iserlohn and in the neighbouring city of Wuppertal for three years and plans had already been laid for Brigade Headquarters and its two Foot Guards battalions to move to Munster in the spring of 1968. Undeterred by the proposed shortness of its sojourn, the 2nd Battalion Scots Guards took over Aldershot Barracks from the 1st Battalion Coldstream Guards and set about the by then seemingly routine task of having to refurbish a barracks long starved of money for even the most basic of maintenance. Unfortunately for those serving in BAOR in 1967, and on later tours in the Command, the lack of resources to allow living and working accommodation to be properly cared for was to become a frequent and depressing refrain.

4th Guards Brigade was part of 4th Division within 1st British Corps. The Corps, along with others within Northern Army Group, was responsible for defending a section of the Inner German Border to the east of the River Weser valley and to the south of the city of Hanover. The battalion's area of responsibility was over 100 miles from Iserlohn and, in the event of an attack by the forces of the Warsaw Pact, it would have been required to move eastwards to previously reconnoitred battle positions, leaving its families to be evacuated to Britain as speedily as those left in charge could arrange it. While such a scenario was happily never put to the test during the forty years of the Cold War when NATO sought to deter the Soviet Union and her Warsaw Pact allies from invading Western Europe, all training in BAOR was directed towards perfecting the means to counter such an invasion. For the infantry this meant being capable of operating in close co-operation with armour and on arrival in

NORTH SEA

BALTIC SEA

Kiel

SCHLESWIG
HOLSTEIN

Neustadt

Hamburg

Wilhelmshaven

Bremen

Soltau

Bergen Hohne

GERMAN
DEMOCRATIC
REPUBLIC

BERLIN

LOWER SAXONY

Osnabrück

Hanover

NETHERLANDS

Bielefeld

Münster

Hameln

Magdeburg

NORTH RHINE
WESTPHALIA

Sennelager

Harz Mts

Dortmund

Iserlohn

River Elbe

Hubblerath

Wuppertal

Düsseldorf

Sauerland

Inner
German
Border

Cologne

Vogelsang

FEDERAL

BELGIUM

REPUBLIC

River Rhine

LUX.

Frankfurt

OF   GERMANY

CZECHOSLOVAKIA

FRANCE

BAVARIA

Munich

Major Training Areas

Miles

0   50   100

Germany

70

Germany the battalion was organized as an infantry battle group and paired to work with one of the two armoured regiments in the Brigade. In practice this entailed not just mastering the handling and maintenance of the eighty-five armoured personnel carriers (APC) allocated to an infantry battalion but also learning and understanding armoured tactics. The battalion inherited from the Coldstream Guards the well tried but obsolescent Saracen wheeled APC but these were replaced in May by the tracked FV432 built by Alvis which had been progressively introduced into service in BAOR from the mid 1960s.

Relationships between British units stationed in the principal garrison towns in Germany and with the local people were usually amicable, although, as with any group of men or women living in an unfamiliar country, there were occasions when tempers frayed and things were said or done which might later come to be regretted. On such occasions the media usually tried to exploit the incident by leading a campaign to have a unit's freedom restricted but, other than in cases of wild excess, the BAOR authorities did not usually allow themselves to be influenced by such clamour. Any fears that Colonel Swinton and his new Sergeant Major, RSM Marchant, may have had that their battalion might clash with neighbouring British units within Iserlohn Garrison were quickly dispelled and the battalion's relationship with the other British battalion there, the 1st Battalion The Royal Highland Fusiliers, started well and continued that way for the few months that the two battalions served alongside each other.

Of equal if not greater importance was the manner in which a battalion established itself with the German population amongst whom it lived. Unless everybody understood from the outset that, regardless of the circumstances that had brought the Army to Germany in 1945, they were 'guests' in a foreign country, differences in culture and temperament could easily be exaggerated to a point where the misguided on either side might take it upon themselves to impress their manliness upon the other. Happily, thanks to the firm control exercised by the Sergeant Major and his company sergeant majors and the good sense shown by the guardsmen, there were few incidents to disturb the peace in Iserlohn and the local police quickly realized that any soldier wearing a jacket and tie was almost invariably a Scots Guardsman and, if on occasion a little the worse for wear, only had to be conveyed to Aldershot Barracks by police car where appropriate action would be taken. A third ingredient in this heady cocktail of international relationships was provided by the close proximity of a Canadian Brigade; however, in this instance the battalion's visit to Base Gagetown the previous year paid real dividends and the good liaison established then was built upon with success.

Much of the battalion's first year in 4th Guards Brigade was absorbed in learning about armoured warfare, a military science that could only be practised on the larger training areas or across the German countryside when special permission to exercise had to be obtained from the civil authorities. During 1967 the battalion trained over the three main training areas most frequently

71

used by BAOR units at Sennelager, Soltau and Vogelsang, on the latter during a period of bitterly cold and snowy weather in April when the final exercise had to be curtailed for fear of bogging in the battle group's Saracens and tanks. In between these periods of training platoons and companies travelled around Germany either to train or enjoy themselves and soldiers who had never previously been outside their own home town soon realized that there was a different world across the English Channel. On 23 May Lieutenant Malcolm Ross and his platoon returned from their attachment to the Irish Guards in Aden, having earned plaudits from their Commanding Officer for the manner in which they had conducted themselves while on active service in the Protectorate.

Also in May Major Ferguson and CSM Edmiston took Right Flank to Copenhagen to train with the Danish Life Guard when all the delights of that hospitable city were seemingly put on display, while other platoons visited Berlin to relieve those on duty there or went to patrol the Inner German Border to demonstrate a NATO presence opposite the wire and watchtowers which delineated that most inhuman of all international boundaries. Meanwhile Battalion Headquarters took part in endless command post exercises when communications were tested and imaginary battles were fought with chinagraph pencils rather than weapons and battle procedure was practised at different levels of command without a single rifleman being deployed on the ground; such exercises had their value and important lessons could be learnt but to the true professional they were a poor substitute for the real thing. Nonetheless the latter came as well when in late September Headquarters 4th Division staged Exercise ROB ROY, one of the largest manoeuvre exercises ever to be held in Germany when 4th Guards and 20th Armoured Brigades were pitted against the Canadian Brigade. Masterminded by the Divisional Chief of Staff, Colonel David Scott-Barrett, and painstakingly planned, the exercise practised several phases of war and allowed the battalion its first real run with its new APCs across the German countryside in the vicinity of the Weser Valley.

The logistics of ensuring that a mechanized battalion is kept running have always been complicated and for the Quartermasters an entirely new method of operational replenishment had to be learnt. Major Donald Whyte and Captain Fred Adams and their staffs had to ensure the provision of ammunition, fuel and rations to the companies and the battalion's affiliated squadron of armour at any time of the day or night whatever the weather or the battle situation and often with inadequate knowledge of the whereabouts of those they were trying to re-supply. Co-ordination of this effort fell mainly to the Headquarter Company Commander, Major George Nickerson, who spent endless hours trying to arrange all the abstruse requirements of the battle group over high frequency radio communications that were often rendered totally unworkable by atmospherics. George Nickerson, who throughout his long service in the Regiment carried the somewhat predictable nickname 'Pants Off', was the epitome of the best sort of regimental officer; lovable for the very qualities of eccentricity that made him the personality that he was, his whole life was the Scots Guards and his happiest time in a long career at regimental duty was undoubtedly his period as the Captain of Right Flank in the 2nd Battalion in the mid 1950s when incidentally he was instrumental in saving the Colours during a fire in the Officers' Mess at Hubblerath. Many are the stories of him but none exemplifies his whimsical sense of humour better than the occasion in Iserlohn when the officers of the battalion were being instructed in the mechanics of nuclear fire planning by a somewhat self-important Gunner colonel; having explained in considerable detail the action to be taken immediately prior to a friendly strike, a procedure which entailed everybody lying face down on the ground with their hands over their heads, the latter called for questions. After ruminating on what he had just heard George asked, 'What happens if the missile is a blind and fails to explode?' and, before the startled colonel, whose authority on matters of nuclear detonations had never before been questioned could reply, George followed with the supplementary question, 'How long do we have to remain in this undignified posture?' His love of the straightforward things in life and his pleasure in being a Scots Guardsman were his hallmarks and he died in a tragic accident in 1987, a much respected regimental officer who carried the distinction of having almost certainly been the most senior major in the British Army when he retired.

Exercise ROB ROY completed, the battalion returned to barracks and prepared for the move to Munster in early 1968. On 3 November an armoured parade was held to welcome Major General Vernon Erskine Crum as the new Commander 4th Division; the parade, which involved a drive past by all the battalion's tracked APCs and wheeled transport and included the Colours being carried in one of Battalion Headquarters' vehicles, went smoothly although Major Nickerson mistook the barrack petrol pumps for the Divisional Commander and saluted them in error! General Erksine Crum's arrival to command the Division was followed three months later by the appointment of Brigadier Michael Gow to take charge of 4th Guards Brigade, thereby ensuring a continuous line of Scots Guards commanders from platoon to Division. General Erskine Crum soon made his mark in Germany as he had done wherever else he had served and the Battalion Sergeants' Mess in particular 'found him so friendly for a general'. A man of very considerable intellect – once described by Major General Lord Ismay as possessing 'a wise head on a young body' – he exuded great qualities of leadership and understanding and, had he not died prematurely after taking up the appointment of GOC Northern Ireland in 1971, would surely have gone to the very top of the three armed services.

A Farewell to Iserlohn Parade on which Major Mark Carnegie-Brown and a *Münster* small detachment represented the battalion, was held on 18 January, whereupon Brigade Headquarters and the battalion moved to Münster, a cathedral and university city with a large British Garrison some fifty miles to the north of Iserlohn, which was to be home to the Foot Guards battalions based in Germany throughout the 1970s. The battalion was sorry to leave Iserlohn after only a year

73

and after working so successfully to cement good relations with the local German people and other military units. As if to drive the point home Waterloo Barracks in Münster presented an even greater challenge to the battalion than had Aldershot Barracks a year earlier; comprising single storey huts of stark simplicity which had been built on the cheap in 1953 to last only ten years, the barracks were in serious need of refurbishment which took place only slowly over the next ten years, while some of the Married Quarters, for which demand had grown considerably in recent years, presented a most unattractive prospect after Iserlohn. Needless to say the battalion set to to sort out its inheritance while embarking upon its second training season in Germany. This followed much the same pattern as that of the year before with companies and platoons travelling all over Germany, patrolling the border, learning to float their APCs in the River Weser near Hameln and exercising with the remainder of the Brigade when the opportunity arose. On 10 July Colonel John Swinton handed over command to Lieutenant Colonel John Acland and departed to the Ministry of Defence before taking over as the Lieutenant Colonel Commanding in 1970.

Reference has already been made in the last chapter to the re-organization of the Infantry as part of a wider exercise to reduce the size of the Army. The first phase of the re-organization was implemented at the beginning of 1968 following which in July it was announced by the Ministry of Defence that there would be a further tranche of reductions which would take effect in 1971. While successful efforts had been made to exclude a battalion of the Foot Guards from the first round of reductions, it became increasingly clear during 1968 that it would not be possible to sustain the argument in the face of the proposed contraction of many distinguished regiments and in July it was announced that the 2nd Battalion would go 'into suspended animation' on 1 April, 1971. As a result Colonel Acland's first task upon assuming command was to inform his battalion of this sad decision. At the same time he consulted the battalion as to where people wished to spend their final year. The response was generally for Windsor and this was in due course arranged.

By 1968 training facilities for units in BAOR were becoming harder to obtain in theatre; ranges and manoeuvre areas were in ever greater demand from regiments and battalions which had been re-equipped with Chieftain tanks and FV432 APCs and which naturally wished to deploy their new and more sophisticated equipment under as realistic conditions as possible. At the same time pressure was being exerted by Britain's NATO allies for a greater share of existing areas while the German Federal authorities were placing a growing number of restrictions on the use of non-military land and convoy movement over week-ends. In order to alleviate this seemingly insoluble problem Head-quarters BAOR arranged for infantry battle groups to fly to Libya to train in the desert south of Tobruk and, within the space of a year, the 2nd Battalion Scots Guards twice visited North Africa as part of an all arms battle group.

Training in Libya

The first exercise took place in August, 1968, and the battalion supported by a squadron of the 13th/18th Royal Hussars equipped with Ferret Scout Cars, a

74

Royal Artillery battery and a Royal Engineer troop trained for four weeks under conditions of intense heat, dust and scorching wind; indeed on one day a temperature of 158 degrees was logged by the Survey Troop, apparently the highest temperature ever recorded in Libya. On that day Colonel Acland and the training staff were laying out the final plans for the battle runs to be undertaken by each company. He recalls that, if he attempted to speak when facing the Sahara to the south, the burning wind dried up his mouth instantly and speech became impossible. Companies and the squadron lived in their own camps in the desert and conducted a wide range of training which culminated in a battle run lasting forty-eight hours and covering ten miles when they were supported by all the battle group's heavy weaponry. This final training was constrained by an absolute minimum of safety restrictions and realistic battle conditions were created by a team of controllers led by the Commanding Officer and the Second-in-Command, Major Blair Stewart-Wilson. The value of such training was immense and everybody appreciated the opportunity to train with all weapons firing live ammunition, something that the majority had not experienced before. Writing after the exercise Colonel Acland recorded that '.... perhaps the most touching thing about the whole Libyan exercise was the evident pleasure of guardsmen, troopers, gunners, sappers and private soldiers in being able to exert themselves on training which they found worthwhile and realistic.' Success in training was made possible by the dedication of those responsible for the battle group's replenishment and the maintenance of its vehicles which worked relentlessly under appalling conditions of heat, sand and rock. The Light Aid Detachment under AQMS Bacon worked wonders in keeping the APCs running, while Captain Jim Forsyth and the administrative staff supplied the battle group with all its daily needs, including a requirement for 2,500 gallons of water for 800 men utilizing vehicles well past their best.

Sandstorms were a common occurrence and strange things happened to people when they became enveloped; CQMS Davis of G Company when near the site of the Second World War Knightsbridge Box position swore that he saw 'infantry in steel helmets' all around him. Snakes, scorpions and camel spiders abounded in the desert, the latter being attracted to noise as Sergeant Fullerton, the Police Sergeant, discovered when he found one crawling over his face as he lay in his sleeping bag. Perhaps the month away was best summed up by Captain Fred Adams, the Technical Quartermaster who worked tirelessly to keep the battle group fleet of vehicles running and who, at the end of the desert training, remarked to the Commanding Officer that he had seen 'the light of battle in the soldiers' eyes'.

Shortly after he had told the battalion that it was to go into suspended animation in April 1971 Colonel Acland consulted RSM Marchant about how the battalion should approach the remaining two and a half years of its existence. They agreed that the battalion 'should go out with a bang', undertaking all that was asked of it, however difficult or tiresome, and entering every competition so that no one would be able to reproach it for not maintaining high morale to the end. As a result the battalion trained hard both inside and outside Germany, played a full part in all that took place in Münster and set out to win all the sporting events for which it entered. Boxing was one sport towards which the battalion adopted a single-minded attitude to winning; following a period of intensive training the novice team beat the 2nd Battalion Grenadier Guards, its neighbour in Munster, in the 4th Division Championships in December, 1968. It was a thrilling contest and the battalion team recovered from being five bouts to one down to win six bouts to five. The heroes of the night were Lance Sergeants Hughes and Stewart, Lance Corporal McCue and Guardsmen Duffy, Brownwood and Johnson. Reinforced by boxers of proven ability from the 1st Battalion and supervised by Sergeant Fullerton, the team went on to achieve further success both during the remainder of the battalion's time in Munster and later at Windsor. In Germany they were runners up to the King's Regiment in the 1969 BAOR Championships. Much previously unknown talent was discovered, among it Guardsman Rigg and Lance Sergeant Speed, the latter ultimately becoming an Army boxer.

1969, the battalion's last full training season, took the same course as the previous two years. Ski-ing in Bavaria and the Harz Mountains, training at Sennelager, an exchange visit by G Company under Major Hugh Laing to Denmark and a test exercise for all the rifle platoons followed one another as such events usually did at that time in BAOR where the training cycle changed little from one year to the next and was therefore utterly predictable. Within the battalion a number of changes took place, the most important being the replacement as Adjutant of Captain Michael Scott by Captain Kim Ross, although the former quickly returned to take over G Company. In late May the battalion paid a second visit to Libya, this time to train there with the 14th/20th King's Hussars, its 'paired' armoured regiment; training in the desert took the same form as that of the previous year although the rules governing safety were rather less relaxed than before. The battalion's three rifle companies worked with their respective armoured squadrons which this time were mounted in Centurion tanks and were supported by the other affiliated units of the battle group. The training was again well worthwhile and on return Colonel Acland wrote to Lieutenant Colonel Peter Cavendish, his opposite number in command of the 14th/20th Hussars in the following terms, 'All of us who were in Libya with you realize how uniquely lucky we have been to have had this five-week training period together. From the point of view of co-operation between our two regiments it was, I reckon, worth five years in BAOR.' Undoubtedly the training paid off and standards of battlecraft and the tactical handling of armoured vehicles improved almost overnight, something that could never have been achieved in BAOR where restrictions on training often resulted in even the most basic of exercises having to be curtailed. The battalion left Libya just as a coup to oust King Idris from his throne was being mounted, following which no further British Army training was able to take place there, a sad loss for units in Germany.

17. "By 1986 training facilities for units in BAOR were becoming harder to obtain in theatre... Headquarters BAOR arranged for infantry battle groups to fly to Libya to train in the desert south of Tobruk and, within the space of a year, the 2nd Battalion twice visited North Africa." (Page 74)

18. "A farewell parade in Waterloo Barracks in February when the new Divisional Commander, Major General David Fraser, a Grenadier, took the salute, brought the 2nd Battalion's tour to an end in mid-March, 1970." (Page 77). The battalion command vehicle, *Ben Lawers*, passes the saluting dais; Captain Malcolm Ross is commanding the vehicle, while Lieutenants Andrew Bacchus and Alasdair Laing, escorted by Drill Sergeant Dargie, Colour Sergeant Sollars and Sergeant Howden, are carrying the Colours.

19. "Much previously unknown talent was discovered, among it Guardsman Rigg and Lance Sergeant Speed, the latter ultimately becoming an Army boxer." (Page 76). Sergeant Speed defeating his opponent from the King's Regiment in the Finals of the BAOR 1969 Boxing Championships.

20. "F Company arrived in Hong Kong with its families at the end of October and moved into Stanley Fort alongside the 1st Battalion Irish Guards." (Page 87). The Company provided a Guard, under the command of Major Johnny Clavering, for the 1970 Queen's Birthday Parade. Marching past behind him are Lieutenant Alasdair Laing, CSM Hope and Sergeant Lazenby.

21. "Because of the paucity of warning for its deployment the battalion had scant opportunity to train for internal security operations." (Page 84). A 2nd Battalion platoon practising riot drills in Armagh, Northern Ireland in July, 1970.

22. "Much of the time passed by Scots Guardsmen on the streets of Northern Ireland's towns and cities… has been interminably dull, although always overshadowed by the threat of a sniper's bullet or a terrorist bomb." (Page 90). Routine checks by a 1st Battalion patrol in the Clonard district of West Belfast in the autumn of 1971.

23. "Eventually the battalion disembarked at Belfast and, amidst considerable confusion, moved to Londonderry where it took over responsibility for the City Centre." (Page 97) A patrol of the Reconnaissance Platoon of the 2nd Battalion leaving a base in Londonderry City in August, 1972.

24. Right Flank of the 2nd Battalion, followed by Support Company and watched by recruits from the Guards Depot, leads the 2nd Battalion from Brookwood Station to Elizabeth Barracks, Pirbright, at the end of the battalion's Belfast tour in March, 1974. In the immediate foreground are Captain Simon Rose and CSM Carnegie, while on the left of the leading file are Lance Sergeants Hammel and Harper, both future RSMs.

25. "At the end of November, 1965, 9 Company relieved Left Flank at Serudong Ulu and the latter became the battalion reserve company at Kalabakan." (Page 50). An aerial view of the 1st Battalion's Serudong Ulu base showing a 105mm Howitzer bottom left.

26. Right Flank's Serudong Laut base in Sabah.

27. "Patrols of several weeks' duration, usually comprising a platoon, trained on a regular basis in and around the Jebel Akhdar Mountains of Northern Oman." (Page 80). Lieutenant Edward Woods' 11 Platoon of the 1st Battalion rests while on patrol near Saiq in 1970. The Omani in the foreground is their guide.

28. "In addition to state and other ceremonial duties the Regimental Band carries out a large number of external engagements, including visits overseas…". (Page 220). The band and members of the Pipes and Drums visited Italy in July, 1984, and were received by His Holiness Pope John Paul II at his summer palace at Castel Gandolfo. The Director of Music is Major Donald Carson.

While the battalion was training in North Africa, F (Support) Company under Major Johnny Clavering, travelled to Guyana for six weeks to undertake jungle training, a form of warfare new to ninety per cent of the company. The company took with it a number of attached sub-units from within the 4th Guards Brigade and was based at Takama, 130 miles from Georgetown in savannah country bordered by thick jungle. Each platoon and troop undertook three weeks' jungle training and at the end of the company's stay it exercised with the Guyana Defence Force. This was followed by adventure training before everybody flew back to Germany in late August.

The battalion's final six months in Germany were taken up with a round of exercises, competitions, sporting events and an overland expedition to the Valley of the Assassins in Iran led by Captain Anthony Leask and 2nd Lieutenant Nicholas Barne; travelling through Europe to Istanbul and thence to the Elburz Mountains north of Tehran, the party were unlucky to encounter appalling weather which prevented it from climbing it's objective, the 17,000 foot Throne of Solomon. However, the twelve men selected to go had the expedition of a lifetime even though some of them may not have appreciated exactly where they were; on arrival in Greece Lance Corporal Patterson, the expedition cook, dispatched a postcard to Master Cook Richardson in Münster triumphantly proclaiming 'We are now in Grease'!

On the sporting side the battalion achieved further successes in the boxing ring, while the squash team won both the BAOR and Army competitions in early 1970. Captain Iain Mackay-Dick led the team which included Captains Campbell Gordon and Peter Le Marchand, 2nd Lieutenant Nicholas Barne and Sergeant Downham. Squash was a sport at which the Regiment had hitherto not excelled and to win two major titles in one season was no mean achievement.

A visit by Her Royal Highness The Duchess of Gloucester in November and a farewell parade in Waterloo Barracks in February when the new Divisional Commander, Major General David Fraser, a Grenadier, took the salute, brought the battalion's three year tour to an end and in mid-March, 1970, it moved to Victoria Barracks, Windsor for its final year. Although the battalion left Münster on a high note with many successes to its name most were glad to leave behind the frustrations associated with trying to maintain high standards of training and operational readiness in a Command where realistic training was every year becoming that much harder to achieve.

29 November, 1967, saw the withdrawal of British troops from Aden after 129 years of colonial rule. For the four previous years the Army and the RAF had endeavoured to maintain a security policy which would allow the British Government to hand over the former protectorate to a federation of local tribal leaders; however, a ruthless nationalist movement, encouraged by Egypt and strongly supported by the local population, had rendered the achievement of such an aim increasingly unlikely and in 1966 Britain decided to cut her losses and to withdraw in as good order as possible the following year. A consequence of this decision was that in 1967 the control of Britain's residual forces in the

1st Battalion Sharjah 1970

77

Middle East was passed to Headquarters British Forces Persian Gulf in Bahrain. The latter's command included two infantry battalions, one in Bahrain and the other at Sharjah in the Trucial States. The presence of these battalions, together with the temporary basing of RAF strike aircraft on Masira Island in the Sultanate of Oman, was intended to demonstrate Britain's continuing support for the Gulf State rulers, particularly those who governed the seven Trucial States for whose external affairs Britain had been responsible since 1892. However, this new arrangement was not to endure for long and, after only a short period, it was decided that Britain would withdraw completely from the Middle East in 1970 when the Trucial States were to come together as an independent nation titled the United Arab Emirates. As a result when the 1st Battalion Scots Guards flew to Sharjah in February that year and took over from the 1st Battalion Queen's Own Highlanders it was destined to be the last battalion to serve there.

Once again an inability to recruit sufficient soldiers into the Regiment required the 1st Battalion to have to be reinforced for the nine months that it was to be based in Sharjah, the reinforcement on this occasion being undertaken by 2 Company, 2nd Battalion Grenadier Guards, commanded by Major Dermot Blundell-Hollinshead-Blundell whose father had served in the Scots Guards both before and during the Second World War. Further Household Division representation was provided by A Squadron, The Life Guards, which, like the 1st Battalion, was undertaking an unaccompanied tour from Windsor as part of Britain's residual presence in the Gulf. All three elements of the Division were based in the same camp adjacent to the RAF Station outside the town of Sharjah.

The battalion was complete in Sharjah by mid-February and a training programme designed to renew basic military skills, many forgotten during a long period of public duties, while at the same time preparing everybody for desert operations, was immediately set in train. Colonel Murray de Klee, a forthright and practical soldier who relished the freedom to command his battalion in the field uninterrupted by other than an occasional order from his superiors, knew better than most that physical fitness was the key to a man's ability to survive and to be effective in the waterless, parched deserts of the Trucial States and the Oman which border that great sand sea, the *Rub al Khali* or Empty Quarter of Saudi Arabia. He determined to get every man in his battalion really fit and for the first month there were no exceptions to the rule that everybody should undertake a run or a period of hard physical training each day; this policy paid dividends as was shown later when the battalion was put through several periods of demanding training without suffering avoidable casualties from heat-stroke or dehydration.

Training during the nine months in Sharjah was divided into three periods. The first concentrated upon improving personal skills up to platoon level, while, during the middle part of the tour when the weather was at its hottest, the emphasis was placed upon teaching guardsmen specialist skills and ensuring

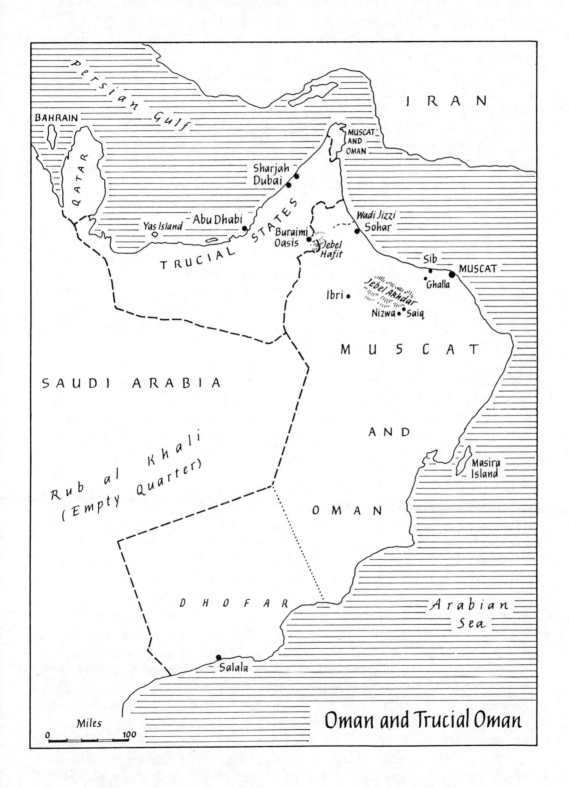

Oman and Trucial Oman

that those who needed them obtained their educational qualifications. Finally towards the end the battalion undertook a range of exercises designed to test it in operating under the harsh conditions found in the desert and among the rocky, inhospitable mountains of the Oman.

One of the ways in which British battalions could support the rulers of the Gulf States was by training in their countries when opportunities arose. 'Flag-waving' expeditionary forces may be more readily associated with the days of the Indian Empire but they are a good way of describing the sort of activities carried out by companies and platoons during their nine months in Sharjah. Patrols of several weeks duration, usually comprising a platoon, trained on a regular basis in and around the Jebel Akhdar Mountains of Northern Oman, the first such patrol being provided by the Reconnaissance Platoon led by Captain Jeremy Cox in April. Based upon Saiq, 6,000 feet up the *jebel*, platoons spent their time training and discovering an area totally different from the deserts of the Trucial Coast while well away from the watchful eye of their company commanders. Earlier B (Support) Company under Major Michael Whiteley, an old Oman hand as a result of earlier service with the Sultan of Muscat's Armed Forces (SAF), and CSM Knight executed a march through Northern Oman visiting places hitherto unknown to Scots Guardsmen but which were familiar enough to those British officers who had served in the area in the 1950s and 60s when the Sultanate had been threatened by the territorial ambitions of its neighbours or by internal insurgency. Buraimi Oasis, the Wadi Jizzi, Muscat and Nizwa were all visited and guardsmen were introduced to the way of life and customs of the tribesmen among whom they found themselves; arab feasts or *fadhls* when the visitor sits cross legged beside his host who might be a local *sheikh* or a *wali* (a governor) can sometimes be a bit of an ordeal, especially when invited to consume an enormous pile of boiled rice and goat, the eyes of which are carefully extracted and given to the senior guest as a mark of respect.

While B Company familiarized itself with the Oman, Right Flank under Major John Arthur flew to Yas Island off the Abu Dhabi coast to clear it of unexploded munitions prior to the area being surveyed for oil and gas exploration and Left Flank commanded by Major Anthony Milner-Brown exercised in Bahrain. Later 2 Company also visited the island to act as the standby company, while Left Flank travelled to Cyprus in June to take part in an exercise designed to test the security of the RAF Station at Akrotiri. The battalion was deliberately kept busy, a sound policy when a unit is overseas without its families and in a place which can offer little entertainment other than that which is self-generated. Most enjoyed the challenge of intensive training and the chance to play competitive sport, while others undoubtedly relished the challenge of learning about an area so seemingly devoid of life and interest but which was rich in history and traditions spanning centuries. Some serving in the battalion in Arabia in 1970 were no doubt aware of those Englishmen who, fascinated by the Arab and his nomadic lifestyle, had gone before them to chart the sands or to cross allegedly uncrossable deserts by camel in order to discover places previously unknown. In the aftermath of the Second World War that great Arabist Wilfrid Thesiger had ridden across the Empty Quarter disguised as a tribesman to better understand the ways of a people who have always captivated the British. In 1970 people like Major Whiteley and Major John Bryden, the Battalion Paymaster whose previous military service had taken him to Iraq, India and Malaysia, equally relished the freedom of the desert and would have had little difficulty understanding Thesiger's motives in undertaking his journey. Meanwhile, much further south in Dhofar Captain Andrew Joscelyne witnessed history in the making when on 23 July, 1970, he was present in Salala when Sultan Said bin Taimuir was deposed by his son Qaboos in a bloodless Palace revolution. Sultan Said refused to recognize that changes elsewhere in the Middle East would in time reach the Oman and that it was therefore perhaps better to lead the accompanying programme of reform than to be overtaken by it. His son Sultan Qaboos has proved a wise and effective leader and is still on the throne today.

SAF, an Army still officered by seconded and contracted officers in 1970, received considerable support from battalions serving in the Gulf. The Training Depot at Ghalla was commanded by Major John Cooper, an erstwhile Scots Guardsman who served in the Special Air Service Regiment during the Second World War, and a number of officers and NCOs assisted him in training the Arab and Baluchi recruits who passed through his hands. The first to serve with SAF were 2nd Lieutenant Julian Lancaster and Sergeants Hardie, Wells and Gault. Writing twenty-three years later, Major Cooper commented that 'he felt the battalion should take great credit for sending these British NCOs with their wonderful adaptability in dealing with an enormous language problem and with boys from local tribes who had a total lack of education'. Meanwhile in July Colonel de Klee determined to test the training accomplished by his battalion up until that time and organized Exercise GAZALA GALLOP, a period of sustained training which involved the battalion being flown to Buraimi before deploying to hunt down a band of dissidents in the foothills of Jebel Hafit. Before the battalion left Sharjah some 'old hands' who thought they understood desert operations expressed doubt as to the wisdom of such an exercise at the hottest time of the year and forecast that the battalion would suffer forty per cent heat casualties within four days. Needless to say the critics were confounded, the battalion suffering only one casualty evacuation during the entire exercise – a guardsman suffering from a suspected appendicitis whom the Commanding Officer decreed should have his appendix removed. If he was ill enough to warrant air evacuation he was ill enough to undergo emergency surgery.

The final months in Sharjah saw no relaxation in training or sporting activities. 166 people travelled away from the Gulf to places as far afield as Iran, Malaysia and Mombasa in order to undertake adventure training; in early October Headquarters Land Forces Gulf set a final test exercise which involved the battalion landing from the sea to the north of Sohar in Oman and then fighting its way up the Wadi Jizzi towards Ibri; Exercise BUGLE CALL allowed the battalion maximum scope to show what it had learnt during its time in the theatre and it took full advantage of the opportunity by capturing the last of the enemy twenty-four hours before the exercise was due to end, appropriate evidence of what had been achieved during the previous eight months.

Another finale of a different sort came on 22 October when the battalion staged a searchlight tattoo in front of 2,500 people, with Sheik Khalid, the Ruler of Sharjah taking the salute. Drill squads, a replica of the Tower of London built by the Royal Engineers to enable a performance of the Ceremony of the Keys to be enacted, massed bands and pipers with the Regimental Band and that of the Royal Irish Rangers combining, RAF guard dogs and a musical drive by the Transport Platoon, all produced by the Second-in-Command, Major Iain Ferguson, set the seal on a thoroughly enjoyable tour. Two days later the advance party left for home followed three weeks afterwards by the rest of the battalion which went on leave prior to re-assembling at Pirbright in the New Year, 1971.

The nine months in Sharjah gave the 1st Battalion a golden opportunity to demonstrate what can be achieved when the determination to succeed exists. From the outset Colonel de Klee knew that he had to give the battalion a real challenge if it was not to fester and become bored in the spartan environment of Sharjah airfield. He drove his officers and guardsmen hard, setting a programme of training and exercises which kept everybody busy from dawn till dusk and which demanded total participation; as a result and not surprisingly the battalion passed every test set it and left at the end of the tour 'with its tail up' and at a peak of efficiency.

While firm leadership from the top set the direction and ensured that momentum was never lost, a strong supporting team deserves credit for the way in which it underpinned the Commanding Officer's lead. Captain Lachlan Maclean, the Adjutant, and Major Gordon Mitchell, the Quartermaster, both like Colonel de Klee former members of the Special Air Service Regiment, and RSM Smith were all men sympathetic to their leader's aims and style of command and they administered the battalion in a way that allowed the latter's plans to be successfully fulfilled.

When Colonel Archie Fletcher flew to Sharjah on his farewell visit as the Lieutenant Colonel Commanding in late June he arrived to be greeted by the Commanding Officer and his Sergeant Major both 'exuding a smartness which, after a long flight, immediately raises a man's morale and causes others to want to achieve similar standards.' However, perhaps the final comment on the Sharjah tour should go to Major Bryden: 'After Chelsea came a nine-month unaccompanied tour in Sharjah. Once again I was most impressed by the battalion's professional switch from London duties to desert conditions. Personally, as Paymaster, I found the tour bliss. No wives within 4,000 miles to pop into the pay office and bother us and no pay problems at all.'

2nd Battalion Windsor 1970 The 2nd Battalion's final year at Windsor was destined to be an exacting one and Colonel Acland and his staff set out to keep everybody busy and involved right up to the time when the battalion would pass into suspended animation. Public duties were rightly the priority along with training and sport and the planning of where every man should go come 31 March, 1971, a task which involved the Adjutant and ORQMS Heybourn in much hard work; however, what was not known in March, 1970, was that an emergency tour of duty in Northern Ireland in late June would disrupt some of this planning. The Commanding Officer's approach to public duties was that, once the battalion had learnt the fundamentals of mounting the Queen's Guard and the Windsor Castle Guard, rehearsals should be kept to a minimum and that ceremonial requirements should not intrude upon the battalion's other activities. Remarkably neither RSM Marchant nor his two drill sergeants, Drill Sergeants Dargie and Cameron, nor any of the company sergeant majors, CSMs E. Lawrie, Hope, Milne and Phillips had previously organized public duties; as a result the Adjutant, Captain Kim Ross, used his own collection of model lead soldiers to help instruct the battalion as to what was required of them!

On 8 May Her Majesty The Queen visited Victoria Barracks and spent nearly two hours talking to members of the battalion, a gesture which, in view of the latter's approaching date of suspended animation, was greatly appreciated. On 13 June the battalion's Queen's Colour was trooped on the Queen's Birthday Parade which was commanded by Colonel Acland; never an enthusiast for the ceremonial side of soldiering, there must have been moments when the guardsmen wondered whether he would survive the test of memory which the role of Field Officer in Brigade Waiting requires. He admits that he 'got through due to the ingenuity of the Sergeant Major', but has however never revealed just what such a statement means. Major James Dunsmure commanded the Escort while Lieutenant Andrew Bacchus carried the Colour which, before being handed over to him by RSM Marchant, was held by Sergeant Fullerton escorted by Lance Corporals Abernethy and MacKay. Naturally the occasion when a battalion troops its colour before its Sovereign for the last time is likely to be a sad one and so it was in June, 1970, although the 2nd Battalion's pride in itself and its determination to go out in style assuaged some of the feelings of dejection that some understandably felt. One spectator who described herself with touching simplicity as 'an English Civilian' wrote to the battalion afterwards: 'In all the years that I have watched the Ceremony of Trooping the Colour, I don't think that I have ever seen it so proudly done. The 2nd Battalion Scots Guards really shone. I have a feeling they planned to go out in a blaze of glory and well they did. It must be awful when your battalion or regiment comes to an end, but if you all served as well and as proudly as you did today you have been wonderful and we are indeed the losers.'

Staff planning for 1970 had resulted in the decision that the battalion should *Ulster* train in Kenya in the summer of that year and when on 19 June the exercise was cancelled at short notice because of a requirement to reinforce Northern Ireland, the advance party commanded by Major M.B. Scott had already departed to set

83

up the training. Deployment to Northern Ireland took place on 29 June, the battalion travelling by sea from Liverpool where, because of a lack of transport, it was forced to march from the station to the docks in the course of which some bystanders pelted the column with missiles, a foretaste of the reception likely to be accorded the Regiment in Ulster at various times over the next twenty-three years. Equally others offered advice as to what the battalion might do with the Irish! On arrival in the Province the battalion was placed initially under command of 5th Infantry Brigade and based at Long Kesh, although it was subsequently deployed into Belfast to support 24th Infantry Brigade, at the time commanded by Brigadier Peter Leng, a former Scots Guardsman. Because of the paucity of warning for its deployment the battalion had had scant opportunity to train for internal security operations and what little training could be done in the time available concentrated on learning the skills required to snatch ringleaders out of a riot and other tactical expedients which had been developed over the previous two years to deal with civil unrest in Northern Ireland.

The battalion had initially been warned for deployment to Londonderry and carried out a reconnaissance there but, in the event, it was about the only place it did not go. South-West Belfast, Armagh and Pomeroy, the latter when it was necessary to 'police' an Orange Day march when a Protestant group of 25,000 exercised its right to march through a village inhabited by 2,000 Catholics, were all secured as part of a heavy programme of patrols, searches and check-points designed to maintain the rule of law at a time when most of those living in Ulster seemed intent upon destroying it. The tour lasted three weeks and the battalion returned to Windsor on 18 July having gained several successes, but, more importantly, having achieved Colonel Acland's direction to his company commanders that 'whatever the situation he would not have men in his battalion put at risk because commanders felt inhibited by published limitations on their freedom of action'. Although only a short tour, it was the first of a number of operational deployments to be carried out by the Regiment in Ulster in the Seventies and Eighties.

Almost immediately on return to Windsor the task of dividing the battalion into the four groups into which it was to be organized before 1 April, 1971, began. As a result of considerable foresight and some nimble negotiation by Colonel John Swinton, the Lieutenant Colonel Commanding, and his team at Regimental Headquarters it had already been agreed by the Ministry of Defence that, when the 2nd Battalion went into suspended animation, some of the manpower which became available would be retained in Scots Guards companies and used to reinforce understrength Foot Guards battalions serving overseas. Consequently while some members of the battalion were earmarked to join the 1st Battalion and others to form the 2nd Battalion Scots Guards Company destined to be based in Edinburgh, two separate companies were formed, one – F Company – to deploy to Hong Kong to support the 1st Battalion Irish Guards and another – S Company – to deploy to British Honduras for a six-month unaccompanied tour prior to joining the 2nd Battalion Grenadier Guards at

Caterham. From late July onwards these groups gradually began to form while the battalion continued to discharge its commitment to public duties.

Few people would be surprised if the impending dismemberment of a happy, efficient and well motivated battalion did not cause its members to doubt the wisdom of those responsible for the decision and as 1 April, 1971, approached every opportunity was taken to lobby senior officers and politicians on the subject. However, it became clear by the beginning of 1970 from the response to this lobbying that the only possibility of a reprieve lay in a change of Government. In June, 1970, the Conservative Party won the General Election and a few weeks later confirmed the decision to disband six infantry battalions already taken by their predecessors. While he probably recognized that there was by then no chance of a reprieve Colonel John Acland, never one to back away from an issue if he felt it should be addressed, wrote a letter to the *Times* which was published on 15 August, in which he castigated those responsible for leading the Army in the Ministry of Defence for 'being incapable of looking beyond their own noses' by failing to recognize the consequences of their decision to reduce the size of the Army at a time of heavy commitment and when all arms, but particularly the Infantry, were experiencing severe over-stretch. Not surprisingly the letter gained Colonel Acland few friends in high places but it received considerable support in the Press – one paper running the headline 'Guards CO carpeted by Brass Hats' – while earning the author 'the displeasure of the Army Board'! It also struck a chord with many of his contemporaries who were at the time struggling with the twin dilemmas of overcommitment and under recruitment.

As 31 March, 1971, approached the battalion started to break up. F Company commanded by Major Johnny Clavering, was the first to leave, departing to join the 1st Battalion, Irish Guards in Hong Kong on 24 October, 1970; one hundred all ranks strong the company was destined to remain with the 'Micks' for fifteen months. CSM Hope and CQMS Beck were the senior ranks in the company. Despite the loss of the company, life in the battalion continued in much the same way as before; successes at boxing and football were achieved, while on 22 December the battalion played a major part in the preparation and implementation of the funeral of Field Marshal Viscount Slim at St George's Chapel. Major Mark Maxwell-Hyslop commanded a Guard of Honour while Captain Iain Mackay-Dick and CSM France led the bearer party. The next company to leave the battalion was S Company commanded by Major M.B. Scott with CSM France, recently awarded the British Empire Medal, and CQMS Simmonds as its senior ranks. The Company, which took its designation from the independent S Company which was attached to the 2nd Battalion Coldstream Guards in Italy from March, 1944, until March, 1945, left on 6 January at a strength of 180 all ranks to serve a six-month unaccompanied tour in British Honduras. The final reorganization commenced in the middle of March when the 2nd Battalion Company began to form at Victoria Barracks under the command of Major Michael Scott whilst at the same time all those destined to join the 1st Battalion moved to G Company.

26 March was the date selected by Colonel John Acland for the battalion's final parade. Earlier he had decided that it was not an occasion for a large parade with a member of the Royal Family present but that it would be more appropriate to stage a smaller one to thank the people of Windsor and the many local members of the Scots Guards Association for their kindness and hospitality during the previous twelve months. Accordingly the battalion paraded in Victoria Barracks with the 2nd Battalion Company in the centre, G Company on the right and Headquarter Company on the left. Both the Commanding Officer and his Adjutant, Captain Malcolm Ross, were mounted. Escorted by Colonel John Swinton, the Mayor of Windsor inspected the battalion after which it marched past the Guildhall where the Mayor, flanked by his aldermen, took the salute. Prior to this both Colonel Acland and the Mayor had addressed the parade. In his speech the Commanding Officer spoke of the sense of loss felt by all ranks at the demise of the battalion, thanked the Mayor for the generous welcome given it by the people of Windsor and commented that the warmth of that welcome and their reception in the town over the past year had 'done much to lift from their hearts much of the sorrow and bitterness they might have felt'. In reply the Mayor spoke of the battalion's long association with Windsor and commented that it was probably the first occasion upon which a Mayor of the Royal Borough had had to say farewell to a Foot Guards battalion about to be placed in suspended animation. In his speech he recalled the times when the 2nd Battalion had served at Victoria Barracks and made special mention of Bella and Bertha, the two Flanders cows acquired by the battalion in 1914 which, after the First World War, grazed on the Green in front of the Officers' Mess. He ended with the words: 'We in Windsor salute you, we wish you well wherever you may go but we shall never forget you.' Five days later the 2nd Battalion ceased to exist in its previous form and the 1st Battalion moved into Victoria Barracks; at the time few could have expected that exactly 200 days later the 2nd Battalion would be restored to the order of battle.

The 1st Battalion re-assembled at Elizabeth Barracks, Pirbright on 4 January, 1971, and immediately set about the task of once again undertaking public duties in London and at Windsor. At the same time the process of assimilating those members of the 2nd Battalion earmarked to join his battalion at the end of March preoccupied Colonel de Klee and his staff; thanks to sensible co-operation between the two Commanding Officers and their Sergeant Majors few problems were encountered and those which did arise were speedily resolved. On 12 January forty-seven men from Pirbright went to Windsor to join S Company and between then and 31 March the 'new' 1st Battalion began to take shape as a result of which the final move to Windsor and the take-over of Victoria Barracks was accomplished with little disruption. It helped that a planned change of Adjutant and Sergeant Major in the 1st Battalion took place at the same time as the move and Captain Iain Mackay-Dick and RSM Cameron, both from the 2nd Battalion, took up those appointments.

Two events dominated 1971 for the 1st Battalion. The first was a tour of operational duty in West Belfast starting in late August for which the battalion had been warned on its return from Sharjah; the second was Exercise BATTLE ROYAL, a review by Her Majesty The Queen, accompanied by His Royal Highness The Duke of Edinburgh, of Household troops in their fighting role at Long Valley, Aldershot, on 9 August. The idea of a review originally came from The Duke of Edinburgh who had suggested to the Major General at the time, Major General Michael Fitzalan Howard, that in some way the Household Division should demonstrate to the public how its operational duties complemented those occasions when it undertook State ceremonial in support of the Monarch. The theme of the review was that elements of the Division would first parade as they would have done in 1887 when Queen Victoria held her Golden Jubilee Review, following which there would be a demonstration of modern battle, involving members of all seven regiments of the Household Division supported by aircraft of the RAF. At the end of the review, which was organized and controlled by Colonel John Swinton, The Queen was to view a static display.

The 1st Battalion, under its Commanding Officer, provided 240 men in ceremonial guard order to take part in the 1887 scene. This group 'formed square' while the Household Cavalry pursued a defeated enemy, after which the infantry advanced, followed by the guns of The King's Troop, Royal Horse Artillery. The 1971 scene comprised a battle during which the Guards Parachute Company parachuted into Long Valley, following which a Coldstream and Life Guards battle group, supported by a company of Grenadiers carried in Puma helicopters, routed an enemy force holding a bridge. Judged from Horse Guards the review was no doubt fully justified and was deemed to have achieved its purpose of showing the Division in an operational setting.

However, Colonel de Klee was less convinced of the value of such an exercise, and understandably so since at the same time as he was required to rehearse for BATTLE ROYAL he was also trying to train his battalion for its forthcoming tour in Ulster. In the early days of the present campaign against terrorism in Northern Ireland there were none of the sophisticated pre-tour training arrangements which have since come to be taken for granted and few people outside those who had actually served in the Province appreciated the real nature of the military situation there or how the Nationalist movement was working to make Northern Ireland ungovernable, in the process placing an enormous burden on the Security Forces. Small wonder that Colonel de Klee, who had been warned that his battalion was to take over one of the toughest areas of Belfast only three weeks after the Long Valley Review, should have felt frustration and anger at the lack of support he received when trying to train his battalion for what was after all a totally new and unfamiliar role.

F Company arrived in Hong Kong with its families at the end of October and *F Company* moved into Stanley Fort alongside the remainder of the 1st Battalion Irish *Hong Kong* Guards commanded at the time by Lieutenant Colonel Tony Plummer who had commanded 3 Company when it was part of the 2nd Battalion Scots Guards in

Kenya in 1963 and 1964. Security duties for infantry battalions in Hong Kong covered a wide range of contingencies, principally in support of the police, and the company immediately set about learning the geography of the colony and practising riot drills and other procedures for dealing with street violence which was never far beneath the surface of the many townships in Hong Kong and the New Territories. The other main duty allocated to the British and Gurkha battalions stationed in the colony was to assist in maintaining security along the border with China and all battalions undertook tours patrolling the wire and checking incursions. For this a high standard of discipline was necessary, since the smallest event could quickly escalate into an incident of international proportions, as the Irish Guards discovered to their embarrassment later in the tour when a party inadvertently crossed the border into China.

Interspersed with these routine and sometimes tedious duties Major Clavering's Company took part in various exercises with the rest of the battalion and dispatched officers and guardsmen all over the Far East to train or explore, including to South Korea in June, when an F Company party, twenty strong, commanded by Lieutenant Angus Cheape with Colour Sergeant Lazenby as his deputy, provided the British element of the United States Honor Guard at Panmunjom. Life with the Irish Guards was never dull and F Company played hard, taking part in all the usual battalion competitions, including the Colony Dragon Boat race and parading on St Patrick's Day to receive their shamrock, alongside the 'Micks'. Early in February, 1971, 7 Platoon, commanded by Lieutenant Andrew Bacchus, went with CSM Hope to Crest Hill in the New Territories just to the south of the Sino-Hong Kong Border to refurbish the Scots Guards Star which had been constructed by the 2nd Battalion in 1927. Apart from occasional visits by individual Scots Guardsmen this was the first occasion that a large party from the Regiment had climbed up to the Star, the stones of which needed re-setting and painting in order to show them off to proper effect. After three tours on the border and having won the Langton Trophy, a much-cherished Irish Guards competition, F Company was summoned to return to Britain in early 1972, leaving Hong Kong after a hectic and enjoyable fifteen months with the Irish Guards who had looked after them superbly.

S Company British Honduras

Meanwhile S Company had completed their six-month tour in British Honduras returning to Britain in August, 1971. The company's time in the Caribbean had been extremely enjoyable and, as was only to be expected with a company commanded by an old jungle hand like Major M.B. Scott, the emphasis was on training and learning to live and operate in the close country adjacent to the border with Guatemala. Guatemala had long laid claim to British Honduras, asserting it to be one of its provinces and British troops had been deployed to deter a possible Guatemalan aggression since the 1960s. By the time S Company arrived at Airport Camp outside Belize City the garrison had reduced from a battalion to a company group in strength, the latter's primary role being to delay any Guatemalan advance eastwards from the border until reinforcements from Britain could be flown in. The company had also to be prepared to disperse anti-Guatemalan rioting in the capital as well as providing teams of soldiers to assist with disaster relief in the hurricane season; fortunately for S Company this season did not start until September by which time it had left for home.

Airport Camp, adjacent to the only major airfield in the country provided reasonable accommodation and was about fourteen miles from Belize City. Walking out for the company was almost non-existent and what was to be had in the bars and shops there was over-priced and usually of such a dubious nature as not to be worth the risk of purchasing it; besides girls of easy virtue, drugs were freely sold in the market while nearly everything that a person might actually want was usually out of stock. Like Lieutenant Colonel de Klee in Sharjah a year before, Major Scott kept his guardsmen busy with jungle training 'up country' and adventurous expeditions amongst the *cays* along the coast while most commanders in the company were sent to the US Army Jungle Warfare School in Panama on the pre-Vietnam course; meanwhile back at Airport Camp CSM France maintained an iron grip on the discipline of the company. Old jungle warriors who had seen service in Kenya, Malaya and Borneo such as Sergeants Little, Nicol and Inglis, all agreed that the jungle in British Honduras was some of the nastiest that they had ever encountered, while operating in it was made that much more difficult by the absence of any locally based helicopters. Patrols and expeditions usually lost communication as soon as they entered the jungle and some emerged as much as seven days overdue, something which worried Garrison Headquarters but caused Major Scott little anxiety since he had total faith in his soldiers and their ability to operate in such a wilderness area.

Towards the end of August S Company returned to Britain and was attached to the 2nd Battalion Grenadier Guards at Caterham, Major Richard Jenner Fust taking command from Major Scott on arrival home. The company was to remain with the Grenadiers undertaking London public duties until January, 1972, when it was ordered at short notice to move to Redford Barracks, Edinburgh.

CHAPTER SIX

NORTHERN IRELAND, BELIZE AND MECHANIZED INFANTRY

1st Battalion: Windsor-Münster
2nd Battalion: Edinburgh-Pirbright-Belize-Münster

14 August, 1969, witnessed the first deployment of British troops onto the streets of Northern Ireland when the 1st Battalion The Prince of Wales's Own Regiment of Yorkshire was sent to Londonderry to support the Royal Ulster Constabulary (RUC), following rioting in that city in the aftermath of the annual Apprentice Boys March. From that time to the present day units of the British Army have found themselves continuously engaged in the Province, initially as protectors of those Northern Irishmen whose civil rights were threatened by the actions of others of a different religious or political persuasion, and, later, in countering a vicious terrorist campaign mounted by the Irish Republican Army (IRA). This campaign, which has lacked for little by way of support or resources from the international terrorist fraternity, began as a movement to defend the Roman Catholic minority in Northern Ireland from their Protestant antagonists but later emerged in its true colours as the catalyst for the creation of a united Irish Republic by the incorporation of the six counties of Ulster into Eire. Any discussion of the history of Northern Ireland or the relationship between the Protestant and Catholic peoples who make up its population can become fraught with difficulty and this regimental history will confine itself to recording the part played by battalions of the Regiment in the affairs of the Province since 1969.

Not including the three-week emergency tour undertaken by the 2nd Battalion in 1970 and already described in Chapter Five, battalions of the Regiment have since 1971 served in Northern Ireland no fewer than twelve times upon emergency or 'roulement' tours of from four to six months in duration, whilst the 1st Battalion undertook a residential tour of twenty months in the Province in 1980/81. Much of the time passed by Scots Guardsmen on operational duty on the streets of Northern Ireland's towns and cities or amongst the hedgerows and fields of its countryside has been interminably dull, although always overshadowed by the threat of a sniper's bullet or a terrorist bomb.

Northern Ireland

Rather than describe every tour of duty in the Province in equal detail, this history will confine itself to relating instances of operational interest and success, while not ignoring those occasions when tragedy struck.

On return from Sharjah the 1st Battalion had been warned for an emergency tour in West Belfast commencing in late August, 1971. As recorded in the previous chapter, the preparation and training for the tour was inadequate, something which might have been avoided had those responsible for dispatching the battalion been better informed of the situation on the streets of Belfast at the time. Neither did it help Colonel de Klee that the successful command team which he had developed in Sharjah should be dissipated on arrival back in Britain; indeed his Second-in-Command and all his company commanders changed shortly before the tour began. The battalion arrived in Belfast ten days after 'Internment' when the Security Forces had mounted an operation to arrest as many as possible of the known hardcore terrorists from both communities, an operation which had been only partially successful since, although it netted some 'baddies', it undoubtedly drove many previously uncommitted republicans into the hands of the IRA. Such was the high level of terrorist activity that, when he handed over his battalion's Tactical Area of Responsibility (TAOR),

1st Battalion
West Belfast

91

Lieutenant Colonel Geoffrey Howlett, the Commanding Officer of the 2nd Battalion The Parachute Regiment, commented that the Scots Guards 'had bought the hot seat' and Colonel Murray de Klee himself admitted that 'the battalion didn't know if it was on its head or its tail' to start with. Sniping attacks, the bombing of patrols with petrol and nail bombs and attempts to destroy military posts with larger explosive devices all confronted the battalion during its first weeks, while any operations undertaken by the Security Forces were invariably met by rioting and other forms of civil unrest. Inserted into this maelstrom of bigotry and hatred not previously encountered by the Army on the streets of a British city, it took the 1st Battalion a little time to find its feet; not only was the battalion quite unprepared for such a situation but there was a real lack of information as to who the opposition were and how, once identified, they should be dealt with.

The battalion deployed with its Headquarters at the Springfield Road RUC Station and its four companies stationed across a large area of Catholic West Belfast; Right Flank and G Company had responsibility for the Clonard and Rodney-St James districts respectively, both areas of dense back-to-back housing which provided little scope for innovative patrolling to counter the terrorist, whereas Left Flank had charge of the Ballymurphy and Turf Lodge areas comprised of more modern semi-detached houses or blocks of flats which permitted much wider use of 'fire and movement' to combat the terrorist.

Meanwhile B Company under Major Michael Smart looked after the Beech-mount area. Every company commander had a different situation with which to deal and, while Battalion Headquarters had an important role to play in co-ordinating activity, operations in Belfast in 1971 and subsequently have invariably been managed and led at company level. Major Peter Johnson in the Clonard had a particular responsibility for policing the 'Peace Line' separating the Catholic community of the Springfield and Falls Road areas from the Protestants of the Shankill; dealing with irate crowds often led by political leaders like Ian Paisley could be intimidating and there were many unpleasant encounters in the early days of the tour until Right Flank developed a philosophy for controlling them and got to know who in the two communities should be called upon to help defuse trouble.

Meanwhile Major Michael Nurton and Left Flank found themselves in a situation bordering upon open war with the people of the hard Republican Ballymurphy and Turf Lodge areas; sniping attacks, bombings, riots and gun battles, especially round the flats adjacent to the Monagh roundabout, became matters of routine and involved platoons in almost constant activity. Tactics for dealing with situations previously not envisaged had to be developed on the spur of the moment and platoon and section commanders in Left Flank and the other companies had to think fast and act courageously if they were to prevail in their task of maintaining order in such an anarchic environment.

When not on duty companies were housed in makeshift bases in schools or factories protected by corrugated iron sheeting and wire to prevent bombs being

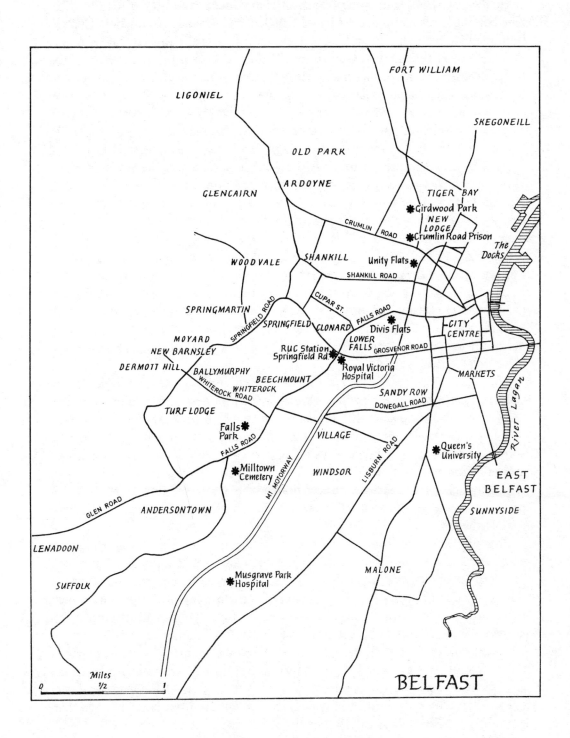

LIGONIEL

FORT WILLIAM

SKEGONEILL

OLD PARK

ARDOYNE

GLENCAIRN

TIGER BAY

✳ Girdwood Park

NEW LODGE

✳ Crumlin Road Prison

WOODVALE

SHANKILL

CRUMLIN ROAD

Unity Flats ✳

The Docks

SHANKILL ROAD

SPRINGMARTIN

SPRINGFIELD ROAD

CUPAR ST.

FALLS ROAD

SPRINGFIELD CLONARD

Divis Flats ✳

CITY CENTRE

MOYARD

LOWER FALLS

NEW BARNSLEY

RUC Station Springfield Rd ✳

GROSVENOR ROAD

DERMOTT HILL

BALLYMURPHY

Royal Victoria Hospital ✳

WHITEROCK ROAD

BEECHMOUNT

WHITEROCK

MARKETS

SANDY ROW

TURF LODGE

DONEGALL ROAD

Falls Park ✳

VILLAGE

LISBURN ROAD

Queen's ✳ University

EAST BELFAST

FALLS ROAD

Milltown ✳ Cemetery

WINDSOR

SUNNYSIDE

GLEN ROAD

ANDERSONTOWN

M1 MOTORWAY

River Lagan

LENADOON

MALONE

SUFFOLK

Musgrave Park ✳ Hospital

Miles

0   ½   1

BELFAST

93

lobbed over the walls; apart from meals and television, the hours between duties were filled by sleep, something that most guardsmen found little difficulty with. The battalion was administered by its Echelon at Carmoney from where Captain Campbell Graham and his staff met all needs whatever the time of day or night.

A week after taking over, Guardsman Telford of G Company became the first battalion casualty when wounded whilst on patrol in the Beechmount. On 14 September Guardsman Maguire was fatally wounded by a sniper whilst on sentry duty in Left Flank's Vere Foster School base and every company sustained attacks on patrols or bases during September and early October. In late September G Company under Major Anthony Leask ceased its role of brigade reserve and moved to a new base in the grounds of the Royal Victoria Hospital which was to become known to generations of soldiers as the RVH. During October Right Flank sustained two particularly vicious attacks when first an Observation Post in Cupar Street close to the 'Peace Line' and later a platoon base in the Springfield Road were attacked by the IRA by the expedient of inserting a bomb into a neighbouring building; in the first attack the bomb was planted in a shop and the resulting explosion killed Guardsman Hall, while Lance Sergeant Whittle lost an eye and five other guardsmen were wounded. In the second Guardsman Booth, a cook attached to 1 Platoon, was killed when workmen repairing the adjacent house secreted a bomb in a breeze block and, despite being searched, managed to insert it into a wall and later to detonate it by remote control.

Throughout this initial period of intense activity and not a little confusion Colonel Murray de Klee led his battalion with calmness and resolute courage; recognizing from the start that the situation in which the battalion found itself was one where his company commanders would have to take the lead, he allowed them to do so while always being on hand to offer support, wise advice and encouragement. On 5 October he handed over command to Lieutenant Colonel Richard Mayfield who continued the work so ably begun by his predecessor and which eventually allowed the battalion to go on to the offensive against the IRA.

Brigadier Frank Kitson, a shrewd but taciturn officer with very considerable experience of low intensity operations, commanded 39th Infantry Brigade which had responsibility for operations in Belfast. His principal contribution towards the restoration of order and the attrition of terrorists lay in the priority which he accorded to the gathering and assessment of information and its conversion into hard intelligence to be used against the IRA and other extremist groups. Thanks to his lead, the companies of the 1st Battalion soon began to learn about the people in their areas and, by a combination of the deft handling of suspects and a subtle approach to operations, there started a flow of intelligence which eventually became a torrent. Many people were involved but none more so than Captain Jonathan Allen, the Battalion Intelligence Officer, who developed an excellent rapport with the RUC Special Branch. Intelligence gained following well targeted arrests led invariably to the disclosure of further information about terrorist involvement or caches of weapons or explosives which, during the second half of its tour, enabled the battalion to get right on top of its task with a resultant drop in the level of terrorist activity. Such was Brigadier Kitson's close involvement that on several occasions Major Nurton, sleeping late after a long night commanding his guardsmen on the streets, awoke to find the Brigade Commander sitting on his bed and impatient to ask about various suspects arrested during the night by Left Flank!

On 17 October Guardsman Hamilton of Left Flank was shot dead by a sniper while on foot patrol in the Ballymurphy. During the tour the battalion lost five guardsmen killed and forty-eight all ranks wounded by sniper fire or explosions, a rate of attrition which gave great cause for concern throughout. Immediate medical cover on the streets was provided by those trained in first aid, supplemented by company medical orderlies, normally the battalion pipers; Lance Sergeant Davidson and Lance Corporal Banks were the G Company orderlies and Major Leask credits them with saving a number of lives by the promptness of their action. However, it was the close proximity of the RVH and the Musgrave Park Hospital, the former probably the best accident hospital in Europe in the 1970s, which really ensured that casualties received the highest standard of treatment in the shortest possible time. Many Scots Guardsmen owe a considerable debt to the men and women of the Army Medical Services and the National Health Service who worked so tirelessly to save lives, many of which might otherwise have been lost.

November saw the mounting of a series of battalion-level operations the purpose of which was to detect the considerable quantities of arms and ammunition known to be hidden throughout the battalion area; on one occasion G Company found 10,251 rounds of ammunition and over the tour in excess of 100 weapons were discovered. On 27 November Guardsman Nicholls of G company was shot and killed in the St James area, the last fatality to be suffered by the battalion before it handed over its area to the 1st Battalion The King's Own Scottish Borderers at the end of December and returned to Windsor. So ended a tour which had begun less than auspiciously but which finished on a high operational note with each company striving to outdo the next with its successes against the IRA. Colonel Mayfield attributed the success of the tour to three factors: the manner in which Brigadier Kitson coerced and encouraged everybody including the RUC to work together to defeat the terrorist; the success of the battalion's own intelligence efforts and, most importantly of all, the extremely high standards of alertness, initiative and leadership displayed by all on the ground particularly at platoon and section level. To these might be added the manner in which the battalion and the companies handled the media; outside scrutiny of military operations is always a sensitive and difficult subject as generations of Army officers know well from their experience in Ulster but, despite its pre-occupation with the battle against the IRA, the battalion contrived to use the Press to its advantage by shrewd and open handling whenever possible.

Writing several years later the Commanding Officer recorded the battalion's feelings on leaving Belfast: 'When we went home we really thought that the IRA were on their last legs and that Northern Ireland would soon be peaceful again; after all, vast numbers of terrorists were locked up, the IRA had lost enormous quantities of arms and ammunition and their morale was very low. How wrong we were!' Padre Keith Crozer who was with the battalion throughout the tour spent his days 'moving around the various locations .... attending to welfare work .... chatting, talking, moving on .... visiting local clergy of different persuasions to establish contact and "build bridges".' Twenty years later he wrote: 'It had been a difficult tour, yet without question it was also a successful one. The initial difficulties and problems of settling in were overcome. This in my opinion was due in no small measure to the quality and intensity of the training from the Guards Depot onwards. Discipline held when there was immense pressure and the battalion more and more began to gain and keep control of its area.'

The 2nd Battalion Company

When the 2nd Battalion went into suspended animation on 31 March, 1971, the 2nd Battalion Company entrusted with that battalion's Colours and commanded by Major Michael Scott with CSM Phillips as his company sergeant major moved to Redford Barracks, Edinburgh, to undertake public duties. After some debate within Household Division circles it had been agreed that the company would not go to Pirbright as originally mooted but to Scotland where it would be well placed to recruit on behalf of the Regiment. In the event the company carried out public duties in Edinburgh and in London in almost equal proportions to recruiting and training. In early May it acted as enemy to 24th Airportable Brigade on an exercise in Kintyre designed to practise the latter's amphibious landing capability prior to a major exercise in the Caribbean. Following this, the company had been warned to undertake a six-month tour of duty as the resident company in Gibraltar in the summer of 1972; however, this plan was destined never to be fulfilled since in the early autumn came the news that, in view of the continuing high level of military commitment in Northern Ireland, the Government had decided to restore four infantry battalions to the Army's Order of Battle. The 2nd Battalion Scots Guards was to be one of those four battalions.

2nd Battalion re-forms

Lieutenant Colonel Tony Boam had been selected to command the Guards Depot but in January, 1972, he was appointed instead to re-form the 2nd Battalion and his place at Pirbright was taken by another Scots Guardsman, Lieutenant Colonel Iain Ferguson, who took up his appointment there in September. Meanwhile when Colonel Boam arrived in Edinburgh early in the New Year he found practically no one other than Lieutenant John Kiszely and RSM Dargie there to help him with his task of planning the structure of his new battalion. However, with so many former members of the Regiment having remained as badged Scots Guardsmen after April, 1971, it did not take long to build up numbers again.

F Company came home from Hong Kong on 24 January, while a week later the 2nd Battalion Company arrived after a spell of public duties at Windsor, and in early February S Company moved north from Caterham. On 21 April a service to mark the reformation of the battalion was held in St Giles' Cathedral and on 1 May it mounted its first Edinburgh Castle Guard. Everybody was delighted to be together again as a battalion and some even forgot the fact that it had been suspended for nine months; the returning independent companies had to be split up on arrival back in Edinburgh in order to allow Headquarter and Support Companies to form and Colonel Boam's first priority was to meld his battalion together before an operational tour in Ulster in October.

Meanwhile ceremonial duties had to continue in Scotland and Left Flank, commanded by Major Robin Buchanan-Dunlop, travelled to London to provide Number Eight Guard on the Queen's Birthday Parade on 3 June. The battalion became officially operational on 1 July and two days afterwards Her Majesty The Queen, accompanied by Her Royal Highness Princess Anne, attended a garden party at Redford Barracks and met a large number of soldiers and families. Shortly afterwards the battalion moved to Kent to train for its tour in Ulster.

Considerable improvements had been made to the arrangements for training battalions for service in Northern Ireland since the 1st Battalion's tour a year previously. The existing ranges at Hythe had been converted to represent the type of conditions to be found in an urban environment, while the former married quarters at Lydd, last occupied by the Regiment when the 1st Battalion was based there in 1956, had been developed to provide an area where urban tactics could be practised. Indeed some of the training in Rype Village was often more challenging than situations encountered on the streets of Ulster and could result in serious casualties, no bad thing in that it gave commanders greater confidence in their ability to handle such events when they arose for real.

On 24 July, having only just returned to Edinburgh, the battalion was placed at twenty-four hours notice to move to Ulster for an emergency tour; however, it did not become clear for a few days that this earlier than planned move was to be part of a large build-up of troops in the Province as a prelude to the mounting of Operation MOTORMAN in order to eliminate the 'no go' areas established during the summer of 1972 by the IRA in Belfast and Londonderry.

The battalion left Edinburgh on 27 July still not knowing to which area of Ulster it was to be sent; equally unclear was the Captain of HMS *Fearless* upon whose ship the battalion was embarked, when he left the Clyde the next day, his sealed orders not being specific in such matters. Eventually the battalion disembarked at Belfast and, amidst considerable confusion, moved to Londonderry where it took over responsibility for the City Centre. 31 July saw the mounting of Operation MOTORMAN, or CARCAN as it was codenamed in Londonderry, when eight infantry battalions supported by an armoured engineer squadron re-occupied the Bogside and Creggan areas of the City. The operation was entirely successful, the 2nd Battalion playing only a minor role in support of the Bogside assault battalions while continuing to control the City.

2nd Battalion
Londonderry

12 August provided the first real test when the annual Apprentice Boys March was held; this event, long cherished by the 'loyalist' Protestant community as a memorial to those who had successfully defended the City for 105 days in 1689 against the forces of King James II was an occasion when Protestants from all over Northern Ireland and further afield could congregate to demonstrate their pre-eminence over their Catholic neighbours. Again the day passed without major incident, although passions were aroused on both sides and members of the battalion saw at first hand the naked bigotry and hatred which percolates so much of what happens in the Province three centuries later.

In early September, life having returned to normal or at least to what passes for normal in Northern Ireland, Headquarters 8th Infantry Brigade, commanded by Brigadier Pat McLellan, a Coldstreamer, decided to reduce military deployment in the city, as a result of which the 2nd Battalion handed over the City Centre to the 3rd Regiment Royal Horse Artillery and took over the Bogside and Brandywell areas from the 3rd Battalion The Royal Regiment of Fusiliers. The latter were both low-lying areas of dense Victorian back-to-back housing dominated to the east by the old city walls and to the west by the more modern Creggan Estate; indeed the Bogside originally took its name from the fact that until relatively recently the River Foyle used to flow through it. In order to cover the area Battalion Headquarters and Left Flank moved from the Victoria Police Headquarters and a neighbouring disused bus station to an abandoned factory in the Bogside (which had once manufactured ladies' underwear), unfortunately losing close contact with the police as a result, while G Company was based just inside the City walls and Right Flank in a newly built camp beside the Craigavon Bridge.

Undoubtedly the luckiest man of the tour was Guardsman Spinks of G Company who on 5 September was hit in the back by an armour-piercing round while on patrol in the Bogside. The round struck the metal part of a baton gun slung across his back and disintegrated against his protective flak jacket leaving him unharmed other than bruised; when he regained consciousness he found himself lying amongst some rosebushes and thought 'this is what heaven must be like'.

The months of September and October saw all companies under sustained pressure from the IRA who were determined to avenge the elimination of the 'no go' areas. Major Johnny Clavering and Right Flank encountered considerable problems in the Brandywell and in the space of a month five members of the company were shot, of whom two, Guardsmen Van Beck and Lockhart were killed. Elsewhere G Company under Major Richard Jenner Fust and Left Flank under Major Robin Buchanan-Dunlop also came under pressure from the gunman and the bomber. On 14 September Lance Corporal Harker, attached to the battalion from the Royal Electrical and Mechanical Engineers, was fatally wounded while on duty at the Bogside Gasworks, a post protected throughout the tour by the Reconnaissance Platoon under the leadership of Lieutenant Angus Cheape and Sergeant Little and which received never-ending attention

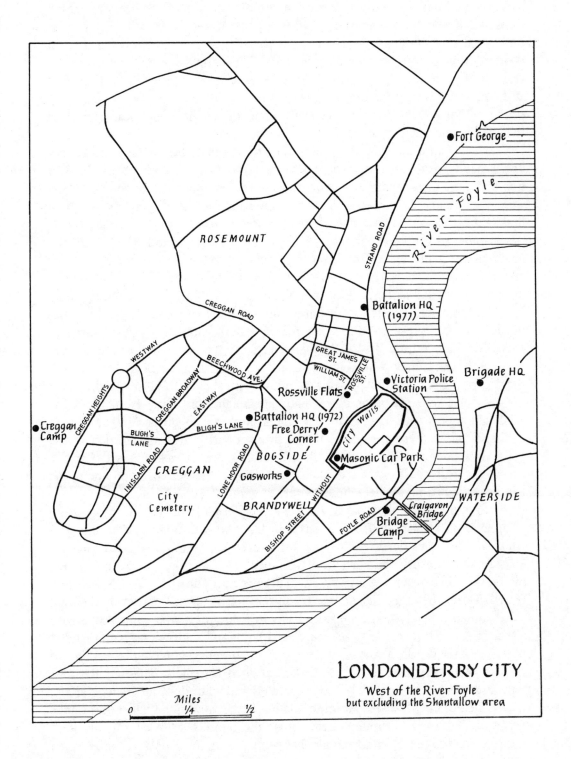

Fort George

ROSEMOUNT

River Foyle

STRAND ROAD

CREGGAN ROAD

WESTWAY

CREGGAN HEIGHTS

BEECHWOOD AVE.

CREGGAN BROADWAY

EASTWAY

Battalion HQ (1977)

GREAT JAMES ST.

WILLIAM ST.

ROSSVILLE ST.

Brigade HQ

Rossville Flats

Victoria Police Station

Creggan Camp

BLIGH'S LANE

BLIGH'S LANE

Battalion HQ (1972)

Free Derry Corner

City Walls

INISCARN ROAD

CREGGAN

LONE MOOR ROAD

BOGSIDE

Gasworks

Masonic Car Park

City Cemetery

BRANDYWELL

STREET WITHOUT

BISHOP STREET

FOYLE ROAD

Craigavon Bridge

WATERSIDE

Bridge Camp

LONDONDERRY CITY
West of the River Foyle
but excluding the Shantallow area

Miles

0   1/4   1/2

from the hoodlums of the IRA who hated the presence of such a post in the heart of the Bogside. On one occasion a crowd of football supporters returning from the Brandywell managed to burst open the gates. A volley of rubber bullets led to a quick retreat when one of the ringleaders was hit in the chest; a good example of the use of minimum force. Throughout the tour patrols in the vicinity of such local landmarks as Free Derry Corner, the Rossville Flats and William Street were guaranteed 'aggro' from bystanders, such places being part of the folklore of the struggle between the people of the Republican areas and the 'occupying' Security Forces.

Slowly but surely during the course of October the battalion started to get the upper hand, although not without further loss when Lance Sergeant McKay was killed by a sniper on 28 October. New tactics adopted following contacts were continually developed and by the time the battalion came to return to Scotland on 28 November the whole area was as quiet as could be expected. While most of the credit should go to patrols on the ground which bore the brunt of the daily aggro and danger there were others who contributed not insignificantly to the success of the tour. Among them were those who tried to develop a rapport with the local population by establishing community links and, while this effort often went unrewarded, by the end there were signs that the attempt was appreciated in some quarters. Both battalion padres, Padre Bill Jones and Father John Williams, involved themselves in this effort and among those with whom they dealt were the five Peace Ladies of the Bogside who for a short period gained national media attention with their efforts to win peace for the area and to wean their more moderate neighbours away from the IRA. Medical support was another area of crucial importance and a number of men in the battalion owed their lives to the prompt and professional action of the battalion's doctor, Captain Peter Brown and Colour Sergeant Baird. Captain Brown, an enthusiast in the true sense, remains a cherished member among the band of attached personnel who have served with the Scots Guards.

Writing in the battalion paper *The Rose and Thistle* at the end of the tour the Commanding Officer said: 'The battalion has had a difficult and trying tour which has at times been tedious, has often been frustrating and has called for considerable bravery, patience and tolerance .... The 'Bog' today is a much safer place than when we arrived .... There is no doubt that 2SG is well and truly back on the map. Let no one try to remove us again!' However, the final word should possibly go to the Rear Party in Edinburgh who had to cope with all the sad consequences of attacks on the battalion in Londonderry; commanded by Lieutenant Clarke Brown, who arrived on commissioning and expecting to be sent on leave three days before the battalion hurriedly departed Redford Barracks and 'found himself left with ten dogs and a hundred cars to look after', it consisted of only himself, Accommodation Sergeant Major Walker and Lance Sergeant Delamere. Through their efforts the families were continually kept informed and in touch with what was happening to their menfolk, a contribution almost as important as what was happening across the Irish Sea.

The 1st Battalion celebrated New Year, 1972, at home, having returned from Belfast two days before. The battalion re-assembled at Windsor at the end of January and immediately plunged itself into a heavy round of public duties which were to be its preoccupation for the nine months before it moved to Germany and a new role as a mechanized battalion. A memorial service was held on 1 February in Holy Trinity Church for the five guardsmen killed in Northern Ireland at which Lieutenant Colonel Simon Bland represented the Colonel of the Regiment. Thereafter public duties in London and at Windsor, Guards of Honour for Queen Juliana of the Netherlands and the President of West Germany and two Guards on the Birthday Parade kept the battalion busy, although in parallel it undertook a period of Spearhead in April and made contingency plans to move into the London Docks in the event of a national strike. Nothing could have better exemplified the flexibility and versatility of the soldier than all these different activities; battalions stationed in London District have always been expected to be 'a jack of all trades', but matters were exacerbated throughout the Seventies by the ever changing situation in Northern Ireland which frequently required reinforcement at little or no notice.

In late May His Royal Highness The Duke of Windsor died. A vigil at the lying in state in St George's Chapel involved five officers including the Commanding Officer. In September the battalion started to turn its attention to Germany and a number of special courses were run, principally for those who had been selected to command and drive APCs in BAOR; these courses were held at Bordon and Chobham and were part of a training package devised by the Director of Infantry to assist battalions converting to the mechanized role. As the complexities of armoured warfare increased the package was continually refined and by the early Nineties involved up to fifty soldiers transferring between battalions. Meanwhile the battalion continued with its ceremonial role and on 2 September a bearer party commanded by Captain Roddy Gow took part in the funeral of His Royal Highness Prince William of Gloucester in St George's Chapel. On 10 November the battalion mounted its last Windsor Castle Guard, just ten days after the introduction at the Royal Palaces of night-time tactical sentries who were in future to 'patrol' their beats and to use pocketphones to communicate with the guardroom. By the end of the first week of December the battalion was complete in Waterloo Barracks, Münster, sad to have left Windsor but looking forward to serving in 4th Guards Brigade, at the time commanded by Brigadier John Swinton.

Regrettably there was to be little time for the battalion to settle into and absorb the intricacies of its new role. Already warned for an operational tour in an area adjacent to the Northern Ireland border with the Republic, the battalion only managed some low level training before it placed its FV432 APCs in the hands of the Rear Party, trained at Tin City, the Germany equivalent of the Hythe-Lydd ranges situated on the edge of the Sennelager training area, and moved to Ulster by air on 3 May. On arrival the battalion found itself under command of 3rd Infantry Brigade and responsible for a large swathe of Counties Armagh and Tyrone, as well as for a number of medium-sized provincial towns. Battalion Headquarters, where RSM Cooper had relieved RSM Cameron the previous October, Support Company commanded by Major Michael Smart and Left Flank under Major Kim Ross were all based in Gough Barracks, Armagh, while Major Thomas Boyd-Carpenter's Right Flank was co-located with Brigade Headquarters in Lurgan and C Company, redesignated from G Company on the reformation of the 2nd Battalion, looked after the Dungannon-Coalisland area under the watchful eye of Major Anthony Leask.

*1st Battalion
Armagh*

The situation that the battalion found in May, 1973, was vastly different from that which it had left behind in Belfast eighteen months previously; the Government's policy of internment had undergone very considerable modification, many terrorists had been released, random arrests had to be fully justified and the morale of the RUC was at a low ebb after five years of constant pressure and countless casualties. In addition there was little hard intelligence to build upon and companies had to work hard to gather information about their areas and those living there. The pattern of terrorist activity had also changed, with fewer shooting incidents and more reliance by the IRA on attacking the Security Forces through remotely controlled bombs placed in culverts or hidden in hedgerows, or mortar attacks on military bases or police stations.

1973 was also a time of growing protest, with innumerable marches staged to draw attention to the plight of those in the Maze Prison or to champion the cause of the Civil Rights Movement or the Orange Order; some of these marches led to clashes when the police and the military attempted to steer them away from sensitive areas. Holding the ring has always been a thankless task and so it proved in the summer of that year as Ulstermen marched and counter-marched through towns such as Armagh, Dungannon and Portadown. By comparison with 1971 it was a dull, almost uneventful tour although the battalion worked hard and produced some significant results, particularly in the area to the west of Lough Neagh. However, as the battalion handed over to The Hampshire Regiment and flew back to Germany on 4 September few people can have been under any illusions that the 1973 tour was more likely to provide the pattern for future tours in the Province than that of 1971. A pointer to the future had come early in the tour when Colonel Mayfield had called upon the Archbishop of Armagh. The Cardinal told him that the Roman Catholic people of the area compared their situation in the Province to that which obtained in the Channel Islands during the German occupation of the Second World War – an inauspicious omen from one so well placed to know what people were thinking.

*2nd Battalion
Pirbright*

Three months after returning from Londonderry the 2nd Battalion moved south from Edinburgh to Elizabeth Barracks, Pirbright, to undertake ceremonial duties similar to those just completed by the 1st Battalion. Prior to leaving Redford Barracks the battalion held a Memorial Service in St Giles' Cathedral on 31 January for the four members of the battalion who had died in Londonderry; the Moderator of the General Assembly, Dr Selby Wright preached and, as at Windsor a year previously, Lieutenant Colonel Bland represented the Colonel of the Regiment.

The summer of 1973 was taken up with the usual round of public duties, Guards on the Birthday Parade and a Guard of Honour for the President of Nigeria on 12 June. On 31 July Major Jeremy Cox commanded the last picquet to be mounted at the Bank of England in Threadneedle Street; originally established in 1780 at a strength of 534 soldiers during the Gordon Riots, the picquet in 1973 consisted of only twelve men. Until the early 60s the Bank Picquet used to march from its barracks in the West End, a distance of some four and a half miles, only going by transport at times of inclement weather. Rumour had it that on occasion the picquet had completed its journey by Underground, although if caught out the officer in charge had to be able justify his actions to a normally unsympathetic Adjutant.

In the autmn the battalion once more put away its ceremonial tunics and prepared for an operational tour in West Belfast which was to see it looking after the same 'patch' as the 1st Battalion in 1971. By 28 November the battalion had taken over its area from the 3rd Battalion The Royal Green Jackets, with Battalion Headquarters at the Springfield Road RUC Station, Left Flank under Major Jonathan Seddon-Brown in the Clonard, Major Jeremy Cox's G Company in Whiterock, Support Company commanded by Major Iain Mackay-Dick in Springmartin and Right Flank responsible for the Ballymurphy-New Barnsley area under Major Murray Naylor. No sooner had the battalion seen the departing riflemen away than there occurred in Right and Left Flank's areas a series of hijackings of buses and other vehicles, some of which were constructed into makeshift barricades and later burnt. All were cleared once the Ammunition Technical Officer (ATO) had checked them for explosives, but the pattern of the night's events indicated an early bid by the IRA to test the mettle of the new battalion and to see how it would react.

2nd Battalion West Belfast

Throughout the tour there was a steady level of terrorist activity. The battalion's TAOR was larger and less parochial than that covered in London-derry and each company area had different situations with which to contend; Support Company dealt with a mainly Protestant population and had the difficult task of supervising the daily exodus of 'loyalist' workers from Mackie's Engineering Works on the Catholic side of the Springfield Road back into their own areas to the north. Elsewhere the republican people of the Ballymurphy and Beechmount served up a daily diet of aggro and invective some of which would be used to distract the Security Forces from IRA operations going on elsewhere; the IRA's tactics were more sophisticated than had been the case in the Bogside and some well planned sniping incidents were mounted against the battalion, one of which was thwarted by the quick reactions of a multiple patrol led by 2nd Lieutenant Henry Llewellyn in Ballymurphy Drive on 11 January when a gunman contrived to snipe at a patrol between two houses and across three streets. On New Year's Eve Guardsman Daughtery of G Company was shot by a sniper in Whiterock, a single shot, which passed through the

103

observation slit at the rear of the armoured vehicle in which he was travelling, killing him instantly; Lance Sergeant Cation was wounded. A consequence of this incident was that the gunman, a fifteen-year-old boy had to be detained in a women's prison, the original plan to place him in a special home in Ballymurphy having understandably been vigorously opposed by Colonel Boam.

Thanks to hard work by the Intelligence Section led by Lieutenant Douglas Erskine Crum and an excellent relationship with Special Branch good work was done in all areas and a number of suspected terrorists were charged or served with interim custody orders, a form of detention pending further inquiries. Occasionally information gained from intelligence sources had bizarre consequences such as on 22 February when a source hinted that an incident was planned that day in the Ballymurphy. Alerted to the possibility of attack a multiple patrol commanded by Sergeant Stoddart of 2 Platoon quickly discovered a car in a private garage in Dermott Hill made up to resemble a Military Police vehicle with an authentic RMP sign bolted to its roof. Suspicions aroused, ATO was called and quickly confirmed the presence of 150 lbs of explosives; clearly the patrol had stumbled upon a potential car bomb destined for a police station or military base. Once made safe, the car had to be taken for forensic examination, but this proved impossible since it could not be moved out of the garage without its Military Police sign hitting the lintel above the door thereby knocking it off. Such are the ways of the Irish terrorist!

At the end of March the battalion was relieved by the Cheshire Regiment and returned to Pirbright. It had been a successful and interesting tour, in some respects almost stimulating, with plenty to do but without the battalion ever being over-extended. Patrols showed restraint and courage on the streets and casualties were light, with only one fatality. Some injuries stemmed from constant hard patrolling on concrete surfaces and across waste ground, and some people, like CSM Carnegie of Right Flank, damaged themselves quite badly when they fell. Leaving base as a member of a four-man patrol with his Company Commander, Major Naylor, Lance Corporal Shuttleworth and Guardsman Lazenby and racing across open ground outside the entrance to the Vere Foster School the Company Sergeant Major tripped heavily, much to the delight of Guardsman Cowan on sentry at the gate who reported to the Operations Room that, 'The four-thirty Ballymurphy Stakes have just begun and CSM Carnegie has fallen at the first fence!'

Relationships with the media were again tested during the tour and Captain Peter Le Marchand, the Public Relations Officer, achieved a reasonable balance whereby the Press were encouraged to see what was happening but were not allowed to get in the way. NCOs and guardsmen were usually spontaneous and therefore genuine in their comments, while officers, because they thought about what they were going to say, often appeared stilted and lacking conviction.

1st Battalion　　Return from leave in early October enabled the 1st Battalion at last to get to grips with learning its business as a mechanized battalion and minds were concentrated by the prospect of a battle group exercise at Suffield in Western

Canada in September 1974. The British Army Training Unit, located some fifty miles north-west of the town of Medicine Hat in Alberta, had been established in the early Seventies to provide space and scope for the exercising of armoured battle groups, something which had become increasingly difficult in Germany and could no longer be carried out in Libya following King Idris's overthrow. The training area at Suffield was administered by a small British staff and covered hundreds of square miles upon which live firing of all but the heaviest weapons was permitted and where battle groups could manoeuvre almost without restriction. Exercises designed to train commanders and soldiers in every phase of war had been prepared and battle groups exercised under the direction of the Commandant of the Training Unit, although their own Brigade Commander was invited to attend for part of the time.

Prior to Canada the battalion trained in Germany both on its own and with other arms. Soltau, Vogelsang and exchange training for Left Flank in Denmark all occupied the rifle companies while Battalion Headquarters took part in the inevitable Command Post Exercises held to a regular pattern and designed to exercise every commander from Corps to Battle Group level. On 8 May, 1974, Colonel Richard Mayfield handed over command to Lieutenant Colonel Christopher Airy, a former Grenadier Guardsman who came from the National Defence College. Colonel Mayfield left the battalion and the Army after a highly successful tour during which he led his soldiers with quiet determination, firm when he needed to be and always conscious of his responsibilities to those whom he commanded. During his time he twice took the battalion to Northern Ireland, being rightly decorated with an award of a DSO after the 1971 tour.

Colonel Airy was unknown to the battalion and indeed to the Regiment and there were probably many who viewed the arrival of an outsider, let alone a Grenadier, to command a Scots Guards battalion with at best suspicion and at worst dread. However, when the selection process failed to provide a Scots Guardsman to command after Colonel Mayfield a number of steps were taken to ensure that the right person from outside the Regiment was chosen. First, Colonel MacGregor, the Lieutenant Colonel Commanding, consulted widely within the Household Division as a result of which his opposite number commanding the Grenadiers generously volunteered to allow Colonel Mac-Gregor to select whomsoever he felt to be best suited to command the 1st Battalion from among those Grenadier officers at the time recommended for command. Secondly, following the selection of Colonel Airy every effort was made by Colonel MacGregor and others to prepare him for his 'new' regiment while Colonel Airy's own personality made it that much easier for him to win the support of his new guardsmen. From his own experience Colonel Airy always envisaged that he would find an empathy with the Scots Guards whose Warrant Officers he has described 'as the best in the Household Division' and he felt at home from the moment he walked into the battalion. He handled his first meeting with the battalion by telling everybody assembled in the Messroom in Münster that 'once a Grenadier, always a Grenadier but that he was the exception to that rule and now his buttons were proudly worn in threes'. He reinforced this first good impression some days later when, after talking with one of the Quartermaster's storemen, the guardsman concerned asked 'leave to carry on, sir please'; questioned as to whether he had just come from the Guards Depot and having been told that he had, Colonel Airy told the guardsman that 'he had picked up some very bad habits!'

Suffield

Having been Brigade Major Headquarters 4th Guards Armoured Brigade (as that formation had now been designated) Colonel Airy quickly determined to raise the profile of the battalion's mechanized training and every opportunity was taken to increase its knowledge of armoured warfare. Exercise KOHINOOR in Canada was only to involve Right Flank commanded by Major Malcolm Ross and Battalion Headquarters, the other elements of the battle group being two squadrons of the 5th Royal Inniskilling Dragoon Guards, a Royal Artillery battery, a Royal Engineer field troop and transport and medical support. The training was exciting and, after the frustration of trying to exercise on inadequate areas in BAOR, was enjoyed by all. Apart from a nasty accident in which Lance Sergeant Lawson lost a leg when caught in the backblast of a hand-held rocket launcher, and the burning of the Command vehicle during a night move, the exercise passed without incident and the battle group returned to Germany on 16 October to be reunited with the rest of the battalion which had been exercising in Germany under command of Headquarters 4th Guards Armoured Brigade in its absence.

Previous to the 1st Battalion training in Canada the Regiment learnt that its twenty-fifth Colonel, His Royal Highness The Duke of Gloucester, had died aged seventy-four years on 10 June, 1974. The third son of King George V and Queen Mary, Prince Henry became Colonel of the Regiment in 1937 on the accession of his brother, King George VI, to the throne. He served for thirty-seven years as Colonel, a loyal and devoted Scots Guardsman who took an unfailing interest in the affairs of the Regiment no matter where battalions were or what they might be doing. During the last years of his life when he became too ill to undertake his duties as Colonel, Princess Alice deputised for her husband on a number of occassions, in the process gaining the respect and admiration of all in the Regiment who encountered her. On 12 September Her Majesty The Queen announced the appointment of His Royal Highness Prince Edward, Duke of Kent, as the twenty-sixth Colonel of the Regiment and on 8 November he paid his first visit to the 1st Battalion. Following this visit the battalion again interrupted its BAOR training programme and prepared for an operational tour in Belfast in April, 1975. Training at Tin City was professionally supervised and RSM Cooper commanded the 'enemy force' with great verve; regrettably Guardsman Smith and Drummer Clark were killed in Tin City when an oil stove overturned and the building they were in quickly caught fire.

1st Battalion North Belfast

Deployment to North and Central Belfast took place in early April, 1975, and by the 4th the battalion had taken over from the 1st Battalion The King's Own Royal Border Regiment. Although there was some overlap with that part of Belfast covered by the 1st Battalion in 1971 and the 2nd Battalion in 1973, the area was mostly unknown, there having been regular boundary changes between battalions of 39th Infantry Brigade since 1973. C Company, commanded by Major Alastair Morrison, were given the hard Protestant Shankill area to look after, while Major Michael Whiteley and Left Flank sought to control the equally hard Republican Falls district. Right Flank, with Major Campbell Gordon in command, was based in North Howard Street Mill in the Clonard while Support Company, under Major Jeremy Warren, shared the Albert Street Mill with the Echelon, commanded by the Quartermaster, Captain Frank Smith. Support Company had responsibility for the Divis Flats, that vast, rambling building covering several acres with interconnecting stairways and balconies which made following up any incident so hard.

The tour followed a pattern which, six years after the first troops were deployed into Northern Ireland, had become well established. Companies took over their areas, established contact with those people who were important or could be of use, learnt their way around and then set about dominating their areas and maintaining order while trying to root out known terrorists or perpetrators of violence. Searches to find weapons and explosives, inter-factional shootings – usually between different groups of the same terrorist tendency – and marches by one cabal or another to protest at some supposed wrong or other, were the daily fare of all companies. Robberies, at the time the principal source of terrorist funds, were a constant headache, while the bombing by one side of pubs or betting shops frequented by the other ensured that the sectarian temperature always ran high. It was a tour when there were a number of small incidents but nothing major occurred, itself testimony to the deft way in which the battalion approached its task.

The battalion returned to Münster in early August and after leave and some training prepared to hand over to the 2nd Battalion and to move to London to Chelsea Barracks. Of the battalion's three years in BAOR approximately eighteen months had been spent either serving in Northern Ireland or preparing to do so, hardly a satisfactory return on the investment made in mechanized training and courses. However, the 1st Battalion was probably not alone in feeling that it had had insufficient opportunity to demonstrate what it could achieve in the mechanized role. For units of other arms which had to train to operate in Ulster as infantrymen the waste of skills and the time spent re-learning basic drills after a tour was potentially most damaging.

Hardly had the 2nd Battalion returned to Pirbright after leave than on 3 May, 1974, command of the battalion changed with Lieutenant Colonel James *2nd Battalion* Dunsmure taking over from Colonel Tony Boam. Like Colonel Mayfield in the 1st Battalion, Colonel Boam's period in command had been dominated by Northern Ireland and he had had the additional and most important task of reforming the 2nd Battalion, a task completed speedily and without fuss. The summer of 1974 was filled by a wide variety of duties and ranged from ceremonial in London, and in July in Edinburgh when Right Flank under Major Naylor mounted the Holyroodhouse Guard for the week of the Queen's visit to the City, to a month of Operation TRUSTEE when elements of the battalion were on standby to support the Metropolitan Police in the event of a terrorist incident at Heathrow Airport, and training on Salisbury Plain in October.

Following the death of the Colonel in June Right Flank mounted a Guard of Honour in the Horseshoe Cloisters at Windsor Castle during the subsequent State Funeral in St George's Chapel. Another incident of a very different nature occurred on 17 July when a bomb exploded in the White Tower at the Tower of London; one woman died and eighteen were wounded and the Tower of London Guard commanded by Captain Ewen Cameron turned out to assist the Police and Emergency Services, winning considerable praise from the Resident Governor. This was not to be the last occasion when skills learnt on the streets of Northern Ireland would have to be put to use in mainland Britain.

Towards the end of 1974 the battalion was warned for an emergency unaccompanied tour in February, 1975, in Belize, the former Caribbean colony the name of which had been changed from British Honduras in June, 1973. Belated notification of the tour meant that some consequential internal reorganization of the battalion had to be carried out at short notice in late November; only Battalion Headquarters and two full-strength rifle companies were required and Colonel Dunsmure selected Right and Left Flank for the tour, leaving G Company under Major Iain McKay at Pirbright, although it was planned that as many soldiers as possible would be 'trickled through' Belize during the seven months that the battalion was to be in the Caribbean. Shortly after the reorganization had been completed His Royal Highness The Duke of Kent paid his first visit to the battalion. During the first week of February, 1975, the battalion flew to Belize to relieve the 1st Battalion The Light Infantry.

Belize Changed perceptions of the threat posed to Belize by Guatemala had caused a revision of plans for the defence of that country since S Company had provided the Garrison in 1971 and on arrival Right Flank under Major Anthony Milner-Brown and CSM Carnegie deployed to Holdfast Camp near the border, while Battalion Headquarters and Left Flank, the latter commanded by Major Ian McLaughlan and with CSM Hardie, were based at Airport Camp close to Belize City. Contingency plans also required the establishment of various platoon camps in addition to the two principal bases and platoons rotated through these on a regular basis, the tour in Belize being divided into four seven-week cycles.

In addition to carrying out operational duties all platoons undertook military training in the area of Mountain Pine Ridge, while jungle warfare courses were run at Sibun by a team commanded by Lieutenant Henry Llewellyn. However, probably the real advantage to be gained from a tour in Belize lay in the potential for adventure training; a base set up at St George's Cay by Major Anthony Forbes and still in use nearly twenty years later, provided instruction in sailing, subaqua diving, canoeing, fishing and survival both inland in the jungle and on a desert island. Canoeing expeditions involved crossing several

29. "Tumbledown is a low limestone ridge rising to around 2,500 feet at its highest point." (Page 146). This photograph, taken from Mount Harriet, shows the 2nd Battalion's objective and the ground across which it advanced on the night of 13 June, 1982.

30. "Back at San Carlos Colonel Scott was warned on 4 June, 1982, that the battalion was to be moved to Bluff Cove the next day to relieve 2 PARA." (Page 138). The battalion embarking in LCUs at San Carlos jetty for the short passage to HMS *Intrepid* and the subsequent move to Bluff Cove. Stores for the Task Force can be seen in the foreground.

31. "Late on the morning of 14 June it became clear that the Argentinians wished to discuss surrender terms." (Page 152). Helicopters land in that area of Tumbledown occupied after the battle by Battalion Headquarters and G Company. Goat Ridge can be seen on the right beyond the smoke.

32. "Stunned by their spectacular success in defeating a well trained battalion of regular Argentenian Marines… in the immediate aftermath of the battle most people experienced understandable feelings of euphoria and relief." (Page 153). Some members of 7 Platoon G Company on Tumbledown on 14 June.

33. "Early in February, 1971, 7 Platoon of F Company went to Crest Hill in the New Territories to refurbish the Scots Guards Star which had been constructed by the 2nd Battalion in 1927." (Page 88). Guardsman Neilly and McIntyre returning to Lo Wu with one of the mules used to carry stores for the task.

34. "First, however, came the Royal Review of the Regiment by His Royal Highness The Duke of Kent on Horse Guards on 31 May, 1979." (Page 121). The Colour Party of the 2nd Battalion is about to pass the Colonel who is positioned in front of the Arch while other elements of the Regiment await their turn to march past.

35. "The 2nd Battalion crossed the Irish Sea on the night of 28 May, 1980, and took over responsibility for the West Belfast TAOR from the 1st Battalion The Royal Scots the next day." (Page 125). The Colonel visited the battalion during its time in Belfast and is seen here talking to members of 2nd Lieutenant Mark Varney's Platoon of Right Flank at the Woodburn Base. Sergeant Macrae (right) is the Platoon Sergeant.

36. "Father and five sons, all Scots Guardsmen." Sergeant Angus McEwan with his sons Rory, Conal, Neil, Gregor and Fergus pictured at the Guards Depot in January, 1978. All served in the Regiment and three of the brothers — Rory, Gregor and Fergus — were still serving at the end of 1993.

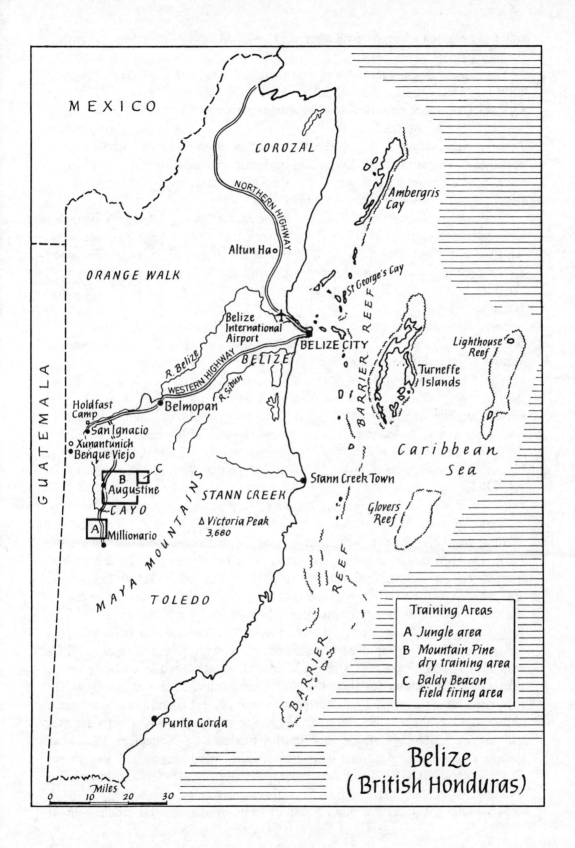

MEXICO

COROZAL

Ambergris Cay

NORTHERN HIGHWAY

Altun Ha

ORANGE WALK

St George's Cay

GUATEMALA

Belize
International
Airport

BELIZE CITY

R. Belize

BELIZE

WESTERN HIGHWAY

R. Sibun

Lighthouse Reef

Holdfast
Camp

Belmopan

Turneffe
Islands

San Ignacio

Xunantunich
Benque Viejo

C

B
Augustine

*Caribbean
Sea*

CAYO

STANN CREEK

Stann Creek Town

MAYA MOUNTAINS

△ *Victoria Peak*
3,680

A
Millionario

*Glovers
Reef*

BARRIER REEF

TOLEDO

BARRIER REEF

Training Areas

A *Jungle area*

B *Mountain Pine
dry training area*

C *Baldy Beacon
field firing area*

Punta Gorda

Miles
0   10   20   30

Belize
(British Honduras)

miles of open sea while survival depended upon soldiers subsisting on what they could dig up or hunt down.

There were no operational alarms during the tour and when Major General Philip Ward, Commanding the Household Division, visited in late March Colonel Dunsmure flew him to Guatemala to visit the ancient Mayan ruins at Tikal. Later in the tour the Reconnaissance Platoon, commanded by Captain Alec Ramsay, drove south to the Punta Gorda area of Belize, while a large expedition set out in early May to climb Mount Victoria, the highest in Belize, only to be defeated by a major forest fire which necessitated its withdrawal by helicopter in a 'Saigon style' rescue operation.

Neither was the ceremonial side of life forgotten and the Queen's Birthday was celebrated on 24 May when the Governor took the salute at a parade upon which Right Flank found the battalion detachment alongside, as the *Battalion Digest* records, 'the Belize Volunteer Guard, the Police, the Prison Service, the Fire Service, the Boys Brigade, the Boy Scouts, the Girl Guides and the Nurses!'

After a changeover of sixty-five men with the Rear Party in mid-May the second half of the tour followed a similar operational and training pattern, although with the additional responsibility for the battalion of having to be prepared to implement plans drawn up to cope with hurricane damage. By 30 August the battalion was back at Pirbright having handed over to The Gloucestershire Regiment, after an extremely successful tour when considerable efforts were made by Colonel Dunsmure and the staff of Battalion Headquarters to ensure that training and leave plans were soundly based and therefore enjoyed by those fortunate enough to be included amongst the 420 Scots Guardsmen to go to Belize.

Münster Public duties and conversion training to prepare the battalion for the mechanized role and its forthcoming tour in BAOR occupied the autumn months and early in the New Year, 1976, the battalion took over Waterloo Barracks, Münster, from the 1st Battalion. Some members of the latter battalion were so well entrenched in Germany that they did not wish to return to Chelsea, and where it suited both battalions that they be allowed to stay, they did so thereby providing some useful mechanized expertise for the 2nd Battalion. The battalion quickly settled into a barracks which it had vacated only six years before and started to familiarize itself once again with a fleet of tracked APCs which it had taken over as new in 1967 and which had subsequently been passed from one Foot Guards battalion to another until returned to the 2nd Battalion nine years later. Efforts to get to grips with mechanized training started at once although, like the 1st Battalion in 1973, the prospect of Northern Ireland training in September and a tour in the Province in November somewhat dampened enthusiasm. Nonetheless companies were dispatched to ski on Exercise SNOW QUEEN in Bavaria and some worthwhile mechanized training took place over the more traditional BAOR training areas.

In parallel the battalion quickly found itself immersed in a whole host of routine tasks which are the lot of a battalion stationed within 1st British Corps in peacetime: Ammunition Site Guards, assistance to non-infantry units earmarked to serve in Northern Ireland, Border patrols, study periods and command post exercises all had to be undertaken, thereby further dissipating the effort which might otherwise have been directed towards learning how to operate as a mechanized battle group.

On 1 September 4th Guards Armoured Brigade, commanded by Brigadier Desmond Langley, was disbanded in a move to abolish the brigade level of command in the British Army in order to save manpower and streamline operational procedures. As a result the two brigade headquarters in the 2nd Armoured Division were re-designated as smaller task force headquarters, although each continued to discharge garrison responsibilities in Munster and Osnabrück. Headquarters 4th Guards Armoured Brigade became Headquarters Task Force C and at a disbandment parade on 1 October 2nd Lieutenant Iain Duncan-Smith carried the Regimental Colour while 2nd Lieutenant Patrick Crichton-Stuart's platoon of G Company represented the battalion.

In mid-June Sergeant Majors changed when RSM Bunton relieved RSM T. Forrest while on 16 September, with the battalion well established in Waterloo Barracks, Colonel Dunsmure handed over to Lieutenant Colonel Murray Naylor. Less than a month later training for Northern Ireland began with the battalion being put through its paces at Tin City, following which in the middle of November it moved to Londonderry to replace the 1st Battalion The Queen's Regiment in the Creggan and Shantallow areas of the city. A month later Brigadier Bryan Webster, Commander 8th Infantry Brigade and the local Divisional Chief Superintendent decided that TAORs within Londonderry should be rationalized; as a result the 2nd Battalion became responsible for the hard Republican areas of the Creggan, Bogside and Brandywell, places that many people already knew well from the 1972 tour, while the Shantallow was handed over to the Blues and Royals operating in the infantry role. Battalion Headquarters was co-located with the RUC at Divisional Headquarters in the Strand Road, while Left Flank was based in Creggan Camp – better known to the locals as Piggery Ridge – first under Major Ian McLaughlan and later under Major Malcolm Ross with CSM Mackenzie, while G Company commanded by Major Ewen Cameron and with CSM Fowler occupied the Masonic Hall Car Park, the same location as in 1972. Right Flank, commanded by Major Robin Buchanan-Dunlop with CSM Fraser, started by sharing Fort George with the Echelon, but after a month moved to the Bridge Camp, its 1972 base, where in February 1977 Major Michael Scott took command.

By the time that the 2nd Battalion came to serve in Londonderry for the second time the operational tempo in the Province had stabilized to a level where there was always plenty to do to pre-empt violence and maintain security but terrorist incidents were few and far between; however, when they did come they tended to be well planned and savage. The pattern of life within the battalion was much the same as for previous tours with a crop of successes as

111

well as some narrow escapes and bizarre incidents. The tour was well summarized in the words of the Commanding Officer writing in the *Rose and Thistle* in early March, 1977: 'All of us will return to Münster with different memories of our time in 'Derry; the boredom of sangars; the thrill of a find and the sensation of a good arrest; the rubbish everywhere; the attitude of local people; the distastefulness of searching occupied houses; the weather; the relief after a shooting incident without casualty .... our experience has doubtless done us all a lot of good and each of us will leave a wiser and more experienced man .... We can also claim to be leaving our part of 'Derry a quieter place than we found it'.

During the first half of 1977 8th Infantry Brigade was a Guards Brigade in all but name, comprising of the Scots Guards and the Blues and Royals on emergency tours in Londonderry City, the 2nd Battalion Coldstream Guards under the command of Lieutenant Colonel Malcolm Havergal as the resident battalion in Ebrington Barracks and the 1st Battalion The Royal Hampshire Regiment in Ballykelly. Brigadier Webster met all suggestions for a change in designation with stoicism, although he did wear a khaki beret when visiting company bases on Christmas Day! Meanwhile the battalion's relations with the RUC were excellent, the move to co-locate at Police Headquarters in Strand Road proving something of a breakthrough; however, the constable who requested permission to use the photocopier in the Intelligence Cell may not have thought so when he discovered that he had inadvertently fed the document he was supposed to be copying into the shredder! On 15 March the 1st Battalion The Prince of Wales's Own Regiment of Yorkshire arrived to relieve the battalion which returned to Germany in the same aircraft.

1977 was to be a busy year in Germany, and once the battalion had completed a period of leave and been reunited with its FV432s, battle group training began in earnest with Exercise MEDICINE MAN at Suffield as the immediate objective. Unfortunately in 1977 all battle groups deployed to Canada in the same configuration of two armoured squadrons and one mechanized company, and as a result only about half the battalion was able to experience the excellent training opportunities provided on the prairie. Colonel Naylor selected G Company as the battle group mechanized company – primarily because the company had not gone to Belize in 1975 – while B Squadron 4th Royal Tank Regiment and A Squadron 5th Inniskilling Dragoon Guards and B Company, 1st Battalion Princess Patricia's Canadian Light Infantry, commanded by Major Ray Crabbe, provided the other three combat teams.

Prior to departing for Canada the battalion and all other elements due to be part of the Suffield battle group trained at Soltau. On 28 June Major General Frank Kitson, Commander 2nd Armoured Division visited the training. Always an astute observer of life, while watching Major Michael Scott's Right Flank demonstrating close bridge garrison procedures to the remainder of the battle group, he espied through his binoculars a soldier standing a long way off apparently without purpose and inquired of the Commanding Officer what he might be doing. Having been told that he was one of the sappers responsible for battle simulation he commented, 'I don't think so, I think he's having a pee!'

On return from Soltau the battalion provided a Colour Party at Her Majesty *Suffield* The Queen's Review of the Army at Sennelager on 7 July. Lieutenant Simon Duffin and 2nd Lieutenant Richard Coke carried the Queen's and Regimental Colours respectively, while Drill Sergeant Milne and Sergeants Mackie and Howie escorted them. A month later the 2nd Battalion Scots Guards Battle Group flew to Calgary for what was to prove some of the best training ever undertaken while stationed in Germany. Since the 1st Battalion had exercised there in 1974 considerable refinement had taken place and battle groups spent most of their time deployed in the field with training in one phase of war leading without interruption into another. It was exhilarating to manoeuvre across the prairie without fear of restriction and to be able to call for all levels of fire support and everybody learnt more about operating as a battle group than they would ever have done anywhere else. The British Army remains lucky to have the facilities of Suffield which will become more important as restrictions on training in Europe become ever tighter. After three weeks practising every phase of war the battle group returned to Suffield, cleaned up its vehicles and dispatched itself on leave or adventure training to the four corners of Canada and the United States. It had been a thoroughly worthwhile exercise during which soldiers came as close as it is possible in peacetime to operating under realistic battle conditions. No one returned to Germany in September without a better understanding of how each arm and service in the battle group dovetailed with the others to produce an efficient fighting unit. Writing several years later Brigadier Langley, who visited the battalion in Canada, said, 'The armoured battle was a very different scene and Suffield provided the most testing and comprehensive training in existence. Careful preparation and planning, well learnt drills and quick thinking were all at a premium. The battalion succeeded in this role as well as in Northern Ireland and won for itself a high repuation.'

A facet of life for all units in Germany in the 1970s was how hard they worked despite the fact that Britain was at peace with her neighbours. While the demands of Northern Ireland went some way to providing an explanation for the frenetic pace, they did not tell the whole story. Life in Germany has always been busy – in particular for commanders – and the 2nd Battalion's programme over the winter months of 1977 and 1978 tell their own story; courses, ski-ing, training at Sennelager and a patrol exercise in the Eifel Mountains near the Belgian border, the conversion of F Company to be a fourth mechanized company under Major Randall Nicol, a battalion level trial of the Army's new Clansman radios and St Andrew's Day, when Major Tony Philipson took the salute following Church Parade, all came and went and were generally enjoyed despite the sometimes unkind rigours of a German winter.

New Colours had last been presented to the battalion in Edinburgh in 1965 and there was considerable discussion during 1977 as to where and when the 2nd Battalion should next parade for that purpose. Outside the battalion it was generally assumed that the parade would be held on the battalion's return to London in the Spring of 1979. However, within the battalion there were different opinions and, having taken soundings, Colonel Murray Naylor presented to the Lieutenant Colonel Commanding, Colonel de Klee, the alternative view that, should Her Majesty The Queen approve, the parade should be held in Germany in 1978 at a time when the battalion could devote itself to making it a unique occasion. In the opinion of the battalion the alternative, a parade in London in the early Summer of 1979, sandwiched between a number of other important ceremonial events was thought to be less satisfactory. Firm views were expressed with those advocating London citing the fact that Foot Guards battalions only received new colours in capital cities and advising that the Regiment should not deny itself the chance of a Royal occasion in Britain, while those wishing to see the parade held in Germany pointed to the precedent of the 1st Battalion's parade at Pirbright in 1964, while emphasizing how much more enjoyable a parade in Germany would be for the battalion and its families. The matter was placed before Her Majesty The Queen and she approved the holding of the parade in Germany and commanded His Royal Highness The Duke of Kent to represent her.

Presentation of New Colours

The parade was held on 20 April, 1978, at Schloss Nordkirchen, an imposing eighteenth century building and the former palace of the Bishops of Munster, described locally as 'the Versailles of Westphalia', and situated some twenty miles south-west of Waterloo Barracks. Watched by over 1,000 spectators, many of whom had come from Britain, the battalion paraded on the lawns in front of the Palace and received the Colonel with a Royal Salute. Following the inspection the Old Colours, carried by Lieutenants Julian Crowe and Iain Duncan-Smith and escorted by Drill Sergeant Downham and Colour Sergeants Milloy and Sulley, were marched off parade. The battalion then formed three sides of a square. The New Colours, carried onto parade by Captain Frank Lawrie and Captain Clarke Brown, were placed upon the drums and consecrated by the Reverend Farquhar Lyall, Assistant Chaplain General Scotland, and a former chaplain to the 1st Battalion, assisted by the battalion's own chaplain, the Reverend Peter Meager. Thereafter the Colours were handed by the Colonel to 2nd Lieutenants Chisholm Wallace and Johnny Stewart, after which the Colonel addressed the battalion and the Commanding Officer replied. The Colours were subsequently marched to the centre of the battalion which then reformed and marched past. Following the parade everybody repaired to Waterloo Barracks for lunch and a succession of parties that went on for three days. Right or wrong as the original proposal to hold the parade in Germany may have been, from the standpoint of the 2nd Battalion 20 April was a resounding success. While the author of this history can only be biased in the matter, he can do no better than to quote what he himself wrote in the *Scots Guards Magazine* at the time: 'History was created on 20 April and such a parade held in Germany demonstrated the Household Division's continuing ability to achieve the highest standards in anything which it chooses to undertake. For those of us who were fortunate enough to be present it was a day to be remembered as well as one to be thoroughly enjoyed.'

Exercise KEYSTONE in October when the 2nd Armoured Division exercised across Lower Saxony was to be the battalion's last major exercise in BAOR before its three-year tour ended in April, 1979. In the New Year and as a preparation for what might be its operational role in Britain the Commanding Officer staged a counter-insurgency exercise in the Sauerland for each company in turn in some of the coldest weather experienced by the battalion; Major Iain Mackay-Dick's Right Flank was the winning company with 2nd Lieutenant Niall Bowser commanding the most successful platoon. Thereafter the battalion's faithful APCs and other vehicles were prepared for handover to the 2nd Battalion Grenadier Guards and on 5 April the battalion left Munster for Chelsea Barracks to serve alongside the 1st Battalion which had by 1979 been resident there for three years. Thus ended an enjoyable tour in BAOR when, despite the frustration of inadequate training opportunities, much had been accomplished. Throughout, the families had once again supported the battalion to the hilt, entering into everything and sharing the good times with the bad. Like Captain Don Dalgarno, the Families Officer of the 1st Battalion before them, Captain Clarke Brown and later Lieutenant Ewan Lawrie looked after the 2nd Battalion's families with enormous dedication and understanding. The Wives Club thrived under the close watch of Mrs Naylor and Mrs Bunton, who by the end could cope with most situations, although even they were defeated the day that Guardsman Cocker's wife, invited to try her hand at the controls of an APC and although closely supervised by Guardsman Turner, drove it straight through the wall of the Signal Platoon Stores, achieving in a matter of seconds damage beyond even the Commander-in-Chief's powers of financial 'write-off'! Aghast at what had happened, they immediately reported to Major Kim Ross, the Second-in-Command, who merely laughed.

CHAPTER SEVEN

LONDON AND ALDERGROVE

1st Battalion: London-Aldergrove
2nd Battalion: London

1st Battalion
1976
The handover of Waterloo Barracks in Münster to the 2nd Battalion completed early in January, 1976, the 1st Battalion Scots Guards moved to Chelsea Barracks to begin a tour of public duties which was to keep it in London for four years with little relief other than a planned operational tour in Ulster and, towards the end of its time, a two-month-long exercise in Kenya. Preparations for duty mounting at the Royal Palaces and the Tower of London had to be completed in less than three weeks, but the fact that it was only three years since the battalion had left Windsor meant that sufficient residual experience remained at a senior level and RSM Cooper was particularly fortunate to be able to draw upon Drill Sergeant Stephenson's considerable knowledge of public duties when practising for the battalion's first Queen's Guard on 16 February.

Meanwhile Colonel Christopher Airy was anxious lest his guardsmen's professional keenness should become tarnished as a result of an unrelenting round of duties, a particular pressure being the requirement to 'fill in' at short notice in the absence of other London District battalions called upon to serve with little warning in Ulster. Like his successor, Lieutenant Colonel Mark Carnegie-Brown, Colonel Airy saw his priority as the maintenance of a happy and motivated battalion with variety and time to relax built in to all programmes.

The summer months of 1976 passed in a whirl of public duties. Captain John Kiszely, the Adjutant, who had the previous year taken over from Captain Roddy Gow, and RSM Cooper prepared Guards of Honour for visiting Heads of State, two Guards for the Birthday Parade and the battalion for a plethora of lesser but nonetheless important ceremonial and administrative tasks. One of these involved finding the staff to run the Royal Tournament at Earls Court, a duty which at that time always fell to a Household Division battalion in the late summer. A thankless task, it meant many hours of duty helping to check the public into the auditorium while conducting continual searches to deter those who might be tempted to mount a terrorist attack in order to kill or maim, or simply to disrupt a performance.

Earlier, on 26 June, Captain Nicholas Scott-Barrett, accompanied by CSMs

Wilkie and McCombie and Sergeant Richards, had provided the Key Party when his father, Lieutenant General Sir David Scott-Barrett, was installed as the Governor of Edinburgh Castle. Since 1976 a similar ceremony has twice involved senior Scots Guards officers: in 1979 when Lieutenant General Sir Michael Gow became GOC Scotland and in 1993 when Major General Michael Scott assumed the same appointment.

Early in September Colonel Christopher Airy handed over command to Colonel Carnegie-Brown after 'two and a half years of immense happiness' and 'feeling tremendously fortunate to have commanded the battalion'. His departure was preceded by that of Major John Bryden, a former Royal Artillery officer who spent twelve years with the 1st Battalion as its Paymaster, and in July by a changeover in the Sergeant Major's office when RSM Knight succeeded RSM Cooper.

As so often in previous years the battalion was once again short of manpower, retention of young officers being a particular problem, and, despite attempts by the Brigade Major and his staff to alleviate some of the public duties load these shortages compounded the battalion's difficulties and often frustrated attempts to provide interesting alternative activities when soldiers were not on duty. There was, however, the compensation of being in the heart of the West End and, however irksome public duties might sometimes be, those off duty could quickly lose themselves down the King's Road and elsewhere. In fairness it should also be said that a number of soldiers, although never very many, actually relish the 'ceremonial life' both for its glamour and the predictability of the duty roster.

The Silver Jubilee in 1977 marked the twenty-fifth anniversary of Her Majesty The Queen's accession to the throne and a number of special events involving the battalion were held in London and elsewhere. First, however, on 20 April the battalion paraded on the lawns of Buckingham Palace and was presented with New Colours by The Queen on a day which promised heavy drizzle but later cleared sufficiently to ensure that nobody got too wet. 400 members of the battalion were on parade as the Old Colours carried by 2nd Lieutenants Mark Bullough and Peter Acland were marched off, watched by His Royal Highness The Duke of Kent, attending his first such parade as the Colonel, following which the New Colours were consecrated by the Reverend Farquhar Lyall, Assistant Chaplain General Scotland and the battalion's Padre in Malaya from 1964 to 1966. The Queen then handed the Colours to Lieutenant John Treadwell and 2nd Lieutenant Tom Fitzherbert. Although the weather detracted from the spectacle and 400 pairs of boots did the Buckingham Palace lawns little good, it was a happy occasion and was rounded off with lunch for 3,000 guests in Chelsea Barracks.

On 17 May The Queen paid a Jubilee visit to Glasgow and the battalion mounted a Guard of Honour in Cathedral Square. Major Michael Nurton commanded the Guard while 2nd Lieutenant Acland carried the State Colour, recently refurbished by the East Kent Guild of Embroiderers, but only after a police car had covered the forty-six miles from the centre of Edinburgh to the centre of Glasgow in a record one hour conveying the Ensign's colour belt which had been inadvertently left behind. The Police arrived ten minutes before The Queen. While the majority of Left Flank found themselves participating in the Guard of Honour the remainder of the company led by Major Michael Smart re-enacted the march of the Earl of Montrose of December, 1644, by following the latter's route from Blair Atholl to Inverary Castle. In May, 1977, the march covering 103 miles was completed in four days, the party generally receiving a more hospitable welcome than their forbears in 1644, although the Duke of Argyll was understandably startled and not a little aggrieved when the detachment arrived at the front gates of Inverary Castle complete with a BBC Television team about which he had not been warned.

The Silver Jubilee Service of Thanksgiving was held on 7 June and the battalion provided ten half-companies to line the Mall for the procession to St Paul's Cathedral. Four days later the battalion's Queen's Colour was trooped on the Queen's Birthday Parade. Colonel Carnegie-Brown was the Field Officer, Captain John Kiszely the Adjutant in Brigade Waiting, while Major Nurton commanded the Escort with 2nd Lieutenant Tom Fitzherbert as the Ensign and CSM Fullerton and CQMS Wight as right and left guides respectively.

No sooner was this period of intensive ceremonial duty completed than the battalion found itself preparing for a month of Spearhead duty during which in early August it moved by sea to Northern Ireland to cover Her Majesty The Queen's visit to the Province. Initially located in Belfast the battalion was used to reinforce units in that City, while Right Flank, with a platoon of Grenadiers under command, was sent on 8 August to support the 2nd Battalion Coldstream Guards during the Royal visit to Coleraine, a far cry maybe from Cathedral Square in Glasgow or Horse Guards Parade but a Royal Guard nonetheless. On 14 August the battalion was stood down and returned to London, the visit having passed without major incident.

Laying up of the battalion's Old Colours in the Kirk of the Holy Rood in Grangemouth on 22 October, training in Britain and, for each rifle company in turn, for a month in Cyprus, meant that, when public duties permitted, the battalion took full advantage of opportunities to get away from Chelsea Barracks. An international incident was narrowly averted in Cyprus on 26 October when a party of ten led by an NCO from Left Flank strayed into Turkish-controlled waters while sailing off Famagusta; fortunately Brigadier John Acland was at the time in command of the Army element on the island and was able to smooth ruffled Turkish feathers and those arrested were released unharmed. The incident was potentially a serious one and demonstrated the speed at which events can escalate when a nation decides to exploit a silly mistake for political ends.

In November the London Fire Brigade went on strike in concert with their colleagues elsewhere. Operation BURBERRY was mounted, with the Services, assisted by the Metropolitan Police, being drafted in to take the place of the striking firemen. Deployed initially to Mill Hill in order to cover North London and later operating out of Chelsea Barracks for Central London, companies provided cover for nearly two months working shifts of twenty-four hours at a time. Fortunately, with the exception of a major pub fire in Finchley, the battalion had only relatively minor incidents to handle, although the four 'Green Goddess' fire engines on duty at any one time certainly proved their worth.

Throughout this period of aid to the civil authorities the battalion continued to mount London duties, once more demonstrating the versatility of the modern guardsman who can one minute find himself parading in the Forecourt of Buckingham Palace and the next risking his life while trying to save a burning building. While the 1st Battalion provided crews and vehicles for BURBERRY, Regimental Headquarters, deploying operationally for the first time since 1945, commanded the Eastern Sector from Armoury House in the City. This was one of Colonel de Klee's last duties as Lieutenant Colonel Commanding and he handed over his appointment to Colonel Iain Ferguson in April, 1978.

The first half of 1978 followed a similar sequence to 1977, with plenty of Queen's Guards and other duties, including the Birthday Parade. A much-needed change of focus was provided for the battalion in the second half of the year in the form of an operational tour in Northern Ireland. In the meantime two retirements of note took place. On 8 June the Quartermaster, Captain Frank Smith, left the battalion after a fine career which he followed with another which eventually took him to a seat in the boardroom at Robert Fleming and Co, the Merchant Bankers in the City. He was replaced by Captain George Cooper.

Two months later, as the battalion was preparing for an operational tour in Northern Ireland, the Sergeants' Mess dined out Lance Sergeant Murray, thirty-eight years in the Regiment and for most of them responsible for delivering and collecting mail within the 1st Battalion. The 'Murray Bird', as he was always affectionately known, had more scrapes with authority than anybody else in the Regiment in his time, but came through them all more or less unscathed, a true Scots Guardsman and a regimental character the likes of which are seldom seen these days. He was one of the last, if not the last, junior NCO in the Regiment to wear Second World War medals. He also passed part of the war as a prisoner of war.

Following training at Hythe and Lydd the 1st Battalion moved to Ulster to *1st Battalion* relieve the 1st Battalion Queen's Own Highlanders in the Armagh TAOR, an *Armagh* area well known to those who had served with the battalion in 1973. With Right Flank under Major Nurton in Dungannon, C Company with Major Andrew Joscelyne in Cookstown and Left Flank commanded by Major Michael Smart in Middletown, Battalion Headquarters, with whom B Company under Major Nicholas Barne was co-located in Armagh, had responsibility for a huge area of rural Ulster. Map reading was complicated by the close proximity of the border with the Irish Republic, while the rolling countryside of small fields surrounded by impenetrable hedges further reduced the chances of successful navigation. No sooner had the battalion taken over than it was faced with the need to assist in controlling a large march which set out from Coalisland to Dungannon to commemorate the original Civil Rights March of 1968. However, the tour was mainly notable for the number of explosive devices with which the battalion had to deal. Planted in the form of car bombs or incendiaries, the latter often hidden in cassettes, devices were usually placed in town centres to cause as much damage as possible in order to destroy the commercial potential of the target, as well as to disrupt the lives of those who lived there. By the end of the tour the battalion had dealt with over fifty explosive devices and innumerable hoaxes which could cause just as much disruption. Shooting incidents were rare and an effective patrolling programme by all companies prevented the IRA from adopting a more offensive stance, while at the same time leading to the discovery of not insignificant quantities of weapons, explosives, clothing and subversive literature, all part of the terrorist inventory.

St Andrew's Day, when it had been planned to dine out RSM Knight prior to his replacement by RSM Beck, provides a good example of the way in which a skilfully co-ordinated operation to cause disruption and damage could be mounted by the IRA. A number of blast incendiaries and a pub bomb in C Company's area in the early evening were followed by devices in Dungannon and Moy, a 200 lb car bomb in South Armagh with which B Company had to deal, and a suspected device in Dyan. In total eleven bombs or incendiaries were planted in the battalion area, effectively tying down each company in turn, causing considerable damage and further eroding the confidence of the local population, both Catholic and Protestant. Needless to say the farewell celebrations for RSM Knight were somewhat disrupted. On 29 December the battalion handed over to The Royal Regiment of Wales and returned to London just in time for Hogmanay.

At the end of January, 1979, Colonel Mark Carnegie-Brown handed over command to Lieutenant Colonel Thomas Boyd-Carpenter. To spend the whole of your command in London with public duties as your battalion's principal role, albeit with an operational tour in Ulster, must rate as 'drawing the short straw' and it is much to Colonel Carnegie-Brown's credit that his battalion achieved as much as it did during a period of considerable pressure and while numbers were low. Nor did the pressure ease when he had gone, since on 21 February the battalion had to provide twenty ambulance crews to cover the central parts of the capital during a twenty-four hour strike by members of the London Ambulance Service, another example of military aid to the civil authority. During their duty, the crews answered fifty-four emergency calls, Lance Sergeant Paterson being the first into action in Edmonton. Despite the battalion's preoccupation with operational and ceremonial duties, the 1978/79 football season was an extremely successful one for the battalion team which, coached by Drill Sergeant Paterson and captained by Lance Sergeant Legdon, won the Infantry Cup, beating the Gordons at home and the Welsh Guards in Berlin in the space of a week. The team was also the runner-up in the Army Cup Final.

2nd Battalion
1979
On 5 April the 2nd Battalion passed its operational role in 1st British Corps to the 2nd Battalion Grenadier Guards, and returned to London to serve

in Chelsea Barracks alongside the 1st Battalion. Not since 1932 had both battalions been stationed together in Chelsea and their nine months there in 1979 before the 1st Battalion left to undertake a residential tour in Ulster proved most agreeable for both. On 11 May Colonel Murray Naylor handed over command of the 2nd Battalion to Lieutenant Colonel Johnny Clavering and the battalion began preparations for a very heavy period of ceremonial duty. First, however, came the Royal Review of the Regiment by His Royal Highness The Duke of Kent on Horse Guards on 31 May. It was the first time that the Regiment had been able to gather on British soil since he had become Colonel on 9 September, 1974, a very good reason to parade for his inspection and endorsement.

The parade took very nearly the same form as that in 1961. The two battalions, led by their pipers, marched from Chelsea Barracks, while detachments from the Royal Military Academy, Sandhurst, the Infantry Junior Leaders Battalion, the Guards Depot, the newly formed Infantry Demonstration Battalion at Warminster and a party from the Scots Guards detachment of the Lothian Battalion of the Army Cadet Force marched from Wellington Barracks. 1,102 serving soldiers were on parade, accompanied by 220 members of the Third Guards Club and 280 members of the Scots Guards Association, commanded respectively by Major General Digby Raeburn and Colonel George Ramsay, the senior Branch President. Five senior serving officers, all of whom had commanded battalions of the Regiment, were mounted and were in attendance on the Colonel. The Lieutenant Colonel Commanding, Colonel Iain Ferguson, accompanied by the Regimental Adjutant, Major Peter Johnson, commanded the parade which was witnessed from the Major General's office above the Horse Guards Arch by Her Majesty Queen Elizabeth The Queen Mother and Her Royal Highness Princess Alice, Duchess of Gloucester, both widows of former Colonels. Following the parade the Colonel led the Regiment down the Mall where he took the salute opposite Marlborough Gate. Afterwards there was a reception at Burton's Court and dances at the Hyde Park Hotel and in Chelsea Barracks. Major Bruce Bell made history by parading in 1979 in the same appointment as he had held in 1961 when he had commanded Headquarter Company in the 2nd Battalion. After the Review one member of the Association wrote: 'As one privileged to have been on the last Colonel's parade in 1961, I thought I would never see the like again but this was an action replay.'

1979 Royal Review

Colonel Ferguson commanded the Queen's Birthday Parade on 16 June with Major Johnson as the Adjutant in Brigade Waiting. The 2nd Battalion Queen's Colour presented the previous year in Germany and carried by 2nd Lieutenant Rory Scott was trooped; Major Iain Mackay-Dick commanded the Escort and Major Kim Ross Number Two Guard, while Major Julian Lancaster and Major Andrew Joscelyne commanded Numbers Three and Four Guards provided by the 1st Battalion. RSM Bunton was the Sergeant Major of the battalion finding the Escort, his last act before handing over his appointment. However he

Both Battalions Chelsea Barracks 1979

sustained an injury to his leg two weeks prior to the parade and his place on the two rehearsals was taken by Drill Sergeant MacKenzie, possibly the first time that a drill sergeant has drawn his sword on such an occasion.

From the middle of June until late October when the 1st Battalion departed to train in Kenya both battalions were heavily engaged on public duties principally in London, although Major Julian Lancaster commanded a detachment drawn from the Flank Companies of the 1st Battalion which went to the Isle of Man at the end of June to be present when Her Majesty The Queen attended celebrations to mark the millenium of the Tynwald, the Manx Parliament. On 5 September both battalions paraded for the funeral of Lord Mountbatten who had been assassinated by the IRA while on holiday in Donegal. A month later, after four years of public duties, the 1st Battalion mounted its last Queen's Guard and flew to Kenya on Exercise GRAND PRIX.

With Battalion Headquarters based at Nanyuki, companies deployed in the vicinity of Mount Kenya in order to undertake a wide range of training, including live firing of all weapons and a platoon test exercise run at Dol Dol by Major Peter Johnson, the Second-in-Command. The scope provided by such training afforded Colonel Boyd-Carpenter the opportunity to see how officers and NCOs performed and to decide where best to place them in the battalion for the forthcoming residential tour in Northern Ireland. After the main training had been completed, it was planned that each platoon would be launched on an expedition somewhere in Kenya. Unfortunately this phase of the exercise coincided with the deployment of the Commonwealth Monitoring Force commanded by Major General John Acland to Rhodesia and uncertainty over the availability of RAF transport aircraft to return the battalion to Britain caused some training to have to be abandoned or severely curtailed. Fifteen years later it remains a matter of speculation as to whether there were plans to employ the battalion in a role in connection with the Monitoring Force but, if so, they were never made known officially.

Despite this disruption most people got to the coast for some relaxation and a party from C Company found themselves staying in a smart hotel in Malindi occupied, apart from themselves, by almost equal numbers of German and Italian tourists. One guardsman, observing a German poised on the hotel diving board and preening himself before 'take off', crept up behind him and pulled down his swimming trunks at the *moment critique*. Following this incident the Germans formed up *en masse* and demanded that the Scots Guards be banned from the hotel, thereby causing the Italians to make a counter-demand that they be allowed to stay and 'to do it more often'. Eventually sufficient aircraft were found to move the battalion home and by 21 December everybody with the exception of a small rear party was back in Chelsea Barracks and ready to celebrate Christmas without the prospect of having to mount duties, the first time in four years.

While the 1st Battalion exercised in Kenya the 2nd Battalion continued throughout 1979 to discharge its share of London duties with little or no opportunity for training or other relaxation. The prospect of constant duty mounting did not unduly concern Colonel Clavering who accepted that such was to be the battalion's role for at least the next three years and that there was no alternative but to get on with it. Like any commanding officer he naturally resisted pressure to do more than he considered to be fair and in briefing his guardsmen, he could point to an operational tour in Belfast in the Summer of 1980 and an exercise in Kenya similar to that just undertaken by the 1st Battalion in the Spring of 1981, both in their different ways ideal means of giving a public duties battalion 'a change of air'. Within the battalion he was supported by a strong team: Major Kim Ross, the Second-in-Command, was always on hand to help iron out any conflicts in the administrative system, while Captain Alec Ramsay, Adjutant since 1978 and who was relieved by Captain Tom Fitzalan Howard in late November, and RSM Wilkie all ensured that the battalion's public duties commitments were managed in a way that resulted in standards being maintained with minimum fuss. In all of this they were assisted by the way in which their guardsmen got on with the job.

On 1 November a large detachment from the 2nd Battalion travelled north to Edinburgh as a prelude to parading in Ayr on 3 November. That morning the battalion's Old Colours were laid up in the Auld Kirk before a congregation of 750 people. The Lieutenant Colonel Commanding read the lesson, while Colonel Clavering handed over the Colours to the Minister for safe custody in his church. In the afternoon the battalion provided a Guard of Honour commanded by Major Campbell Gordon outside the Sheriff Court House in Wellington Square when the Freedom of the District of Kyle and Carrick was conferred upon the Regiment. Many serving and former Scots Guardsmen attended both occasions, the Ayr Branch of the Association being there in strength and providing excellent support to the battalion.

Return to Chelsea was followed by another heavy round of public duties which continued until 3 February, 1980, when the battalion mounted its last Queen's Guard before preparing to deploy to Northern Ireland at the end of April. This tour necessitated the battalion once again deploying at a strength of four rifle companies and on 15 February F Company was re-formed under command of Major Robin Whyte with CSM Singler as his company sergeant major. Earlier, on 29 November, 1979, Major General Lord Michael Fitzalan Howard, who had commanded the battalion from 1955 to 1957 and who had been the Major General from 1968 to 1971, was appointed Colonel of The Life Guards in succession to the late Lord Mountbatten.

After nearly a year sharing Chelsea Barracks with the 2nd Battalion, the 1st Battalion and its families moved to Alexander Barracks, Aldergrove on 15 March for a twenty-month tour of duty relieving the 1st Battalion The Green Howards in 39th Infantry Brigade. Alexander Barracks lie just to the east of Lough Neagh and are contained within an area occupied by the RAF Station adjacent to Belfast Airport. On arrival the battalion assumed the role of Province reserve, deploying companies to assist units across Northern Ireland when

1st Battalion Aldergrove 1980

123

operational circumstances demanded, but having no territorial responsibilities of its own, a situation which was to endure for the first half of the tour.

As soon as the battalion had assumed its new role Right Flank was deployed to Belfast City Centre to work with the 27th Field Regiment Royal Artillery in patrolling and manning the security system established to protect the commercial and shopping centre of Ulster's principal city. Thereafter platoons of all companies found themselves involved in a roulement which took them to a number of bases across Belfast. As might be expected, the lack of a specific role for the battalion and the routine 'renting' of companies to other units caused considerable frustration in Battalion Headquarters whose responsibilities were largely administrative until arrangements were made by which the battalion was allocated a TAOR of its own.

'Pacing' the battalion to ensure a sustainable balance between operations, routine military training, sport and leisure occupied the attention of Colonel Boyd-Carpenter and RSM Beck for much of the time. Unlike previous tours in Ulster when battalions of the Regiment had deployed for four months knowing that they would be operating intensively for the whole period, the life of a resident battalion had perforce to be run at lower speed with due allowance being made for activities other than operations. As a result the battalion had two seconds-in-command, Major Peter Johnson being responsible for training and 'peace' activities, while for much of the tour Major Malcolm Ross, in addition to commanding Headquarter Company, focused on operations. Consequently operational commitments, normally accepted without question by a roulement battalion, could be sensitively dovetailed into the wider programme of a battalion undertaking a longer residential tour, an arrangement which brought benefits for married and single soldier alike.

Alexander Barracks was shared with the Northern Ireland Army Air Corps Regiment, a disposition which worked well especially at Sergeants' Mess level. Life for single men living in barracks was not uncomfortable and there were a number of compensations for those who found themselves working a constant cycle of operational duty. Because the barracks were within the perimeter of the RAF base there was no internal guard commitment and single soldiers in particular were well remunerated, receiving free accommodation and food as well as other allowances which service in Northern Ireland attracted. Certainly no one in the battalion saw fit to purchase his discharge under such circumstances.

Meanwhile the battalion's families, who, notwithstanding the operational nature of the deployment to Ulster, had been strongly encouraged to accompany their husbands to Aldergrove, quickly settled into their new homes, most of which were in Antrim. The security implications of housing them away from barracks and outside a protected military environment were well understood and the risks inherent in transporting people back and forth to Aldergrove were never ignored.

The news which came soon after arrival in Aldergrove that the battalion's next posting after Ulster was to be a tour in Hong Kong did much to boost the spirits of everybody, including the families, not that morale was ever a problem during the battalion's deployment at Aldergrove. Much of the credit for keeping the families happy rightly went to Captain Bill Stuart, who, following the example of his predecessors in both battalions of the Regiment, dedicated himself totally to their welfare, while the battalion was usually too busy to worry about whether or not it was enjoying itself.

In early March it was announced that the 2nd Battalion would also move to Northern Ireland for a residential tour at Ballykelly in County Londonderry when its time in Chelsea ended in December, 1981, although this move was later cancelled, with consequences which no one could possibly have foreseen at the time. However, the battalion's attention was by then firmly fixed upon its forthcoming four-month roulement deployment to West Belfast at the end of May. Following the by then standard package of Northern Ireland courses and training at Lydd and Hythe, the battalion crossed the Irish Sea on the night of 28 May and took over responsibility for the West Belfast TAOR from the 1st Battalion The Royal Scots the next day. This was to be the 2nd Battalion's fourth roulement tour to Northern Ireland since 1972 and its second to Belfast; on arrival it found itself covering much the same area for which it had been responsible in 1974 and in addition a large stretch of the south-western suburbs of the City. From the Shankill in the north to Twinbrook in the south was a distance of seven kilometres and Colonel Clavering's four companies, with 18 Battery Royal Artillery commanded by Major Crawford Stoddart and based in North Howard Street Mill under command, had to work hard to cover the TAOR which a few years previously would have been allocated two or three battalions. Right Flank, under Major Niall Crichton-Stuart and CSM Kaye, looked after the Lenadoon-Suffolk area, F Company, with a Coldstream Guards platoon as reinforcement and commanded by Major Robin Whyte with CSM Singler, covered the Beechmount-Whiterock neighbourhood, while G Company, led by Major Iain Dalzel Job and CSM Field, was based at Glassmullen in order to patrol the Andersontown estate. Left Flank occupied the new Moyard base from where Major Anthony Leask, on his third tour of operational duty as a company commander in the Province, and CSM Croucher, sought to control the hard Republican areas of New Barnsley, Ballymurphy and Turf Lodge. In order to discharge its responsibilities across such a large and potentially volatile area the battalion was reinforced both operationally from other units within 39th Infantry Brigade, including at times by the 1st Battalion at Aldergrove, and by individual officers and soldiers who had joined at Chelsea for the duration of the tour. In addition to the Coldstream platoon in F Company, an officer from the Irish Guards and The Royal Signals both served on the streets commanding Scots Guardsmen.

A feature of the 1980 tour was the excellent relationship which obtained between the Police and the Army at RUC Divisional Headquarters in the Springfield Road where Battalion Headquarters was located. Chief Superintend-

*2nd Battalion
West Belfast*

125

ent Jimmy Crutchley, a former Irish Guardsman, and Colonel Clavering and their staffs worked closely together to police an area which could only be successfully controlled if the two arms of the Security Forces were determined that their operations should be carefully co-ordinated.

When the battalion arrived in early May West Belfast was generally quiet, the people of the area seemingly passively accepting that violence by one faction or another and an accompanying Security Force presence were likely to remain a feature of their lives until politicians in London, Dublin and Belfast could find ways of bringing the conflict to an end. For the battalion a highly proficient IRA team of gunmen and bombers, dubbed 'The Ballymurphy Gun Team', of some fifteen hardcore terrorists posed the greatest threat. In addition 'cowboy' attacks on patrols, civil disturbances following a protest march or a show of support for those detained in the Maze Prison, erupted at regular intervals and kept everybody alert and ready to respond. Constant patrolling, searches and the manning of checkpoints and observation posts ensured that the battalion and the RUC remained on top of events and on 2 September a joint operation planned by Left Flank and the Police successfully arrested 'The Ballymurphy Gun Team', thereby eliminating a particularly well motivated terrorist group.

Earlier, at the beginning of August, the battalion had been put under considerable pressure when Province-wide demonstrations to mark the anniversary of Internment were initiated by the Republican movement; hijackings, the construction of barricades and hooligan behaviour were met by firm counteraction and, after five days and nights of some of the worst rioting Belfast had seen for some years, the troubles subsided.

On 11 October the tour ended, the battalion handing over to the 1st Battalion The Royal Regiment of Fusiliers and sailing in LSL *Sir Bedivere* for Liverpool. During the four and a half months in 39th Infantry Brigade the battalion had been well supported by its sister battalion at Aldergrove, the 1st Battalion not only reinforcing the 2nd on the streets but also providing sustenance in a variety of other ways, all of which exemplified how good the relationship between the two battalions had become. When the 2nd Battalion sailed out of Belfast Lough the Pipes and Drums of the 1st Battalion played it away from the quayside, while Colonel Boyd-Carpenter, his Adjutant, Captain Charlie Grimston, and RSM Beck were also present to say their goodbyes. Sadly tragedy struck as *Sir Bedivere* crossed the Irish Sea when Guardsman Connell of Left Flank was lost overboard and, despite a detailed search, was never found. The incident, which was never satisfactorily explained, threw a pall of sadness across the whole battalion.

On a happier note Major General Glover, the Commander Land Forces in Northern Ireland, wrote to the Major General in the following terms about the battalion's performance in West Belfast: '2SG's recent stint here coincided with the annual aggro associated with the Anniversary of Internment and also with a period when we were deliberately re-shaping the Army's stance. The former called for an astute, sensitive response. The battalion met these two contrasting demands with impeccable skill. I was always much impressed by the sturdy professionalism of the guardsmen and by their sheer good sense. They contrived to put proper pressure on the known terrorists and to leave well alone, unharassed and undisturbed, all those unconnected with the men of violence. In short they got it right.'

While the 2nd Battalion was endeavouring to uphold the rule of law in West *1st Battalion* Belfast the 1st Battalion continued to reinforce units across the Province, although its attention was primarily focused upon Belfast itself. Over the period of the Anniversary of Internment the Anti-Tank Platoon, commanded by Lieutenant Mark Turner, found itself operating under command of the 5th Heavy Regiment Royal Artillery in the City Centre and at 0150 hours on 9 August was deployed to the Unity Flats to disperse a crowd of youths threatening an Observation Post. Having successfully broken up the mob by firing three volleys of baton rounds, the platoon was redeployed to the New Lodge area where it came under sustained attack from a large crowd throwing bottles and stones. Several members of the platoon were injured when a blast bomb was thrown, whereupon, quoting the *Battalion Digest*, 'While the injuries were being taken care of, Guardsmen Ritchie and Young, who both identified the bomber, ran out through the base line and into the crowd. They arrested the blast bomber even though they were still being subjected to stoning from the crowd. The behaviour and discipline of all those present ensured that the injuries were minimal and that a secure base line was quickly reformed.' Thereafter the platoon continued to deal with similar incidents for the next three hours, being shot at more than once, a not untypical example of the type of situation confronting platoons during the first days of August, 1980, and demonstrating the courage of soldiers often deployed in small numbers to deal with crowds many times larger and out of control.

Between 27 September and 11 October Left Flank, commanded by Major Nick Potter, deployed complete to North Howard Street Mill, under command of the 2nd Battalion, the first time any company of the 1st Battalion was given its own area to control. Following this a wide variety of operations and training opportunities arose and all companies managed to leave Ulster to train in Scotland. Industrial action by the Prison Officers Association in December resulted in guardsmen being deployed in turn to guard the Foyle Prison near Coleraine, a thankless task involving long hours spent in watch towers continually bombarded by sleet and hailstorms blown across from Donegal. Earlier the battalion had been warned to be prepared to provide a fire-fighting service in North and West Belfast in the event of a Fire Service strike, another example of the demands that were heaped upon resident battalions in Northern Ireland which had to be able to respond quickly and efficiently to all possible contingencies.

The operational pattern for the 1st Battalion was set to change during 1981, but the year began with companies still deploying in support of other units; in March C Company, commanded by Major Edward Woods, moved to Fermanagh for a fortnight as part of an operation to prevent the assassination of off-duty policemen and soldiers of the Ulster Defence Regiment, a matter of constant concern to the authorities. With Company Headquarters based in Newton Butler, platoons were deployed to the area of the border with the Republic and patrolled extensively to deter action by the IRA; several contacts were reported but all proved to be negative except for one on 15 March when a covert van containing members of the Anti-Tank Platoon and driven by CSM Shearer drove over a 200 lb bomb which partially detonated. Fortunately nobody was hurt but the incident graphically illustrated the risks involving movement by vehicle along routes near the border which were open to easy interdiction by IRA groups based in the Republic.

Meanwhile within 39th Infantry Brigade plans were being made to relieve the battalion of its Province reserve role and to give it its own area of North Belfast to control. A small Operations Room was to be established at Girdwood Park Base and from it a Scots Guards company and a company from one of the roulement battalions in Belfast would patrol the New Lodge and Ardoyne districts. Once this plan was implemented companies based at Aldergrove would rotate through a two-week period of duty at Girdwood. At the same time the battalion's Close Observation Platoon was to operate under the direction of Brigade Headquarters with Major John Holmes, the Company Commander of B Company, co-ordinating its operations at battalion level.

Throughout the time the battalion was in Aldergrove Major Holmes made a significant contribution to intelligence-gathering across the whole 39th Infantry Brigade area, working most successfully with the RUC and other military units; as a result his own commanding officer always felt himself to be far better informed than most others, including Brigade Headquarters, about what was likely to happen. When the move into North Belfast finally took place it gave the 1st Battalion a much more satisfying role, although everybody found themselves working harder and most guardsmen spent almost fifty percent of their nights on duty, something which was considered to be acceptable in view of the operational situation pertaining in Belfast at the time.

On 28 March Colonel Boyd-Carpenter's tour of duty came to an end. A compassionate man of considerable intellect – known to many members of his battalion as 'The Silicon Chip' for his ability to analyse and store information apparently in a matter of seconds – he bequeathed to his successor, Lieutenant Colonel Ian McLaughlan, a battalion at a high peak of efficiency with, after a first year of disjointed operations as Province reserve, a real job to do in North Belfast. Before he left the battalion a lunch was held in Alexander Barracks when five of the six Scots Guards lieutenant colonels at the time serving in Northern Ireland sat down together. Apart from Colonel Boyd-Carpenter and his successor, Colonel McLaughlan, there were present three commanding officers of Ulster Defence Regiment battalions: Lieutenant Colonel Michael Whiteley commanding the 1st Battalion in Ballymena; Lieutenant Colonel Robin Buchanan-Dunlop the 8th Battalion in Dungannon and Lieutenant

Colonel Michael Nurton the 9th Battalion in Antrim. Not present was Lieutenant Colonel Kim Ross, at the time Military Assistant to the GOC Northern Ireland. It must be unique for any regiment to provide at the same time three commanding officers of another regiment and this success was added to when two years later Colonel Nurton was succeeded at Antrim by another Scots Guardsman, Lieutenant Colonel Jonathan Seddon-Brown, and Lieutenant Colonel Anthony Leask followed Colonel Buchanan-Dunlop in command of the 8th Battalion at Dungannon.

The final six months of the 1st Battalion's tour in Ulster saw a considerable increase in tension across the Province, following the decision of certain convicted terrorists to go on hunger strike in the Maze Prison. A campaign of civil disobedience and rioting staged by the supporters of this action came to a head in early May when Bobby Sands, the leader of those on strike and nominally a Westminster Member of Parliament, although he never took his seat, died in prison. For the next month street violence and insurrection affected nearly every area of Ulster and the Security Forces met challenge after challenge as their authority and mettle were tested. Nowhere was this more pronounced that in North Belfast when at one time the entire battalion was deployed at Girdwood Park or at other bases in the City, from where patrols operated day and night to control events. The battalion TAOR covered three Police Divisions and Colonel McLaughlan deployed a company in support of each to combat the threat of sniping and bombing attacks and to assist in the immediate follow-up of an incident. The attacks on the Security Forces were too numerous to record here but the fact that, despite a number of casualties including one guardsman badly wounded by a blast bomb in the Ardoyne but saved by the prompt reaction of a paramedic, there were no deaths is again testimony to the manner in which the 1st Battalion set about its job in those difficult and demanding days.

On 28 May the Prime Minister, Mrs Margaret Thatcher, visited Girdwood to thank the Security Forces for 'their courage, forbearance and steadfastness'; she looked every man she met in the eye, shook his hand firmly and thanked him for what he had done.

In June RSM Beck handed over to RSM Macfarlane, leaving the battalion briefly before being commissioned and returning as the Transport Officer. A wise man, much respected and trusted, RSM Beck was the ideal person to take the battalion to Northern Ireland where the twin pressures of operational demand and security constraints could so easily have boiled over had they not been so well controlled by those in charge. RSM Beck was a key member of this team and, judging by the results in 1981, it is hardly surprising that he is today a Lieutenant Colonel Quartermaster, having originally joined the 2nd Battalion in Kenya in 1963.

During July and August rioting and attacks on patrols again broke out as three more Republican prisoners in the Maze went on hunger strike and subsequently died. Although some of these attacks were as vicious as those experienced in May, one patrol in Etna Drive on 20 August sustaining four casualties following a blast bomb attack, while two days later three NCOs were wounded in a similar incident, the level of violence was less pronounced and subsided once the hunger strike was abandoned.

At the end of September His Royal Highness the Colonel visited Aldergrove and Girdwood and met a large number of the battalion and its families. Six weeks later without any further operational alarms the battalion handed over its TAOR and Alexander Barracks to the 1st Battalion The Royal Green Jackets and went on leave prior to flying to Hong Kong in time for Christmas, its task in Ulster successfully completed.

2nd Battalion Once re-established in Chelsea and this time sharing the barracks with the 1st Battalion Irish Guards, the 2nd Battalion immersed itself once more in public duties. In February, 1981, it was announced that the battalion's posting to Ballykelly would not take place, a decision which at the time elicited no marked reaction, probably because days later the battalion departed to train in Kenya for six weeks. For their part the battalion's wives were rather pleased. The prospect of Ballykelly did not appeal while for some the thought of losing a well paid job in London appealed even less. Exercise STRIDENT CALL followed a not-dissimilar pattern to the 1st Battalion's Exercise GRAND PRIX in 1979 and in the words of Colonel Clavering provided 'a marvellous break from public duties'; training concentrated upon improving basic infantry skills and companies rotated through a series of exercises held in the vicinity of Mount Kenya and Archer's Post. Companies and platoons were made to operate with the minimum of transport and other support under harsh conditions and the experience gained in Kenya in 1981 was to prove invaluable a year later when the battalion found itself fighting in the equally inhospitable but totally different environment of the Falkland Islands.

This training was followed by a period of leave at the coast and a number of adventure training camps all of which were established close to Game Reserves and organized by Lieutenant Chisholm Wallace. Platoons assisted the Park Authorities by renovating boundary fences or clearing fallen timber blocking roads and bridges and, in the Aberdares Reserve, participated in anti-poaching patrols in return for which they were allowed unrestricted access to game lodges and parks. In parallel the pipers and drummers beat retreat across Kenya, always a popular event and especially appreciated by those expatriates still living in the country.

The battalion went to Kenya at a strength of 650, of which 150 were attached for the duration of the exercise, the latter including a platoon of the Irish Guards commanded by Lieutenant Michael Morrisey who had served with the battalion in Belfast. St Patrick's Day on 17 March was celebrated in true 'Mick' style, when, as recorded by the Adjutant, 'the Commanding Officer presented shamrock on behalf of Her Majesty Queen Elizabeth The Queen Mother'.

A Guard of Honour for King Khaled of Saudi Arabia at Victoria Station on 9 June found by Right Flank and commanded by Major Douglas Erskine Crum and the provision of Numbers Seven and Eight Guards on the Birthday Parade four days later meant that the battalion was again involved in ceremonial duties as soon as it returned to London. As Her Majesty The Queen rode up the Mall towards Horse Guards just before 1100 hours on 13 June a man in the crowd fired six blank rounds in her direction from a starting pistol. Lance Corporal Galloway of Left Flank, who was streetlining in the vicinity immediately forced his way into the crowd and apprehended the man involved and held him at the point of his bayonet until joined by the police. The Queen, momentarily startled by the incident, carried on as if nothing untoward had happened while for the next few days Lance Corporal Galloway attracted considerable media attention! Sadly there was no official recognition of his brave conduct by Buckingham Palace. The remainder of the summer months was taken up with more ceremonial duties, including the wedding of Their Royal Highnesses the Prince and Princess of Wales, and some training on Salisbury Plain.

Earlier in July the battalion had taken steps to strengthen its links with HMS *Ardent*, a Royal Navy Amazon Class frigate with which the Regiment was twinned, whose Captain at the time was Commander Alan West. Not every unit in the Army was fortunate to have established such close links with a Naval ship and considerable efforts were made to cement the link. Unfortunately *Ardent* was to be sunk with heavy loss of life during hostilities in 1982.

The last six months of 1981 saw a number of personalities change in the Regiment, principal amongst them Colonel Iain Ferguson who handed over his duties as Lieutenant Colonel Commanding in the late Summer to Colonel James Dunsmure and went to become the Deputy Chairman and Director of the Royal Tournament, that annual event at Earls Court when the three Services parade before the public with each in turn taking the lead in portraying the work and traditions of its men and women. Preceding him by a few days was RSM Wilkie who was relieved in mid-June by RSM MacKenzie, while in the middle of October Lieutenant Colonel Michael Scott assumed command of the 2nd Battalion from Colonel Johnny Clavering. It was perhaps ironic that the latter's final week in command should be overshadowed by an IRA atrocity outside Chelsea Barracks when the coach carrying the dismounting Tower Guard, found by the Irish Guards for the last time before moving to Germany, was blown up by a terrorist device. Several Irish Guardsmen were seriously injured, as was Lieutenant Fred Moody, the 2nd Battalion Families Officer, who was passing at the time. For Colonel Clavering, whose own tour in Ulster a year previously had been so successful, it must have been a stark reminder that the ability of the terrorist to strike remained as lethal as ever.

CHAPTER EIGHT

WAR IN THE SOUTH ATLANTIC

2nd Battalion: London-The Falkland Islands

1982
On 16 March the Sultan of Oman, Sayid Qaboos, began a three-day state visit to Britain. The 2nd Battalion provided a number of half-companies to line the processional route and Colonel Michael Scott and Captain Mark Bullough, his Adjutant, were mounted, since the former was in command of all troops in The Mall. A suspect car bomb was found in the vicinity of the route and as a result the Royal Procession was diverted along Birdcage Walk, an occurrence unprecedented even in 1982. As a consequence the street liners had to be dispersed in order to remove them from possible danger and Colonel Scott held what was in effect a mounted 'O' Group in The Mall; RSM MacKenzie later recalled the difficulty of trying to hold a serious conversation with officers mounted on horses.

While the battalion was concentrating on such ceremonial duties, events which were to have a profound influence on the lives of its soldiers were unfolding elsewhere. For a number of years the Argentinian Government had claimed sovereignty over the Falkland Islands in the South Atlantic some 300 miles from the South American mainland. Although the islands had been first settled by the British as far back as 1766 and had thereafter been incorporated into the British Empire, their colonial status had long been disputed by Argentina. After 150 years of comparative peace, and despite the strongly expressed views of the islanders that they wished to remain under British rule, throughout the Seventies and early Eighties the Argentinian Government had pressed its claim, finally threatening military action if some accommodation was not reached.

On 2 April, 1982, Argentinian Special Forces landed near the capital, Port Stanley, and, following spirited resistance by the small Royal Marine detachment based there, quickly overwhelmed the defences. In London news of the invasion and subsequent surrender by the Governor, Mr Rex Hunt, was initially received with disbelief and subsequently with anger. A highly charged debate in the House of Commons on 3 April was followed by an announcement from the Prime Minister that a naval task force was being prepared as a prelude to

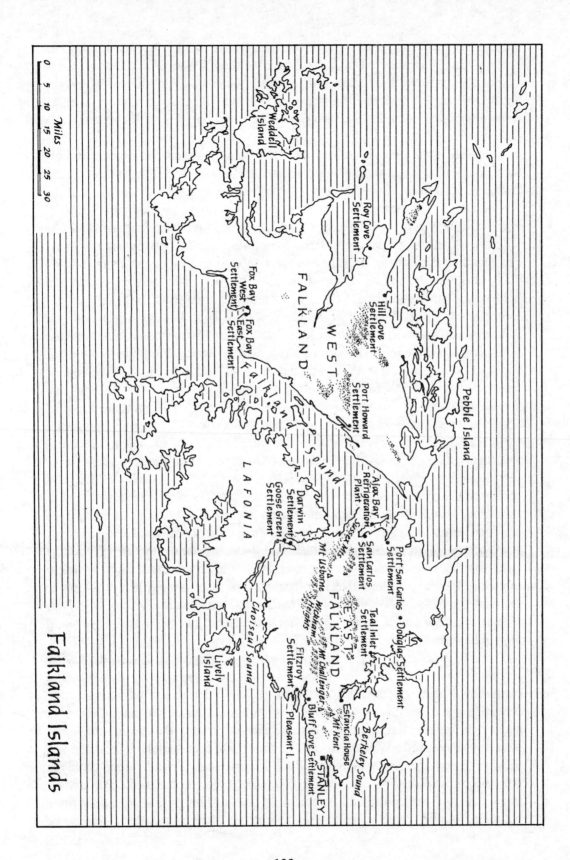

Falkland Islands

the mounting of an operation to retake the Islands. Within the week a Carrier Battle Group, commanded by Rear Admiral Sandy Woodward and comprising a large fleet of Royal Navy and civilian ships, began an 8,000 mile voyage to the South Atlantic. A few days later 3rd Commando Brigade, made up of three Royal Marine commandos and two parachute battalions, followed aboard the SS *Canberra*.

Even before the brigade sailed, plans to assemble a second brigade to follow the Commandos south were being discussed in London and it was soon decided that the UKLF 'out of area' brigade, 5th Infantry Brigade at Aldershot, was the logical choice to command such a force. At this juncture nobody knew what its task would be nor indeed whether either it or 3rd Commando Brigade would be required to fight to retake the islands. There was a strong presumption in many quarters that diplomatic negotiations or a move by the Argentinians to back down in the face of a clear British determination to recover territory considered to be sovereign would obviate the need to resort to arms.

5th Infantry Brigade, commanded by Brigadier Tony Wilson, a former Light Infantryman, normally consisted of the 2nd and 3rd Battalions of the Parachute Regiment and the 1st/7th Gurkha Rifles. Since the two parachute battalions had already been dispatched under command of 3rd Commando Brigade, immediate decisions had therefore to be made in respect of their replacements and early on the 1st Battalion Welsh Guards at Pirbright was selected to join the Brigade. This was an entirely logical decision since the battalion had just completed a period of Spearhead duty. However, selection of a second battalion was less easy and involved the staffs in the Ministry of Defence and at Wilton in a series of complicated assessments, during which every battalion within UKLF was considered. Brigadier Christopher Airy, at the time the Assistant Chief of Staff at Wilton, recalls 'his staff doing their sums on "baulk" for units about to go to or return from Northern Ireland, overseas exercises, regimental commitments and Spearhead, etc, something which was done constantly in the selection of units for any commitment. It was obviously right to continue these clear-cut rules for Operation CORPORATE. In any event when we applied our rules to the need for the selection of a second battalion, 2SG was clearly the one. It was as simple as that but of course it was not actually simple and it raised problems for public duties.'

The Major General, Major General Desmond Langley, had already readily agreed to the selection of the Welsh Guards; there were in April, 1982, five battalions within London District and it was calculated that, taking into consideration other known commitments, public duties could still be covered, albeit that the number of Guards on the Queen's Birthday Parade in June might have to be reduced. When a second London District battalion was selected these pressures inevitably increased, but, not wishing to plead public duties as a reason for not acceding, General Langley accepted the decision, although he knew that to mount public duties for other than a short period with only three battalions would bring considerable problems. Much later there was some internal Army criticism of the decision to send what some saw as an 'elitist' force of Marines, Parachutists, Guardsmen and Gurkhas to the Falklands, but such sentiments were hardly justified, given that the planning was logical and widely discussed, and that the execution of it was sustained satisfactorily.

Colonel Scott and his battalion were of course unaware of such deliberations. Although the Commanding Officer was warned in confidence on 6 April of the possibility of involvement, it was not until 15 April that the battalion was officially informed that a week later it would become part of 5th Infantry Brigade for possible deployment to the South Atlantic. Within the battalion the immediate reaction was one of heartfelt relief that the Major General's Inspection scheduled for the next day was cancelled. The transition from public duties began at once and the battalion started to re-role and to equip itself as quickly as the staff could locate equipment and weapons not normally held such as, for example, Clansman radios and .50 Browning machine guns. A series of Treasury inspired economy measures over preceding years meant that 5th Infantry Brigade, unlike 3rd Commando Brigade, did not possess a full complement of supporting units and these had to be identified and prepared at the same time as the Brigade was attempting to organize and train itself for operations in a theatre about which relatively little was known. While some subsequent criticism of the way in which the Brigade staff operated was no doubt partly justified, the fact that many of its administrative units had to be provided from elsewhere and in some instances de-stocked and then re-stocked to suit the Brigade's requirements should not be overlooked.

At Chelsea the battalion got on with its preparations with the minimum of fuss. Few really believed that they would actually leave Britain (a view apparently shared at a high level within the Ministry of Defence) and, if they did, the battalion's role was expected to be that of garrison troops, the Argentinians being assumed to have surrendered long before 5th Infantry Brigade could arrive to influence events.

From 20 April to 3 May the brigade trained at Brecon under ground conditions as similar to those in the Falkland Islands as it is possible to find in Britain, although the weather was far too good and not at all like that usually encountered during a Falklands winter. At company level the training was tough and testing and soldiers learnt to operate with minimum support and to become self-reliant and confident in the constant use of live ammunition. Major John Kiszely, who commanded Left Flank, told his guardsmen that the more that people said that they would not go to the Falklands, the more probable it was that they would and that they should prepare accordingly. Although Colonel Scott felt that his soldiers had learnt a lot very quickly, including about themselves, he found the training somewhat disjointed and unsatisfactory in that it did not put commanders and staffs at battalion level under any form of pressure. Return to London on 3 May was followed by last-minute preparations and three days' leave to enable people to say farewell to wives and relatives before at 0300 hours on the morning of 12 May the battalion paraded on the square at Chelsea Barracks to travel to Southampton to embark in RMS *Queen Elizabeth 2*.

Departure from Britain

At 0400 hours – with a real dash of style – General Langley and his ADC arrived at Chelsea Barracks on horseback to wish the battalion well, while, in the words of Padre Angus Smith, 'We were very touched when the officers of the 2nd Battalion Grenadier Guards came with champagne to toast our departure'. At Southampton the battalion embarked in the *QE2* along with the majority of 5th Infantry Brigade and in mid-afternoon the ship sailed, being given an emotional send-off by many families and friends as well as by the Regimental Band. Once clear of the Solent all on board settled into a routine which provided for almost non-stop training; map reading, first aid, aircraft recognition and battle procedure were all practised, while fitness training round and round *QE2*'s deck with each man completing a daily stint of anything up to two hours was a constant activity for everybody. To many it seemed bizarre to be going to war on a major cruise liner, especially as the conditions on board were far from spartan and the crew attentive to a fault, and this added to the air of unreality that afflicted many people who still could not quite come to terms with the fact that they might soon be fighting the Argentinians.

Although, before leaving Britain it had been made abundantly clear that 5th Infantry Brigade was going south as a reserve for the Commander Land Forces, Major General Jeremy Moore, and not simply to garrison the islands once captured, many still envisaged not sailing beyond Ascension Island. News of what was happening elsewhere filtered through to *QE2* via the BBC World Service and people learnt of the diplomatic efforts to reach a settlement before a major military clash could occur. They also learnt of the Task Force's success in destroying Argentinian shipping, the raid on Pebble Island on 14 May when the Special Air Service Regiment destroyed a number of enemy aircraft and the tragedy when a Sea King helicopter lost power and crashed killing twenty men of the same regiment.

20 May was Ascension Day and appropriately *QE2* arrived off Ascension Island that morning. Owing to the threat of hostile submarine activity the *QE2* and her escorts did not anchor and the opportunity to get men ashore to stretch their legs and for the Quartermasters and their staffs to check on the battalion's freight and vehicles which were being carried on one of the accompanying car ferries, was lost. This was a particular blow since stores and freight had been loaded in Britain without much thought and several discrepancies which had come to light after leaving Southampton could have been rectified at Ascension had the opportunity been provided. General Moore and his staff came aboard *QE2* at Ascension and this, coupled with a realization that United States Secretary of State Haig's shuttle diplomacy stood increasingly little chance of finding a peace formula acceptable to both sides, caused most of those aboard *QE2* to recognize that they were probably not going to turn around. Training continued as the ship sailed south but the weather became progressively colder.

136

On 22 May came the news of 3rd Commando Brigade's landings the previous day at San Carlos, followed almost at once by the disclosure that HMS *Ardent*, the Regiment's affiliated ship, had been sunk in Falkland Sound. On 23 May 5th Infantry Brigade was placed on active service, dispelling any lingering doubts that the battalion might still not be involved. Four days later *QE2* arrived off Grytviken in South Georgia and rendezvoused with *Canberra* which was to take the Scots and Welsh Guards on board for the last stage of their long voyage from Southampton. The original plan had been for *QE2* to take 5th Infantry Brigade direct to the Falkland Islands but, in the light of the successful Argentinian attack on the *Atlantic Conveyor* and the loss of HMS *Coventry*, *Antelope* and *Ardent* between 22 and 25 May, it was decided that *QE2* should not be risked so close to the battle zone, a matter of great disappointment to her crew but a wise decision nonetheless.

'Cross decking' between *QE2* and *Canberra* completed, the ship sailed at 2000 hours on 28 May for East Falkland, although not before the battalion pipers had welcomed aboard *QE2* the survivors of Ardent who were returning to Britain. As *Canberra* steamed towards the battle zone there came the news of 2 PARA's heroic battle at Goose Green and the progress of 3 PARA and 45 Commando advancing on foot towards Port Stanley.

Canberra sailed into San Carlos Water on the morning of 2 June and within a *San Carlos* short time the battalion, along with the 1st Battalion Welsh Guards, had been disembarked and landed across Blue Beach adjacent to the San Carlos Settlement. Before leaving *Canberra* Colonel Scott and his company commanders were briefed by the Second-in-Command on the deployment to be adopted on landing. Major Mackay-Dick, who had transferred to HMS *Antrim* while the battalion was still on the *QE2* in order that he could liaise with the 5th Infantry Brigade staff, had arrived at San Carlos three days earlier and had been given orders by Brigadier Wilson that the battalion was to dig in about a mile to the east of the settlement and await further instructions.

Once ashore Battalion Headquarters and the companies started the frustrating work of trying to prepare a defensive position capable of withstanding attack from the air in peat soil so wet that even a trench a foot deep quickly became inundated; work on the position continued for the three days that the 2nd Battalion was at San Carlos and in the end the protection it afforded depended more on earth butts built up using peat and stones than on trenches.

San Carlos Settlement was also the Maintenance Area for 3rd Commando Brigade, a mass of containers and palletized loads seemingly dumped at random in what had quickly become a sea of mud. The area was guarded by 40 Commando Royal Marines which, now that 5th Infantry Brigade had landed, fully expected to be released in order to join its sister commandos further to the east in the battle for Port Stanley.

Elsewhere on 2 June there were other developments. That day Mrs Thatcher told the Argentinians that a battle for Port Stanley could be avoided if they agreed to a phased withdrawal over a ten to fourteen day period. At the same time 3rd Commando Brigade had begun to consolidate its positions some fifteen miles to the west of Port Stanley with 42 Commando by then firm on Mount Kent, a feature which dominated most of the ground to the east, and with 3 PARA complete at Estancia House. To their south, Headquarters 5th Infantry Brigade and the 1st/7th Gurkha Rifles, which had landed two days before the remainder of the brigade, had established themselves in the Darwin area.

Meanwhile, back above San Carlos Settlement, the 2nd Battalion Scots Guards remained in its newly completed positions, uncertain as to the plans of Brigadier Wilson or General Moore. Colonel Scott fully expected his battalion to be ordered to take responsibility for the security of the Maintenance Area, thereby releasing 40 Commando for other tasks. In the meantime, after two days ashore, the Welsh Guards set out to march east over the Sussex Mountains to join those elements of 5th Infantry Brigade which were beginning to assemble in the Darwin area in order to open up an axis along a southern route towards Port Stanley. This well-intentioned endeavour to save time and ease the strain on grossly overloaded sea and air transport resources unfortunately failed and the battalion had eventually to return to San Carlos.

However, while this attempt was being made, other developments had taken place on the southern flank when the settlement at Bluff Cove was secured without a fight. On learning that Argentinian Forces were no longer occupying either Fitzroy or Bluff Cove Brigadier Wilson had immediately ordered B Company of 2 PARA to fly forward from Goose Green to secure Bluff Cove. This bold move completed without incident, other than for the fact that the Chinook helicopter carrying the parachutists was nearly brought under fire from a friendly Observation Post located high up on Mount Challenger which was unaware that 5th Infantry Brigade was operating so far to the east, it became imperative that the successful securing of Bluff Cove should be reinforced as quickly as possible. In one stroke 5th Infantry Brigade had placed itself alongside 3rd Commando Brigade to the north and, once fully deployed, would be in a position to play an equal part in the final battle. Brigadier Wilson was determined that this advantage should not be lost.

Back at San Carlos Colonel Scott was warned on 4 June that the battalion was to be moved to Bluff Cove the next day to relieve 2 PARA. This move, which was to be followed twenty-four hours later by a similar operation to get the Welsh Guards forward, began at dawn on 5 June with the battalion moving to Blue Beach. By mid-afternoon it was eventually embarked on HMS *Intrepid*, one of two Assault Landing ships in the Task Force which carried four integral inshore landing craft known by their abbreviated designation as LCUs. These craft were moored within *Intrepid*'s stern dock during a passage and, once floated out, could land troops and stores inshore either across a beach or alongside a jetty. Once aboard the battalion was able to dry out after three days of heavy rain and incessant wind, for many this being the first opportunity to clean up since they had landed on 2 June.

However, before *Intrepid* sailed the Commanding Officer was summoned to fly forward to a Brigade 'O' Group at Darwin and command of the battalion duly passed to Major Mackay-Dick who was to control the move to Bluff Cove. Colonel Scott had been looking forward as much as anybody to drying out on *Intrepid* after three nights exposed to the Falklands weather above San Carlos and while there was no option but for him to join his Brigade Commander, seeing the looks of intense disappointment on the faces of Major Roger Gwyn, his Artillery Battery Commander, and Captain Tim Spicer, the Battalion Operations Officer, he charitably left them behind and flew alone to Darwin.

The plan for the move to Bluff Cove was in theory straightforward and involved *Intrepid* carrying the battalion around the south-western extremity of East Falkland as far as a point somewhere to the north of Lively Island from where her four LCUs would complete the last thirty miles to Bluff Cove. *Intrepid* sailed at last light and at 2230 hours, having reached a position south of Lively Island but still some distance short of the previously arranged drop-off point, proceeded to transfer the battalion, its equipment and ammunition into her four LCUs. The earlier decision not to go beyond a point to the north of Lively Island had been prompted by a wish not to hazard any of the Task Force's capital ships by exposing them to attack from a shore-based Argentinian Exocet missile system earlier identified in the Port Stanley area. Taken at the highest level back in Britain, this decision was doubtless fully justified; however, the eventual decision to transfer the battalion into LCUs some miles south of the original drop-off point added considerably to the length of time that the battalion had to endure sea and weather conditions for which those craft were not designed, and has never been fully explained.

Half an hour before midnight the four LCUs sailed out of *Intrepid*'s stern dock and the latter departed with her escorts to return to San Carlos. Command of the LCUs was vested in Major Ewen Southby-Tailyour, a Royal Marines officer with considerable experience of the Falkland Islands shoreline and the hundreds of small islands and inlets which litter their coastal waters. Packed tightly with up to 130 men in each LCU, the small flotilla set off unescorted and without any information as to what it might expect to encounter en route. Shortly after getting his LCUs under way Major Southby-Tailyour told Major Mackay-Dick, 'We will make it to Bluff Cove. It will be a long passage. . . . If we see another ship it will be Argentinian. There is no food. Smoking can take place below the level of the catwalks.' Thus began a voyage estimated originally to take no more than two hours and which, had the earlier drop off-point been used, would probably have taken around four hours under good conditions but which in the end involved over seven hours' exposure to the worst elements of the South Atlantic. However the battalion was on its way and that was all that mattered.

The first of several alarms came approximately two hours after leaving *Intrepid* when a number of starshells burst over the flotilla. Having been assured by the Navy that there would be no friendly ships in the area, it was assumed that the fire was coming either from an Argentinian warship, something which seemed unlikely in view of the small part that the Argentinian Navy had played in the War since the sinking of the battleship *Belgrano* on 2 May, or from ground forces on East Falkland.

Major Mackay-Dick who was in the LCU carrying Left Flank and some of Battalion Headquarters recalls that, 'About two hours after setting out we saw flares to the west which seemed to be coming from the land. Then we started hearing whistles over our heads and realized that someone was firing starshells at us and they were coming closer. As no friendly ships were supposed to be in the area we were worried that the starshells might be Argentinian, and all the machine guns, which we had placed along the sides of the landing craft were manned in case we came under air attack. It was still a very clear night and the possibility of a Pucara [Argentinian ground attack aircraft] attack from Port Stanley could not be discounted, particularly as we were vulnerable to Argentinian radars operating on the high ground west of Stanley.' RSM MacKenzie, aboard the same LCU, remembers the incident vividly with someone saying after the second starshell had burst, 'They'll fire two of those and then the real one comes,' a prediction which fortunately proved to be mistaken.

Twelve years after the incident it is impossible to be sure of what exactly happened, but certain facts are not disputed. There were no Argentinian ships in the area, nor, despite the justifiable fears of those on the LCUs, was there a serious threat of enemy air attack. However, there were two Royal Navy warships in the vicinity of Lively Island – HMS *Cardiff* and HMS *Arrow* – and it was these which would appear to have illuminated the LCUs by firing starshells. How or why these ships came to be in the area unbeknown even to the Task Force's Commodore Amphibious Warfare, the officer responsible for sanctioning *Intrepid*'s operation that night, will probably never be known. In war, communications can become difficult, assumptions have to be made, incorrect deductions are later drawn and as a result a disaster of the sort which so nearly befell the battalion, can easily occur.

At the time none of this was clear to Major Southby-Tailyour or Major Mackay-Dick and, following hurried consultations, the latter attempted to make contact with Brigade Headquarters to clarify the situation. Fearful of further attack and the loss of his valuable complement of guardsmen, Major Southby-Tailyour advised putting into Choiseul Sound in order to hide his landing craft among the islands there. After due consideration and having been reassured by the Brigade staff that the battalion was expected by 2 PARA that morning at Bluff Cove, Major Mackay-Dick decided that they should press on; his appreciation led him to conclude that little would be gained from turning into Choiseul Sound where they were just as likely to be caught in the open in daylight and that to move in that direction ran the risk of a clash with the Gurkhas who were in the process of clearing the area either side of the Sound of remaining Argentinian troops. His final contention that in any event the ships which had fired at the flotilla had not been identified as enemy was confirmed

37. "We tried to sleep with sleeping bags and ponchos. It was freezing cold and almost strange and unreal after the toils and struggles of the previous night." (Page 153). Padre Angus Smith on Tumbledown after the battle.

38. "Confirmatory Orders were given in the afternoon, soldiers checked and re-checked their equipment, plans were rehearsed and, when nothing more remained to be done, everybody simply waited for H Hour." (Page 148). In the Assembly Area below Goat Ridge. Guardsman Clark and Captain Tim Spicer, the Battalion Operations Officer, are on the left.

39. "When at 1130 and 1145 hours a second and third wave of four Skyhawks came in to attack, the battalion, already at Red Alert, was ready for them." (Page 143). Lance Corporal Urban of the Corps of Drums mans a general purpose machine gun, pintle-mounted for use in the anti-aircraft role.

40. "The battalion transferred to four VC10 aircraft to fly to RAF Brize Norton and the greatest welcome any battalion of the Regiment has received for many a long year." (Page 155). The Colonel greets the returning 2nd Battalion. Behind him is Colonel James Dunsmure and on his left Major Iain Dalzel Job. Also in the photograph are, left to right, Admiral Fieldhouse (in overall command of operations in the South Atlantic), General Kitson (C in C UKLF) and Major General Langley (GOC London District).

41. "Its new home was Stanley Fort, a spacious barracks perched at the end of a peninsula on the south side of Hong Kong Island in one of the less heavily inhabited areas of the Colony." (Page 156). The 1st Battalion on parade at Stanley in 1982.

42. "The intention was that the battalion should advance the length of Lantau Island clearing enemy positioned on the various peaks which lay along its axis." (Page 161). Lieutenant Malcolm MacGregor leads his platoon through a Chinese village during Exercise CROSSED KUKRIS.

43. "Throughout its time in Cyprus the battalion was involved in all ceremonial occasions and in both 1984 and 1985 the Regimental Colour was trooped on the Queen's Birthday Parade." (Page 168). Major General Sir Desmond Langley inspects the 2nd Battalion on parade, accompanied by Lieutenant Colonel Iain Mackay-Dick. Captain Johnny Stewart, the Adjutant, is on the left.

44. "1987 was the turn for the 2nd Battalion's Queen's Colour to be trooped." (Page 181). 2nd Lieutenant Willie Swinton is the Ensign and Lieutenant Alastair Mathewson the Subaltern of the Escort. The Birthday Parade that year was the first occasion that Her Majesty The Queen did not ride on parade and the last upon which the self-loading rifle was carried.

soon afterwards when two British warships closed on the LCUs and, having received an affirmative response to a signalled challenge, turned away to the south-east.

The flotilla of LCUs then continued on its way, encountering increasingly heavy seas which broke over the sides of the open landing craft drenching all those standing on the vehicle decks. Rest was impossible and, as the wind got up and an unpleasant swell started to run, the journey became a nightmare. At 0545 hours, two hours after it was expected, the battalion was finally put ashore at Bluff Cove in pouring rain. For many the voyage was the worst part of the whole campaign, one guardsman remarking afterwards, 'Those LCUs were awful and it's a wonder we weren't all thoroughly sick. I suppose the fact that we were all so alone and cold and didn't know whether we might not be fired on at any moment kept our minds off feeling ill.' Major Mackay-Dick expressed similar sentiments about the voyage, 'I, personally, was wearing six layers of clothing on my top half and four on my legs, and even I, who had spent most of the time on the bridge was soaked through to the skin. Perhaps we were lucky that the weather was foul when we landed because it prevented enemy air attacks and it gave us the chance to dry out in the sheep-shearing sheds and the Kilmartins' house at Bluff Cove.'

In war those who take risks do so in order to win or to exploit an advantage already within their grasp; after the unplanned capture of Bluff Cove, it was obviously imperative that 5th Infantry Brigade should be brought forward as quickly as possible. Moving the battalion in *Intrepid* was sensible but was it right to transfer it into LCUs so far from its objective and to send it unprotected into waters not previously cleared and without ensuring that friendly ships in the area were warned of its presence? The gamble paid off but the credit for getting the battalion to Bluff Cove in one piece, if not necessarily fit to fight, must lie with those who that night exercised skilled seamanship in navigating a difficult shoreline and those who made the courageous decision to push ahead when the easier option might have been to turn into Choiseul Sound.

Bluff Cove is a small settlement of no more than half a dozen houses and *Bluff Cove* outbuildings, the largest of which are used for shearing sheep. Colonel Scott landed at the Settlement from Darwin shortly after the battalion and his immediate impression was that his soldiers were 'exhausted, soaking wet, cold, weighed down by their loads which were equally wet and that they would probably be incapable of fighting until they had dried out.' His orders were to relieve 2 PARA in the immediate vicinity of Bluff Cove and then to extend the defensive perimeter towards Mount Wall pending the arrival of other units of 5th Infantry Brigade.

However, his first priority was to get the battalion back on its feet after its seven and a half hour voyage in the LCUs. He therefore gained agreement from Brigadier Wilson to deploy only part of the battalion to secure Bluff Cove, while rotating the remainder through the Kilmartins' shearing sheds to dry them out.

As a result 2 PARA were relieved and withdrawn to Fitzroy and the battalion began to build a defensive position around the Settlement to protect the immediate bridgehead from air and ground attack.

With the exception of Left Flank which was deployed to an area of higher ground across the inlet to the east of Bluff Cove, the rest of the battalion soon dried out and, having recovered its equilibrium, on 7 June G Company replaced Left Flank which was withdrawn to the Settlement. Left Flank had passed a wretched night battered by constant wind and driving rain but had suffered not a single case of exposure, a tribute to the way in which Major Kiszely and his junior commanders led and encouraged their guardsmen as they prepared their positions. When Colonel Scott gave Major Kiszely his orders on 6 June he had made it abundantly clear that a shortage of helicopter support and the presence of a sizeable stretch of water between Left Flank's position and the rest of the battalion made it unlikely that he would be able to come to his assistance if he encountered difficulties. Minds concentrated, the company set to with a will and in the words of their Company Commander 'their performance that night gave him a great feeling of confidence for the future'. During the battalion's seven days at Bluff Cove it was given unstinting help by the local settlers who provided landrovers and trailers to help move ammunition and stores around the area and made their homes and buildings available; Kevin and Diane Kilmartin, Tim Dobbyns and Mike Mackay begrudged the battalion nothing and will long be remembered for the support and advice they gave.

On 7 June orders were given for the battalion to patrol to the east of Bluff Cove in order to locate and destroy two suspected Argentinian 105mm guns and a radar. This was the first offensive mission given to the battalion and the task was entrusted to the Reconnaissance Platoon commanded by Captain Rory Scott. The platoon deployed the same day and, following a careful reconnaissance of the area, established a firm base and Observation Post at Port Harriet House from where it was able to watch the Argentinian positions on Mount Harriet less than 3,000 yards to its north. During the forty-eight hours that the platoon was at Port Harriet House it was unsuccessful in locating the enemy guns or radar, despite a close search of the target area. In all probability they had been moved by the Argentinians before the platoon was tasked to find them and no firm information as to their whereabouts was ever given to the battalion. However, the real value to accrue from the operation came from the intelligence which the platoon was able to obtain from the excellence of Port Harriet House as a vantage point from which to observe the enemy positions in the area.

Late on 8 June a party commanded by Major Richard Bethell, Headquarter Company Commander and an officer who had recently served with the Special Air Service Regiment, was dispatched in two civilian landrovers to make contact with Port Harriet House and insert a four-man Special Air Service Regiment patrol into the area to supplement the intelligence-gathering operation. Unfortunately one of the vehicles hit an anti-personnel mine, blowing off a wheel, and the party had to withdraw to find an alternative route forward; unsuccessful in this second attempt, they eventually withdrew to Bluff Cove having failed to get through to the Reconnaissance Platoon.

The driving rain and powerful wind of the previous few days abated on the night of 7 June and, as so often with the Falklands weather, they were replaced with blue skies and clear visibility. During the night a second attempt to move the remainder of the Welsh Guards from San Carlos had been successful and by dawn on 8 June LSLs *Sir Galahad* and *Sir Tristram* were both anchored off Fitzroy discharging soldiers and stores for 5th Infantry Brigade. Offloading was still in progress when shortly after 1100 hours five Argentinian Skyhawk aircraft turned west over Port Pleasant and attacked the two vessels which at the time were undefended by any anti-aircraft system. As a result both ships were hit, *Sir Galahad* quickly catching fire, and frantic efforts were made by everybody who could be spared to help with the rescue of the wounded and dying from both vessels. Fifty people lost their lives in the attack, including thirty-eight members of the 1st Battalion Welsh Guards Group, and over ninety people were wounded. Minutes before the aircraft began their bombing run TSM Taylor, a member of the Technical Quartermaster's staff at A2 Echelon at Fitzroy, had been dispatched to *Sir Tristram* to collect supplies urgently required at Bluff Cove; at the time of the attack his landing craft was alongside *Sir Galahad* and, unhurt himself, he helped to get a number of people off the burning vessel. The tragedy at Fitzroy has been fully documented elsewhere and it is not for this regimental history to analyse what happened or why, or to pass judgement; suffice it to say that mercifully no Scots Guardsmen were killed or wounded in the attack, although 8 June will remain in the collective memory of the battalion as a day when fate struck a cruel blow against the Task Force and particularly against its sister battalion, the Welsh Guards. The aircraft which caused such devastation at Fitzroy arrived almost without warning and the battalion at Bluff Cove had no time to react.

When at 1130 and 1145 hours a second and third wave of four Skyhawks came in to attack, the battalion, already at Red Alert, was ready for them and during the course of about thirty seconds over 18,600 rounds were fired at the Argentinian aircraft. Even Pipe Major Riddell fired his SMG and at least two and possibly a third aircraft were claimed as having been shot down by the battalion. Lance Corporal Winfield, firing a .50 Browning machine gun, was personally credited with one confirmed kill. The third wave of Skyhawks saw a wall of tracer ahead and dropped their spare fuel tanks and five parachute-retarded 500 lb bombs just in front of Right Flank's position. This was the first occasion on which the battalion took the offensive since landing on East Falkland and, as well as causing people to feel that they had at last become involved in the fight against the Argentinians, it helped to avenge the dreadful events of a few hours earlier at Fitzroy.

On 9 June Brigadier Wilson met his commanding officers to discuss the part to be played by 5th Infantry Brigade in General Moore's plan for the final

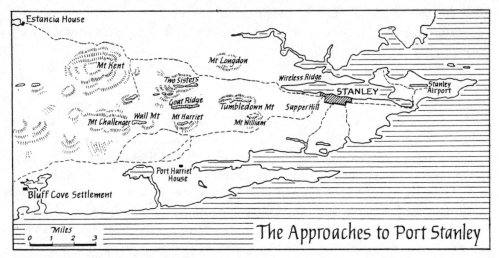

The Approaches to Port Stanley

advance to Port Stanley. This was to be a two-phase operation, with 3rd Commando Brigade attacking Mounts Harriet and Longdon and Two Sisters on the night of 11 June, following which the next night 2 PARA was to capture Wireless Ridge and 5th Infantry Brigade was to secure Tumbledown Mountain and Mount William and then to exploit forward to Sapper Hill. At his meeting on 9 June Brigadier Wilson directed that, in conjunction with the 3rd Commando Brigade attacks to the north on the night of 11 June, the 7th Gurkhas were to patrol against the enemy holding Tumbledown and William with the aim of securing both features if the opportunity arose. If they were unsuccessful, the Scots Guards and the Gurkhas were to be prepared to mount attacks on Tumbledown and William respectively from a south-westerly direction on the night of 12 June.

Planning for the attack on Tumbledown Mountain

Colonel Scott returned to Bluff Cove and pondered the task given to his battalion, in all probability the only major engagement that it was likely to fight before Port Stanley was reached. A map appreciation told him that the capture of Tumbledown could result in the remaining Argentinian positions becoming untenable, since Tumbledown and William to its south dominated the main approaches to the town. At this stage there had been no ground reconnaissance by the battalion of the enemy positions on Tumbledown and there was no contact intelligence other than that gained by the Port Harriet Observation Post over the previous forty-eight hours. In particular little was known about the extent or depth of the Argentinian minefields, estimated to have been laid to the south and south-west of Tumbledown; what information there was on the minefields had been discovered by the Reconnaissance Platoon, earning it a commendation from Brigadier Wilson who described it as 'some of the best intelligence we ever received'. The Commanding Officer therefore decided to hold a briefing for his subordinate commanders and, wishing to include the Reconnaissance Platoon Commander, sent a helicopter to Port Harriet House to bring him to Bluff Cove, despite the fact that such a move could risk compromising the Observation Post.

144

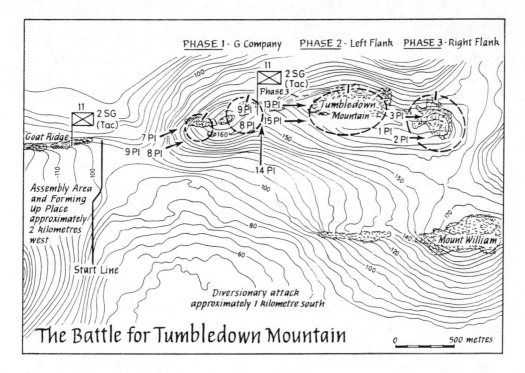

PHASE 1 - G Company   PHASE 2 - Left Flank   PHASE 3 - Right Flank

The Battle for Tumbledown Mountain

0   500 metres

The briefing was held in the loft above the Kilmartins' garage and the Commanding Officer gave those present details of the overall plan and the battalion's role in the 5th Infantry Brigade operation. Information was sifted and options were discussed in the light of what information there was, but it was probably the advice of the Royal Engineer Troop Commander, Lieutenant Peter McManus, which carried the greatest weight. In his view it would take most of the night to clear lanes through the minefields south of Tumbledown and, if his time appreciation was correct, this would mean the battalion being exposed to the enemy at the foot of the Tumbledown feature at first light on the morning of 13 June. Moreover, the Argentinians were known to be well entrenched with several machine guns covering the minefields to the south, this seemingly being the direction from which they expected to be attacked. Clearly such an attack in daylight would stand little chance of success and, having heard all opinions and having studied what little intelligence there was, Colonel Scott concluded that the battalion must approach Tumbledown from a different direction. Consequently he was later to recommend to Brigadier Wilson the alternative of a night attack from due west using the area between Mount Harriet and Goat Ridge from which to launch it, dependent upon 42 Commando securing those objectives on the night of 11 June. As if to reinforce the view that an attack from the south or south-west would stand little chance of success, the Argentinians had started to mortar Port Harriet House while the helicopter sent to collect Captain Scott was lifting from the ground.

After several rounds had landed uncomfortably close to the house Sergeant Allum, the Platoon Sergeant, who had assumed command in Captain Scott's

145

absence, decided that his position was no longer secure and that he must withdraw, but, because of problems with his radio, was unable to communicate his decision to Battalion Headquarters. 'We dashed out and began running chased by mortar rounds. Luckily the soft ground reduced their effect but all the same we felt very vulnerable. Our bergens were slowing us down and so we ditched them. . . . Then we saw thirty to forty Argentinians coming down off Mount Harriet. They were obviously doing a follow-up and, although they were out of effective range, we harassed them with our two light machine guns.' Eventually Sergeant Allum managed to make contact on the radio and artillery fire was brought down on Mount Harriet, but not before he and two others had themselves suffered shrapnel wounds. After breaking clean they avoided the minefield and made their way to the shoreline where Captain Scott, who had flown back from Bluff Cove as soon as the full extent of the threat to his platoon became known, met them. The three wounded were evacuated direct to Fitzroy by air after which Captain Scott extricated the remainder through another minefield to an RV with Lieutenant Innes Kerr's troop of the Blues and Royals. This was the battalion's first close engagement with the enemy and the fact that there had been casualties was not lost on the battalion. Nobody could be in any doubt that they really were at war.

Brigadier Wilson quickly agreed to Colonel Scott's recommended alterations to the plan and at 1000 hours on 11 June gave formal orders. Assuming a successful attack by 3rd Commando Brigade that night, the Scots Guards and the Gurkhas were to assemble behind Goat Ridge during 12 June; thereafter the battalion was to assault Tumbledown from the west and, once successful, 1st/7th Gurkhas were to attack William from the north, having passed around the eastern flank of Tumbledown. The Welsh Guards were to be in reserve to be ready to exploit forward to Sapper Hill, while, at the same time as the Scots Guards attacked Tumbledown, 2 PARA was to attack Wireless Ridge.

Tumbledown is a low limestone ridge rising to around 2,500 feet at its highest point. It runs west to east for approximately one and a half miles and the north face of the feature is very steep and difficult to climb. Observation showed that the western end was strongly held by an enemy company interspersed with a number of heavy machine guns with another company toward the eastern end.

However, since the eastern end of Tumbledown could not be observed from any ground held by friendly troops and because air photographic cover was inadequate, this was never confirmed. Finally there were scattered pockets of enemy to the south of Tumbledown which were assumed to be covering the minefield and the approach which the battalion would have taken had the original Brigade plan been followed. Because of the risk of a clash with 42 Commando attacking Harriet and in order not to alert the Argentinians to the direction from which they were to be attacked, it was decided not to patrol against the enemy on the night of 11 June.

Colonel Scott's plan, given to his company commanders at 1530 hours, was for a three-phase operation with companies attacking through each other in turn. G Company was to lead and to take the western section of the mountain, Left Flank the central area and the Right Flank the far end. In order to maintain surprise the attack was to be silent until first contact with the enemy when fire support from the artillery, three mortar platoons and two frigates would be available to strike predetermined targets. Finally Colonel Scott briefed Major Bethell to lead a diversionary attack against Argentinian positions on the southern side of Tumbledown Mountain adjacent to the main track to Port Stanley. The aim of this attack was to draw the attention of the Argentinians to the south and to lead them to believe that it was from that direction that the main attack was coming.

Orders given, the battalion set about preparing itself for battle. All the usual preparations were made and the A2 Echelon at Fitzroy, commanded by Captain Ewan Lawrie, had the task of bringing the battalion's last-minute requirements forward, using local tractors and trailers; this task was made more difficult because a connecting bridge had been blown by the Argentinians and could only be crossed on foot. Consequently every store had to be unloaded, carried across and reloaded on the far side. Captain Lawrie said afterwards, 'It was a time-consuming business but I wanted to make sure that the battalion lacked for nothing when the moment came.' Nor did it, and every man finally went into battle with more than enough ammunition to enable him to do what was required.

An hour before first light on 12 June the battalion was ready to move from Bluff Cove to Goat Ridge. The 3rd Commando Brigade attacks of the previous night were all going as planned although 3 PARA was still involved in a long and costly fight to capture Mount Longdon. Of more immediate interest to the Scots Guards was the capture of Mount Harriet by 42 Commando in a brilliantly executed operation thereby paving the way for their own attack on Tumbledown. Throughout the day the battalion waited at Bluff Cove but no helicopters arrived to lift them forward and at 1600 hours Colonel Scott was summoned to Fitzroy to learn what the delay was.

The one resource which was always in shortest supply throughout the Falklands Campaign was the helicopter. Ground vehicle movement being virtually impossible and movement by sea being restricted by tides and coastal conditions, helicopters provided the only real means of moving men, ammunition and equipment around the battlefield and the amount of lift available to the Land Force Commander had been sharply reduced with the sinking of the *Atlantic Conveyor* on 25 May. When Colonel Scott arrived at Brigade Headquarters late on 12 June he learnt that a higher priority had been placed on re-supplying 3rd Commando Brigade after its attacks of the previous night and that consequently there would be no move forward for his battalion that day. He also knew that the artillery ammunition to support his attack had not, by that stage, been flown forward to his guns. He therefore discussed with Brigadier Wilson the implications and, despite considerable pressure from General Moore to mount the attack on Tumbledown at the earliest opportunity in order to relieve the pressure on the Commando Brigade, some of whose units had by then been on the mountains for nearly a fortnight and were now being regularly shelled by the Argentinians, both finally agreed that an attack in daylight was not feasible and that the operation should be postponed twenty-four hours until the night of 13 June. This decision was reluctantly accepted by the Land Forces Commander.

The postponement of twenty-four hours proved to be a godsend. Since nobody in the battalion had previously been able to view Tumbledown, the delay enabled all commanders to go forward to Goat Ridge to observe the objective and such enemy positions as could be identified. The fact that commanders were able to see the ground may well have made the difference between success and failure and it certainly instilled confidence in those who were to lead the attack. As the battalion was flown forward all commanders down to section level were therefore taken up to Goat Ridge while in the Assembly Area companies dug in and awaited final orders. Intermittent shelling occurred during the day, Lance Sergeant McGeorge of Right Flank being wounded early on, the first occasion that the battalion had experienced shelling other than at Bluff Cove when G Company had been attacked briefly. Confirmatory orders were given in the afternoon, soldiers checked and re-checked their equipment, General Moore and Brigadier Wilson both visited the Assembly Area, plans were rehearsed and, when nothing more remained to be done, everybody simply waited for H Hour, alone with their thoughts about the events in which they were about to be caught up.

The Diversionary Attack

At 1845 hours Major Bethell's force for the diversionary attack, consisting of thirty men made up from two sections of the Reconnaissance Platoon under Sergeant Coull and some members of Headquarter Company under Drill Sergeant Wight and CSM Braby, began to move from the western end of Mount Harriet. Their mission was to make such a demonstration as to lead the enemy on Tumbledown into thinking that an attack on their positions was coming from the south rather than the west.

Since for most of the day those taking part had been involved in preparing underslung loads carrying ammunition for the battalion's move to the Assembly Area, there had been little time to prepare, but the commanders had viewed the approximate area of the positions against which they were to patrol. Moving with a troop of the Blues and Royals in support, Major Bethell's patrol set out along the general line of the Stanley road and made good progress until it encountered a well concealed position which, following further investigation, Major Bethell concluded was the position which he had earlier identified from Mount Harriet. The presence of enemy was confirmed by snoring heard coming from one trench and Major Bethell gave orders for a quick attack; at this moment an Argentinian sentry engaged the platoon's assault group and a fire-fight began, with some enemy positions in rear joining in to support those being attacked. Eventually the forward trenches were silenced and cleared of enemy,

148

although not without the loss of Drill Sergeant Wight and Corporal Pashley from the Royal Engineers, both of whom had been killed in the first moments of the battle. After an hour and a half of intermittent fighting and having sustained four wounded and with ammunition running low, Major Bethell assessed that the immediate positions had been effectively cleared and that his group should withdraw. While he and Piper Duffy remained to cover the withdrawal, CSM Braby and Sergeant Coull proceeded to pull the rest of the patrol back. During this operation an Argentinian soldier rolled a grenade down the front of his trench and the resultant explosion wounded Major Bethell and Piper Duffy, both of whom, however, managed to withdraw and join up with their colleagues. A slow and painful withdrawal then commenced, with the patrol being mortared and sustaining two further casualties from mines. Around 0200 hours the patrol made contact with the Blues and Royals troop which came forward to pick up the wounded and, despite having a vehicle immobilized by an anti-personnel mine, evacuated the patrol to 42 Commando's Regimental Aid Post from where the wounded were flown to Ajax Bay. Although sadly expensive in the number of those killed and wounded, post-war interrogation confirmed that the patrol had almost certainly achieved its aim of deluding the Argentinians into believing that its operation was the prelude to a major attack on Tumbledown from the south-west.

While Major Bethell's diversionary attack was still in progress, G Company, commanded by Major Iain Dalzel Job, left the Assembly Area behind Goat Ridge and moved forward the 1,500 yards to the start line for the main attack, a stock fence earlier secured by the Reconnaissance Platoon. The night was very dark and cold with temperatures below zero and flurries of snow blown so fiercely by the wind that on occasions they appeared to be falling horizontally. After crossing the start line at 2100 hours, the company fanned out into extended formation with 7 Platoon under Lieutenant Michael Joynson on the left and 8 Platoon under 2nd Lieutenant Charles Page on the right. 9 Platoon, under command of Lieutenant Charles Blount, moved behind them in reserve. Progress was slow across the spongy peat ground most of which was waterlogged or criss-crossed by small 'stone runs' of rocks which could easily cause a man carrying a heavy load of ammunition to stumble and damage a leg or ankle. Although soldiers were only wearing belt order, each was heavily laden with rockets, grenades and belts of machine-gun ammunition. The battlefield was lit up by flares from the east and the occasional burst of mortar and shell fire, but after about an hour the leading elements of the company were firm on the western extremity of Tumbledown without contact with the Argentinians. 9 Platoon then passed through and with 8 Platoon on its right moved forward to secure the company's second objective which lay in the dead ground between the western and central sections of the feature. Again this position was unoccupied, the defenders having apparently evacuated shortly before G Company's arrival. Phase One had been entirely successful. Earlier as he moved forward to the start line, Colonel Scott was informed over his radio by Brigade

Phase One –
G Company

149

Headquarters that Tumbledown had been reinforced by an additional Argentinian Company. Since he did not see any merit in alarming people at this late stage, he rejected the idea of telling his Company Commanders.

Phase Two –
Left Flank

At approximately 2230 hours Left Flank passed through G Company and started to climb the main feature of Tumbledown. 13 Platoon under 2nd Lieutenant James Stuart and 15 Platoon under Lieutenant Alastair Mitchell moved on the left and right respectively as they began to advance into the lower crags. Lieutenant Anthony Fraser's 14 Platoon was in reserve some 300 yards behind them. 15 Platoon was the first to be engaged by the Argentinians and a quickly mounted attempt to dislodge them led by Lance Sergeant Dalgleish was beaten off. During this action the platoon was engaged by several semi-automatic weapons and was bombarded by some very accurate shell and mortar fire which continued for most of the battle. In trying to work its way forward the platoon was subjected to a heavy weight of rifle and machine-gun fire from the high ground about 300 yards to its front. Further attempts at movement left a number of casualties, including Guardsman Stirling killed, and the Platoon Sergeant, Sergeant P Jackson, wounded.

13 Platoon on the left had been brought under fire at about the same moment as 15 Platoon. Engaged by snipers hiding in the rocks and equipped with night sights, sections tried to fight through; Lance Sergeants Davidson and McGuinness both led attacks using anti-tank rockets and white phosphorous grenades to blast the enemy positions, destroying a number in the process, but the Argentinians would not be budged and put up a stiff fight firing on their attackers from the crags above. As the battle continued, Sergeant Simeon and Guardsman Tanbini were both killed and Lance Corporal Eyre and CSM Nicol, who had gone forward to assist the platoon, were wounded. Major Kiszely, who had placed himself between his two leading platoons, controlled the battle as best he could, monitoring the actions of his platoon commanders and trying to manage the fire of the artillery and mortars in order to give them the suppressive fire support without which they were unlikely to get forward, given the determined resistance they were encountering. For the next two to three hours, principally for technical reasons on the gun positions and mortar lines, but also because it was often impossible to differentiate between the fall of friendly and enemy rounds, Major Kiszely and Captain Willie Nicol, his Forward Observation Officer, were unable to bring down sufficiently accurate fire to get the Argentinians' heads down and so give their own platoons the opportunity to move forward. The problems were eventually resolved at about 0230 hours when accurate fire was finally brought down on the enemy.

Throughout the time that Left Flank was pinned down, Colonel Scott was under intense pressure from his Brigade Commander to restore the momentum of the attack. Responding patiently and courteously, he explained the situation and what was being done to rectify it. Equally, when talking to Major Kiszely he listened carefully, never berated and quietly encouraged, 'When he spoke to me on the radio, Colonel Mike was calm, steady and logical, but I could tell that he was under great pressure from above. I told him what was happening and what I was doing about it. . . . He said something like, "Right, you know the urgency. You're the man on the ground and I back your judgement but don't hang about." I drew strength from his confidence in me and I consciously used the same tone of voice on my own radio net to my platoon and section commanders.'

As soon as the artillery had corrected onto the enemy positions and, judging that the initiative had probably now passed to him, Major Kiszely pushed his platoons forward again. He knew that time was running out and that following his attack Right Flank still had to take its objective. Thereupon, with 14 Platoon having been ordered to prepare to move forward to assist, Lieutenant Mitchell led 15 Platoon, supported by Company Headquarters, in an assault upon the enemy's forward position. Capitalizing upon this success, 15 Platoon then moved around to their right and with Company Headquarters again in close support, overran several enemy at the rear of the position. Lance Sergeant Mitchell, who had led his section so gallantly, was killed in this attack. There then followed a series of engagements during which pressure was maintained on the enemy, with guardsmen skirmishing forward in small groups using grenades and bayonets to winkle the Argentinians out of the rocks. When the final objective was reached only Major Kiszely and six men remained and a burst of machine-gun fire immediately cut down and wounded three of them, including Lieutenant Mitchell. Vulnerable to attack, the four who remained held the summit of Tumbledown for some fifteen minutes until 14 Platoon and the remnants of 13 Platoon closed up in time to beat off a half-hearted and belated Argentinian counter-attack. As the company's casualties were being evacuated, the stretcher party received a direct hit from a mortar bomb, killing Guardsmen Malcolmson and Reynolds, the latter already wounded in the final attack. Thus ended an epic battle when, against all the odds, a well prepared enemy, sited on dominating and often insurmountable crags, was overwhelmed by men determined to win. Left Flank's action had taken over seven hours and the company killed over thirty enemy, capturing another twenty for the loss of seven of its own killed and twenty-one wounded.

At 0600 hours with the lights of Port Stanley clearly visible ahead, Right Flank commanded by Major Simon Price, moved through Left Flank to take the eastern end of Tumbledown. 3 Platoon under 2nd Lieutenant Robert Lawrence on the left and 2 Platoon under 2nd Lieutenant Mark Mathewson on the right led the advance, with 2nd Lieutenant Viscount Dalrymple's 1 Platoon in support. The enemy were firmly lodged high up on two promontories of rock and, on commencing their attack, the leading platoons engaged them straightaway, an action which gained them an initial lodgement. However, following this early success, the company was unable to make further progress, being held up by strong enemy positions sited on the spine of the nearest promontory of rocks. Guardsman Pengelly was driven back, wounded, after he attempted to dislodge the position, following which Major Price went forward to co-ordinate

Phase Three – Right Flank

a further attack leaving CSM Amos to organize a number of prisoners who had been taken. At this juncture Sergeant R. Jackson, discarding his rifle, climbed up a crag and threw a grenade which destroyed the Argentinian machine gun holding up the advance. The way was then clear for 3 Platoon, supported by a group led by Captain Ian Bryden, the Company Second-in-Command, to move around the northern side of the feature, fighting from rock to rock and crag to crag against a succession of snipers. This group, after losing four men wounded, including 2nd Lieutenant Lawrence shot in the head, managed to go firm at the far end of the position. The Company Commander's group then cleared the centre rocks and that part of 2 Platoon led by Sergeant Robertson advanced across the grassy area between the two parts of the enemy position; they finally arrived above what subsequently proved to have been the Argentinian administrative area and cleared out the remainder of the enemy who started to withdraw in disorder down the hill.

As the platoons re-organized on the position they came under fire from a machine gun on an outcrop of rock to their north and for a while it looked as if a counter-attack might be mounted against the position. Despite a force of forty Argentinians having been placed there for that very purpose, it never properly materialized, mainly because Lance Corporal Campbell's section raked the position with fire from above. For the loss of five members of the company wounded, by 0815 hours Right Flank was able to claim success in clearing the last of the enemy off Tumbledown, thereby securing the final significant feature before Stanley.

Once firm on its objective, Right Flank set about the task of gathering and treating its wounded, a task made more difficult by continuing enemy shelling. Once Captain Miller, the Artillery FOO had come forward, he was able to engage the Argentinians retreating towards Stanley, although, as soon as it became clear that he was witnessing a rout, he was ordered to stop firing. Meanwhile the Gurkhas were beginning their attack on Mount William and the Welsh Guards were moving forward to take Sapper Hill.

However, for Major Price, evacuating his wounded had now become his greatest concern; the Battalion Regimental Aid Post was at least two miles to the rear and, despite the best efforts of the pipers who performed miracles in caring for their charges, a helicopter was the only realistic means by which badly wounded men could be evacuated in time to save their lives. Because of the continuing enemy shelling large helicopters would almost certainly have been put at considerable risk had they flown forward and for a time it seemed that nothing could be done to assist the evacuation process. Eventually, however, Captain Sam Drennan, a former Scots Guardsman who had transferred to the Army Air Corps, flew his Scout helicopter into a saddle behind Right Flank's position, ignoring the dangers posed by shelling, and, making several trips, managed to evacuate all the wounded. For this gallant and totally unselfish act he was subsequently awarded a Distinguished Flying Cross.

Late on the morning of 14 June it became clear that the Argentinians wished to discuss surrender terms. All units were ordered to remain where they were and the battalion set about preparing a defensive position on Tumbledown against the contingency of the talks breaking down and hostilities being resumed. Stunned by their spectacular success in defeating a well trained battalion of regular Argentinian Marines and having fought arguably the toughest action of the whole campaign, in the immediate aftermath of the battle most people experienced understandable feelings of euphoria and relief. Theirs had been a great victory and no one could ever take it away from them.

However, as the day wore on and as the adrenalin drained away to be replaced by cold and tiredness, thoughts turned to those who had died or had been so badly wounded that they might not survive. The battalion remained on the mountain the night after the battle. In the words of Padre Smith: 'We tried to sleep with sleeping bags and ponchos. It was freezing cold and almost strange and unreal after the toils and struggles of the previous night. The wind blew through the crags as it had done for thousands of years before.'

At 2100 hours on 14 June General Menendez, the Argentinian Commander, *Aftermath* surrendered to General Moore. The next day, amidst all the chaos and destruction that is the inevitable consequence of war, British troops moved into Port Stanley and preparations were begun to accept the Argentinian surrender on West Falkland. Late in the afternoon the 2nd Battalion was flown to Fitzroy where the sheep-shearing sheds provided an opportunity to dry out, clean up and rest after the battle. There was much speculation as to how soon people would be returned to Britain, although it was apparent even at that stage that some units would have to be retained on the islands to secure what had just been won at such cost and that this was unlikely to be the Commandos and Parachutists because of their longer and greater involvement in the conflict.

On the evening of 16 June twenty-five members of the battalion flew to Ajax Bay where Padre Smith conducted a funeral service for the eight Scots Guardsmen and one sapper killed in action with the Scots Guards. They were buried in simple graves overlooking the sea and remained there until their bodies were repatriated to Britain for re-burial.

After three days at Fitzroy the battalion, pending its dispersal across the Falklands, was moved to the ferry MV *St Edmund* in Port Stanley Harbour. It had been decided that the battalion was to remain in the islands until replaced by another from Britain and consequently it was given a number of tasks to undertake. The Anti-Tank Platoon, under Captain Jeremy Campbell-Lamerton, went to garrison South Georgia, Right Flank moved to Ajax Bay to guard 500 Argentinian prisoners, while towards the end of June the rest of the battalion deployed to West Falkland, to Port Howard, Hill Cove and Roy Cove where people relaxed, tidied up the battlefield, collected abandoned Argentinian equipment and, as guardsmen do the world over, brought order and decency to places where it had ceased to exist. Nowhere was this truer than at Ajax Bay where the prisoners were held under circumstances of considerable squalor at the abandoned refrigeration plant; by a mixture of persuasion and leadership Right Flank induced them to improve their own conditions and guarded them until they were finally returned to Argentina.

Meanwhile Colonel Scott had the additional problem of not being able to tell his battalion when it was to return home. Until almost the end of July there was to be no news even of when a decision was likely to be made, the latter being linked to the arrival of a new commander and his assessment of the force levels required to secure the islands. For some it became difficult to accept this frustrating delay although most of the battalion stoically acknowledged that there was little that could be done to alleviate their situation and that others were working to resolve matters as fast as they could.

As the battalion got on with life on West Falkland and at Ajax Bay other problems started to arise. Guardsman Williams had disappeared on the night of 13 June and had consequently been listed as 'missing presumed dead'. Despite intensive searching all efforts to find him or his remains yielded nothing. Williams later turned up on East Falkland the day after the battalion finally sailed from Port Stanley; however, his disappearance and subsequent absence for six weeks remain a mystery to this day.

Another source of irritation for those left to languish in the Falklands, once the majority of the Task Force had returned to Britain, was the appearance of a number of reports in the media which were critical of 5th Infantry Brigade's performance during the campaign. While most of these were seen to emanate from the pens of reporters who had accompanied the Commando Brigade, they were nonetheless damaging and caused considerable distress to those by implication criticized. Although reporters who had been with the battalion, such as A.J. McIlroy of the *Daily Telegraph*, had produced accurate and balanced reports of the battalion's involvement, they were insufficient to counteract the more sensational dispatches of those determined to view the outcome of the war from a limited and biased perspective, and without acquiring first hand knowledge of what had gone on in places and at times not witnessed by themselves personally. However, the damage had been done and it was only when General Sir Edwin Bramall, the Chief of the General Staff, wrote to the Major General on 13 July that the record was put right. Writing about the exploits of the Household Division the CGS said, 'I want to place firmly on record the magnificent way in which all three Regiments of the Division performed, which was in the best traditions of the Brigade of Guards and the Household Cavalry.' Meanwhile about the Regiment he wrote: 'The Scots Guards carried out an attack on the key objective of Tumbledown, where the enemy was well trained, well equipped and determined, and consisted of the Argentine crack troops, their Marines. It was a long, hard fight. . . . It was only by the utmost determination, courage and gallantry that, despite considerable casualties, they ultimately took their objective. . . . It was a really magnificent achievement.' He went on to write: 'Units of the Household Division have done an outstanding job by any standards, and have justified a thousandfold the confidence we all placed in them. They can fully take their place alongside those of the previous generation who fought with so much glory in the past; and they have earned the admiration of all of us for their professionalism, courage and spirit and shown to the world the incomparable quality of the Household troops and the strength of the regimental system'. CGS concluded by expressing his heartfelt thanks on behalf of his colleagues on the Army Board and the Army as a whole.

Towards the end of July Major General David Thorne arrived as the new Commander in the Falkland Islands. He quickly made his decision concerning future force levels and within days it was announced that the 2nd Battalion Scots Guards would leave the islands before the end of the month. Before departing, a cross to commemorate those who had fallen in battle was erected and dedicated at the eastern end of Tumbledown Mountain. Constructed by Pioneer Sergeant Major Hope in the form of a simple wooden cross with the names of those killed inscribed on a brass plaque at its base, it stands looking out across the battlefield, an abiding reminder of what guardsmen went through in June 1982 to uphold the cause of freedom and right. On 31 July the MV *Norland* sailed from Port Stanley, arriving at Ascension Island on 8 August where the battalion transferred to four VC10 aircraft to fly to RAF Brize Norton and the greatest welcome any battalion of the Regiment has received for many a long year.

CHAPTER NINE

HONG KONG AND CYPRUS

1st Battalion: Stanley Fort
2nd Battalion: London-Episkopi

1st Battalion
Hong Kong
1981

By 16 December, 1981, the 1st Battalion was complete in Hong Kong, having taken a month's well deserved leave at home after its demanding twenty-month tour of duty in Northern Ireland. Its new home was Stanley Fort, a spacious barracks perched at the end of a peninsula on the south side of Hong Kong Island in one of the less heavily inhabited areas of the Colony. With the exception of the battalion, the remainder of the Gurkha Field Force, the brigade-sized formation, which embodied all operational units in Hong Kong, was almost entirely made up of battalions and supporting units found from within the Brigade of Gurkhas. The Headquarters and the majority of the Field Force were located at Sek Kong in the New Territories, a three-hour journey by road from Stanley which involved passing through the teeming conurbations of Victoria and Kowloon, both with enormous Chinese populations. To some in the battalion this wide separation may have been viewed as an advantage, although history has generally shown that units detached from their parent headquarters other than by a small distance tend to fare less well than those closer to the seat of power. When a battalion is the only British unit in a formation which is predominantly staffed by tough Nepalese hillmen from the foothills of the Himalayas whose skills and culture are so very different from those of its own soldiers, it is arguably a double disadvantage to be so isolated.

The battalion took over at Stanley from the 1st Battalion Queen's Own Highlanders, its operational role being to support the police in the maintenance of law and order, in the case of the single British battalion, primarily on Hong Kong Island. Since the Communist takeover of China in 1949 the internal situation in the Colony had rarely been peaceful and periodic violence, usually orchestrated from Peking, had broken out on a number of occasions over the previous thirty years. However, in late 1981 the situation was generally quiet and, in the light of negotiations soon to be embarked upon by the British and Chinese Governments in order to establish the terms under which the Colony was to be handed back to China in 1997, it was likely to remain that way.

A more immediate preoccupation for the battalion was the rotational commit-

ment to maintain security along the border between Hong Kong and Guangdong Province, a task which involved a complete battalion deploying to prevent illegal immigrants attempting to cross into Hong Kong from the Chinese Republic. The first of four tours undertaken by the battalion while stationed at Stanley was scheduled for April, 1982, and once Christmas and the New Year were over, Colonel McLaughlan began the training for this deployment.

December is probably the best time of the year to arrive in Hong Kong and it did not take the battalion and its families long to adjust to a climate which at that time of year was not unlike that of the French Riviera. After the pressure of constant operational duty in Ulster everybody was looking forward to a less frenetic pace and the chance to relax and enjoy the mysteries of the Far East, this having been the picture of life in Hong Kong which had reached Aldergrove. Unfortunately the reality was somewhat different and, during their two years in the Colony, Scots Guardsmen more often than not found themselves working as hard as they had in Belfast in order to meet the operational and training commitments placed upon the battalion. Brigadier Bob Hodges, the Deputy Commander British Forces who lived at Stanley and saw a lot of the battalion during its first months there, summarized its situation in the following words, '1SG arrived in Hong Kong from a two-year operational tour in Ulster.

157

I suspect that they were under the impression that Hong Kong would provide a welcome change in the pace of battalion life and that they would have an opportunity to relax with their families. They faced a rude shock as they found that they were subjected to lengthy tours on the Border and much separation. As the only British battalion in a Gurkha brigade, they also encountered a culture which revolved around shooting, running up and down hills, preferably carrying heavy loads, and khud races. The Guardsmen had firm views on all of this, especially when invited to take part in exercises starting on 1 January!'

There is little doubt that when it arrived in Hong Kong the battalion harboured an unrealistic view of what was expected of it. An unfortunate combination of circumstances centred loosely upon an operational requirement which was more extensive than anticipated, the unfamiliar style of the Gurkha Field Force where the British battalion could so easily become the 'odd man out' and the demands of an expatriate British population which assumed that the Stanley battalion would meet every request for assistance, contrived to make the battalion's first year an uncomfortable one. While some mistakes were made by the battalion and while it may not have got its public relations quite right to begin with, it must be said that for some time before the Scots Guards arrived in 1981 the importance of the military relative to other sections of society had been waning, this decline in the Army's standing in the Colony being in rough proportion to the growing influence enjoyed by those who managed and led the great finance houses which are today so much part of Hong Kong's life and the foundation of its burgeoning prosperity.

Such was the level of affluence in the Colony that life for a single guardsman or junior NCO subsisting on his pay alone permitted only passing contact with the fleshpots of Kowloon or Victoria, while for those families who could not be housed at Stanley and who therefore lived in high-rise flats amongst the Chinese community, life when the weather was at its most humid and the man of the house was away on duty on the border sometimes verged on the intolerable. It is against such a background that the activities and achievements of the 1st Battalion must be judged; deployment to the Far East entailed a way of soldiering not previously experienced and one for which the battalion was neither psychologically nor physically well prepared when it arrived in the Colony.

Colonel McLaughlan's team, on arrival at Stanley, was virtually unchanged from that which had performed so well in Ulster. RSM Macfarlane was to remain with the battalion throughout the tour, as were the two Quartermasters, Captain Jim Bunton who replaced Captain George Cooper when he was seconded to the 7th Gurkha Rifles in August, 1982, and Captain Ian Beck. Captain Charlie Grimston was succeeded by Captain Rory Ingleby-Mackenzie as Adjutant after two months and Major Jeremy Warren became Second-in-Command shortly after arrival in the Colony.

An early visitor to Stanley was the Right Reverend Robert Runcie, the Archbishop of Canterbury, who spent much of 5 January with the battalion and its families. The Archbishop, who had served with the 3rd Battalion in North-West Europe where he had won a Military Cross, was accompanied by Mr Terry Waite, his special emissary, who was later to be kidnapped by Muslim Fundamentalists in the Lebanon and held prisoner for a long period before finally being released in November, 1991. All who met both the Archbishop and Terry Waite were much impressed by their vitality and openness.

The battalion's first tour of border duty lasted for six weeks and involved companies being deployed along the fence separating Hong Kong from China, while also patrolling some of the islands adjacent to the Chinese mainland in conjunction with the Royal Navy and the Royal Hong Kong Police. Operational plans involved the Army in apprehending any illegal immigrants managing to cross the hinterland fence who, once arrested, were handed over to the police; thereafter they were invariably sent back to China, no doubt to an uncertain future. Although the vast numbers who had tried to cross over in previous years had dwindled to a trickle, in 1982 up to ten illegal immigrants a night might still be caught, with some so desperate to escape to Hong Kong that they tried more than once to enter the Colony. Major Martin Snow, who commanded Left Flank, remembers being implored by a Chinese dentist not to hand him and his niece over to the police; the man became so overwrought that he finally grabbed Major Snow and CSM Young by the legs to avoid removal.

If an illegal immigrant succeeded in reaching Kowloon his chances of being detected were remote, but few managed to do so, mainly due to the efficiency with which operations were conducted along the border. It was tedious and distasteful work for the battalion, with the companies being deployed in 'penny packets' along the fence line from where they could observe an incursion and react to detain those involved. Weapons and ammunition were carried, but there was little or no danger of an engagement and contact with the Chinese Army patrolling its side of the border to catch potential escapees before they reached the wire, was avoided at all costs.

Battalion Headquarters was based below the Scots Guards star on Crest Hill at Lo Wu from where Colonel McLaughlan and RSM Macfarlane would visit positions along the border by bicycle. Boredom was a problem, but some people developed unexpected interests, Lance Corporal Davey of Left Flank becoming an expert on the birds which frequented the marshes beyond the border. Major General John Chapple, the Commander British Forces and himself a keen ornithologist, was visiting border posts on one occasion and asked what a particular bird was. Without a moment's hesitation Lance Corporal Davey replied, 'A Swinhoe Egret, sir!'

Ceremonial duties in Hong Kong invariably came the way of the single British battalion and the 1st Battalion found itself heavily involved in a number of parades throughout its two years in the Colony. Sir Murray Maclehose, the Governor of Hong Kong, was due to leave on completion of his tour at the end of April and the Battalion spent considerable time rehearsing his farewell parade only to have it cancelled when the Governor suffered a mild stroke days before his departure. However, in May a detachment drawn from across the battalion and commanded by Captain William Barne with PSM Boyle as the Guard Warrant Officer went to Seoul as the British platoon in the United Nations Honor Guard Company, a commitment which lasted until the middle of August.

While, socially, life in Hong Kong for the battalion's more junior ranks was limited by the expensive nature of entertainment and the lack of any sizeable group of Europeans to whom they could relate, the Officers' and Sergeants' Messes both developed very agreeable life-styles and each in its own way established a sound rapport with a myriad of civilian friends. Brigadier Hodges commented on how popular the battalion was with Hong Kong Society 'who respected the very positive contributions made to collect money for a range of charities.' He has also written that, 'whenever they entertained it was with great flair and style. As such I know that they are still remembered with respect and affection.' A good example of this generous approach – too generous to some minds – came on 22 May when the Officers' Mess organized a party for the Samaritans which raised £10,000 and was an enormous success. On this occasion the Commanding Officer dressed as a monk and remained unrecognized for most of the night, while General Chapple having taken the salute at the earlier Beating of Retreat, changed out of his uniform and re-appeared dressed in a long tunic looking like a wizened old Indian who bore an uncanny resemblance to Pandit Nehru!

Although the battalion played hard during its two years in Hong Kong it also worked hard, the Field Force Commander, Brigadier Morgan Llewellyn, being determined that standards of fitness should match those of the Gurkha soldiers whom he commanded. As well as a second tour of duty on the border in November and December, there were exercises to practise plans for controlling civil unrest in Hong Kong's townships, while shooting and the firing of the battalion's support weapons all took place regularly.

In late August Right Flank, under Major James Napier and CSM McDonald, flew to Malaysia for a month's jungle training, the first of a number of excursions which, during 1982 and 1983, were to take companies away from Hong Kong as far afield as Brunei, Fiji and Australia, as well as on three occasions to Malaysia. Stanley possessed excellent sporting facilities and the football and rugby teams, led respectively by Captain Ian Beck and Captain Mark Turner, performed remarkably well against both military and civilian opposition. Not so successful was the battalion's participation on Dragon Boat Day, a Chinese holiday when a boat organized by Lieutenant Malcolm MacGregor won its first heat in a race across the harbour, but, following a six hour wait and considerable socializing, failed to make progress beyond the next round. However, the most travelled in the battalion were the Pipes and Drums who during the course of their first twelve months in the Far East visited Indonesia, the Philippines, Korea and Japan, where under the direction of Pipe Major Banks they played in Tokyo and Osaka during a British Business Fortnight attended by the British Prime Minister, Mrs Margaret Thatcher. The latter, the main purpose of whose tour in the Far East was to lead negotiations over the future of Hong Kong in Peking, later visited the Colony and, despite an exhausting schedule, found time to visit Stanley to meet members of the battalion and their families, an event which was as usual stimulating.

A busy year was rounded off with a visit by Their Royal Highnesses the Colonel of the Regiment and The Duchess of Kent in late October, to be followed a day later by sixty members of the Scots Guards Association and their wives whose time in Stanley was certainly memorable. Finally it must be recorded that 1982 was notable for the fact that, as far as the author can ascertain, the Regiment involved itself in a sport in which it had not previously indulged when thirteen members of the 1st Battalion entered the Hong Kong Judo Championships, the only European team to do so. The team, which was coached by Lance Corporal Mullen, won more medals than any other, Guardsmen Moon and Japp both winning Gold Medals while Guardsman Anderson and Lance Corporals Harrison and Wright achieved Silver or Bronze awards. The following year they went to compete in Tokyo.

1983 did not begin well. No sooner had Hogmanay passed than the battalion *1983* deployed on Exercise CROSSED KUKRIS, an exercise set by the Field Force Commander and designed to test the battalion operating on light scales. Following a landing by minesweeper, the intention was that the battalion should advance the length of Lantau Island clearing enemy positioned on the various mountain peaks which lay along its axis. An ill-thought out and badly controlled exercise encountered problems from the outset when weather more reminiscent of the Falkland Islands than Hong Kong curtailed most of the planned helicopter support. The battalion suffered an unpleasant night on the aptly named 'Bloody Butcher' mountain without any realistic administrative support and, with several soldiers suffering from exposure and exhaustion, an exercise which should have been an opportunity for the battalion to demonstrate its undoubted skills merely became a test of endurance. No doubt lessons were learnt on both sides and it is to be hoped that the Field Force Commander and his staff pondered the wisdom of mounting further such exercises. The exercise was probably the nadir in relations between the battalion and its superior Headquarters; with the wisdom of hindsight it is easy to be critical of the way in which those most closely involved handled their relationships. The successful juxtaposition of units and headquarters within the hierarchy of the Army's command structure has never been easy and invariably relies upon the interaction between key personalities. The 1st Battalion was not the only battalion to experience difficulties on arrival in Hong Kong and other British battalions before it had had to cope with similar pressures when pitchforked into what can only be described as a military and civilian 'goldfish bowl'.

If 1982 was the year when the battalion familiarized itself with every aspect of life in Hong Kong, 1983 was a year of fragmentation with, for most of the time, at least one company outside the Colony. C Company, under Major Edward Woods, and later under Major Tom Fitzalan Howard, exercised in

161

Malaysia and Fiji, while Right Flank, commanded by Major James Napier, went to Brunei and Left Flank, by then commanded by Major Douglas Erskine Crum, flew to Malaysia for a month in March. At the same time Battalion Headquarters went to Brisbane to represent the British Army in a five-nation CPX which also involved the Australian, New Zealand, Malaysian and Singaporean Armies.

A third tour on the border in mid-June and the dispatch of a second Guard Platoon to Korea the same month, this time commanded by 2nd Lieutenant Dominic Vail, with Drill Sergeant MacDonald as the Detachment Warrant Officer, completed what was by any standards a hectic six months. The border tour was notable for a marked decrease in the number of illegal immigrants attempting to enter Hong Kong, the drop being attributed partly to increased security in Guangdong Province and partly to a realization by those seeking to enter the Colony that, without an identity card, their chances of finding work were minimal. On 26 July Colonel Ian McLaughlan completed his tour in command and handed over to Lieutenant Colonel Kim Ross for the final seven months of the battalion's time in the Far East.

Hong Kong weather in 1983 swung from one extreme to another: the wettest ever summer, the most rain to fall in any twenty-four hours, the hottest ever October and the driest November on record. In addition on 8 September Hong Kong suffered a very severe storm when Typhoon ELLEN crossed the South China Sea and hovered for ten hours a few miles to the west of Stanley Fort. Whilst by no means the worst typhoon to be experienced by Hong Kong, ELLEN did immense damage and resulted in a number of deaths in the Colony. Fortunately no member of the battalion or its families was hurt, although the intensity of the storm blew in windows and caused a number of air-conditioning units to implode in married quarters and elsewhere; for the families, in particular those of Right Flank and C Company whose husbands were away from Stanley at the time, siege by typhoon was a frightening experience as they battled to keep their homes intact. The unluckiest man was Padre Stephen Blakey whose church was devastated in the storm, causing the loss of many church and personal artefacts.

The last six-week border tour ended on 28 November, 1983, with the battalion accounting for 169 illegal immigrants, an average of four a day or one wretched infiltrator caught for each 1,500 to 2,000 man hours spent peering at the border fence, hardly a satisfactory return for the taxpayer's money. Unfortunately the tour was marred by a stupid incident when two members of C Company absconded from their posts on the border and attempted to hijack an aircraft at Kai Tak Airport; they were eventually talked out of taking such action by a Hong Kong Police Officer and no damage was done other than to the battalion's reputation which regrettably never really recovered with the Colony media who were understandably critical. For their part the military authorities played the incident in a low key leaving Colonel Ross to sort out matters within the battalion.

It was sad that such an incident should occur just as the battalion was preparing to leave Hong Kong and at a time when in many areas it had built a good name for itself; an excellent exercise with the 2nd Gurkha Rifles in mid-December when Left Flank swapped battalions and showed its Gurkha hosts that anything they could do Left Flank could do equally well or better, a 'mini' Birthday Parade at Stanley when Brigadier Llewellyn took the salute and the winning of the Field Force seven-a-side Rugby competition for the third year running – a relief because the cup had already been sent home to Pirbright – and the Garrison Football Cup, all combined to ensure that the battalion completed its tour on a high note. In mid-February, 1984, the 1st Battalion The Cheshire Regiment arrived in the Colony and the 1st Battalion returned home.

Enough has already been written to show that the battalion's two years in the Far East were not always as successful as those serving in the battalion would have wished them to be. The reasons for this have already been alluded to and do not require repetition. It must also be said that much was achieved that allowed the battalion to enhance a reputation for competence and co-operation gained before arrival in Hong Kong. Success in the field of sport, a willingness to 'take part and to have a go' and to contribute time and effort towards a host of social occasions in the Colony should not be lightly dismissed, since in the early 1980s they provided some of the markers by which the lone British battalion was judged by people in Hong Kong.

Probably the greatest accolade of the tour belongs to the guardsmen and junior NCOs of the battalion who, despite the lack of a social life of the same variety and intensity as that enjoyed by many of their seniors, generally behaved themselves impeccably throughout. On his departure Colonel Ross was told by Mr Roy Henry, Commissioner of the Hong Kong Police, that 'the battalion had had less incidents than any other during his time in post'. However, it is a fact of life that the modern day Army is a competitive place and weaknesses, once identified, are usually ruthlessly exposed, however inaccurate or unjust such initial perceptions might be; that the 1st Battalion managed to swim through the Hong Kong 'goldfish bowl' as well as it did was no mean achievement.

2nd Battalion Return to Britain

A well merited six weeks' leave followed the 2nd Battalion's homecoming from the South Atlantic, on completion of which everybody returned to Chelsea Barracks on 23 September, 1982, to resume the duties of a public duties battalion. Not surprisingly the battle to recover the Falkland Islands from Argentina continued to be a topic of enormous interest and pride for the Nation long after the last troops had returned from the South Atlantic and, whether they wished it or not, key members of the battalion at once found themselves involved in many discussions and presentations describing the campaign and its lessons. Thanks to its seven-week sojourn on West Falkland and at Ajax Bay after hostilities had ended, few if any Scots Guardsmen had returned home psychologically scarred by what they had been through, the period of enforced relaxation out of the public eye having provided an opportunity for people to adjust and to come to terms with what they had so recently experienced. On return to Chelsea the battalion wished for no more than to be able to pick up the threads of a routine so unexpectedly interrupted five months earlier.

However, life is never that simple and the Falklands War was destined to occupy the headlines for many months to come. At national level a Parliamentary Inquiry by a committee of Privy Counsellors chaired by Lord Franks to investigate the circumstances leading up to the Argentinian invasion, the Government's plans to ensure the future security of the islands and a bitter controversy concerning the circumstances surrounding the sinking of the Argentinian battleship *Belgrano*, along with a host of lesser matters, all ensured that the public were not allowed to forget quickly what had happened. Within Chelsea Barracks a more balanced view prevailed and the battalion soon reverted to its former role, mounting public duties again for the first time on 14 November. Previously in mid-October there had been justifiable pride when it was learned that twenty-four members of the battalion were to be honoured for gallant and distinguished service during the Falkland Islands Campaign, the list including the names of Lance Sergeant Mitchell and Guardsman Reynolds, both of Left Flank, who received posthumous awards. A further award which gave particular pleasure was that of an MBE to Captain Fred Moody who had had the awesome responsibility of looking after the battalion's families while their menfolk were in the South Atlantic. A day later the Corporation of the City of London held a parade to salute the return to the Task Force upon which the Commanding Officer led a detachment of three officers and twenty-seven soldiers drawn from throughout the battalion. On 12 November a Memorial and Thanksgiving Service was held in St Giles' Cathedral, Edinburgh, in memory of those who had lost their lives in the South Atlantic and to give thanks for the safe return of the battalion. The service was attended by the Colonel, and Padre Hutch Whiteford, Chaplain to the 2nd Battalion in 1945, gave the address; Colonel Scott read the 27th Psalm, the opening verse of which contains the immortal words 'The Lord is my light and my salvation; whom shall I fear? The Lord is the strength of my life; of whom shall I be afraid', the same words as he had read when the cross on Tumbledown Mountain commemorating the battalion's dead had been dedicated at the end of July. RSM Mackenzie read the roll of honour and, following the service, a Guard of Honour with both Battalion Colours marched past the Colonel outside the Cathedral.

Throughout the remainder of the autumn there were to be further reminders of the recent conflict with Argentina and the consequences which had followed in its wake. Most were happy and dignified events as when on 1 December in the garden of Buckingham Palace His Royal Highness Prince Philip, Senior Colonel of the Household Division, presented all those in the Division who had served in the Falklands and those attached from other regiments and corps with their South Atlantic Medals. He was accompanied by the Colonels of the three Regiments involved. Twenty-three officers and 425 soldiers of the 2nd Battalion were on parade. Another happy occasion occurred in mid December when Mr

Richard Scriven, a former officer of the Regiment and in 1982 the Master of the Salters Company, generously entertained forty-five members of the battalion to a Falklands lunch in his Company's Hall in the City of London. Each Scots Guardsman present was given an inscribed tankard.

A matter of an altogether different and more disturbing nature also started to manifest itself towards the end of the year, when for reasons which still remain unclear, Lieutenant Robert Lawrence, badly wounded with a head injury during the final phase of the assault on Tumbledown, chose to mount an attack against the Government's handling of the war and, as he saw it, the plight of the casualties. Whether motivated by frustration or by a deeper desire to castigate those he deemed responsible for leading the Nation into needless conflict, Lieutenant Lawrence, supported by his father, conducted a sustained campaign to air his views. While the immediate object of his attack appeared to be 'authority' and not the Regiment, the fact that he proceeded as he did, aided and abetted by others including the BBC, which in 1986 produced a dramatised film entitled 'Tumbledown', caused great distress to many of his erstwhile comrades in the battalion.

One of the final acts of 1982 was the funerals of the eight Scots Guardsmen to be killed in the Falklands. Allowed the right to decide whether they wished the remains of the deceased to be brought back for burial in Britain, the relatives all elected that they be repatriated. As a result, during the last week of November eight funerals were held, seven in Scotland and one, that of Guardsman Tanbini, in Liverpool, at all of which Padre Angus Smith officiated. His words, written long afterwards, give a certain poignancy to the eight occasions, while succinctly summarizing what the battalion's involvement in the war had meant to those involved. 'As we stood, in the words of Alfred Tennyson, "revolving many memories", we each had our own thoughts, memories and emotions; sorrow for what we were doing at that moment and a fierce pride because the object of the exercise had been achieved. Tumbledown Mountain had been liberated in a gallant night attack. Port Stanley was visible again. In the language of the Argentinian Commander, General Menendez, our victory had finally convinced him that it really was all over. In this respect the deceased had contributed and given their all to this desirable and legitimate result. "Greater love hath no man than this, that he lay down his life for his friends."'

1983 1983 was to be the battalion's last full year in London, since it had already been announced that in January, 1984, it would move to Cyprus to assume responsibility for the security of the Sovereign Base Areas. However, for most of 1983 attention was still focused on public duties with only a brief interlude for training, although the battalion football team, managed by Colour Sergeant Allender, and the boxing team, trained by Sergeant Pettit, both reached the UKLF Finals in their respective sports. Otherwise it was a case of a never-ending succession of Queen's Guards and other Royal Duties, including Numbers Three and Four Guards on the Queen's Birthday Parade, commanded

165

respectively by Majors Andrew Joscelyne and Julian Lancaster, and in October two Guards of Honour within the space of a week. Major Nick Potter, the new Captain of Right Flank, commanded both Guards, the first for President Machel of Mozambique and the second for the King of Tonga, while 2nd Lieutenant Ian Campbell-Lamerton carried the Regimental Colour and CSM Amos and CQMS Wood were the right and left guides respectively.

Meanwhile a bizarre and totally unforeseen incident had earlier befallen the Corps of Drums and Pipes and Drums of the battalion which, while on a recruiting tour north of the Border, were visiting Carlisle on 3 July to play at the local Association Branch Outing held at the Racecourse. Just before 1700 hours as they were about to beat retreat, both bands were subjected to an unprovoked attack by a group of twenty local youths and a most unpleasant fight ensued. Major Tony Harrison, the Carlisle Branch Chairman, recalls 'seeing a pitched battle raging between the youths and Scots Guardsmen Past and Present'. He immediately alerted the police who managed to break up the battle, although not before several tunics, feathered bonnets and a set of pipes had been damaged and eleven guardsmen had been hurt. It was an incident without precedent – and happily one not since repeated – and so incensed was the Mayor of Carlisle at the adverse publicity that the incident had brought upon her city that she immediately opened a fund in aid of the pipers and drummers.

Award of the Falklands Campaign Battle Honours

On 26 October it was announced that Her Majesty The Queen had approved the award of Battle Honours for those ships and units which had taken part in the Falklands Campaign. The Regiment was awarded two Honours: 'FALK-LAND ISLANDS 1982', which was to be borne on the Colours which would in future be decked with a laurel wreath on the anniversary of the Battle of Tumbledown on 14 June. This honour was to be recorded in the Army List in heavy print. A second Honour 'Tumbledown Mountain' was also awarded, but this was not to be borne on the Colours and would only be recorded in the Army List in small print. The most recent previous grant of a Battle Honour to the Regiment had been that of 'NORTH WEST EUROPE, 1944–45' at the end of the Second World War. Six weeks later, and after learning that the part which it had played in the Falklands Campaign had been so appropriately recognized, the battalion mounted its final Queen's Guard with Colonel Michael Scott as the Captain of the Guard, Major Campbell Gordon, the Second-in-Command, as the Subaltern and Captain Andrew Foster, the Adjutant, as the Ensign. During the last week of January, 1984, Chelsea Barracks were handed over to the 2nd Battalion Coldstream Guards and the battalion and its families flew to Salamanca Barracks, Episkopi in Cyprus.

Cyprus 1984

The Island of Cyprus, the third largest in the Mediterranean, was formally annexed to Britain in November, 1914, on the outbreak of war with Turkey. It remained a Crown Colony until 1960 when, following a four-year armed insurgency by EOKA terrorists seeking union with Greece, agreement was reached between the British, Greek and Turkish Governments that Cyprus

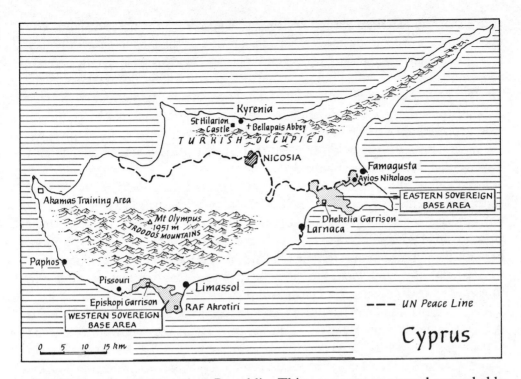

Cyprus

would become an independent Republic. This arrangement proved unworkable in practice and soon led to inter-communal troubles which caused a United Nations Peace Keeping Force (UNFICYP) to be deployed to the Island in 1964 to keep the warring factions apart. However, coups mounted by both the main protagonists eventually resulted in the island being physically divided between the Greek and Turkish Cypriot communities. In 1984 approximately eighty per cent of the population was Greek Cypriot in origin, the remainder being predominantly Turkish Cypriot. Under the terms of the 1960 Agreement Britain retained two military enclaves on the southern side of the island – denoted Sovereign Base Areas (SBA) – that centred around Episkopi and Akrotiri in the west being designated the Western SBA while that encompassing Dhekelia in the east was designated the Eastern SBA.

Salamanca Barracks in Episkopi, a spacious and pleasant camp a few miles to the west of Limassol, has always been the home of the British battalion responsible for the overall security of the two SBAs. A second battalion, the role of which was primarily to assist in manning the UNFICYP 'Peace Line' separating Greeks and Turks, was based at Dhekelia to the east of Larnaca. Routine duties and internal security tasks such as the guarding of sensitive communication sites at Ayios Nikolaos and on Mount Troodos were to be the 2nd Battalion Scots Guards' operational role for its two years on the island, although Cyprus, with hot dry summers and variable warm winters, provided enormous scope for training and sporting activities.

On arrival Colonel Scott warned his guardsmen that, while Cyprus would provide a total and pleasant change after five years in London, they should be

167

aware that the battalion was one of only a few major units on the island. Not only could it expect to be given a large proportion of the jobs to be done, but it would be under the spotlight of local military and civilian scrutiny. In order to add emphasis to this latter point he told the battalion that its predecessor, the 1st Battalion The Argyll and Sutherland Highlanders, had had a somewhat difficult tour and prior to the 2nd Battalion's arrival a rumour had circulated around Episkopi Garrison that 'the Scots Guards were similar to the Argylls but six inches bigger'. He made it clear that such a canard was to be quickly disproved and was not disappointed!

Early on in the battalion's tour it was decided that the British national contingent at the time serving in Beirut should be withdrawn. Cyprus being the nearest base, it was appropriate that the Commander British Forces, Major General Sir Desmond Langley, should command the withdrawal operation. Captain Peter Farrelly and ten members of his Mortar Platoon were embarked to assist with the evacuation, but, after three days at sea, they were stood down, thwarted by bad weather and a change of plan.

Two months after the battalion's arrival Her Majesty The Queen and His Royal Highness The Duke of Edinburgh visited the Western SBA and G Company provided a Guard of Honour, commanded by Major Julian Lancaster, and a quarter guard, commanded by Sergeant Anderson, for the duration of the visit; this was the battalion's only ceremonial commitment of that time and it caused the author of the G Company notes in the 1984 Scots Guards Magazine to boast: 'The only Guard of Honour so far found by the battalion was provided by the Company, ably assisted by F Company and the Regimental Band. We believe that the Flank Companies should realize that without a bearskin it is what's underneath that really matters! Hence our selection.' Throughout its time in Cyprus the battalion was to be involved in all major ceremonial occasions and in both 1984 and 1985 the Regimental Colour was trooped on the local Queen's Birthday Parade when the Commander British Forces represented Her Majesty The Queen.

On 27 April Colonel Michael Scott handed over command to Lieutenant Colonel Iain Mackay-Dick. Colonel Scott's time in command will surely rank as one of the most demanding periods that any battalion of the Regiment has experienced since the Second World War. Having begun his command with little to look forward to other than a further two years of public duties with the possibility of some training overseas, he suddenly found himself and his soldiers pitched into perhaps the most complex and difficult operation undertaken by British Forces since 1945. That the battalion, unprepared in April, 1982, for the commitment so hurriedly placed upon it, should have responded as it did and should have subsequently acquitted itself so well, is testimony to his leadership and the direction he gave. Colonel Mackay-Dick's arrival coincided with a number of other changes at the top of the battalion: Major Andrew Joscelyne took over as Second-in-Command from Major Campbell Gordon, while Major Julian Crowe took command of Left Flank and Major Patrick

Gascoigne arrived from Hong Kong to command Headquarter Company, later moving to Right Flank. Meanwhile Captain Johnny Stewart had already taken over as Adjutant from Captain Andrew Foster prior to the battalion leaving London. Later in the autumn RSM Clemison was to replace RSM Mackenzie.

The battalion's two years in Cyprus followed a pattern which sought to maximize every opportunity to train, while ensuring that individual members of the battalion and, most importantly their families, enjoyed their time on the island to the fullest extent possible. Against the background of an operational role which required the battalion to be able in an emergency to secure all British military installations in the two SBAs and to be ready to protect British nationals island-wide, Colonel Mackay-Dick devised a policy which divided his battalion's time between the discharge of its operational responsibilities, training and sport.

With Cyprus still relatively unaffected in 1984 by the spread of international terrorism, the battalion, while always ready to react to the unexpected, was able to follow a routine which allowed maximum use to be made of the excellent training facilities and the myriad of adventurous training and sporting opportunities that the island and its coastline had to offer. Windsurfing, sailing, swimming, water ski-ing, canoeing and tennis (and ski-ing in the Troodos Mountains in the winter) to mention but some, were among the sports which people were able to enjoy, some for the first time in their lives, and many became real experts in their chosen recreation.

Whilst the staff in Headquarters British Forces worked a morning only routine, Colonel Mackay-Dick did not think that this was appropriate for a battalion of young men whose average age was twenty-one and who were extremely keen to be kept occupied in their operational role and to take advantage of the outstanding opportunities for training, adventurous training, travel and all forms of sport which existed in Cyprus. He therefore devised a routine which ensured that, if men were not involved on operational duties or field training, they were to be occupied in the afternoons in adventurous training or sporting activities. The battalion therefore ran its own courses on such afternoons and men were allowed to choose whatever activity or course they wished. The Commanding Officer's overriding principle in all of this was that people should get out and do something constructive and, most of all, enjoy themselves, while at the same time learning a new skill. It was a system that worked well, one example of its success being that four members of the battalion won the Cyprus Board Sailing Team Championships in 1985 against stiff competition from the RAF, only one year after the battalion's arrival in Cyprus and having never boardsailed in their lives before.

It would be easy to draw invidious comparisons between the situation encountered by the 1st Battalion in Hong Kong in 1982 and 1983 and that of the 2nd Battalion two years later in Cyprus. However, any parallels which people might be tempted to draw would necessarily be superficial. As this chapter has already made clear the 1st Battalion's arrival in the Far East after a demanding operational tour in Ulster was followed by two years when there was little pause from an almost non-stop round of military duty and training when for much of the time the battalion was the subject of close and often critical inspection by people unfamiliar with or ignorant of the pressures that life in the colony could exert upon the lone British battalion. Similar pressures were not present in Cyprus, where, by comparison, the 2nd Battalion had perhaps fewer obligations to the local people and was not involved in as heavy an operational commitment. Most important of all, those responsible for preparing the 2nd Battalion for its tour of duty in Cyprus were able to learn from the 1st Battalion's experience and nobody was allowed to leave Chelsea Barracks in January, 1984, believing that he was about to embark upon 'a sunshine tour'.

Circumstances were different for the families as well; in Hong Kong those unlucky not to be quartered from the outset in barracks had to endure high-rise living among the clamorous Chinese population of Kowloon. In Cyprus conditions were altogether more satisfactory, with about half of the 2nd Battalion's families living just outside Limassol at Berengaria. While the latter was affectionately known as 'Tenko', after the television serial depicting a Japanese prisoner-of-war camp, because the houses resembled huts similar to those in the film, in reality those who lived there were very happy and generally thoroughly enjoyed the island tour.

Towards the end of the battalion's time in Cyprus history was made when SQMS Foley of the Royal Army Pay Corps paraded in front of Colonel Mackay-Dick on leaving the battalion. Twelve years previously at Windsor he had joined the 1st Battalion when Colonel Mackay-Dick was the Adjutant and subsequently served two full tours with both battalions of the Regiment, just one of many examples of how those attached to the Scots Guards throughout the period of this history have served their parent battalion with devotion and respect, thereby earning an equal measure of gratitude and affection from their Scots Guards colleagues.

1985

For the 2nd Battalion two years in Cyprus passed very quickly. Akamas, in the far west of the island, offered lots of scope for imaginative exercises and the climax of the battalion's training in both years of its tour was Exercise TARTAN CRUSADE when it deployed as an all-arms battle group, complete with its own armoured car support provided by a squadron of the 15th/19th The King's Royal Hussars, to fire all its weapons and to practise a wide variety of operations. Other support included artillery, engineers, helicopters, RCT landing craft, Hercules transport aircraft and Harriers and Jaguars from RAF Akrotiri while, according to Captain Stewart's Battalion Digest, in 1984 six donkeys from a local village were also pressed into service on the battalion's behalf.

Being one of the only two teeth arm major units within the Cyprus Command the battalion was left to get on with arranging and executing its own training, both General Langley and his successor, Air Vice Marshal Ken Hayr, taking the line that so long as Colonel Mackay-Dick and his guardsmen provided satisfactory coverage of the battalion's routine operational commitments they should be trusted to manage their own training without excessive outside interference, a refreshing difference of approach from those senior commanders who in peacetime tend to over-supervise their units, often stifling good ideas and initiative as a result.

While at Episkopi the battalion entered for nearly every sporting and adventurous training event and won a considerable number of them. A major success in mid-October, 1985, was the battalion's performance during the Cyprus Walkabout, a misleadingly named two-day mountain double marathon orienteering exercise, when the battalion took eight of the first nine places. The winning team, which incidentally beat the previous best time set two years earlier by the Argylls by a whole hour, comprised Lieutenant Jonathan Perks, on attachment to the battalion from the Royal Signals, Lance Sergeant Fleck and Piper Marshall. It provided a fitting climax to an extremely active and happy tour, described by Major Ewan Lawrie, the Quartermaster, 'as the best two years of my life. The guardsmen were not allowed to get bored, exercises were highly organized and the families loved it, as did the single men', whilst RSM Clemison, who having earlier served in Hong Kong with the 1st Battalion, was well able to appreciate how much more fortunate the 2nd Battalion was, commented on returning to Britain that 'the tour had been good fun; there was not much high profile soldiering but the battalion was sad to leave although two years were probably long enough'. However, lest the reader should assume that the tour was a continuous stream of successes it is worth recording that in November 1985 the battalion sent its rugby team to Israel to play a friendly match against a local fifteen who beat them by sixty-four points to nil!

Three months later, at the end of February, 1986, the battalion returned to Britain, this time to Cavalry Barracks, Hounslow and a tour of public duties which was to last six years. Two years in Cyprus had seen the battalion at the peak of efficiency, a fact which did not escape the notice of the Colonel when he visited in May, 1985. On return to York House he wrote to Colonel Mackay-Dick in the following words: 'I can't remember ever seeing a battalion that was livelier, happier and fitter than yours and I found it a great stimulus to talk to all those eager guardsmen who were plainly extracting the maximum value out of their time in Cyprus and taking full advantage of all the multifarious opportunities available to them. My visit gave me much pleasure as well as making me feel very proud.'

CHAPTER TEN

PUBLIC DUTIES, ARMOURED INFANTRY AND THE GULF WAR

1st Battalion: Pirbright-Hohne
2nd Battalion: Hounslow

1st Battalion
1984

Within a month of re-assembling at Elizabeth Barracks, Pirbright on 5 March, 1984, the 1st Battalion found itself mounting public duties for the first time in four years, whilst also providing a platoon on standby to assist the Metropolitan Police in the event of a security incident at Heathrow or Gatwick Airport. Operation TRUSTEE was by 1984 a familiar role for battalions and regiments serving in the London area and military support for the police was rehearsed at regular intervals, especially at times of international tension when a terrorist attack was assessed as a possibility. When deployed, guardsmen generally enjoyed the duty, although confinement to Pirbright Camp for long periods at a few hours' notice could be irksome. Operation TRUSTEE was a commitment which fell naturally to the Army and London District was the obvious formation to command the troops needed to watch over its execution.

For the first year of the battalion's time at Pirbright, the Guards Depot, located in the adjoining Alexander Barracks, was commanded by Lieutenant Colonel Malcolm Ross. Both he and Colonel Kim Ross determined that the Depot and the 1st Battalion should work closely together to improve some of the more austere aspects of 'Pirbright Life' and some positive ideas originated as a result.

During Colonel Ross's time as Commandant, the Depot found itself caught up in yet another round of structural and financial reorganization; restrictions on numbers of recruits, ideas for reshaping the training machine and the arrival at the Depot of junior leaders from the Parachute Regiment to train alongside their Household Division counterparts, all occurred during his period in command and inevitably added to the difficulty of providing a steady supply of trained soldiers for battalions, several of which were desperately short of manpower. That the storm was successfully weathered was in no small part thanks to Colonel Malcolm Ross's leadership and experience gained during

45. "However, of greatest importance was the journey to Scotland to receive New Colours from Her Majesty The Queen at Hopetoun House on 27 June, 1988." (Page 183). Accompanied by the 2nd Battalion Families Officer, Captain Cyd Loveday, The Queen meets soldiers and their wives after the parade. Here she is seen talking to PSM Anderson and his wife.

46. "At Hohne the 1st Battalion began 1990 with the prospect of a heavy year in BAOR during which it would first train as a battle group in Canada." (Page 189). The 1st Battalion Battle Group on the prairie at Suffield on completion of Exercise MEDICINE MAN in May, 1990.

47. Warrior Infantry Fighting Vehicles in a leaguer on the Soltau training area, a scene well known to anybody who has participated in exercises across the North German Plain. This photograph was taken in October, 1990, the last time that the 1st Battalion was to train through the Rheinsehlen 'dustbowl'.

48. "The battalion's involvement was very limited, with the rifle companies moving from leaguer to leaguer across the barren gravel plain over which the advance into Iraq took place." (Page 195). C Company of the 1st Battalion in Assembly Area RAY prior to the Gulf War land offensive.

49. "Even before command passed, two Scots Guards patrols had had contacts with the IRA and thereafter the pace never really slackened for the whole period of the tour." (Page 200). Major Charles Page directs Right Flank's operations in North Belfast in May, 1992.

50. "The crowning event for everyone associated with the Scots Guards in 1992 was the Review of the Regiment by Her Majesty The Queen, its Colonel in Chief, in celebration of its 350th Anniversary." (Page 202). Accompanied by the Colonel and Brigadier Michael Scott, The Queen inspects the parade in Holyrood Park.

51. "Both Commanding Officers and both battalions' Colours were on parade, as was the State Colour, carried by Lieutenant Giles Taylor, the first occasion when all five Colours possessed by the Regiment have paraded together." (Page 203). On the right Lieutenant Simon Orwin carries the 2nd Battalion Queen's Colour and 2nd Lieutenant Marcus Barnett the Regimental Colour. The State Colour is on the left.

52. "In January, 1993, Major Andrew Bell took Left Flank of the 2nd Battalion to exercise in the Oman." (Page 206)

previous training appointments at Pirbright, Oswestry and at the Royal Military Academy, Sandhurst.

The 1st Battalion's tour at Pirbright was to last for four years until February, 1988, when it was planned that it should move to Germany in the mechanized role. In the meantime the 2nd Battalion was also soon to return to Britain – to Hounslow in March, 1986 – from where it was to undertake public duties for five years until moving to Edinburgh in early 1992. Thus for a period of eight years a battalion of the Regiment, and for two of them both battalions, was to be engaged upon ceremonial duties with only occasional breaks for operational deployment or overseas training. The growing tendency towards longer tours of duty within London District was to give rise to some disquiet within the Household Division where it was feared that, unless very carefully managed, such tours could result in staleness and disillusionment and the diminishment of opportunities for adventure and excitement, the very ingredients of a military life which young people find so attractive and which help every soldier to endure the relatively mundane routine of a public duties battalion. It was small consolation that the policy which gave rise to this situation had originated from a laudable wish on the part of the Ministry of Defence to reduce turbulence for both soldiers and their families by retaining units for longer in a particular role or station. However, it escaped nobody's notice that the same policy also allowed the costs involved in providing training for the numerous changes of role undertaken by the Infantry and Royal Armoured Corps to be considerably reduced.

Over the whole period covered by this history those responsible have sought ways of reducing the state ceremonial and public duties commitment in London and at Windsor. This is not the place to enter into a long description of how this difficult process of retrenchment has been conducted, but some facts will help to illustrate the extent of the changes which have taken place. In 1956 it required three officers and forty Warrant Officers, NCOs and guardsmen to provide the daily Queen's Guard. In addition the Bank of England Picquet required another one officer and eleven soldiers. The Queen's Birthday Parade that year would have comprised 600 all ranks in eight Guards supported by over 400 bandsmen, drummers and pipers, whilst troops from the Household Division would have also lined the Mall and 'kept the ground' around Horse Guards Parade with an inner line of sentries. Full Guards of Honour at a strength of three officers and ninety-nine soldiers were regularly mounted for visiting Heads of State or at the annual State Opening of Parliament, although smaller Guards at the Ministry of Defence had not by then been instituted. It is also worth noting that, so long as sufficient manpower was available, a Scots Guards Guard of Honour went to Edinburgh every year in the late 1950s and early 1960s as a matter of course. In addition to these ceremonial duties guardsmen supported the Royal Family in a number of other ways such as by providing orderlies at Garden Parties or baggage parties to move the Royal luggage whenever the Royal Family left London for an appreciable period.

Since 1956 many changes have taken place. Most have been designed to ease the commitment on the soldier at a time of ever-increasing military involvement both at home and abroad, although some measures have been prompted by the need to provide a greater degree of security for the Royal Family. Successive Major Generals and their staffs at Horse Guards have sought ways to reduce the load on the Household Division's soldiers. They have had to conduct delicate negotiations with those other Government agencies which maintain an interest in how ceremonial within the Capital is conducted while at the same time persuading Her Majesty The Queen, an acknowledged expert on the subject, of the rightness and efficacy of any proposed changes. It would fill a chapter to record all the alterations that have taken place over the last forty years but it is worth recording that by 1993 the Queen's Guard had been reduced to three officers and thirty-two soldiers with the Tower of London Guard supplementing the Guard Changing Ceremony at Buckingham Palace before proceeding to the Tower to mount duty there. Battalions and regiments outside the Household Division and the RAF now provide troops to mount ceremonial duties on a regular basis and assist with street lining on state occasions. Ceremonial sentries at the Royal Palaces have since 1972 adopted a tactical disposition during the hours of darkness. Forty-eight-hour guards are now mounted throughout the winter months, and, depending upon whether The Queen is in residence or not, at other times as well. The Bank Picquet was discontinued in 1973 while ground-keeping around Horse Guards ceased in 1964. However, following decisions taken by the Government in 1991 to reduce the size of the Army by thirty percent by April, 1995, a radical review was initiated in 1992 to ascertain what scope existed for further reductions in the ceremonial commitment in order to match an impending reduction in the number of Foot Guards battalions from eight to five. As a result one sentry post was removed at each of the three Royal Palaces and the Tower Guard is to be considerably reduced after 1994. State ceremonial is also to suffer cutbacks with the Birthday Parade being cut down permanently to six Guards and with London State Visits in future being confined to one a year, with the distance between streetliners for all state occasions being increased from six to nine paces. Some more minor but equally important changes have also been agreed. It is to be hoped that this latest round of cuts will be accepted as being the limit beyond which it would be wrong to go; any demands for further reductions will inevitably call into question the viability of public duties and state ceremonial in their present form, and will cause those most closely involved to examine the continuing ability of the Household Division to provide Her Majesty The Queen and her family with a level of support unquestioned in the past.

It is against the background of much of what has been written in the preceding paragraphs that the life of the 1st Battalion at Pirbright – and two years later that of the 2nd Battalion at Hounslow – must be seen. After the demands of four busy years, first in Ulster and later in Hong Kong and with a high degree of separation in both stations, the 1st Battalion needed time to

174

build up its stamina again. Public duties provided exactly the right military environment for this; training was kept to an essential minimum and, within the scope permitted by the duty roster, the battalion was given ample opportunity to relax and enjoy being at home again. RSM Macfarlane prepared the battalion well for a heavy summer of ceremonial, including the provision of Numbers Five and Six Guards on the Birthday Parade commanded respectively by Majors James Napier and Douglas Erskine Crum. The Sergeant Major completed his time with successful Guards of Honour for the Amir of Bahrain in April and President Mitterand of France in October before handing over to RSM Fowler who came to the battalion from a secondment as RSM at the Nigerian Army Staff College. The only routine public duty which he had undertaken prior to his appointment was at the Tower of London, but, with the assistance and guidance of the Garrison Sergeant Major London District, RSM Dumon of the Coldstream Guards, RSM Fowler soon learnt the requirements of his job.

Two successive Easters found elements of the battalion deployed to support the police and the RAF in protecting the two United States Air Force Cruise Missile Sites in Britain, at Greenham Common in 1984 and at Molesworth in Cambridgeshire in 1985. Both deployments involved the battalion being held in reserve. At Molesworth the police manned the perimeter of the base and guardsmen therefore had little or no contact with the so called 'peace women' and their supporters who marched to besiege the bases, while at Greenham Common soldiers patrolled inside the perimeter and could therefore attempt to establish some dialogue with 'the opposition'. Deployment to Molesworth was more exciting than that at Greenham, with 10,000 people marching to the airfield where they attempted to pull down the wire around the base; although the battalion had no direct involvement with the protesters it did at least have the satisfaction of being able to deploy its night viewing devices to detect those attempting to infiltrate the police!

An event of an altogether different nature had taken place at Pirbright in mid November, 1984, when Colonel Ross arranged a lunch party to say farewell to Major Fred Adams who was retiring from the Army, having spent his final tour as the Housing Commandant responsible for all married families in the Pirbright Cantonment; described as 'the greatest gathering ever of Household Division Quartermasters, past and present' over fifty people turned out to say goodbye to one of the Regiment's most popular and revered personalities. Major Jim Bunton, the Quartermaster of the 1st Battalion and the organizer of the event afterwards wrote some lines of poetry to commemorate it for the 1984 *Scots Guards Magazine* and these are reproduced below:

> You were there when we 'lunched' Fred out!
> The Quartermaster cadre from all about.
> You came from far and you came from near,
> To have a chat and quaff a beer.

The Cavalry! The Grenadiers!
'Nulli Secundus', these are our Peers?
'The Taff', 'The Mick' and of course 'The Jock'.
These are the Guards, no man can mock.

We gathered in Pirbright at the mid-day hour,
In groups of two, or three, or "fower",
Old friends were there, a glorious host
A lesson in loyalty for the rest, I boast.

The insults flew both thick and fast,
A result of friendships old and past,
We heard of 'Salerno' and 'Medenine'
'Monte Camino' and 'Pirbright Green'.

Old fights were fought and stories told,
But the men who spoke will ne'er grow old.
You are our Regiments, strong and true,
Our History written by such as you.

We felt a humble, simple pride,
At being there, on the inside.
A success it was, there is no doubt,
The day we all 'lunched' Fred out.

1985 followed much the same form as 1984 although both Right and Left Flank managed to leave Britain on some excellent overseas training. Right Flank under Major John Cargill and CSM R. Walker spent an extremely successful and professionally satisfying month in the Oman early in the New Year training with both the Omani Army and Air Force under the most realistic circumstances. Later, in the early autumn, Major James Greenfield and CSM Kelly took Left Flank to train near Udine in North-East Italy, while a mechanized infantry company of Italians came to Pirbright in exchange, to be hosted by C Company. Otherwise public duties and a period of training at Otterburn kept the battalion busy until the end of the year when Colonel Kim Ross ended his tour in command and handed over the battalion to Lieutenant Colonel John Kiszely. Few commanding officers can have achieved quite such a close rapport with their battalion as did Colonel Ross who will long be remembered by those serving both within the Regiment and outside it for his deep interest in every aspect of the Scots Guards and his total commitment to those under his command. His thirty-two years service came to an end in 1993 with the achievement of the rank of Brigadier and a permanent place in the heart of every Scots Guardsman who had served with him, and in the hearts of many others who knew him only by repute.

Cavalry Barracks in the outer London Borough of Hounslow has seen many different occupants, including Headquarters Eastern Command, since their construction in the 1790s and the arrival of the 2nd Battalion in March, 1986, therefore caused little stir. Built in the style of the times and with scant modernization since, the barracks, occupied because Victoria Barracks at Windsor were being rebuilt, offered little in the way of late Twentieth Century comforts and presented a bleak prospect after Episkopi. However, undaunted by such a perspective, the battalion soon got down to the job of preparing for its first public duty on 18 April, the performance of ceremonial duties being relatively easy since the battalion had only been away from London for two years and memories had had little chance to dim in the intervening period. Hounslow was by no stretch of the imagination a perfect station; situated at the eastern end of the northernmost runway of Heathrow Airport the noise of incoming jet aircraft disrupted most conversations, while the fact that a majority of the battalion's families were quartered in Windsor made the conduct of battalion social life awkward, particularly for the more gregarious members of the Sergeants' Mess. The battalion's re-initiation into public duties proceeded smoothly enough and on 14 June the Queen's Colour of the 1st Battalion was trooped on The Queen's Birthday Parade. Colonel Johnny Clavering exercised his privilege as the Lieutenant Colonel Commanding to command the parade (the last time that the holder of that appointment was to do so) and the 1st Battalion provided the Escort and Number Two Guard, commanded respectively by Major Tim Spicer and Major Simon Price while 2nd Lieutenant James Prior, whose father had commanded Right Flank of the 2nd Battalion in Kenya in 1964, carried the Colour. CSMs Callachan and Crockett were the right guides of the two 1st Battalion Guards while Major Niall Crichton-Stuart was Adjutant of the Parade and Majors Patrick Gascoigne and Julian Crowe commanded Numbers Three and Four Guards found by the 2nd Battalion. RSM Fowler was Sergeant Major of the Parade. A year later these roles were to be reversed with the 2nd Battalion's Queen's Colour being trooped and with the 1st Battalion providing Numbers Three and Four Guards.

1986 was an important year for the Regiment for a number of reasons. On 24 June the Colonel in Chief, Her Majesty The Queen, accompanied by His Royal Highness The Duke of Edinburgh and the Colonel, attended the Sesquicentennial Dinner of the Third Guards Club held in the Savoy Hotel. A month later the 2nd Battalion provided fourteen half-companies to line part of the processional route along the Mall on the occasion of the wedding of His Royal Highness Prince Andrew to Miss Sarah Ferguson. Colonel Clavering, accompanied by the Regimental Adjutant, was responsible for the sector of streetliners from Admiralty Arch to Westminster Abbey; unfortunately just after the Procession had passed them on its return journey to Buckingham Palace, the Lieutenant Colonel's horse, Bugle Boy, collapsed and died beneath him. However, the presence of two Scots Guards battalions on the public duties roster did not last for long and, following the Birthday Parade, the 1st Battalion ceased to carry out any ceremonial duties as a prelude to deploying to Northern Ireland for a tour of duty in South Armagh. Meantime the 2nd Battalion continued to commute from Hounslow to the centre of London occupying a prominent position in the Brigade Major's ceremonial programme.

On 10 October Colonel Mackay-Dick, having seen his battalion well settled into Cavalry Barracks, handed over to Lieutenant Colonel Julian Lancaster. In passing it should be mentioned that earlier in the year the appointment of Major General had been filled by Major General Christopher Airy, a former Commanding Officer of the 1st Battalion who had started life in the Grenadier Guards. During the time that General Airy commanded the Household Division, the Grenadier Guards appointed a Scots Guards Officer, Lieutenant Colonel Andrew Joscelyne, to command the 2nd Battalion Grenadier Guards. When he assumed command of the 1st Battalion from Colonel Ross, Colonel Kiszely considered that he was faced by two immediate challenges; the first, that of ensuring that the Escort and Number Two Guard achieved the highest possible standards on the 1986 Queen's Birthday Parade, he soon dismissed, since he knew that, prepared by RSM Fowler, the guardsmen would deliver their best. His second challenge was to make certain that the battalion went to Ulster as well prepared as possible. South Armagh had long been an area of particular danger and unpleasantness for the Army and the RUC, its close proximity to the border with the Irish Republic and its population by people with strong republican tendencies ensured that the area was unlikely to be well disposed towards the Security Forces. The scale of the challenge had become apparent for all to see as the years progressed and Security Forces casualties in South Armagh mounted.

1st Battalion South Armagh

The battalion deployed on 10 September with Battalion Headquarters, C Company and the Echelon at Bessbrook Mill, Right Flank and part of B Company at Crossmaglen and Left Flank at Forkhill. It inherited a company of The Prince of Wales's Own Regiment of Yorkshire and a platoon of Coldstream Guards from the outgoing 2nd Battalion The Royal Anglian Regiment and at the end of September was joined by Support Company, 1st Battalion Grenadier Guards. If nothing else this order of battle demonstrates that the military approach to operations in Northern Ireland had by 1986 become one of maximum flexibility with units and sub-units being deployed regardless of capbadge at little notice to reinforce those areas which offered the best potential for operations against the IRA. The 1st Battalion's mission was to prevent terrorist activities in that area adjacent to the border for which it was responsible and to interdict those routes through its TAOR used by the IRA to re-supply its active service units across the rest of Ulster. Close co-operation with the RUC and on some occasions through the latter to the Irish Republic Garda was essential if the actions of a skilful and motivated enemy were to be neutralized.

178

Well trained at Lydd and Hythe and later at Stanford, where rural conditions were not too dissimilar to those found in South Armagh, the battalion soon got to grips with its role in Ulster. Operations along the border were mainly conducted on foot with patrols being inserted by helicopter. Road vehicles were hardly used since their vulnerability to attack by remotely controlled mines and booby traps was such as to make them more of a liability than an asset. Helicopters, although increasingly at risk from hand-held surface to air missile systems acquired by the IRA, were invaluable and all movement into and out of the battalion area was by air. Indeed Bessbrook Mill is alleged now to be the busiest heliport in the world, all air movement in and out of the base being controlled by an officer specifically appointed for the purpose. In 1986 Captain Ronnie MacKenzie fulfilled the task, carrying the radio appointment title of 'Buzzard' to indicate the nature of his responsibilities.

The rifle companies located in Crossmaglen, Forkhill and Bessbrook covered the border area with patrols of varying duration tasked to watch for terrorist movement while the majority of B Company manned the 'high rise' watchtowers established to give uninterrupted surveillance of approaches and areas assessed as being used by the IRA. Operations resembled a game of cat and mouse and a mistake by one side would quickly be capitalized upon by the other; alertness and discipline were essential since a momentary lapse could jeopardize the lives of a complete patrol. Although there were a number of mortar attacks on all the battalion's bases and frequent operations had to be mounted to clear suspected or real explosive devices planted by the IRA, more often than not on the main Belfast to Dublin railway line, the battalion, unlike its predecessors, suffered no casualties during its time in South Armagh, a fitting tribute to the way in which it had been prepared for its task and the manner in which at all levels it operated while in the Province. Equally very few members of the IRA have ever been killed or captured by the Security Forces in South Armagh, a fact which demonstrates all too clearly the skill of the terrorist and the degree of local support for the movement in that area of Northern Ireland.

On 21 January, 1987, the battalion handed over its responsibilities to the 1st Battalion The Royal Hampshire Regiment and returned to Pirbright. Although the battalion lost no one to the IRA whilst in South Armagh, it suffered one death during its time there when at Bessbrook Mill on 21 October Major Duncan Nicol died in his sleep. A Scots Guardsman since 1958, Major Nicol had recently returned to the 1st Battalion to command Headquarter Company. Although both older and more senior than all the other officers in the battalion, including Colonel Kiszely, he, like both Major George Nickerson and Major Bruce Bell before him in the 2nd Battalion, had been prepared to return to the battalion to undertake an appointment of a nature well below expectations because it helped the Regiment that he should so do. A kind man whose dry sense of humour always amused but never wounded, his death was a great blow to the 1st Battalion and to all his many friends in the Regiment.

Return from leave in mid-February, 1987, was followed by a hectic spring and summer of public duties. Royal duties in London and at Windsor, Guards of Honour, Numbers Three and Four Guards on the Queen's Birthday Parade when the Queen's Colour of the 2nd Battalion was trooped, various inspections and, most important of all, the presentation of New Colours by Her Majesty The Queen on 24 June, were all crammed into little more than four months.

Presentation of New Colours

The Presentation of Colours in the garden at Buckingham Palace was as always a special day; blessed with fine weather, over 400 members of the battalion paraded in front of The Queen, watched by a large number of their families and invited guests, demonstrating once again just how smoothly and efficiently a battalion of the Household Division can put aside an operational role and four months later achieve equally high standards, this time of drill and turnout, in the presence of its Colonel in Chief. After the parade several members of the battalion, their wives and representatives of the Association, who always support such regimental occasions so loyally, were presented to The Queen. Following these important events the pace eased, although the battalion continued to undertake a wide range of duties until 28 September when it mounted its last Queen's Guard before putting away its tunics and beginning conversion training in readiness for its planned move to Germany and the role once again of a mechanized battalion.

2nd Battalion 1987

For the 2nd Battalion the fifteen months from March, 1987, to July, 1988, followed a very similar pattern of events to those experienced by the 1st Battalion a year before. However, before trooping its Colour in June, a welcome diversion in the form of a six week exercise in the United States came its way. Fort Lewis in Washington State was home to the US Army 1st Corps, a formation of 50,000 soldiers, based in the centre of an extensive training area where nearly every phase of war could be practised. Exercise TRUMPET DANCE allowed the battalion a break from public duties and in some small measure helped to persuade a number of soldiers that it was worth remaining in the Army.

By the Spring of 1987 the battalion was already aware that, following a long period of public duties, there was the possibility of a residential tour of duty in Ulster and it was a prospect that did not thrill everybody. Consequently many guardsmen had converted on to a 'notice engagement' which permitted them to leave the Army at any time provided that they had given the requisite period of warning of their intention; in a sense they were hedging their bets against the future not providing the degree of stimulation they wanted and it naturally concerned Colonel Lancaster. For him Exercise TRUMPET DANCE and a subsequent roulement tour in Northern Ireland in the autumn could only help to persuade his guardsmen that, although they faced at least three years of public duties, there were other more exciting commitments to look forward to.

Six weeks in the United States did provide a tonic and the battalion trained and played hard with everybody disappearing at the end to every corner of the continent for a few days' leave. The training facilities at Fort Lewis were

180

excellent and the people of the area welcoming to a fault; when Major Iain Dalzel Job went on the local radio to promote his 'Take a Jock' idea by which he hoped to persuade local residents to invite members of the battalion into their homes, the response was overwhelming. For his part RSM Clemison only remembers playing golf for much of the time but acknowledges that much serious training did take place and that everybody returned to Hounslow considerably refreshed and ready for the next bout of ceremonial duties. Before leaving the United States a party led by the Commanding Officer visited San Francisco as guests of the US 6th Army and presented a Union Flag to the Mayoress. They also entered a team for a local marathon and the Pipes and Drums beat retreat.

1987 was the turn for the 2nd Battalion's Queen's Colour to be trooped and, Colonel Clavering having commanded in 1986, it fell to Colonel Lancaster to command the parade. Captain Michael Joynson was the Adjutant in Brigade Waiting, while Majors Rory Ingleby-Mackenzie and Euan Kelway-Bamber commanded the Escort and Number Two Guard respectively. 2nd Lieutenant Willie Swinton carried the Queen's Colour, while RSM Clemison, whose last parade it was before leaving the battalion on commissioning, was the Sergeant Major. The 1st Battalion provided Numbers Three and Four Guards commanded by Majors James Napier and Johnny Stewart. It was the first occasion upon which Her Majesty The Queen did not ride on parade, travelling instead to Horse Guards in a carriage and watching the parade from a dais positioned in front of the Arch. It was also the first time that the five Foot Guards Lieutenant Colonels paraded not as Colonels but in the rank of Lieutenant Colonel, their appointments having been downgraded the previous year by the Ministry of Defence. For the Regiment this meant that Lieutenant Colonel Michael Whiteley had taken over from Colonel Clavering the previous February. The parade was also the last upon which the self-loading rifle was carried, that weapon having earlier been replaced throughout the Army by the smaller, more compact and easier to handle SA80 5.56mm assault weapon. At the time there was some speculation as to how easy it would be to drill with the latter but once the combined intellects of the senior Warrant Officers in the Household Division had been brought to bear on the problem, it was easily resolved.

The 1987 Regular Army Rifle Meeting took place at Bisley in early July. Captained by Captain Simon Thornhill and coached by Colour Sergeant Gwynne, the battalion came a very creditable second; shooting has never been a skill at which either battalion of the Regiment has ever excelled consistently and to achieve such a good result entailed much hard work and not a little skill.

Following this, the battalion ceased mounting public duties and began its preparations for a tour of duty in South Armagh, moving to that area of Northern Ireland just eight months after the 1st Battalion had returned. It occupied the same base locations with Battalion Headquarters, F Company and the Echelon at Bessbrook Mill, while Right Flank under Major Rory Ingleby-Mackenzie and CSM MacRae went to Crossmaglen and G Company with Major

*2nd Battalion
South Armagh*

181

Andrew Foster and CSM Rankin deployed to Newton Hamilton. Left Flank, under Major Euan Kelway-Bamber and CSM Hammel, was at Forkhill. The tour passed in much the same way as the 1st Battalion's the year before with every company and platoon working hard to ensure that pressure was maintained upon the IRA and that they were afforded no opportunity to strike against the Security Forces. There were few incidents of any note and Colonel Lancaster concluded at the end of the four months that it was almost as if the enemy had decided not to risk taking the battalion on. This may sound like a boast but it was undoubtedly the case that if a battalion determined 'to sit on the IRA hard' it usually sustained few if any casualties and left its area more peaceful at the end of its time.

One aspect of cross-border movement which the battalion did witness at first hand was the blatant smuggling of a wide range of commercial products backwards and forwards across the border in order that those involved could benefit from generous subsidies which some trade between countries of the European Community attracted and because of pricing differences between the North and South of Ireland. Such traffic was openly manipulated in order to gain maximum benefit, most notably by the IRA themselves who throughout the present campaign have regularly subsidized their funds from this and other illegal activities. Along the border heavy goods vehicles would be driven into farms which had access to both countries and, having qualified for a subsidy, would be driven back again. On one day the 2nd Battalion logged sixty such vehicle movements. It seemed that little could be done to prevent such flagrant manipulation of the rules and, while it was fortunately not the Army's task to prevent such activities, it nonetheless affronted those whose job it was to maintain the rule of law in an area that has rightly come to be dubbed 'bandit country'.

The battalion handed over to 40 Commando Royal Marines on 24 February and returned to Hounslow. Apart from a soldier of the Royal Welch Fusiliers who was seriously injured in a mortar attack while his company was serving under the battalion's operational command there had been no casualties. However, while at Newton Hamilton Lance Corporal Lindsay of G Company was diagnosed as suffering from motor neurone disease and had to be evacuated; a guardsman of great potential and incidentally an Army footballer, he later died, a tragic loss to the Regiment. Before the tour began RSM Harper had taken over as Sergeant Major, thereby returning to Bessbrook for the second time in the year having been there with the 1st Battalion as a Drill Sergeant, while Adjutants had also changed when Captain Mark Bence-Trower had taken over from Captain Michael Joynson a month before the deployment. It had been hard work getting the battalion up to standard to prepare it for what has always been considered to be the toughest operational area in Northern Ireland, but, once that standard had been reached the battalion, like the 1st Battalion before it, delivered what was needed.

Returning to Hounslow from leave in mid April the battalion plunged immediately into public duties and over a period of little more than three months mounted two full Guards of Honour for visiting Heads of State, the King of Norway and the President of Turkey, with both Guards commanded by Major Ingleby-Mackenzie, paraded in the presence of Her Majesty Queen Elizabeth The Queen Mother to mark the twentieth anniversary of the granting of the freedom of the Borough of Windsor to the Household Division and provided Numbers Four and Five Guards on the Birthday Parade.

However, of greatest importance was the journey to Scotland to receive New Colours from Her Majesty The Queen at Hopetoun House, the family seat of the Earls of Linlithgow to the west of Edinburgh, on 27 June. The gardens at Hopetoun provided an ideal setting for such a parade and the spectacle of the battalion marching on to the main lawns around the lake was very dramatic. Appalling traffic chaos on the route into the grounds was not allowed to mar what was a most successful day and in the evening a Third Guards Club Dance took place in Hopetoun House whilst the Sergeants' Mess held a ball for over 1,000 people at the Royal Highland Showground at Ingliston. The only sadness was the fact that the battalion was in Scotland for less than ten days and that very few of the families could afford to make the long journey north from Hounslow. It is also worth noting that 29 June was the first occasion when a battalion of the Regiment drilled in front of The Queen with the new SA80 assault weapon which was carried on parade at the slope rather than being held parallel to the body as was the case with the self loading rifle. *Presentation of Colours*

The 1st Battalion's final act before handing over Elizabeth Barracks to the 1st Battalion Welsh Guards was to lay up its Old Colours at St Columba's Church, Pont Street in London on 4 February, 1988. A number of senior Scots Guardsmen were present and the Colours were carried up the aisle by 2nd Lieutenants Charlie Mayfield and David Leslie, escorted by RSM Amos and Sergeants Goodall, McDonald and Nelson, after which Colonel Kiszely handed them to the Minister of the Kirk for safekeeping. *1st Battalion Hohne*

A fortnight later the battalion and its families moved to Campbell Barracks, Hohne, to begin a five year tour as one of two mechanized battalions in 22nd Armoured Brigade of 1st Armoured Division. Until 1984 Foot Guards battalions serving in BAOR had usually been based in Munster Garrison, but, following a number of unrelated changes within 1st British Corps, this practice had been gradually discontinued and in 1984 the Welsh Guards had become the first Guards Division battalion to serve in Hohne, a sizeable garrison to the south-west of the Lüneburger Heide, equidistant from the great industrial cities of Hamburg and Hanover and only about forty miles from the Inner German Border. The barracks were very different from those in Munster which were single storey and of poor standard, whilst those in Hohne had been built in the 1930s to accommodate the Wehrmacht for whom Hitler spared little or no expense. The battalion's families were housed either in barracks or in the neighbouring town of Bergen and, once they had adjusted to their new surroundings, generally enjoyed their five years there. Hohne is a place which has never been rated very highly by the British Army but which, if people are prepared to make their own entertainment, can be as enjoyable as anywhere in Germany, as the 1st Battalion was determined to demonstrate from the outset. Sadly it is best known for having been the site of the infamous Belsen Concentration Camp, a gloomy place less than a mile from Campbell Barracks where it is alleged that no birds are ever heard to sing and which, after the Second World War, was razed to the ground and made into a memorial to commemorate those who died at the hands of the Nazis.

The battalion adopted a very positive approach to its mechanized role and during the 1988 training season all three rifle companies flew to Canada to train with other battle groups, something not normally arranged for units in their first year in BAOR. Right Flank, commanded by Major Julian Crowe, and C Company, commanded by Major Tom Fitzalan Howard, both accompanied The Queen's Own Hussars to Suffield in September, while Major Peter Farrelly and Left Flank joined the 4th Royal Tank Regiment on the final exercise of the year in October. The decision to expose the three companies early on to training in Canada, which was both professionally stimulating and physically demanding, paid dividends and by the end of October when Colonel Kiszely handed command of the battalion to Lieutenant Colonel John Cargill, the reputation of the 1st Battalion stood high. While much of the credit for this should rightly go to the Commanding Officer, he was *inter alia* well supported by Captain Ron Clemison and Captain Munro Davidson, his Quartermasters and RSM Amos, a tough and thoughtful man whose previous experience, particularly with the Special Air Service Regiment, made him an ideal choice as Sergeant Major of an infantry battalion in a large station such as Hohne.

The battalion was also fortunate to start its time in 22nd Armoured Brigade under Brigadier Hew Pike, a professional soldier of stature and intelligence who provided wise guidance and support which was invariably helpful without ever being prescriptive. Writing several years later, Major General Richard Swinburn, the battalion's Divisional Commander on its arrival in Hohne, said, 'Battalions, like people, exude character. They have a basic character that spans the years, and on top of that is laid the character of the moment, much influenced by those in command at the time. 1SG had a well founded reputation for high military achievement – "the most able soldiers of the [Household] Division" – coupled with a refreshing lack of pomposity and pretentiousness. This translated at Hohne into the battalion grasping the mechanized role with real professionalism, and making genuine friends with both British and Germans living there. Neither happening might seem remarkable, but few did so, and none so successfully.'

Fermanagh and Tyrone

While Colonel Cargill's principal task during his period in command of the 1st Battalion would be to plan and execute the conversion of its APC fleet from the obsolescent FV432 to the new Warrior Infantry Fighting Vehicle during 1990, his first year was to be dominated by another tour in Northern Ireland, this time along the border in the two south-western counties of Fermanagh and

184

Tyrone. After the usual period of training the battalion deployed in June, 1989, having left its APCs and families in the care of the Rear Party, and settled into a life which principally involved monitoring movement across the border with the Irish Republic either by means of covert Observation Posts, patrols or Vehicle Check Points designed to interdict the passage of terrorists, their arms and explosives. There was little new in the task and indeed it was not dissimilar to the role undertaken by the battalion little more than two years previously in South Armagh; however, what was new was that a different area had to be learnt and the local terrorist and his supporters had to be identified and kept under surveillance. The tour was overshadowed by the constant requirement to prevent illegal movement across the border at places where roads and farm tracks had been blocked in order to hamper IRA operations. Naturally any measure that interfered with the local population's freedom of movement around the area was resented and when the same people also gave their support to the IRA, the potential for conflict was inevitably limitless.

Battalion Headquarters and Right Flank, under Major Crowe and CSM Murray, were based at Lisnaskea, while Left Flank, commanded by Major Farrelly with CSM Williamson, was based at Clogher. B Company, with Major Price and CSM McCavera was in Cookstown under command of the 8th Battalion of the Ulster Defence Regiment (UDR), while C Company, commanded by Major Foster with CSM Spence, was under command of the 4th Battalion of the same Regiment in St Angelo.

Early in the tour a major operation involving the battalion and two other infantry companies was mounted at Lacky Bridge to remove a Permanent Vehicle Check Point close to the border and no longer deemed operationally necessary. Immediately dubbed by the Loyalists as a retreat in the face of republican pressure Operation GILLESPIE generated more political reaction than anything else, but was nonetheless eventually successfully completed. This and other closure operations, constant patrolling to deter all forms of terrorist activity and to provide some semblance of support to the 400 or so 'soft targets' – mainly RUC and UDR soldiers – living locally, and joint operations with the police kept the battalion fully occupied for four months.

On 19 September a proxy bomb driven by a local postman acting under duress was delivered to the Permanent Vehicle Check Point at Kilturk; fortunately the bomb failed to explode, although the initiating device went off setting the van on fire. Lance Sergeant Dykes of Right Flank showed great courage during this incident when, regardless of the danger posed to himself, he rescued two disabled women from a nearby house, for which action he was subsequently mentioned in dispatches.

The tour ended on 17 October without any further major incidents when the 1st Battalion The King's Own Scottish Borderers arrived and the battalion returned to Hohne. The battalion lost nobody killed in Fermanagh, but tragedy struck almost as soon as it returned to Germany. On 8 November 2nd Lieutenant David Leslie was killed driving back to Netheravon whilst attending a course, while on 28 November Guardsman Hewitt was killed in a road accident during training at Soltau when the vehicle in which he was travelling skidded on black ice. Both men had served together in 2 Platoon in Right Flank in Ulster and a combined Memorial Service was held for them in Hohne on 14 February, 1990. Earlier, Captain Harry Nickerson handed over the appointment of Adjutant to Captain David Thompson, while, prior to the Lisnaskea tour, RSM R Walker, the youngest of three brothers to serve in the Regiment, all of whom reached Warrant Officer rank, became the Sergeant Major in place of RSM Amos.

The latter part of 1988 saw the 2nd Battalion heavily involved in public duties although opportunities to indulge in wider military activities also came the way of the battalion. Following a breakdown in industrial relations between the Home Office and the Prison Officers Association, troops were drafted in to assist in securing a number of temporary prisons in July. Right Flank and G Company were both involved at a temporary prison established within Deepcut Camp in Surrey to alleviate overcrowding, their role being to secure the outside of the complex, while provost staff from the three services supervised the prisoners. The work was tedious and boring but it did allow soldiers to see how the Prison Service operated and to appreciate that most problems arising between staff and prisoners usually originated from petty bureaucracy (such as when televisions might or might not be used) and the minor infringement of rules which in themselves were not always very realistic. Since the Prison Service has always tended to recruit heavily from those leaving the Armed Forces, a period of duty at Deepcut may have given those contemplating such a second career cause to re-think any such plans.

While the remainder of the battalion continued with public duties at Hounslow, Left Flank, followed four months later by G Company, travelled to Belize to support the 1st Battalion Irish Guards which was undertaking an unaccompanied tour there. These attachments were arranged by Colonel Lancaster with the assistance of Headquarters London District and proved an excellent way of giving those who wished to go overseas an opportunity to do so, while at the same time persuading some guardsmen that they should commit themselves to the Army for rather longer than the scope provided by the 'notice' engagement. Despite this and other measures the Commanding Officer and his team found themselves continually waging 'a battle to keep people in', a recurring theme of this History and a problem which beset the whole Army in the 1980s and 1990s. The Major General and his staff were as aware as anybody of this problem and did what they could to help; from the 2nd Battalion's standpoint it was especially beneficial to have Brigadier Michael Nurton as Commander 56th London Brigade, the one-star formation which, on behalf of the Major General, planned the deployment and training of all units within London District, while the presence of Lieutenant Colonel Douglas Erskine Crum as the Brigade Major Headquarters Household Division, the first Scots Guards officer to hold that prestigious appointment since his late father in 1954, was also valuable. On 24 April he took command of the battalion from Colonel Julian Lancaster who went to assist in running the new Headquarters Foot Guards which had been established earlier in the year to oversee regimental and administrative aspects of the management of the five Foot Guards regiments. These and other changes affecting the Household Division and the Regiment are set out in detail at Appendix A.

Before leaving the battalion Colonel Lancaster had volunteered a team to take part in a military competition which was to form the basis for a programme about the Army being made by Central Television for the BBC. The terms of the competition demanded stamina and mental dexterity from the competitors but made excellent publicity for the Army and the regiments involved. The 2nd Battalion's four-man team, led throughout by Lieutenant The Master of Falkland and Colour Sergeant Gwynne, won its three preliminary rounds and were runners-up to the 2nd Battalion The Parachute Regiment in the Finals, a result generally agreed to be very fair and one which reflected well on the battalion.

In parallel the battalion laid up its Old Colours at Glamis Castle in mid-March before Colonel Lancaster's departure, provided Numbers Seven and Eight Guards, commanded by Majors Gascoigne and Mathewson, on the Queen's Birthday Parade and mounted Guards of Honour for State Visits by the Presidents of Nigeria and the United States, before leaving for Canada to take part in Exercise POND JUMP WEST at Wainwright in Alberta from 1 August to 15 September. The exercise provided yet another tonic for soldiers satiated by a long period of unrelenting ceremonial and allowed Colonel Erskine Crum to 'try out' his battalion for the first time.

As well as inheriting a retention problem, he had also to prepare the battalion for the prospect of a two-year tour of operational duty at Aldergrove similar to that undertaken by the 1st Battalion in 1980/81. In April, 1989, there had still been no official confirmation of the tour, assumed to begin the following March, but there was sufficient speculation to prompt everybody to make up his or her mind as to whether they viewed the future with pleasure or disquiet; in the event it was decided in September that a move to Aldergrove to be the Province Reserve would not take place and that instead the battalion would remain at Hounslow for another two years with a six-month tour in Ulster in March, 1990, a decision greeted with relief by some and disappointment by others.

Exercise POND JUMP WEST was a great success and the battalion flew to Canada at a strength of 792 all ranks, being joined for its six weeks there by detachments from the principal arms which comprise a battle group, as well as by a platoon from the 2nd Battalion Grenadier Guards. The Commanding Officer kept companies and detachments in the field for most of the time, while training and a most imaginative adventure training package was organized for everybody once their field training was complete. Captain Charlie Stisted, the Second-in-Command of Left Flank, arranged the adventure training which was centred upon Jasper in the Rockies. On return the battalion turned its attention firmly towards preparations for its forthcoming tour in Ulster with training at Lydd and Hythe and subsequently at Stanford in December and January, 1990. At the end of the year RSM Harper handed over his appointment to RSM Wood, while Major Ian Beck, having served as the Quartermaster in both battalions of the Regiment, went to the Guards Depot to hold the same appointment there.

Omagh

The 2nd Battalion's tour in Ulster from March to August, 1990, was unique in two respects. First because the battalion was to serve unaccompanied for six and a half months instead of for four and a half months which had previously been the case, the first British Army unit to do so, and, secondly, because all its companies were to be deployed under command of other battalions and Battalion Headquarters was to be allocated no TAOR of its own to control. As might be expected, such a situation was to prove exceedingly frustrating for Colonel Erskine Crum and his command team and, although the Commanding Officer regularly deputised for his opposite number in command of the 8th Battalion UDR, it was poor compensation for not having one's own 'patch' to run. Such a situation arose because of a wish by Army Headquarters in Lisburn to reinforce the border areas of West Ulster to counter an upsurge in terrorist activity; it was easier to achieve this by superimposing the companies of a reinforcing battalion upon the existing infrastructure of units than to create a new area for the former. It was a great tribute to Colonel Erskine Crum that he accepted this situation so stoically.

Upon arrival in mid-March Right Flank, under Major Patrick Gascoigne and CSM Crawford, deployed to Cookstown under command of the 8th Battalion UDR, whilst Left Flank, commanded by Major Simon Thornhill and with CSM R. Jackson, went to Omagh to operate under command of the 6th Battalion. G Company, with Major Alastair Mathewson and CSM W. Scott, was also under command of the 8th Battalion in Dungannon, while F Company, commanded by Major Johnny Stewart with CSM Anderson, operated from Fort George in Londonderry under the control of the resident battalion there, the 1st Battalion The Royal Hampshire Regiment. Finally the Close Observation Platoon, commanded by Captain Marr, was based in Armagh City and operated in East Tyrone and South Armagh. Battalion Headquarters, the role of which was to administer all its detached sub-units, was based in Omagh where, after the first ten days of the tour, Captain Mark Bence-Trower handed over his responsibilities as Adjutant to Captain Charles Page.

Throughout the tour there was a constant level of incidents, most of them involving sniping attacks, the attempted insertion of proxy bombs into military bases or check points or the planting of improvised explosive devices designed to catch patrols of the Army or police. Companies patrolled hard to deter terrorist activity and searches in all areas discovered various quantities of weapons and explosives. On 5 May the battalion sustained its first casualty when a four-man patrol of the Close Observation Platoon, occupying a covert Observation Point near the border village of Cullyhanna to the north of

Crossmaglen, was attacked by the IRA. During the initial engagement Lance Sergeant Stewart was fatally wounded. Lance Corporal Gray, who was subsequently awarded an MM for his action, immediately returned fire in a very aggressive manner, thereby causing the IRA attack to falter and giving Lance Sergeant Belshaw the chance to take the situation under control after which the latter secured a helicopter landing site in order that Lance Sergeant Stewart could be evacuated. Lance Sergeant Belshaw was later to be awarded a BEM.

As the summer months passed all companies had their fair share of activity and nobody departed from the Province in late September feeling that they had not achieved something. On 4 June a Right Flank patrol led by Major Gascoigne narrowly avoided injury when a command-detonated device exploded in Stewartstown, while on 21 June a 200lb bomb exploded outside the Cookstown Post Office. A week later Guardsman McKenzie was wounded when a patrol from G Company was engaged by gunmen in Pomeroy. Although seriously injured he made a full recovery. On 2 August Drummer Brown whose platoon was attached to F Company, was killed by a car when manning a checkpoint in the Strand Road in Londonderry, while on 5 September a Lynx helicopter carrying six members of G Company crashed when taking off near Dungannon.

It was therefore with some relief that the battalion returned to Hounslow at the end of September. The tour had not been without its problems, most of which stemmed from the command arrangements which permitted Colonel Erskine Crum no direct operational control of his companies. Lieutenant General Sir John Wilsey, who arrived as GOC in the Province during the 2nd Battalion's tour, has recorded his first impressions of meeting the battalion and its Commanding Officer: '2SG was one of my first visits. I met Douglas Erskine Crum and was briefed by him in Battalion Headquarters and then we flew around his outlying companies: Londonderry, Cookstown and Dungannon. I was with him for the best part of four hours; I had never met him before but he struck me as being an exceptionally able Commanding Officer, with a good feel for the situation and a clear understanding of what needed to be done. He also had some bright ideas about the future. Based upon that impression, and as a result of what I heard and saw that day, I thought 2SG were in good form but I sensed that they did not exactly feel that they were well understood or appreciated by the Chain of Command and I put that right.'

At Hohne the 1st Battalion began 1990 with the prospect of a heavy year in *1st Battalion* BAOR during which it would first train as a battle group in Canada and then *1990* over the summer months convert from the role of a mechanized battalion to that of an armoured infantry battalion equipped with the new Warrior Infantry Fighting Vehicle. Little did any member of the battalion realize that before the year was out the battalion would be involved in preparations for a move to Saudi Arabia to join Operation GRANBY, the Coalition Forces operation commanded by the Americans to restore Kuwait to its legitimate rulers.

Meanwhile, 1989 had also seen momentous changes within Europe. These had originated in the Communist-ruled countries of the Baltic Littoral and

Eastern Europe and ultimately led to the collapse of governments in several of the countries concerned, including the Soviet Union, where President Mikhail Gorbachev presided over changes thought to have been inconceivable even five years earlier. Within Germany the Berlin Wall had come down and Chancellor Kohl's Christian Democrat Government had begun moves which would in due course lead to the re-unification of the two halves of the country. For British troops stationed in BAOR, whose whole *raison d'être* for serving in West Germany began to appear less tenable than it had been in the days of the Cold War, life would soon take on new meaning. However, in early 1990 nobody was forecasting what might be the eventual outcome of such changes in the international arena and the 1st Battalion Scots Guards confined its thinking to its exercise in Canada and the planned conversion to the Warrior role.

Exercise MEDICINE MAN across the prairie at Suffield in May probably sounds idyllic to those ignorant of Canadian weather. The battle group, which comprised a normal mix of supporting arms including two squadrons of the battalion's 'paired' armoured regiment in Hohne, The Queen's Own Hussars, undertook the usual live firing exercises although Colonel Cargill, who had once served on the staff at Suffield, noticed that there was more emphasis on testing than training, a retrograde step in view of the increasingly limited training opportunities enjoyed by soldiers in Germany. Training is all about making mistakes and rectifying them, and a philosophy that demands that things be done perfectly the first time, as occasionally happened in BAOR, is unattractive and unproductive since it stifles initiative and leads to stereotype training.

However, in May, 1990, the Scots Guards battle group landed at Calgary Airport in a snowstorm and the first two days on the prairie were desperately cold. Despite close supervision of the training, the battle group enjoyed itself and got good value from its three weeks in the field. Before handing over its vehicles and dispersing on adventure training or leave the battle group paraded on the orders of the Commanding Officer for an aerial photograph; whilst not the first time that such a photograph has been taken, the results were particularly good, doubtless because RSM Walker dressed companies and squadrons from a helicopter by issuing such commands as 'come this way' or 'move to your left' over the Battalion Command Net.

On return from leave the battalion began the complex task of conversion from the FV432 Personnel Carrier to the Warrior Armoured Fighting vehicle. Whilst the former is no more than a tracked personnel carrier or, as sometimes described, a 'battle taxi' protected with a thin coat of armour which simply takes infantrymen into battle, the latter is a highly sophisticated fighting vehicle capable of keeping pace with tanks and other vehicles across country. Built by GKN, the Warrior mounts a 30mm Rarden cannon capable of destroying enemy vehicles of similar design and disabling tanks, while its Hughes Chain Gun can deliver a heavy weight of machine-gun fire in support of an attack.

There were fundamental changes at a tactical level. There was a clear contrast in role, necessary skills and training between those who fought mounted (manning the Warrior turret, manoeuvring and employing its firepower) and those who fought dismounted (the infantry commanders and rifle sections.) The latter now had the option of remaining inside the Warrior for much longer in an attack. Their enhanced protection and mobility enabled them to dismount right on top of an enemy objective with intimate support from the Warrior weapons.

The process of converting the battalion took three and a half months, such was the extent of the technical detail which everyone had to absorb. The process was supported by the Armoured Infantry Training Team set up by the Director of Infantry's staff to assist with conversion. At this time the Armoured Infantry Manning Increment also appeared. These three officers and sixty-nine NCOs and guardsmen (drawn from across the Household Division but predominantly Welsh Guards) provided the additional manpower required within a Warrior battalion. They fitted quickly, completely and happily into the battalion, proving once again the essential closeness of the Foot Guards 'family'.

Conversion training moved into top gear in September and His Royal Highness the Colonel visited Hohne on 10 September to view progress and to try his hand 'with the new toys'. As a former armoured soldier with the Royal Scots Greys he had little difficulty in understanding Warrior and no doubt was able to teach the battalion a thing or two. However, only four days after his visit it was announced by the Government that Britain was to dispatch a brigade to support the American Force being assembled in Saudi Arabia to retake Kuwait which the Iraqi Army had overrun a month before in early August.

President Saddam Hussein, the megalomanic leader of Iraq, had invaded his neighbour to the south on the pretext of liberating the Kuwaitis from their alleged undemocratic and repressive leaders and was clearly unlikely to be removed other than by force. London decided the 7th Armoured Brigade from BAOR would join General Norman Schwarzkopf's Force, a move that inevitably disrupted the 1st Battalion Scots Guards' conversion programme. Between September and the end of 1990 events moved fast within Germany and Britain, with first the 7th Armoured Brigade being dispatched to the Gulf, followed by Headquarters 1st Armoured Division under Major General Rupert Smith who was to command the British Force in the field, and later by the 4th Armoured Brigade. The 1st Battalion became involved, helping to train the infantry who were earmarked to go to the Gulf with the 7th Armoured Brigade and by loaning vehicles whilst its own Warrior training continued. Across the whole of BAOR units of every arm and service were stripped of both their manpower and equipment in order that those regiments and battalions selected to be part of the 1st Armoured Division might deploy at War Establishment. It was a thoroughly unsatisfactory situation, principally brought about by a political failure to call out the reservists earmarked to top up units for their full war roles, and it is to be hoped that such a situation will never be allowed to happen again. The British Army is a most flexible and adaptable organization but sometimes that flexibility and adaptability can be pushed too far.

On 2 October, 1990, West and East Germany came together to form the new

Federal Republic of Germany, an historic event and one of great significance for British Forces stationed in BAOR who had served there for nearly forty-five years as guardians of West Germany's democratic constitution. It was ironic that, as the threat to freedom seeped away in Europe, another should arise in the Middle East. On 7 November the battalion was warned that it might be required to deploy to Saudi Arabia as part of a formation to relieve the 7th or 4th Armoured Brigades should Operation GRANBY need to be extended. Thereafter events moved even faster and on 22 November 2 Platoon of Right Flank commanded by 2nd Lieutenant Charles Stuart was strengthened to a total of forty-five which, if called for, would move to the Gulf as Battle Casualty Replacements (BCRs). A BCR is a trained soldier positioned in a suitable area to the rear of the battlefield; he or she is held ready to replace a soldier wounded or killed in combat. Early in December it was decided that the battalion should assume responsibility for providing all infantry BCRs for the 1st Armoured Division and on 3 December it was placed at seven days notice to move to the Gulf although to what area and with what equipment was never made clear. Warrior conversion training was hurriedly completed and a series of internal and external courses was run to prepare all ranks for their probable role within 1st Armoured Division.

In parallel with these preparations there took place the usual if somewhat muted Christmas and New Year festivities and all those earmarked to go to the Gulf were sent on leave for a few days. It was a time of worry and disappointment for most people; worry on the part of the battalion's families because they had little idea as to what their husbands might be committed once they had left Hohne and disappointment from the guardsmen that they were unlikely to be used as a fighting entity, although such a sentiment was tempered by relief that the battalion was at least to be involved and not left to watch from the sidelines in Germany.

The Gulf War   On 15 January, 1991, having held a final exercise at Soltau and then handed what Warriors the battalion still held to the 2nd Battalion The Royal Anglian Regiment, the advance party flew from Hanover to Al Jubail, a desolate area of sand and scrub dominated by oil wells and refineries to the north of Dhahran on the Saudi Arabian Gulf coast. At 2359 hours the same day the United Nations ultimatum to Saddam Hussein to withdraw his forces from Kuwait expired and on the morning of 16 January the 'air war' against Iraq was launched with strikes against a number of targets across the whole country.

Meanwhile the advance party, having finally been allowed to deplane, was moved away from the airfield upon which it had landed and the Commanding Officer was given instructions to take charge of Blackadder Camp, by all accounts a shambles of considerable proportions, and 'to sort out the BCR system'. Such a directive provided a considerable challenge and Major Ron Clemison, the Quartermaster, and RSM Walker both quickly got to grips with the task. RSM Walker remembers 'being absolutely appalled' by what he found, but, having taken a series of decisions that probably only a Household Division

192

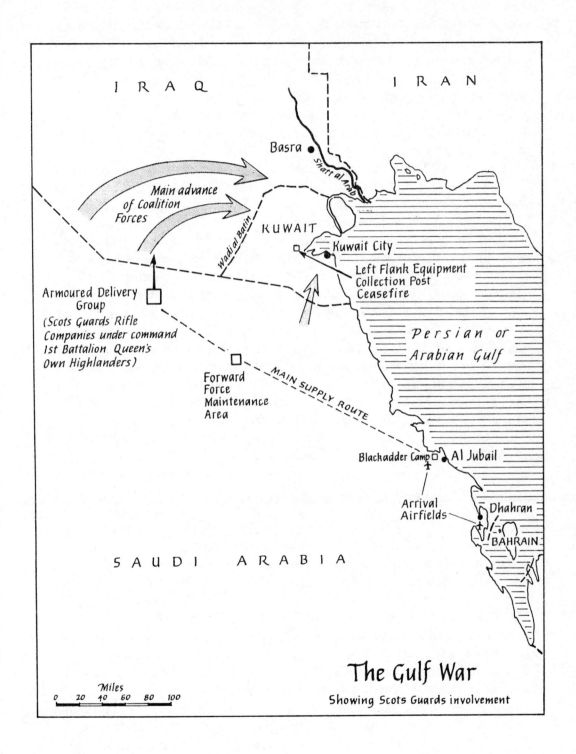

IRAQ

IRAN

Basra

Shatt al Arab

Main advance
of Coalition
Forces

KUWAIT

Wadi al Batin

Kuwait City

Left Flank Equipment
Collection Post
Ceasefire

Armoured Delivery
Group

(Scots Guards Rifle
Companies under command
1st Battalion Queen's
Own Highlanders)

Persian or
Arabian Gulf

Forward
Force
Maintenance
Area

MAIN SUPPLY ROUTE

Blackadder Camp

Al Jubail

Arrival
Airfields

Dhahran

BAHRAIN

SAUDI   ARABIA

Miles
0   20   40   60   80   100

The Gulf War

Showing Scots Guards involvement

Sergeant Major could have taken and in doing so, in the words of the *British Army Review*, 'made himself the most unpopular man in Al Jubail', order slowly emerged from the chaos that had greeted the advance party. By 28 January, when the main body of the battalion arrived from Germany, a more organized welcome awaited it. Despite an almost continuous series of siren alerts predicting Iraqi SCUD missile chemical attacks which had begun the first night the advance party was in Al Jubail and which necessitated everybody spending long hours in protective clothing, Blackadder Camp had been brought firmly under Scots Guards command and a system for registering, organizing and training BCRs was beginning to take shape.

The Regimental Band
However, the 1st Battalion was not the only element of the Regiment to serve in the Gulf during the war against Iraq. As far back as 3 October, 1990, the Regimental Band, which had recently returned from New York and Spain, was warned for duty in the Gulf. After appropriate training at Pirbright and at Saighton Camp near Chester, where all medical unit training takes place, it flew to Al Jubail on 3 November, the first Scots Guardsmen to become involved in the build-up in the area. Throughout its tour the band was attached to 33 Field Hospital where it was divided between such departments as Reception, Treatments, Resuscitation, Theatre and on wards. The band also took its instruments and discharged a number of engagements during its four months in Saudi Arabia. One musician recalls how the band learnt of its forthcoming deployment when Major Robin Whyte, the Regimental Adjutant, briefed everybody at Wellington Barracks: 'The Major General in his infinite wisdom had decided that a Household Division band should be involved (with the Cambridge Military Hospital which formed 33 Field Hospital) and that is how the Scots Guards band found itself preparing to go to war. "Don't get worried", said the Regimental Adjutant, "it's only a contingency plan." He went on quickly to tell us about our exciting programme of training, a package which would include NBC, some shooting and physical fitness ..... He spoke very quickly and seemed quite excited about the whole thing but his expression remained stern. Then he left.'

1st Battalion
Soon after the arrival of the main body, Colonel Cargill was warned that his three armoured infantry companies would be deployed forward to the Forward Force Maintenance Area to join the Armoured Delivery Group which was commanded by Battle Group Headquarters of the 1st Battalion Queen's Own Highlanders. On arrival in the Forward Force Maintenance Area, the companies drew up vehicles and equipment and 'Chobham Armour' was bolted on to the Warriors to give them additional protection. The Scots Guards Battle Group Headquarters and B Company, without the means to exercise its support skills, were to remain at Blackadder Camp to continue the programme of organizing the BCRs which would undoubtedly have been required had the conflict not ended so quickly and with so little injury. It was a depressing prospect for Colonel Cargill and those others of the battalion left behind and the Commanding Officer judged that he must, at the very least, represent that his whole

battalion be allowed to go forward in order that it should be ready to intervene in whatever way might be required of it. However it was not to be and, while his position and that of those who were to remain at Blackadder Camp was fully understood and evoked considerable sympathy in some quarters, there was to be no change to the original order and on 12 February the rifle companies moved forward to join the Queen's Own Highlanders.

The land offensive began on 25 February, 1991, and lasted almost exactly 100 hours, by which time the objective of the Coalition Forces to liberate Kuwait had been successfully achieved and the bulk of the Iraqi Army routed. The battalion's involvement was very limited with the rifle companies moving from leaguer to leaguer across the barren gravel plain over which the advance into Iraq took place. The only part of the battalion to be operationally committed was 2nd Lieutenant Lincoln Jopp's 7 Platoon which was sent to reinforce the 2nd Battalion The Royal Regiment of Fusiliers, following a tragic incident when American A10 aircraft fired on the advancing friendly forces in error.

A cease-fire was proclaimed on 28 February and there then started the massive job of dealing with thousands of Iraqi prisoners as well as clearing up the desert which was littered with abandoned equipment and vehicles. Left Flank, commanded by Major Jan de Haldevang was given the task of collecting all movable enemy vehicles and equipment from the 1st Armoured Division area and moving it to an area north-west of Kuwait City.

Meanwhile Battalion Headquarters had the unenviable task of trying to process the hundreds of BCRs who had flown into Al Jubail during the build-up as a prelude to dispatching them back to Britain and Germany. ORCS Cerson did a first-class job, his computer-based 'tally' system ensuring that those claiming to be BCRs but who had not seen fit to register as such on arrival in theatre did not receive the same priority for return as the genuine article

On 12 March the battalion re-formed at Blackadder Camp and a week later flew back to Germany. Thus ended the Gulf War during which the 1st Battalion suffered frustration and disappointment, yet achieved the highest standards in those tasks which it was ordered to undertake. No doubt the history of the War will in time analyse the methods by which operational reinforcement and logistic support were undertaken and will pass judgement as to the wisdom of breaking up units to bring others up to War Establishment. A political decision to deny the Army traditional methods of reinforcement having been taken early on, it was perhaps inevitable that there would have to be compromises and that these would suit few but those deployed with the two fighting brigades, and probably not even all of them. That the 1st Battalion should be one of the unwitting victims of a system of reinforcement and support which had to be developed as it grew was unfortunate, but then such things tend to happen in war.

During 1990 and 1991 the Ministry of Defence had been developing plans for a reduction in the size and deployment of the Nation's Armed Forces, an exercise generally accepted as inevitable in the light of the ending of the Cold War but which, despite denials, was also driven by the need to make savings in

'Options for Change'

195

the Government's spending plans which in the early 1990s required annual borrowing approaching fifty billion pounds. Work on 'Options for Change', as the planning process was termed, started in February, 1990, and continued throughout the Gulf Conflict although some work was placed in abeyance as the prospect of hostilities grew closer. Notwithstanding this, once the war was over planning resumed and in July, 1991, a number of measures to reduce the size of the Army by around thirty percent to a strength of just below 120,000 were announced in Parliament. Included were plans to cut the Infantry from a strength of fifty-five battalions to thirty-eight (although this was later increased to forty) by a process, principally, of amalgamation. The prospect of such surgery came as no great surprise to present and past members of the Regiment, it having been long accepted by most people that, if single-battalion infantry regiments of the line were to disappear from the Army's order of battle, it would be inconceivable that the three Foot Guards regiments still possessing second battalions, should or indeed could retain them. Arguments about quality, recruiting potential and tradition, while important, were not allowed to obscure the central criteria that equity must as far as possible be applied across the Infantry and must be seen to be applied. It therefore came as little surprise when Mr Tom King, the Defence Secretary, announced in the House of Commons in July, 1991, Government plans for the reductions which included the merging of the 1st and 2nd Battalions of the Regiment before 1 April, 1995. Subsequent staff planning led to decisions which would permit the 2nd Battalion to spend its last eighteen months in Edinburgh, while the 1st Battalion would return from Hohne to the newly rebuilt Victoria Barracks in Windsor in June, 1993, where in December the two battalions would merge to form the 1st Battalion Scots Guards.

CHAPTER ELEVEN

350 YEARS

1st Battalion: Hohne-Windsor
2nd Battalion: Hounslow-Edinburgh

1991 was a year of significant events for the British Army. Although only a few units were involved in the successful campaign to eject the Iraqi Army from Kuwait at the end of February, many more regiments and battalions were to be affected by decisions emanating from the Ministry of Defence's post Cold War 'Options for Change' study, details of which were made known in July that year. Re-established at Hounslow after its 1990 operational tour in Northern Ireland the 2nd Battalion passed a summer of ceremonial duties in the almost certain knowledge that, when announcements were eventually made, its would be among the names of those battalions to be merged or disbanded. With the assistance of a number of senior officers in the Regiment and supported by Major General Robert Corbett, the Major General, Colonel Erskine Crum prepared his battalion for the inevitable decision. Unlike 1971 when only a handful of infantry battalions had been selected for removal from the Order of Battle, 'Options for Change' touched nearly every part of the Army, with arms such as the Royal Armoured Corps sustaining a reduction of almost fifty per cent in their strength as a result of amalgamations. While some regiments, most notably those within the Scottish Division, mounted well organized and vociferous campaigns to preserve their battalions, others accepted the outcome of the Ministry's review with reluctance and a heavy heart but with good grace, recognizing that, however much they might disagree with what was being done, they had little alternative but to accept the consequences. The Scots Guards fell within this latter category.

March, 1991, saw the battalion training in Scotland, principally in the area of *2nd Battalion* Garelochhead but with companies rotating through Guards House at Folda on Tayside to ski. His Royal Highness the Colonel visited the training, once again demonstrating his interest in the Regiment and his willingness to involve himself in its activities whenever a suitable opportunity to do so arose. Prior to the battalion's deployment north of the Border a lunch was held at the Cavalry Barracks in Hounslow to say farewell to Major Jim Grant whose service to the Regiment totalled forty-seven years as a guardsman, RSM of the 1st Battalion,

Families Officer of the 2nd Battalion and finally, after he had retired, for almost ten years as the Welfare and Regimental Funds Officer at Regimental Headquarters, a record unsurpassed and truly an example of devotion to duty.

In early May command of 56th London Brigade changed when Brigadier Michael Nurton was relieved by another Scots Guardsman, Brigadier Kim Ross, while a month later the battalion provided Numbers Three and Four Guards on the Queen's Birthday Parade, the last time it was to parade on Horse Guards before its merger with the 1st Battalion in November, 1993.

However, a rather different event took place on 15 July when the battalion provided the Tower of London Guard commanded by Captain Tom Coke with CSM Dalgleish as the Senior Sergeant and Lance Corporal Morton as the Drummer of the Guard. The Ceremony of the Keys that evening was, for the first time ever, filmed and broadcast live on satellite television and was watched by the Leaders of the Group of Seven Leading Economic Countries of the World, at the time meeting in London, who were hosted for the occasion by the Constable of the Tower, Field Marshal Sir John Stanier. Major Johnny Stewart, the Captain of Right Flank, represented Colonel Erskine Crum at a reception following the Ceremony and found himself involved in a somewhat bizarre encounter with President George Bush of the United States. The President commented upon the excellence of the Ceremony, whereupon Major Stewart responded by saying that 'the President would probably be the last one to see the ceremony since with the course 'Options for Change' was taking, it might soon be that it would be no longer!' Horrified to learn of such a possibility, President Bush sought out the Prime Minister, Mr John Major, and urged him to avoid such a course of action, a move that resulted in Major Stewart receiving an extremely dirty look from an embarrassed Premier.

On 26 September, following periods of battalion training at Thetford and Sennybridge, Colonel Douglas Erskine Crum handed over command to Lieutenant Colonel Tom Fitzalan Howard. The latter was destined to be the last Commanding Officer of the battalion. He was the son of Major General Lord Michael Fitzalan Howard, who was the Commanding Officer of the battalion in 1956 at the start of this History when the battalion came home from Germany to Chelsea Barracks. The same month Captain Charles Page handed over as Adjutant to Captain Willie Swinton who almost immediately found himself involved in planning the battalion's move to Edinburgh in April, 1992.

During the remainder of the year the battalion continued to mount public duties and to undertake its fair share of other ceremonial commitments, while at the same time providing a platoon commanded by 2nd Lieutenant William Inglis with Sergeant Scott to serve in Northern Ireland with the 1st Battalion Welsh Guards; earlier in the year a multiple patrol commanded by 2nd Lieutenant Michael Knollys had undertaken a similar attachment with the 2nd Battalion Coldstream Guards. Both attachments were good examples of the way in which battalions of the Household Division continued to reinforce one another when circumstances demanded it.

Return from Saudi Arabia in March 1991 was followed for the 1st Battalion by leave and a frustrating period when, because of the slow return to Germany of equipment used during the Gulf War, it was impossible to train other than at a very low level. By the autumn the situation had improved and the battalion managed to take part in some formation training with its Warriors, while over 300 soldiers left Hohne to involve themselves in adventure training of one sort or another. Meanwhile, in the late summer long-term plans for the deployment of British Forces in Germany were announced and, *inter alia*, these involved a reduction in the size of the land component of BAOR from three in-theatre divisions to one. This one division was to have its headquarters at Herford with brigades based around Hohne, Sennelager and Osnabrück. These changes, which were to be completed by 1 April, 1995, were to result in the closure and return to the German authorities of a large number of barracks and a reduction in the strength of BAOR by approximately fifty per cent. Embryo plans to form a new NATO Rapid Reaction Corps capable of deploying to areas of potential conflict within the Alliance area were also announced, although these were not to affect the 1st Battalion, which was told on 2 September, 1991, that it would move to Windsor in June, 1993, to be the first occupants of the newly rebuilt Victoria Barracks.

On 4 December, after three years in command, Colonel John Cargill handed over command to Lieutenant Colonel Tim Spicer whose first task would be to prepare the battalion for a six-month tour of duty in West Belfast in May, 1992. Earlier in the summer RSM P. Jackson had replaced RSM Walker as the Sergeant Major. Having spent so much of the last year concentrating upon a conversion programme designed to prepare it for the armoured infantry role, the 1st Battalion needed time to adjust to operating once again in the basic infantry role with the emphasis on patrolling, observation and low level tactics. From the moment that he took command Colonel Spicer concentrated on preparations for the forthcoming tour in West Belfast, placing priority on traditional infantry skills, physical fitness and shooting. The battalion's training between January and the end of April was therefore directed principally at preparations for operations in the urban environment of West Belfast for a period of six months. Before the battalion left Hohne command of 22nd Armoured Brigade changed when Brigadier John Kiszely, a former Commanding Officer of the 1st Battalion, took command early in the New Year.

Deployment across West Belfast involved the use of three principal bases. Right Flank, commanded by Major Charles Page with CSM Goodall and including the Drums Platoon, was at Girdwood Park and looked after the northern part of the battalion area. C Company, led by Major Mark Turner and CSM Kennedy, based itself at North Howard Street Mill along with most of B (Support) Company and patrolled the Falls and Springfield areas, while Left Flank at Whiterock, under command of Major James Stuart and CSM Tasker, covered the Ballymurphy, Turf Lodge and Springmartin districts. In addition a company of the 1st Battalion The Parachute Regiment was placed under Scots

Guards command at Woodburn to control Andersonstown and the south-west areas of Belfast. Finally the Reconnaissance Platoon commanded by Lieutenant Jeremy Orwin manned the three 'tower' Observation Posts at Broadway and the Divis Flats and in the Turf Lodge; these Observation Posts provided a useful 'bird's eye' view of the area and allowed patrols on the ground to be directed to incidents accurately and with minimum delay. It was a large area for one battalion to control and for most of the six months Battalion Headquarters commanded in excess of 900 soldiers wearing a variety of different capbadges; however, a month before the end of the tour the northern part of the area was detached and given to another unit to cover, whereupon Right Flank moved from Girdwood Park to co-locate with Left Flank.

The battalion took over its TAOR from the 1st Battalion The Prince of Wales's Own Regiment of Yorkshire on 7 May. Even before command passed, two Scots Guards patrols had had contacts with the IRA and thereafter the pace never really slackened for the whole period of the tour, during which there were 340 serious incidents involving the battalion and the RUC. In particular two incidents during May set the tone; the first, on 16 May, occurred when a joint RUC/Reconnaissance Platoon mobile patrol was engaged by a Mark 12 Mortar concealed in the back of a car in the Beechmount area. Quick reaction during the follow-up led by Lance Sergeants Burgess and Goodman resulted in an IRA Active Service Unit (ASU) being arrested. A second incident three days later near the Monagh bypass resulted in a patrol led by 2nd Lieutenant Ben Wallace successfully apprehending another ASU which had positioned itself with the intention of 'bombing' his patrol as it passed through a narrow defile. Most of the incidents encountered by the battalion involved sniping attacks, 'coffee jar' bombings using various receptacles filled with Semtex explosive or remotely controlled devices; few patrols experienced an incident free period of duty on the streets, although those committed to protecting the City Centre through the manning of a series of check points found that duty both tiring and irksome.

On 3 August a joint patrol involving Right Flank and the RUC was fired upon in the Antrim Road and Guardsman Shackleton, a married man who had been in the Regiment for seven years, was mortally wounded. His was the only death in the battalion; given the number and sophistication of the attacks on the Security Forces during the tour it is surprising that there were not more casualties, testimony to how thoroughly the battalion had prepared for its time in Belfast and the professionalism and energy which it brought to its task.

On 4 September an incident occurred in the New Lodge area when a terrorist suspect, seen to be acting suspiciously, was apprehended, whereupon he tried to run away. Shots were fired and the man concerned later died. This action led to two members of Right Flank, Guardsmen Wright and Fisher, being arrested and later charged with murder. At the time of writing the case of Guardsmen Wright and Fisher still remains to be finally settled, but the incident neatly illustrates the difficulties faced by soldiers serving on the streets of Ulster's towns and cities who must at all times seek to protect the innocent and interfere as little as possible with everyday life, but at the same time must pursue the evil men of the IRA with every means that can be brought to bear by professional soldiers, yet do so within the law as interpreted by Britain's courts.

The 1st Battalion handed over its TAOR to the 1st Battalion The Green Howards on 5 November and flew back to Hohne. It had been a hard and exhausting tour for everybody and few were sorry to see the back of Belfast, a city with which most Scots Guardsmen had by 1992 come to associate only with squalor, bigotry and the brutality exercised by the modern-day urban terrorist. No doubt if questioned most members of the 1st Battalion would have reserved their greatest contempt for those men and women in the Province who, whilst purporting to seek peace, made little or no attempt to find an accommodation with those of their fellow Ulstermen with whom they differed politically. The tragedy of Ulster has been all too clear to those who have been associated with its fortunes since 1969: tradition, history, religion and politics have confused and, barring an unexpected happening or a political act of unprecedented imagination, would continue to confuse the process of reconciliation so openly desired by the majority in the Province who are as sickened by the carnage and destruction as those in the Army and the police who endeavour to prevent it. It was a depressing note upon which to depart from Belfast Airport in November 1992 and few Scots Guardsmen could at that time have foreseen that, less than two years later, both the main terrorist groups would have declared a ceasefire, an essential prerequisite to the holding of discussions on the future of the Province.

2nd Battalion

The 2nd Battalion's last few months at Hounslow were divided between public duties and preparing for the move to Edinburgh. After five and a half years in a dingy barracks in an area of London well known for its drug culture, and surrounded by ethnic minorities which do not mix easily with their white neighbours, it might be assumed that the Scots Guards would be delighted at the prospect of a move north of the Border. Indeed many were, although a sizeable minority of the families were firmly settled at Hounslow with well paid jobs and had little wish to be uprooted. Equally, many single soldiers did not necessarily relish a return to the land of their birth, having originally enlisted to get away from home in order to seek life's excitements beyond the range of the parental eye. Throughout the thirty-eight years of this History battalions of the Regiment have always tended to view future postings with a mixture of indifference and anticipation, usually setting themselves impossible expectations and then being pleasantly surprised by how much they actually enjoy the tour of duty involved. As if to prove the truth of what has just been written, despite some initial reluctance, the 2nd Battalion's twenty months in Edinburgh were to prove highly popular.

Edinburgh

The battalion mounted its last Queen's Guard on 19 February, 1992, and a month later reassembled in Redford Barracks after a period of leave. It was twenty years almost to the month since the battalion had last been stationed at Redford, the previous occasion being in 1972 when it had re-formed there, having been restored to the Army's Order of Battle following the defence cuts of the previous year. Redford Barracks were not dissimilar to the Cavalry Barracks in Hounslow, being in need of extensive refurbishment, but the battalion was to remain there for only eight months before it moved to nearby Dreghorn Barracks, a former training and administrative camp which had undergone extensive renovation to allow it to be used as a battalion station.

Headquarters Scotland gave the battalion a warm welcome and it soon settled to its new role as the Edinburgh public duties battalion, mounting guard at the Castle and providing Guards of Honour when necessary. Relations between the Regiment and the Scottish Infantry have never been very close, especially when the Scots Guards serve within Scotland, and, despite the welcome from Lieutenant General Sir Peter Graham and his staff, it was inevitable that others might not be quite so pleased to see the arrival of the battalion. Fortunately, prior to the 2nd Battalion's tour in 1992, a number of senior Scots Guardsmen had served within the Scottish military establishment and recollections of the part played by such officers as Colonel James Dunsmure and Brigadier Kim Ross, both senior staff officers at Headquarters Scotland, and Major Campbell Graham and Captain Ernie Marchant, at the Castle and at Redford Barracks respectively, meant that there was a considerable reservoir of goodwill to be drawn upon.

The crowning event for everyone associated with the Scots Guards in 1992 was the Review of the Regiment by Her Majesty The Queen, its Colonel in Chief, in celebration of its 350th Anniversary. Once it became known that the 2nd Battalion would be in Scotland in 1992, Brigadier Michael Scott, the Regimental Lieutenant Colonel (as that appointment had by now been re-designated), determined that, if at all possible, a parade to celebrate such an important anniversary should take place in Scotland's capital city in the presence of The Queen. The original plan was for both battalions to be on parade, but this unfortunately had to be changed when it was announced that the 1st Battalion would be on operational duty over the summer months, although a detachment from the battalion did fly over from Belfast to parade alongside the remainder of the Regiment on 24 June. Regimental Headquarters had also planned that, following the Review in Holyrood Park, the Regiment should march up the Royal Mile to Edinburgh Castle from where everybody would be taken by bus to lunch at Redford Barracks. This plan did not survive the objections of the Lothian and Borders Police who expressed concern on the grounds of security and traffic congestion. As a result it was decided to hold the Review in Holyrood Park, after which everybody on parade and their guests would lunch in marquees erected next to the parade ground. Organization of the day was principally vested in two officers, Major Robin Whyte, the Regimental Adjutant, and Major Julian Crowe who established himself with a Project Team in Redford Barracks from April; his responsibilities included everything from setting out the parade ground in the early hours of 24 June to arranging fifty-seven coaches to convey people to and from Redford.

24 June, despite dawning overcast and seemingly threatening rain, was bright and at lunchtime the sun emerged to make weather conditions almost perfect. Brigadier Scott in his appointment as the Regimental Lieutenant Colonel, commanded the parade. First to march on were various detachments comprising serving Scots Guardsmen not at the time in either battalion and past members of the Regiment; a large contingent from the Third Guards Club with another from the Association was followed by a detachment of serving officers and soldiers who were at the time serving at extra-regimental duty. This detachment included Scots Guardsmen from Sandhurst, the Guards Depot and the Regiment's affiliated Army Cadet Force Detachment. Next came four Guards, three of which were provided by the 2nd Battalion wearing tunics and bearskins, while the fourth (although it paraded as Number 1 Guard) was found by fifty members of the 1st Battalion wearing combat kit. Both Commanding Officers and both battalions' Colours were on parade, as was the State Colour, carried by Lieutenant Giles Taylor, the first occasion when all five Colours possessed by the Regiment have been paraded together. A detachment of the Queen's Bodyguard for Scotland (Royal Company of Archers) was positioned on either side of the Dais.

Preceded by a few minutes by His Royal Highness The Duke of Kent, Colonel of the Regiment, Her Majesty The Queen, accompanied by His Royal Highness The Duke of Edinburgh, was received on parade at 1100 hours with a Royal salute, after which she inspected the parade. Thereafter the Regimental Band, the Pipes and Drums and Corps of Drums of the 2nd Battalion trooped, following which all detachments marched past in quick time. After re-forming in line the parade advanced in Review Order. The Queen then addressed all those on parade and, after tracing the Regiment's long and illustrious history, she made reference to the impending demise of the 2nd Battalion: 'It is a great sadness that after many centuries the 2nd Battalion goes into suspended animation next year but I am confident that nevertheless you will continue to serve the Crown with the same steadfastness and distinction that has been the hallmark of your last 350 years. It was not for nothing that my grandfather once translated your motto "Beware of challenging the Scots Guards".'

In his reply Brigadier Scott said, 'You see before you a cross-section of young and old; past, present and future generations of the Scots Guards. The spirit that binds us together and sustains us through fatigue, fear and anxiety is our pride in our professionalism, our dependence on each other and our self-discipline. . . . We fight well because we are among friends.' He ended by saying, 'We look forward to the next 350 years with confidence and pride, in the knowledge that we can match our distinguished forbears in loyalty and service to Crown and Country.'

The parade then gave three cheers for The Queen after which the four Guards and all detachments marched off parade behind the Regimental Band and The Queen and The Duke of Edinburgh who led the way in a Range Rover. With Their Royal Highnesses The Duke of Edinburgh and The Duke of Kent as the principal guests, over 4,000 people then sat down to lunch in marquees adjacent to Holyrood Park. After lunch all ranks – old or young, General or Guardsman, serving or retired – mingled together to discuss old times, predict the future, pull each other's legs and to bask in an ambience which only a truly happy family can achieve. It was a time to savour the past as well as to anticipate what the future might bring.

For the 2nd Battalion the second half of 1992 was as busy as the first and, once the Review in Holyrood Park was over, everybody got on with a routine which concentrated mainly on those ceremonial duties associated with Scotland's capital city but which permitted some opportunities for training. In his directive for the year Colonel Tom Fitzalan Howard told his company commanders that he wanted them to ensure that their guardsmen both saw and were seen around Scotland and that, in the final two years of its existence, he wished the battalion really to enjoy itself.

During August G Company, under the command of Major James Kelly and supported by the Regimental Band and the battalion's pipers and drummers, took part in the Edinburgh Military Tattoo. The theme of the Tattoo in 1992 was 'The Scots Guards' and Michael Parker, the Producer, so arranged events as to trace the Regiment's history over the preceding 350 years. This was achieved through a series of short cameos depicting major events from the past and involved one group from G Company changing their clothing nine times in three hours. By the end of the month even RSM Spence, who had taken over as the Sergeant Major from RSM Wood after the Review, was prepared to acknowledge that those involved had earned their extra duty pay.

Royal Guard While G Company battled it out on the Esplanade below Edinburgh Castle, Right Flank, reinforced by the other companies and commanded by Major Angus Macpherson and with CSM Gwynne as his Detachment Company Sergeant Major, travelled to Victoria Barracks in Ballater to provide the Royal Guard for Her Majesty The Queen's annual visit to Balmoral. It was only the second time in the history of the Regiment that a detachment had provided the Guard and the commitment and routine were very similar to that in 1967 when the 1st Battalion had provided a similar party under Major Philip Erskine's command. In the main those detached to Ballater enjoyed their three months away from Edinburgh amidst the hills and glens of Deeside, life on the Balmoral moors being infinitely preferable to a constant stream of Castle Guards or even, for some, the show business life of the Tattoo. A Guard of Honour for The Queen on her arrival and departure, attendance on Sundays at Crathie Church, beating on the moors and the occasional Ghillies' Ball all helped to make the time pass. Everybody attended dancing classes supervised by Pipe Major Webster before leaving Redford and as a result people like Guardsman Swanson had no difficulty in dancing with The Queen on three occasions during the course of a single evening. On the other hand Captain James Fairholme was allegedly somewhat at a loss when invited to take the floor with Her Royal Highness The Princess of Wales for a Canadian Hopscotch. Guardsmen were

53. "On arrival at the gates of Dreghorn Brigadier Iain Reid took the salute as the 2nd Battalion entered its new — and what was to be its final — home for the first time." (Page 205). In early November, 1992, Colonel Tom Fitzalan Howard leads his battalion into Dreghorn Barracks. Marching behind him is Major Angus Macpherson while the Quartermaster, Major Munro Davidson, and the Paymaster, Captain Mandy Tindall, are standing behind the Brigade Commander.

54. "For the next six days a succession of platoons found themselves rescuing people cut off by floodwater, building sandbagged river defences." (Page 207). CSM Convery assists with operations to counter the effects of widespread flooding in Perth in February, 1993.

55. "The Colonel handed F Company the Colours of the battalion for safe keeping." (Page 207). On 4 November, 1993, the 2nd Battalion paraded for the final time. The Colonel hands the Regimental Colour to 2nd Lieutenant Andrew Jeffrey. 2nd Lieutenant Hugh Anderson is carrying the Queen's Colour while (left) are Brigadier Kim Ross, the Regimental Lieutenant Colonel, and Colonel Tom Fitzalan Howard.

56. On 5 November, 1991, the Colonel dined on Queen's Guard at St James's Palace with the eleven officers of the Regiment who had served as his Equerry since he assumed the appointment of Colonel Scots Guards in September, 1974. From left to right are Captain Charles Blount, Major Johnny Stewart, Captain John Treadwell, Majors James Napier and Charles Page, the Colonel, Captains Mark Bullough and Michael Campbell-Lamerton, Majors Peter Le Marchand and James Greenfield and Captains Christopher Knollys and Tom Coke.

amazed by the close contact and the relative informality of their relationships with members of the Royal Family, a hallmark of the Royal Guard in recent years. However, it remains to be seen whether the Regiment will ever again provide the Guard in its present form; like so many other facets of modern military life it may be approaching the moment when its utility and future form may need to be carefully and sensitively scrutinized.

In mid-October the battalion deployed to Otterburn and Galloway to train, its first real opportunity to do so in 1992, following which it moved in early November from Redford Barracks to Dreghorn Barracks, newly renovated at a cost to the taxpayer of thirty-six million pounds. The distance between the two barracks is little more than a mile and the battalion marched with its Colours flying and bayonets fixed, permission to do so having been obtained from the Lord Provost of Edinburgh. Dreghorn proved to be a superb new base for the battalion and one which it greatly appreciated during the year that it was to occupy the barracks. The Commanding Officer, Major Julian Crowe, his Second-in-Command and Captain Swinton, the Adjutant, were all mounted for the march to Dreghorn, although the latter experienced some difficulty since the police horse which he rode was more used to separating rival groups of football fans at Ibrox and Celtic Park in Glasgow than following sedately behind the Commanding Officer. On arrival at the gates of Dreghorn Brigadier Iain Reid, Commander 52nd Lowland Brigade, took the salute as the battalion entered its new – and what was to be its final – home for the first time. The last major event of 1992 found the battalion providing support to the Edinburgh Summit Meeting of the Heads of State of the European Community in mid-December, an event which involved it in the provision of a small Guard of Honour on the Esplanade commanded by Captain Rupert Erskine Crum to welcome the statesmen concerned and an Observation Post screen from Captain Caspar Hobbs' Reconnaissance Platoon deployed high up amongst the crags of Arthur's Seat to maintain an operational watch over the Palace of Holyroodhouse where the meeting was held.

The 1st Battalion returned from Northern Ireland in early November, 1992, *1st Battalion* to find that in its absence all but a few of its Warriors had been handed over to another battalion and had already been removed from Hohne. This task had been handled by Captain Ian Amos, the Technical Quartermaster, and the Rear Party and had been executed with a minimum of fuss in a very short time. It meant that for the last seven months of its time in Germany the battalion would be unable to take part in any conventional BAOR exercises and would only be able to train in the dismounted infantry role. Therefore, in order to keep his battalion usefully occupied, Colonel Spicer planned a counter-insurgency exercise to take place in the Sauerland in March. Exercise FOREST CHASE was set against a background of a Balkans-style conflict, a scenario which has unhappily become all too familiar since, and involved the hunting down of groups of partisans by a regular battalion. Supported by a company of the Royal Danish Life Guard and with elements of Headquarter Company, reinforced by

205

Territorial Army Special Air Service Regiment soldiers, as enemy, the battalion deployed from Hohne by Chinook helicopters and then conducted a wide variety of operations against the partisans. It was a hard exercise which achieved its main purpose of challenging the battalion in its last few months in Germany.

On 31 March 22nd Armoured Brigade was re-titled to become 7th Armoured Brigade and the next day the Regimental Band and Pipes and Drums beat retreat as a farewell to Hohne. Previously, in August, 1992, Major General Iain Mackay-Dick had assumed command of 1st Armoured Division at Verden, thereby, as in 1967 when the 2nd Battalion was serving in Iserlohn, ensuring a continuous chain of Scots Guards commanders from platoon to Division. Thereafter the battalion concentrated on preparing for its move to Britain, making Campbell Barracks ready for its successors and beginning the ground-work necessary to ensure a smooth transition to public duties after over five years as a mechanized or armoured infantry battalion in BAOR. On 10 June the last flight left Germany for Windsor and on 14 July, following a hectic rush to get the battalion fitted with tunics when Master Tailor Hatton and his team worked eighteen hours a day to prepare everybody, the battalion mounted its first Queen's Guard at Buckingham Palace.

The contractors responsible for carrying out the rebuilding of Victoria Barracks had done an excellent job and, although the new buildings have been described as 'looking like a cross between a Tesco store and a prison', guardsmen were delighted with their accommodation and the facilities provided for them. It should perhaps be noted that one of those on the staff of Headquarters London District who had been involved in the early stages of the project was Major Bill Wilbur although his successor, Major Ray Giles, oversaw the main work through to its completion. Major Wilbur started life in the Scots Guards as a clerk, rose to be the Superintending Clerk at Regimental Headquarters and was then commissioned, following which he eventually became the staff officer responsible for buildings and works at Horse Guards. However, the project with which he will be mainly associated, will always be the rebuilding of Wellington Barracks where his very considerable contribution is marked by the naming of a flight of steps near the Guards Chapel, 'The Wilbur Steps'.

On 27 August the battalion exercised its right to march through the streets of Windsor with bayonets fixed and its Colours flying to be given a great welcome by the townspeople, many of whom no doubt would have recalled the sad occasion when the 2nd Battalion had paraded in front of the Mayor prior to disbandment in March, 1971. On 21 October General Corbett, the Major General, officially opened Victoria Barracks, but by then plans for the merger of the two battalions and redundancy arrangements were the main pre-occupation for many people, especially Major Andrew Foster, the Second-in-Command, and Captain Jeremy Orwin, the Adjutant. Two days previously it had been announced that the Regiment had been awarded the Battle Honour 'GULF 1991' in recognition of the part that the 1st Battalion had played during operations in that theatre two years earlier.

For the 2nd Battalion its last year of existence was to be as busy as any in its long and illustrious history. In January Major Andrew Bell took Left Flank to exercise in the Oman while in September and October the battalion flew to Canada for its final exercise. It was the second time in four years that the 2nd Battalion was allocated Exercise POND JUMP WEST and such overseas training, ending only a month before the battalion's final parade, gave Colonel Fitzalan Howard the opportunity he sought to keep his battalion fully occupied and stimulated right to the end.

However, the summer months in Scotland had been equally busy with routine public duties and the annual Royal visit to Edinburgh in late June, while on 30 July the battalion paraded with the Regimental Colour and four Guards on the Castle Esplanade when Major General Michael Scott, the GOC Scotland and a former Commanding Officer of the battalion, was installed as the Governor of Edinburgh Castle.

Much earlier in the year, in mid-February a totally unexpected commitment had landed in the battalion's lap when the River Tay burst its banks and inundated a considerable area around Perth. Despite being assured at 1130 hours on Friday 15 February that there was little or no likelihood of the battalion being required for duty and told that he might therefore proceed with his plan to dispatch his guardsmen on weekend leave, at 1215 hours the same day Colonel Fitzalan Howard was telephoned and told to send a company to Perth for immediate flood relief duties. By 1400 hours a composite company was ready to move and for the next six days a succession of platoons rotated through a series of duties which found them rescuing people cut off by the floodwater, building sandbagged river defences and mounting patrols to assist the police in deterring petty looting. As with all such military operations it was carried out with efficiency and good humour although those whose responsibility it was to predict such dangers by reading tide tables and monitoring the wind and weather sustained some damage to their reputations.

On 4 November the 2nd Battalion paraded for the final time. In the presence of His Royal Highness the Colonel and with over 2,000 former members of the battalion around the square, including fourteen previous Commanding Officers and nine former RSMs, and with their families watching, the battalion paraded at Dreghorn on a bright but cold morning. After inspection by the Colonel, the battalion advanced in Review Order. The Commanding Officer then ordered F Company to form, whereupon officers, NCOs and guardsmen selected to serve in the company which was to continue to carry the Colours, traditions and *ésprit* of the 2nd Battalion, left their former companies and formed on the left of the parade. The Colonel handed F Company the Colours of the battalion for safe-keeping, following which Colonel Tom Fitzalan Howard marched the remnants of his battalion off parade to the strains of 'Hielan' Laddie' and the 'Black Bear'; the battalion flag was then lowered and Last Post sounded before F Company, commanded by Major Mark Bence-Trower advanced in Review Order and marched past the Colonel. All present then repaired to the various

207

messes to mourn the loss of a battalion which in their eyes had no equal and whose achievements would live for ever.

Next day a Service of Thanksgiving for the 2nd Battalion Scots Guards was held in St Giles' Cathedral; Guardsman Cameron read the lesson and the Reverend Angus Smith, Chaplain to the battalion eleven years previously at the time of the Falklands War, gave the address. His text was from the words of verses 4 and 5 of the 17th Chapter of the Gospel according to St John, 'I have shown your glory on earth. I have finished the work you gave me to do. So now, Father, glorify me in your own presence with the glory that I had before the world existed'. The Chaplain explained how, like Christ's time on earth, the physical presence of the 2nd Battalion had to come to an end, its work having been completed. He exhorted the congregation to give thanks for the battalion and for all its achievements in war and in peace. The ideals and standards of the battalion, having come from the Regiment, would live on in the Regiment, in the 1st Battalion and in F Company who had received the Battalion Colours for safe custody. He ended with the words, 'Gratitude for the past, an acceptance of current demands, confidence for the future. May these be the basis of our faith and our prayer for ever, Amen.'

On 1 December the remnants of the 2nd Battalion joined the 1st Battalion at Victoria Barracks, Windsor, and merged into a single 1st Battalion. The new battalion was commanded by Colonel Tom Fitzalan Howard with Captain Jeremy Orwin as his Adjutant and RSM Spence as the Sergeant Major. At the same time F Company, commanded by Major Mark Bence-Trower and with CSM Convery, travelled to Wellington Barracks, London, to serve there alongside the 1st Battalion Grenadier Guards.

CHAPTER TWELVE

LOOKING BACK

Throughout history most generations have managed to persuade themselves that they have seen the world and its established practices change more in their time than at any previous period in the evolution of mankind. Such claims are hardly surprising and it is only natural that people who have lived through momentous events should consider the repercussions of those events to be unique to themselves. However, the extent and depth of change in the Twentieth Century has been particularly marked, the speed and complexity of developments across nearly every area of society having often been disconcerting and sometimes devastating. Turbulence experienced over the last half century has resulted in Britain's internal structure and her position in the world being transformed to an extent that conventions, standards and customs taken for granted by people who lived even as recently as between the two Great Wars are now hardly acknowledged. This is not to argue that change is necessarily bad. Far from it, some changes to the way in which Britain has conducted her affairs and looked after her people having been both necessary and long overdue. However, the process by which change is brought about can be damaging to the cohesion and good order of society, even in a country like Britain where the population usually accepts innovation or modification without resort to the barricades.

Britain's Armed Forces have always been affected by developments which reflect the wider fluctuations of society and in recent years they have had constantly to be ready to adapt to sudden lurches in national policy over which they no longer exert any real control, if indeed they ever did. Since 1956 Britain has supervised the return of her once extensive colonial empire to indigenous rulers, has successfully 'fought' and won the Cold War in conjunction with her NATO allies, thereby ensuring the continuing peace of Europe, whilst, since 1968, she has had to conduct a campaign to counter terrorism within the British Isles themselves. All these tasks have been undertaken in the shadow of potential world nuclear conflict and at a time when some of her own citizens have questioned, and continue to question, Britain's role in the world and her support for overseas dependencies such as Hong Kong or the Falkland Islands, which, in their view, should be abandoned. Some of these critics no doubt identify with the remarks of Mr Douglas Hurd, the Foreign Secretary, when he said that 'Britain was trying to punch above her weight' in attempting to maintain a position in the world that is no longer justified. Notwithstanding, in 1994 Britain finds herself with overseas possessions still to defend, a bitter internal conflict in Northern Ireland, which is only just beginning to show signs of possible resolution, and under growing pressure to contribute military forces to operations controlled by the UN in an effort to limit international disputes in territories where she may have little or no direct interest. If all this were not enough, continuous calls for the reshaping of Britain's means of defending herself have led to debilitating and often fruitless examinations of the Nation's defence apparatus, exercises habitually conducted with scant regard for the sensitivities of those involved, while increasingly stringent financial controls have tended to restrict all but the most essential peacetime military activities.

The three Services, but in particular the Army, have shown great resilience in adapting to the challenges posed by national and international change over the nearly forty years covered by this book. Indeed it might fairly be asked what other nation's armed forces could have transformed themselves so successfully whilst at the same time retaining an international reputation for professionalism, impartiality and commitment. Like every other regiment in the Army, the Scots Guards has had to adjust its thinking and approach to meet new demands and new situations. That, as this history sets out to demonstrate, this has been achieved without the loss of a reputation for the delivery of high standards, flexibility and good humour, speaks volumes for the men and women who comprise the regimental family and who have been instrumental in ensuring that within the Regiment the challenges brought about by change have invariably been met and have often been turned to advantage.

This book records several instances when the Regiment has been challenged. Two occasions of an operational nature immediately spring to mind: August, 1971, when the 1st Battalion found itself on the streets of Belfast for the first time, inadequately prepared for a task the complexity of which was generally not understood outside Northern Ireland and yet, after only a few weeks, the battalion triumphed. The other, the 2nd Battalion's involvement in the hurriedly mounted operation to win back the Falkland Islands in 1982, will forever stand as an example of what can be achieved when determination, courage and leadership combine to ensure success.

Since 1956 the Regiment has been involved in the only two wars fought by British Forces and has served full tours of duty in Kenya, Malaysia, Hong Kong and Cyprus and emergency tours in Belize and Sharjah. Battalions have also undertaken innumerable tours of operational duty in Northern Ireland and have undergone conversion to the mechanized role in BAOR six times. Closer to home the Regiment has paraded on Horse Guards to troop one or other of its Queen's Colours no fewer than eight times. Doubtless other regiments can point to a similar record, but few can claim to have discharged their responsibilities to such a consistently high standard.

Of course there have been some failures and it would be a less than honest history which pretended otherwise. Such setbacks as there have been, have usually arisen from a lack of experience or because of misguided intention and have never been allowed to continue beyond a point where lasting damage might occur. No regiment can claim to be without fault and the best acknowledge when mistakes have been made, learn the appropriate lessons and do not repeat the original error.

A useful indicator against which to measure regimental performance can often be the views of those senior officers under whom battalions have served. Where possible these have been recorded to allow the reader to judge for him or herself how a battalion has performed within the milieu of the Army. Another yardstick by which success can be judged is to identify how those who have served as Scots Guardsmen for all or part of their careers have translated the experience gained into other avenues. Apart from the impressive list at Appendix G of those who, since 1956, have reached the rank of major general or above, several former members of the Regiment have gone on to achieve high positions in public life outside the Armed Forces. To be able to record that the last forty years have seen former Scots Guardsmen hold such eminent positions as those of Archbishop of Canterbury, Home Secretary, Lord Chamberlain (on two occasions), Chief Scout and Private Secretary to Her Majesty The Queen, whilst several others have risen to become leaders of industry or the Lord Lieutenant of their county, speaks volumes for the manner in which the Regiment has contributed to the training and development of people who have gone on to achieve success outside military service. This underlying theme of success achieved outside the Regiment, but built upon standards learnt whilst serving, is by no means confined to senior officers. Many others, but most notably a number of officers commissioned during their time in the Regiment to be Quartermasters have, after serving twenty years or more, left to take up appointments in the City of London and elsewhere, holding their own against intense competition from people better qualified and with greater natural advantages than themselves. In both these instances and in the case of all those guardsmen who have left the Regiment to achieve success in other fields, the basis for their performance has been firmly rooted in their experience as soldiers. They all owe the Regiment a great deal.

Many facets of the life of the Regiment have changed since 1956. Whilst the underlying conventions by which battalions and the independent companies of the Regiment have been administered probably differ little in form today from forty years ago, there have been subtle changes of emphasis and outside influences now impinge more upon how the Regiment conducts its life than was formerly the case. The role of Regimental Headquarters in the direct management of Scots Guardsmen has diminished quite considerably and continuity within battalions has reduced, with officers and NCOs spending less time holding key internal appointments, whilst the influence of cultures readily adopted by civilian society has inevitably eroded standards previously considered to be inviolable. Reference is made in Appendix A to changes in the way in which guardsmen are now trained, a far cry from methods practised at the Guards Depot in 1956, and it might be tempting to think that the adoption of such a different approach can only result in standards taken for granted in the past no longer being possible of achievement. However, it would be foolish to make such an assumption; training is an evolutionary process and as, technology tempers tradition in this area as in so many others, different but equally efficacious methods of inculcating standards will doubtless be found. After all it is Scots Guardsmen, in concert with their colleagues in the other regiments of the Household Division, who are now being challenged to mastermind future training at Pirbright and Catterick.

Another area of significant change has been that of the management of the Regiment's families. Not until the 1960s did the Army deem it necessary for a regiment's or battalion's families to be made the sole responsibility of an officer designated as Battalion Families Officer and even then many regiments did not immediately embrace such a concept. Within the Scots Guards a newly commissioned Warrant Officer, almost certainly serving on a Short Service Commission, has since the early 1970s been made responsible for the administration of a battalion's families, a development which has been to the benefit of all concerned. Those filling the appointment have proved themselves to be dedicated and resourceful leaders with an ability to manage the families as effectively as they had previously commanded their guardsmen.

Although Regimental Headquarters may in recent years have lost most of its former authority over its battalions there are areas where its influence is as strong if not stronger than previously. Appendix A shows how the role of the Headquarters in Wellington Barracks has changed, its main task now being to maintain the cohesion of the Regiment by co-ordinating its extramural activities and by providing an essential link between those serving and those no longer in uniform. Despite criticism sometimes heaped upon it by those ignorant of its responsibilities or unhappy at its decisions, Regimental Headquarters has generally served the Regiment well and has always attempted to look after the interests of serving Scots Guardsmen to the best of its abilities.

Helping those whose luck has deserted them after leaving the Regiment is one of the responsibilities of the Welfare Officer at Regimental Headquarters, although he is also responsible for the administration of regimental funds. This latter responsibility has always been a major commitment, particularly so since 1972 when Colonel Sir Gregor MacGregor, at the time the Lieutenant Colonel Commanding, undertook a major review of the regimental funds and investment policy. As a result of his work twenty years later the Regiment is very well endowed and well able to disburse generous financial assistance to those who deserve it.

Within battalions considerable internal organizational change has occurred.

In 1956 Scots Guards battalions were self-contained in as much as they provided all the departments to ensure their own internal smooth running. Regimental cooks, clerks, tailors and tradesmen pioneers all contributed to the well-ordered running of life where the principle of 'if you can fix it yourself, do so' prevailed. Nearly forty years later cooks have been replaced by others provided by the Army Catering Corps now part of the Royal Logistic Corps, while regimental clerks, in company with their colleagues in the Royal Army Pay Corps who have served battalions so loyally since their introduction in the 1950s, have been incorporated into the recently formed Adjutant General's Corps, which now embodies all those responsible for the administration and remuneration of soldiers, whatever their capbadge. Female officers have also made their debut and at various times over the last ten years both battalions have had a female Assistant Adjutant, first from the Women's Royal Army Corps and now from the Adjutant General's Corps, to assist with internal administration. No doubt there will be other developments in this area, since the further emancipation of women within the Services looks set to continue; however, there is no reason to fear such developments so long as sensible guidelines are followed. In general terms the official establishment of a battalion has changed little over the years and the guardsman of the late 1950s would discover that the basic organization is much the same today as in his time.

Attention has sometimes been concentrated upon the relationship between the two battalions of the Regiment. On occasions the rapport has not been as harmonious as might have been expected and, as a very young officer on commissioning in 1957, the author remembers being a little surprised by the attitude of those in the 2nd Battalion who appeared to regard their colleagues in the 1st as virtually belonging to another regiment. Various epithets have been used by some interviewed for this book to describe 'the other battalion', none of which are in the slightest bit important, since from the time when officers and NCOs began to be regularly cross-posted between battalions, most animosities have faded away. A particularly close relationship between the two battalions developed in 1979 when both were stationed in Chelsea Barracks and was subsequently reinforced when a year later they served alongside one another in 39th Infantry Brigade. Meanwhile there are already positive indications that the 'new' 1st Battalion has successfully absorbed the best traditions and characteristics of its two immediate predecessors.

Of far greater importance are the bonds which have always drawn officers, NCOs and guardsmen together regardless of background, education, ability or commitment. Such intangible links exist in every regiment and battalion of the British Army and it would be fallacious to think that they are unique to the Scots Guards. However, through a conjunction of mutual respect and self-discipline generations of officers and soldiers have managed to build an enduring rapport which permits them to respond to one another without advantage or imposition. It is a similar human thread which ensures that a Warrant Officer on commissioning experiences less difficulty in becoming a member of the

Officers' Mess of a Scots Guards battalion than in that of any other regiment of the Household Division.

However, as with all battalions of the Division it is the Sergeants' Mess which has always provided the bedrock upon which the rest of the battalion structure is built and it is because such a stable platform exists that so many of the successful enterprises recorded in this book have been possible of fulfilment. Explanation as to why this should be so is neither called for nor necessary and must remain part of the Regiment's *mystique*; suffice it to say that the bonds which draw all Scots Guardsmen to one another have been forged over many years through a mixture of trust, confidence and respect to fashion a regiment which evokes pride, affection and gratitude in all who have served within its ranks. One former RSM interviewed for this History, on being asked what the Scots Guards had done for him, simply replied, 'Everything'. Few who have had the good fortune to serve in the ranks of Scotland's own Regiment of Foot Guards over the last forty years would disagree.

Appendices

APPENDIX A

COMMAND, ORGANIZATION AND SUPPORT WITHIN THE REGIMENT

INTRODUCTION

Standing Orders of the Scots Guards were last brought up to date and re-published in 1964. They were issued to preserve uniformity throughout the Regiment and to supplement regulations and orders applicable to the Army and the Household Division. They will not be repeated in this short appendix, the purpose of which is to record the principal changes which have been made to the way in which the Regiment has been commanded, organized, trained and supported since 1955 and to cover such activities of the Regiment as may not, for reasons of arrangement, have been included in the main chapters of this History.

COMMAND

Command of battalions and independent companies of the Regiment has throughout the period of this History been vested in the appropriate operational or administrative officer within the chain of command periodically determined by the Ministry of Defence. This is normal military practice. Command of the Regiment for regimental matters has, however, remained with the Lieutenant Colonel Commanding. What constitutes 'regimental matters' has varied from time to time but has generally included responsibility for the records and posting of all ranks, regimental recruiting and publicity, regimental property and funds, the Regimental Association, regimental events and all matters affecting the Colonel. In addition when battalions have been stationed within London District the Lieutenant Colonel Commanding has usually acted as a battalion's immediate superior commander, himself reporting to the GOC, whilst on other occasions he has been made responsible for supervising their military training.

For most of the thirty-eight years covered by this book the command team at RHQ has consisted of the Lieutenant Colonel Commanding in the rank of Colonel, the Regimental Adjutant, the Assistant Regimental Adjutant, who has also invariably held the appointment of Equerry to the Colonel, and the Welfare

Officer who is *inter alia* responsible for the administration of regimental funds. At times a Recruiting Officer has also been appointed. The senior soldier at RHQ is the Superintending Clerk in the rank of WO1 and he manages an office staff comprising military and civilian personnel. In 1955 Colonel Henry Clowes was the Lieutenant Colonel Commanding. In 1986 it was decided that the role of Lieutenant Colonel Commanding, which was re-titled Regimental Lieutenant Colonel from 1989, no longer justified the rank of Colonel and Lieutenant Colonel Michael Whiteley therefore succeeded Colonel Johnny Clavering at the end of the latter's tour in February, 1987.

Further change took place in March, 1989, when it was decided that the five Foot Guards RHQs would be 'brigaded' under a Colonel Foot Guards to whom each would report on matters of a general military and Household Division nature, while continuing to be responsible to a senior serving officer of the Regiment for regimental affairs. The senior officer in question was to discharge his regimental responsibilities in addition to his primary military duties. The first officer to hold this new dual appointment was Brigadier Michael Scott, while Colonel Sir Brian Barttelot, formerly Coldstream Guards, was appointed the first Colonel Foot Guards. In late 1990 Brigadier Scott formed a Regimental Council of most serving senior officers in the Regiment down to and including those holding the rank of colonel, to advise him on matters pertaining to the Regiment.

When in February 1974 Wellington Barracks was closed for re-building, RHQ Scots Guards, in company with RHQ Grenadier Guards, was moved to 4 Bloomsbury Court, High Holborn where it remained until December 1981 when it returned to Wellington Barracks. M Company remains the sub-unit through which RHQ and the Regimental Band are administered. For most of the time covered by this book RHQ has been designated a sub-sector headquarters responsible for undertaking contingency operations in North East London under the auspices of Headquarters London District.

ORGANIZATION

From 9 February, 1946, to 30 November, 1993, there were two regular battalions of the Regiment and their activities since 1 January, 1956, provide the core of events running through this book. On 30 November, 1993, following decisions reached as part of the Government's 'Options for Change' reductions programme, the 1st and 2nd Battalions came together at Victoria Barracks, Windsor to form a single 1st Battalion. Independent companies have also been formed from time to time to fulfil particular military requirements; F and S Companies were re-formed in 1970 as a prelude to the placing of the 2nd Battalion in suspended animation and subsequently served in Hong Kong and British Honduras respectively, both being disbanded when the 2nd Battalion re-formed in 1972, although F Company remained in the battalion order of battle. F Company was again re-formed as an independent company on 4 November,

1993, on the dispersal of the 2nd Battalion and is currently serving at Wellington Barracks, London with the 1st Battalion Grenadier Guards. A 2nd Battalion Scots Guards Company also formed in 1971 to carry the Colours and traditions of that battalion. It disbanded early in 1972 on the reformation of the 2nd Battalion, having been based in Edinburgh for its short life.

No 1 (Guards) Independent Parachute Company remained in the Army's order of battle until 1975. During its twenty-seven years existence the company's role was to provide the spearhead for any airborne assault to be mounted by 16th Parachute Brigade. Since 1956 the company has deployed operationally to Cyprus, Jordan, Borneo and Northern Ireland and a large number of Scots Guardsmen have served in its ranks. Major Mark Carnegie-Brown was the last Scots Guards officer to command the company which he did from February, 1974, to July, 1976. G Squadron 22nd Special Air Service Regiment was formed in 1966 by Major Murray de Klee, himself a former member of No 1 (Guards) Parachute Company. The original intention was that the squadron should be comprised entirely of guardsmen and, although this has never been achieved, a large number of Scots Guards officers and non-commissioned officers have served within its ranks. Along with the remainder of the Special Air Service Regiment the squadron has served in a variety of places and has since its formation been involved in a wide range of operations both at home and abroad. Lieutenant Colonel John Holmes commanded 22nd Special Air Service Regiment from 1989 to 1992, while in their time Majors Hugh Laing, Alastair Morrison and Richard Bethell commanded G Squadron.

TRAINING

Between 1956 and 1961 the initial training of Scots Guardsmen was conducted at the Guards Depot at Caterham and at the Guards Training Battalion at Pirbright. Under the auspices of K Company at Caterham recruits trained in drill, physical training, education and weapon training. Under L Company at Pirbright they learnt fieldcraft and tactics. Meanwhile training of junior soldiers for the Brigade of Guards began at Pirbright in 1958, while junior leaders for the Infantry were trained at the Infantry Junior Leaders Battalion at Plymouth from 1955.

From 1961 to 1993 adult recruit training was consolidated at Pirbright. L Company was disbanded, but K Company continued to exist at the new Guards Depot until 1974 when the Guards Division regimental companies and the Household Cavalry Training Squadron were disbanded and replaced by two divisional companies. This arrangement remained extant until 1993, albeit with some minor modifications, when the Guards Depot was replaced by the Army Training Regiment, Pirbright. The latter is one of five such battalions located across Britain commanded by the Director General Training and Doctrine. Once a recruit's ten weeks at Pirbright are complete he now moves to the Infantry Training Battalion at Catterick for thirteen weeks advanced drill and fieldcraft.

Since 1960 the training of junior soldiers and junior leaders has been conducted at a variety of places and in a variety of different ways; Pirbright for junior soldiers, and Oswestry, Shorncliffe and finally, in 1987, Pirbright for junior leaders. Junior training ceased altogether in 1993. Throughout the period potential officers have undergone instruction prior to sitting the Regular Commissions Board at Westbury, through attendance at the Brigade Squad at Pirbright.

MUSIC

In 1956 the Scots Guards **Regimental Band** was maintained at a strength of seventy-five. By 1993 this had fallen to a total of fifty although the band was still expected to discharge broadly similar musical and military duties. The Ministry of Defence continues to require the Regiment to maintain a band which can provide either a marching band of forty-nine, a concert band of thirty-five, a fanfare team of seven or an orchestra of twelve. In addition to state and other ceremonial duties the band supports the Regiment and carries out a large number of external engagements, both paid and unpaid, including visits overseas to support national enterprise events or to undertake tours. The band is under command of the Regiment, although it is tasked by Headquarters Household Division. Musicians are permitted to undertake outside engagements and several teach on a regular basis.

The band's mobilization role is to provide Grade Three Regimental Medical Orderlies to supplement regular and reserve units of the Army Medical Services for operational duty. This concept was fully tested in the autumn of 1990 when the band deployed complete under Lieutenant Colonel David Price to Saudi Arabia to support British troops preparing to re-capture Kuwait. This deployment is dealt with in more detail in Chapter Ten. Earlier in 1989 members of the band were involved in providing military cover during the Ambulance Service national strike, something which caused His Royal Highness Prince Philip to comment when he saw the orchestra playing at St James's Palace, that he did not believe that a baby delivered by a Scots Guards musician (as had happened with Lance Sergeant Wilson) would survive. During the last forty years the band has been directed by some notable personalities including Directors of Music such as Lieutenant Colonels Sam Rhodes (who held his appointment for twenty-one years) and David Price (the current Senior Director of Music Household Division), Majors Jimmy Howe, Duncan Beat, Brian Hicks and Donald Carson while Band Sergeant Majors since 1956 have included BSMs Mansfield, Williams, Bibby, Davis, Cook and Proctor, the current incumbent. Following the Army's 1992 Band Study which recommended very considerable reductions in the number of military bands, the five Foot Guards bands have been left unchanged in number and role.

Traditional pipe music has not changed at all during this period. Many of the old favourites are still held within the band's repertoire, particularly within the sets used for public duties or marching displays: 'Pibroch of Donald Dhu',

'Cock of the North', 'Glendaruel Highlanders' and 'Blue Bonnets' to name but a few. In the past twenty years both battalions' **Pipes and Drums** have placed much more emphasis on competing at pipe band competitions, although pipers are still encouraged to compete in solo piping events. Pipe Major Macdonald won the Gold Medal in 1964 and Sergeant Donaldson in 1990. Both bands have reached Grade One status in the pipe band world; the 2nd Battalion band under Pipe Major Ingram in 1974 was the first regular army band to achieve such a position, while that of the 1st Battalion in 1985 under Pipe Major Banks did so after winning the Grade Two World Championships at Bellahouston Park in Glasgow. Instruments have changed with the times; the pitch of chanters has sharpened considerably while in the 1970s rope tension drums were replaced by rod tension drums, making the pitch of the side drums sharper.

Pipe bands are established at sixteen pipers although at the time of merger in December 1993 the Pipes and Drums of the 1st Battalion numbered twenty-six pipers and eleven drummers. The military role of the pipers has not changed and on most operations and exercises the majority still carry out the task of stretcher bearer and company medical orderly. However on operations in Northern Ireland some pipers have been regularly employed as riflemen.

The **Corps of Drums** in both battalions have changed little since 1956. They provide the oldest form of military music and continue to rely upon B Flat and F Flat Flutes and side drums as their main instruments. Although old favourites such as 'Prussian Glory' and 'Hazelmere' continue to be played on both major and minor occasions, in recent years Drum Majors have innovated to expand the repertoire of their bands. The establishment of a Corps of Drums stands at a Drum Major and sixteen drummers, the term 'drummer' covering all members of a band regardless of rank. Like Piper Majors, Drum Majors tend to remain a long time in charge of their band and Scots Guards Drum Majors since 1956 have included such well known personalities as Drum Majors Taylor, Abethell, Hickling, Waterston, Davidson and McLintock. Some Drum Majors have gone on to hold senior Warrant Officer appointments such as that of RQMS, while Drum Major McLintock is now RSM of the Royal Military School of Music, Kneller Hall.

Operationally a Corps of Drums usually deploys as a rifle platoon although drummers have been used as assault pioneers and Sustained Fire role machine gunners on occasion. In Northern Ireland a Corps of Drums has usually operated as a platoon, if not commanded by its Drum Major, then under the aegis of an officer or Warrant Officer. For example in 1974 Drill Sergeant Bunton commanded the Drums Platoon with Right Flank in Ballymurphy, West Belfast.

STAFFING

In 1956 battalions of the Regiment employed their own guardsmen as tradesmen pioneers, cooks, clerks, tailors as well as staff in both Officers' and Sergeants'

Messes. Since then many of these roles have been deleted from the official establishment of an infantry battalion, either not being replaced or, as in the case of the regimental cooks, being substituted by soldiers of the Army Catering Corps in 1972, while regimental clerks were absorbed into the Adjutant General's Corps in 1992, along with those members of the Royal Army Pay Corps who formerly served with infantry battalions. Other changes may well be planned although the arrangement by which battalions are supported by armourers and vehicle mechanics of the Royal Electrical and Mechanical Engineers as yet remains unaltered.

SUPPORTING ASSOCIATIONS

The **Third Guards Club** is the Regimental Officers' Dining Club. Formed in 1836 the Club held its first dinner in 1880. Since 1956 the Club has dined annually in London, most often at either the Fishmongers' Hall or The Savoy Hotel, while in 1968 and 1987 a second dinner was held at the Surgeons' Hall, Edinburgh. Major General Sir Digby Raeburn has been President since 1975. In addition to the Third Guards Club there are three other occasions in a year when past and serving officers of the Regiment dine together. Currently organized by Major Ion Calvocoressi the **Desert Dinner** involves those officers of the 2nd Battalion who fought with the battalion in the Western Desert before August, 1942, although, since 1977 those who joined the 2nd Battalion after that date have been invited to attend so long as they served in North Africa. The first dinner was held in 1950 and eighteen people dined in 1994. The **Tumbledown Dinner** is held every year on 14 June, regardless of the day of the week, on the anniversary of the battle of that name and is attended by those officers and NCOs who have since been commissioned, who were serving in the 2nd Battalion at the time of the Falklands Campaign in 1982. The **D-Day Dodgers Dinner** involves those officers serving in the 1st Battalion and S Company in Italy in 1944; their first dinner was held in 1964 and at their last one held in October, 1993, twenty-one out of a possible forty-seven attended. Nowadays the dinner is more normally known as the '1SG Dinner Club'. A dinner involving 100 officers, their wives and brother officers' widows who had served with the **3rd Battalion** was held in the Guardroom at Lambeth Palace on 15 October, 1990, to commemorate the fiftieth anniversary of the formation of that battalion. The Right Reverend Doctor Robert Runcie, the Archbishop of Canterbury and a former officer of the battalion gave permission for the Palace to be used. He told David Bankes who organized the occasion that, if some of the pictures in the Guardroom were covered over, 'you can make the hideous light fittings your target'.

The **Scots Guards Association** has been in existence since 1904. Its membership is open to all who have served in the Regiment whilst a number of serving officers and soldiers are also affiliated to branches. Its purpose is to provide members of the Regiment with a forum in which they can continue to meet while providing a conduit through which any circumstances experienced by those who fall upon difficult times can be brought to the attention of former colleagues. There are now eighteen branches of the Association covering the whole of Scotland and most of England, other than the South Coast and East Anglia. The South Western Branch which meets regularly at Chepstow, gives former Scots Guardsmen living in Wales a chance to meet, while the North American Branch caters for the needs of all those who served in the Regiment who now live in that continent. Since 1956 several branches have been formed or re-formed, including those now established in Edinburgh and the Lothians, Surrey, Berkshire and Buckinghamshire, Durham and Yorkshire, South-West England and North America. During the same period the Leeds Branch closed. At the end of 1993 there were in excess of 1,800 members of the Association, the affairs of which are administered from RHQ by the Superintending Clerk, currently RSM Anderson. The **Scots Guards Warrant Officers' and Sergeants' (Past & Present) Association** formed in 1949 with the aim of maintaining connections between past and present members of the Regiment and of promoting friendship and association with those who are now in civilian life. Membership is open to all Sergeants' Mess Members and serving and past officers of the Regiment can be invited to attend annual dinners. The Colonel dined with the Association in 1976.

ROLL OF HONOUR

of

Officers and Soldiers of the Regiment, and those attached to it, killed in action or on operational duty.

Northern Ireland

1970   Guardsman J. E. EDMUNDS

1971   Guardsman B. W. HALL
           Guardsman G. HAMILTON
           Guardsman N. BOOTH
           Guardsman P. NICHOLLS
           Guardsman S. A. L. T. MAGUIRE

1972   Guardsman J. VAN BECK
           Guardsman G. LOCKHART
           Lance Sergeant T. McKAY
           Lance Corporal C. HARKER, *REME*

1973   Guardsman A. DAUGHTERY

1978   Lance Corporal A. D. SWIFT

1990   Lance Sergeant G. A. STEWART
           Drummer P. BROWN

1992   Guardsman D. J. SHACKLETON

The Falkland Islands

1982   Warrant Officer Class 2 D. WIGHT
           Sergeant J. J. SIMEON
           Lance Sergeant C. MITCHELL
           Guardsman D. J. DENHOLM
           Guardsman D. MALCOLMSON
           Guardsman J. B. C. REYNOLDS, DCM
           Guardsman A. G. STIRLING
           Guardsman R. TANBINI

Other Officers and Soldiers of the Regiment who died whilst serving.

1956   Warrant Office Class 2 C. SMITH

1958   Guardsman W. F. K. HOPE

1959   Guardsman J. C. NUGENT

1960   Lance Sergeant W. McC. MITCHELL

1961   Guardsman R. J. OWENS
        Captain T. P. A. GOSSELIN

1962   Guardsman J. GAY
        Lance Sergeant S. G. RAYMENT
        Guardsman T. PORTER

1963   Lance Sergeant J. PAUL
        Guardsman F. LEYDEN

1964   Lance Sergeant J. MATHESON
        Guardsman J. B. HOME

1965   Guardsman E. J. TOPPING
        Sergeant J. J. HUMPHREY
        Lance Corporal D. A. WATERHOUSE

1966   Captain (QM) R. TILLOTSON
        Lieutenant R. A. J. FANE-GLADWIN

1967   Guardsman M. PATTINSON
        Guardsman J. F. CONNELLY

1968   Guardsman W. SCOTT
        Guardsman W. LOGIE

1969   Guardsman J. FLEMING

1970   Guardsman R. D. YUILLE

1971   Lieutenant General V. F. ERSKINE CRUM, CIE MC
        Drummer H. J. A. SHEPHERD

1972   Captain (QM) J. FORSYTH, MBE
        Guardsman D. HYND
        Drummer J. D. O'BRIEN
        Lance Corporal K. McA. WILSON
        Lance Corporal D. SPEED

1973   Guardsman A. FOTHERINGHAM

1974   Field Marshal HRH The Duke of Gloucester, KG KT KP GCB GCMG GCVO
Lance Sergeant J. PROUD
Sergeant J. M. LANG
Guardsman W. MC. FORSYTH
Guardsman J. C. HUNTER

1975   Drummer R. CLARK
Guardsman B. SMITH
Lance Sergeant T. C. LINDSAY
Guardsman B. W. JOHNSTONE

1976   Lance Corporal T. PINDER

1977   Warrant Officer Class 2 H. RUSHFORTH, *APTC*
Lance Corporal J. P. NEWMAN
Lance Corporal A. SMITH

1978   Lance Corporal D. W. MINTO
Guardsman I. J. S. MCALOON
Guardsman J. A. WOTHERSPOON
Sergeant D. J. NADEN

1979   Lance Corporal G. M. RUSSELL
Guardsman R. S. LONIE

1980   Colour Sergeant E. J. MURRISON, QGM
Lance Sergeant I. HANNA
Guardsman J. F. FERGUSON
Guardsman G. CONNELL

1981   Guardsman R. E. SHENNAN
Guardsman J. P. MCCUTCHEON
Guardsman J. FORT
Guardsman D. A. L. B. Y. NEILLY

1983   Lance Sergeant J. JOHNSTON

1984   Warrant Officer Class 2 R. T. GREWCOCK
Guardsman D. CONN
Guardsman P. TALMAN
Guardsman R. R. FLEMING
Guardsman P. FERGUSON
Guardsman C. D. THOMPSON

1985   Lance Sergeant A. D. TURNBULL
Piper R. FLEMING

1986   Major D. N. D. NICOL OF ARDMARNOCH

1988	Guardsman S. K. KEENAN
	Guardsman S. JOHNSTONE
	Warrant Officer Class 2 G. THORNLEY, *ACC*
1989	Lance Corporal D. T. WINTERS
	Lance Corporal A. M. OVERTON
	Guardsman G. HEWITT
	2nd Lieutenant D. J. LESLIE
1990	Lance Corporal K. M. LINDSAY
	Guardsman C. L. JOHNSTONE
	Guardsman A. K. IRELAND
1991	Guardsman S. MOULDING
1992	Lance Sergeant H. McCOY
	Guardsman A. WASON
1993	2nd Lieutenant G. G. P. ELWES

HONOURS AND AWARDS

Honours and Awards for Service other than in Northern Ireland and the Falkland Islands 1982

1956	*Member of the Order of the British Empire*	Major D. W. Scott-Barrett, MC
1957	*Knight Commander of the Royal Victorian Order*	Major General G. F. Johnson, CB CBE DSO
1957	*Mention in Despatches*	Captain M. P. de Klee Warrant Officer Class 1 A. Young
1958	*Commander of the Order of the British Empire*	Brigadier J. W. H. Gow Brigadier E. B. W. Cardiff, OBE
1958	*Croix de Guerre avec Palme*	Major M. P. de Klee
1958	*Member of the Order of the British Empire*	Warrant Officer Class 1 D. C. Gibson
1958	*Meritorious Service Medal*	Sergeant C. Metcalfe
1959	*Member of the Royal Victorian Order*	Lieutenant Colonel (DoM) S. Rhodes, MBE ARCM
1960	*Member of the Royal Victorian Order*	Major N. D. P. Chamberlayne-Macdonald
1960	*Member of the Order of the British Empire*	Captain (QM) R. H. Thomson, DCM
1961	*Companion of the Order of the Bath*	Major General C. I. H. Dunbar, CBE DSO
1961	*Officer of the Order of the British Empire*	Lieutenant Colonel (QM) A. O'C. Greenwood, MBE
1961	*Member of the Order of the British Empire*	Warrant Officer Class 2 M. McL. Leitch

1962	*Companion of the Order of the Bath*	Brigadier E. B. W. Cardiff, CBE
1962	*Commander of the Order of the British Empire*	Brigadier The Hon M. Fitzalan Howard, MVO MBE MC
1962	*Member of the Order of the British Empire*	Major P. J. H. Leng, MC
1963	*Member of the Order of the British Empire*	Warrant Officer Class 1 A. Suttle
1963	*British Empire Medal*	Warrant Officer Class 2 J. French, MM
1963	*Royal Victorian Medal (Silver)*	Sergeant A. Cox
1964	*Knight Commander of the Royal Victorian Order*	Major R. N. McDonald-Buchanan, CVO MBE MC
1964	*British Empire Medal*	Colour Sergeant L. Richardson
1965	*Member of the Order of the British Empire*	Major A. T. Philipson
1965	*British Empire Medal*	Warrant Officer Class 2 T. Rorison
1966	*Companion of the Order of the Bath*	Major General W. D. M. Raeburn, DSO MBE
1966	*Member of the Order of the British Empire*	Captain (QM) J. Hughes Captain (QM) D. Mc N. Whyte
1966	*Military Medal*	Sergeant W. McGill
1966	*British Empire Medal*	Sergeant S. N. Rochelle
1966	*Mention in Despatches*	Lieutenant Colonel A. I. D. Fletcher Major M. I. V. Bowater Lieutenant J. M. A. Nurton Colour Sergeant J. Dargie Sergeant A. D. Knight
1967	*Officer of the Order of the British Empire*	Lieutenant Colonel A. I. D. Fletcher
1967	*Member of the Royal Victorian Order*	Major S. C. M. Bland
1967	*British Empire Medal*	Colour Sergeant D. Young Colour Sergeant R. Ryves Colour Sergeant W. Gatherum
1968	*Companion of the Order of the Bath*	Brigadier The Hon M. Fitzalan Howard, CBE MVO MC
1968	*British Empire Medal*	Colour Sergeant (Pipe Major) K. Roe Sergeant W. Muir Lance Sergeant G. Murray

1969	*Officer of the Order of the British Empire*	Lieutenant Colonel J. Swinton
1970	*Officer of the Order of the British Empire*	Lieutenant Colonel J. B. Denham
1970	*British Empire Medal*	Warrant Officer Class 2 J. France Colour Sergeant G. Mansfield
1971	*Knight Commander of the Royal Victorian Order*	Major General The Hon M. Fitzalan Howard, CB CBE MVO MC
1971	*Member of the Order of the British Empire*	Major (DoM) J. H. Howe
1971	*British Empire Medal*	Warrant Officer Class 2 (Drum Major) B. Abethell Sergeant F. Colley Sergeant A. Chisholm
1972	*Member of the Order of the British Empire*	Captain (QM) J. Forsyth
1973	*Companion of the Order of the Bath*	Major General Earl Cathcart, DSO MC
1973	*Commander of the Royal Victorian Order*	Major S. C. Bland, MVO
1973	*Member of the Order of the British Empire*	Major T. P. J. Boyd-Carpenter Major D. M. Naylor Warrant Officer Class 1 R. G. Campbell
1973	*Military Cross*	Major A. G. A. Morrison
1973	*British Empire Medal*	Colour Sergeant G. W. Robertson Sergeant G. S. Beveridge
1974	*Officer of the Order of the British Empire*	Lieutenant Colonel M. P. de Klee
1974	*British Empire Medal*	Sergeant D. Goodwillie Sergeant T. Wright
1975	*Companion of the Order of the Bath*	Major General P.J.H. Leng, MBE MC
1975	*British Empire Medal*	Colour Sergeant H. Benton
1976	*Knight Commander of the Order of the British Empire*	Major General D. W. Scott-Barrett, MBE MC
1976	*Member of the Order of the British Empire*	Major J. H. A. Bryden, RAPC
1976	*British Empire Medal*	Lance Sergeant J. I. M. Innes
1976	*Mention in Despatches*	Sergeant W. Blake

1976	*Queen's Commendation*	Warrant Officer Class 1 G. I. Cooper
1977	*Member of the Order of the British Empire*	Major (QM) G. R. Mitchell, BEM Major (QM) C. Graham
1977	*British Empire Medal*	Colour Sergeant M. M. Davidson
1977	*Queen's Commendation*	Lance Sergeant R. McDermid
1978	*Knight Commander of the Order of the Bath*	Lieutenant General P. J. H. Leng, CB MBE MC
1978	*Commander of the Order of the British Empire*	Major General J. H. B. Acland Brigadier T. A. Boam, OBE
1978	*Officer of the Order of the British Empire*	Major A. G. A. Morrison, MC
1978	*Member of the Order of the British Empire*	Major A. de C. L. Leask
1978	*British Empire Medal*	Lance Sergeant S. Mathews
1979	*Knight Commander of the Order of the Bath*	Major General J. M. Gow
1979	*Knight Commander of the Royal Victorian Order*	Major General J. Swinton, OBE Major General W. D. M. Raeburn, CB DSO MBE
1979	*Officer of the Order of the British Empire*	Colonel I. A. Ferguson Lieutenant Colonel J. A. Dunsmure
1979	*Member of the Order of the British Empire*	Warrant Officer Class 1 J. M. Bunton
1979	*Royal Humane Society Testimonial on Vellum*	Lance Sergeant J. C. D. Baines
1980	*Knight Commander of the Order of the Bath*	Major General J. H. B. Acland, CBE
1980	*Lieutenant of the Royal Victorian Order*	Major The Lord Napier and Ettrick
1980	*British Empire Medal*	Colour Sergeant J. Taylor
1981	*Knight Grand Cross of the Royal Victorian Order*	Major General Lord Michael Fitzalan Howard, KCVO CB CBE MC
1981	*Member of the Royal Victorian Order*	Major (DoM) D. R. Beat
1981	*British Empire Medal*	Colour Sergeant H. Shearer
1981	*Queen's Commendation*	Lance Sergeant J. B. Bradley
1982	*Knight Commander of the Royal Victorian Order*	Lieutenant Colonel S. C. M. Bland, CVO

1982	Officer of the Order of the British Empire	Lieutenant Colonel R. D. Buchanan-Dunlop
1982	Member of the Order of the British Empire	Major I. C. MacKay-Dick Major M. C. B. Smart Warrant Officer Class 2 W. F. Fullerton Warrant Officer Class 2 W. Muir, BEM
1983	Knight Grand Cross of the Order of the Bath	General Sir Michael Gow, KCB
1983	Officer of the Order of the British Empire	Lieutenant Colonel J. M. Clavering, MC
1983	Member of the Order of the British Empire	Major (QM) F. Lawrie Major (QM) G. I. Cooper
1983	Lieutenant of the Royal Victorian Order	Lieutenant R. Fellowes
1983	Member of the Royal Victorian Order	Lieutenant Colonel B. A. Stewart-Wilson
1983	British Empire Medal	Sergeant M. J. Allum
1984	Commander of the Order of the British Empire	Major General C. J. Airy
1984	Member of the Order of the British Empire	Major (DoM) D. Carson Warrant Officer Class 1 (Pipe Major) A. MacDonald
1985	Commander of the Royal Victorian Order	Major The Lord Napier and Ettrick, LVO
1985	Officer of the Order of the British Empire	Lieutenant Colonel J. R. Arthur
1985	Member of the Order of the British Empire	Major (QM) W. Wilbur Captain (QM) R. J. C. Mackenzie
1985	British Empire Medal	Colour Sergeant E. J. Smith
1986	Member of the Order of the British Empire	Major (QM) E. Lawrie
1987	Companion of the Order of the Bath	Major General T. A. Boam, CBE Lieutenant R. Fellowes, LVO
1987	Officer of the Order of the British Empire	Lieutenant Colonel A. P. H. Parsons Lieutenant Colonel W. H. M. Ross
1987	British Empire Medal	Sergeant A. Armstrong
1989	Knight Commander of the Royal Victorian Order	Major General C. J. Airy, CBE Lieutenant R. Fellowes, CB LVO
1989	Member of the Order of the British Empire	Major P. E. C. Gascoigne

1990	Commander of the Order of the British Empire	Colonel A. de C. L. Leask, OBE
1990	British Empire Medal	Colour Sergeant I. Gywnne
1991	Knight Commander of the Order of the Bath	Lieutenant The Rt Hon Sir Robert Fellowes, KCVO CB PC
1991	Officer of the Order of the British Empire	Lieutenant Colonel J. T. Holmes, MC
1991	Member of the Order of the British Empire	Major R. A. Ingleby-MacKenzie
1991	British Empire Medal	Sergeant J. Donald
1991	General Officer Commanding's Commendation (Gulf War)	Lance Corporal A. Cooper Lance Corporal J. Marham Musician I. Killoran Musician G. Haynes
1992	Knight Commander of the Royal Victorian Order	Major The Lord Napier and Ettrick, CVO
1992	Companion of the Order of the Bath	Major General D. M. Naylor, MBE
1992	Member of the Order of the British Empire	Captain (QM) R. Walker
1992	British Empire Medal	Colour Sergeant P. Pettit Sergeant S. W. Wolff
1993	Knight Commander of the Order of the British Empire	Lieutenant General The Hon T. P. J. Boyd-Carpenter, MBE
1993	Commander of the Royal Victorian Order	Lieutenant Colonel W. H. M. Ross, OBE
1993	Member of the Order of the British Empire	Lieutenant Colonel N. E. A. G. Cameron Major (QM) I. Beck Warrant Officer Class 2 J. McGowan
1993	British Empire Medal	Colour Sergeant M. F. Tetlow

Honours and Awards for Service in Northern Ireland

1972	Distinguished Service Order	Lieutenant Colonel R. Mayfield
1972	Military Cross	Major J. M. A. Nurton Lieutenant J. T. Holmes
1972	Military Medal	Lance Sergeant A. L. Ball

1972	*Mention in Despatches*	Captain J. H. G. Allen Lieutenant E. A. Woods Warrant Officer Class 2 R. T. Clarkson Colour Sergeant R. Paterson Lance Corporal J. W. Spiers Guardsman S. G. McRonald
1972	*General Officer Commanding's Commendation*	Colour Sergeant R. Chapman Sergeant B. Fraser Sergeant K. G. Taylor Sergeant J. Lawson Sergeant I. A. Kaye Lance Sergeant C. Gibb Lance Sergeant A. J. McClements Lance Sergeant J. Barclay Lance Corporal A. M. Hamilton Guardsman W. Whyte Guardsman J. P. Friel
1973	*Officer of the Order of the British Empire*	Lieutenant Colonel T. A. Boam
1973	*Military Cross*	Major J. M. Clavering
1973	*Mention in Despatches*	Major R. D. Buchanan-Dunlop Major A. de C. L. Leask Sergeant J. P. MacDonald Lance Sergeant J. S. Carlin
1974	*Member of the Order of the British Empire*	Captain J. H. G. Allen
1974	*British Empire Medal*	Sergeant J. Macfarlane
1974	*Mention in Despatches*	Major D. M. Naylor, MBE
1974	*General Officer Commanding's Commendation*	Lieutenant D. V. Erskine Crum Warrant Officer Class 2 P. V. Reynolds Colour Sergeant J. G. Boyle Sergeant R. F. Bibby Lance Sergeant J. Underwood Lance Corporal D. Salkeld
1975	*General Officer Commanding's Commendation and RSPCA Silver Medal*	Guardsman B. Smith
1976	*Mention in Despatches*	Major J. J. D. Cox Captain (QM) F. Smith Lieutenant R. E. Whyte
1976	*General Officer Commanding's Commendation*	Captain (QM) D. Cameron Sergeant D. Wight Lance Corporal A. Lewthwaite

1977	*Mention in Despatches*	Lieutenant Colonel D. M. Naylor, MBE Warrant Officer Class 2 D. Murphy
1977	*General Officer Commanding's Commendation*	Lance Sergeant M. Mackenzie Lance Corporal A. Forbes
1978	*Queen's Gallantry Medal*	Lance Sergeant E. Murrison
1978	*Mention in Despatches*	Captain The Hon R. N. Bethell
1979	*Member of the Order of the British Empire*	Major The Hon R. N. Bethell
1979	*Queen's Gallantry Medal*	Sergeant S. J. Williamson
1979	*Mention in Despatches*	Lieutenant Colonel M. M. Carnegie-Brown Major J. M. A. Nurton, MC Captain J. H. K. Trevaskis Sergeant D. Naden
1979	*General Officer Commanding's Commendation*	Sergeant D. W. Bowes Lance Corporal J. Dadley
1981	*Mention in Despatches*	Lieutenant Colonel The Hon T. P. J. Boyd-Carpenter, MBE Lieutenant Colonel J. M. Clavering, MC Captain J. T. Holmes, MC Warrant Officer Class 1 S. J. Carnegie Sergeant A. W. J. Baker Lance Corporal J. B. P. Owen
1981	*General Officer Commanding's Commendation*	Colour Sergeant J. S. Carlin Sergeant M. J. Allum
1982	*Officer of the Order of the British Empire*	Lieutenant Colonel I. W. MacLaughlan
1982	*Queen's Gallantry Medal*	Sergeant P. McCavera
1982	*Mention in Despatches*	Major W. H. M. Ross Major E. A. Woods Sergeant H. F. Tetlow Guardsman J. Hutchison
1982	*General Officer Commanding's Commendation*	Sergeant J. S. Riseley Sergeant McGowan Guardsman Holmes
1983	*Officer of the Order of the British Empire*	Lieutenant Colonel J. M. A. Nurton, MC Lieutenant Colonel A. G. Ross
1983	*Member of the Order of the British Empire*	Major J. A. S. Lancaster
1984	*Officer of the Order of the British Empire*	Lieutenant Colonel A. de C. L. Leask, MBE

235

1984	*Member of the Order of the British Empire*	Warrant Officer Class 1 (RSM) F. J. Hardie
1985	*Meritorious Service Medal*	Warrant Officer Class 2 J. D. Hope
1985	*Mention in Despatches*	Lieutenant Colonel J. L. Seddon-Brown
1987	*Commander of the Order of the British Empire*	Brigadier M. I. E. Scott, DSO Colonel R. D. Buchanan-Dunlop, OBE
1988	*Mention in Despatches*	Lieutenant Colonel J. A. S. Lancaster, MBE Lieutenant Colonel J. P. Kiszely, MC Guardsman S. Robinson
1988	*General Officer Commanding's Commendation*	Colour Sergeant J. Spence Lance Sergeant S. Goodman Lance Sergeant M. McNally Lance Sergeant R. G. J. Crookdake Piper H. Mcleod
1989	*General Officer Commanding's Commendation*	Captain (QM) G. Fowler Sergeant M. F. Tetlow
1990	*Mention in Despatches*	Lance Sergeant M. B. Dykes
1990	*General Officer Commanding's Commendation*	Colour Sergeant J. Dadley Colour Sergeant T. Steele Colour Sergeant D. Tasker Guardsman J. Fowler Guardsman J. A. MacLachlan
1991	*Officer of the Order of the British Empire*	Lieutenant Colonel D. V. Erskine Crum
1991	*Military Medal*	Lance Corporal K. Gray
1991	*British Empire Medal*	Lance Sergeant J. Belshaw
1991	*Mention in Despatches*	Major P. E. C. Gascoigne, MBE Sergeant A. Bunyan
1991	*General Officer Commanding's Commendation*	Major S. Thornhill Captain The Master of Falkland Captain M. A. de C. Marr Lieutenant C. M. Corson 2nd Lieutenant J. S. McEuen Captain (LE) S. Airey Warrant Officer Class 2 A. C. E. Dalgleish Lance Sergeant K. McGovern
1993	*Officer of the Order of the British Empire*	Lieutenant Colonel T. S. Spicer
1993	*Member of the Order of the British Empire*	Major M. N. D. Turner

1993	Queen's Gallantry Medal	Lance Sergeant S. Goodman
1993	Mention in Despatches	Major C. S. T. Page
		Lieutenant R. B. L. Wallace
		Lance Sergeant L. Burgess
		Guardsman J. Docherty
1993	General Officer Commanding's Commendation	Captain J. M. A. Orwin
		Lieutenant W. D. Glen
		Lieutenant A. J. Fairclough
		Sergeant I. Cameron
		Lance Sergeant W. Rumney
		Lance Corporal W. Hill
		Guardsman D. Hutchinson
		Guardsman S. White

Honours and Awards for Operations in the Falkland Islands 1982

Distinguished Service Order	Lieutenant Colonel M. I. E. Scott
Member of the Order of the British Empire	Captain (SSC) F. J. Moody
Military Cross	Major J. P. Kiszely
	Lieutenant R. A. D. Lawrence
Distinguished Conduct Medal	Warrant Officer Class 2 W. Nicol
	Guardsman J. B. C. Reynolds (*posthumous*)
Military Medal	Sergeant R. W. Jackson
	Guardsman A. S. Pengelly
Mention in Despatches	Major The Hon R. N. Bethell, MBE
	Captain I. A. Bryden
	Lieutenant A. M. Mitchell
	2nd Lieutenant J. D. Stuart
	Lance Sergeant T. McGuinness
	Lance Sergeant A. C. E. Dalgleish
	Lance Sergeant I. Davidson
	Lance Sergeant C. Mitchell (*posthumous*)
	Lance Corporal D. MacColl
	Lance Corporal G. Rennie
	Lance Corporal G. Tytler
	Piper S. W. Duffy
	Piper P. A. McInnes
	Guardsman G. Brown
Commander in Chief Fleet's Commendation	Captain (QM) E. Lawrie
	Lance Sergeant S. J. Williamson
	Piper B. S. H. Rodger

PRINCIPAL APPOINTMENTS

Officers and Warrant Officers who held the Principal Appointments
1956–1993

Lists which are a continuation of those in *The Scots Guards 1919–1955* by
David Erskine start with the last name therein; new lists start from 1956.

COLONEL IN CHIEF

Her Majesty Queen Elizabeth II	1952

COLONELS

25th Colonel	1937

Field Marshal HRH Henry William Frederick Albert, Duke of Gloucester, Earl of Ulster,
KG KT KP GCB GCMG GCVO

26th Colonel	1974

Field Marshal HRH Edward George Nicholas Paul Patrick, Duke of Kent, Earl of St
Andrews and Baron Downpatrick, KG GCMG GCVO ADC(P)

LIEUTENANT COLONELS COMMANDING

Colonel H. N. Clowes, DSO OBE	1954
Colonel W. D. M. Raeburn, DSO MBE	1958
Colonel Earl Cathcart, DSO MC	1959
Colonel A. J. C. Seymour	1962
Colonel G. P. M. Ramsay	1964
Colonel A. I. D. Fletcher, OBE	1967
Colonel J. Swinton, OBE	1970
Colonel Sir Gregor MacGregor of MacGregor, Bt	1971
Colonel M. P. de Klee, OBE	1974
Colonel I. A. Ferguson, OBE	1978
Colonel J. A. Dunsmure, OBE	1981
Colonel J. M. Clavering, OBE MC	1985
Lieutenant Colonel M. G. L. Whiteley	1987

REGIMENTAL LIEUTENANT COLONELS

Brigadier M. I. E. Scott, CBE DSO	1989
Brigadier A. G. Ross, OBE	1993

REGIMENTAL ADJUTANTS

Major G. P. M. Ramsay	1954	Major H. M. Maxwell-Hyslop	1973
Major J. M. Gow	1957	Major M. G. L. Whiteley	1976
Major J. Swinton	1960	Major P. D. Johnson	1977
Major M. P. de Klee	1962	Major J. F. Warren	1979
Major J. B. Denham	1964	Major A. P. H. Parsons	1981
Major B. A. Stewart-Wilson	1966	Major J. J. D. Cox	1983
Major A. J. R. Harrison	1968	Major J. N. A. Crichton-Stuart	1984
Major R. Mayfield	1970	Major J. W. S. Lawrie	1987
Major J. R. Arthur	1971	Major R. E. Whyte	1989

SUPERINTENDING CLERKS

Warrant Officer Class 1 W. Wilbur	1956	Warrant Officer Class 1 R. Paterson	1980
Warrant Officer Class 1 J. Forsyth	1959	Warrant Officer Class 1 D. Vasey	1981
Warrant Officer Class 1 G. West	1963	Warrant Officer Class 1 D. Archibald	1983
Warrant Officer Class 1 C. Butchers	1966	Warrant Officer Class 1 I. Colbridge	1986
Warrant Officer Class 1 J. Louden	1969	Warrant Officer Class 1 S. Airey	1988
Warrant Officer Class 1 C. Brown	1970	Warrant Officer Class 1 R. Gray	1989
Warrant Officer Class 1 T. Ross	1972	Warrant Officer Class 1 J. Hart	1990
Warrant Officer Class 1 R. Clarkson	1974	Warrant Officer Class 1 G. Anderson	1993
Warrant Officer Class 1 D. Cuthill	1977		

COMMANDING OFFICERS

1st Battalion

Lieutenant Colonel T. F. R. Bulkeley, MBE	1954
Lieutenant Colonel Earl Cathcart, DSO MC	1957
Lieutenant Colonel The Hon W. E. H. Lawson	1959
Lieutenant Colonel C. J. R. Duffin	1962
Lieutenant Colonel A. I. D. Fletcher	1963
Lieutenant Colonel Sir Gregor MacGregor of MacGregor, Bt	1966
Lieutenant Colonel M. P. de Klee	1969
Lieutenant Colonel R. Mayfield, DSO	1972
Lieutenant Colonel C. J. Airy	1974
Lieutenant Colonel M. M. Carnegie-Brown	1976
Lieutenant Colonel The Hon T. P. J. Boyd-Carpenter, MBE	1979

2nd Battalion

Lieutenant Colonel The Hon M. Fitzalan Howard, MVO MBE MC	1956
Lieutenant Colonel A. J. C. Seymour	1958
Lieutenant Colonel G. P. Burnett	1960
Lieutenant Colonel G. P. M. Ramsay	1962
Lieutenant Colonel J. M. Gow	1964
Lieutenant Colonel J. Swinton	1966
Lieutenant Colonel J. H. B. Acland	1968

2nd Battalion Company

Major M. I. E. Scott	1971

2nd Battalion

Lieutenant Colonel T. A. Boam, OBE	1972
Lieutenant Colonel J. A. Dunsmure	1974
Lieutenant Colonel D. M. Naylor, MBE	1976

Lieutenant Colonel
I. W. McLaughlan, OBE 1981

Lieutenant Colonel A. G. Ross, OBE 1983

Lieutenant Colonel J. P. Kiszely, MC 1986

Lieutenant Colonel J. J. Cargill 1988

Lieutenant Colonel T. S. Spicer, OBE 1991

Lieutenant Colonel T. M. Fitzalan
Howard 1993

Lieutenant Colonel J. M. Clavering,
MC 1979

Lieutenant Colonel M. I. E. Scott,
DSO 1981

Lieutenant Colonel I. C. MacKay-
Dick, MBE 1983

Lieutenant Colonel J. A. S.
Lancaster, MBE 1985

Lieutenant Colonel D. V. Erskine
Crum, OBE 1988

Lieutenant Colonel T. M. Fitzalan
Howard 1991

F Company

Major M. G. Bence-Trower 1993

ADJUTANTS

1st Battalion

Captain The Lord Napier and Ettrick	1955
Captain P. N. Erskine	1957
Major D. C. Prior	1959
Captain M. I. V. Bowater	1961
Captain T. P. J. Boyd-Carpenter	1963
Major J. A. Dunsmure	1965
Captain M. McN. Campbell of Airds Bay	1967
Captain L. H. C. Maclean	1970
Captain I. C. MacKay-Dick	1971
Captain R. C. Gow	1973
Captain J. P. Kiszely	1975
Captain H. E. O. Balfour	1977
Captain C. J. D. Lawrence	1979
Captain The Hon G. C. W. Grimston	1980
Captain R. A. Ingleby-Mackenzie	1981
Captain E. G. Kelway-Bamber	1983
Captain M. L. B. Varney	1985
Captain G. F. H. S. Nickerson	1987
Captain D. H. Thompson	1989
Captain A. Tetley	1991
Captain J. M. A. Orwin	1992

2nd Battalion

Captain B. A. Stewart-Wilson	1955
Captain T. A. Boam	1957
Captain I. A. Ferguson	1959
Captain A. E. Hopkinson	1960
Captain D. M. Naylor	1963
Captain H. M. Maxwell-Hyslop	1965
Captain M. I. E. Scott	1966
Captain A. G. Ross	1969
Captain W. H. M. Ross	1970
Captain J. L. Seddon-Brown	1972
Captain A. M. H. Joscelyne	1973
Captain D. V. Erskine Crum	1975
Captain A. J. P. M. Ramsay	1977
Captain T. M. Fitzalan Howard	1979
Captain A. W. Foster	1981
Captain J. C. Stewart	1983
Captain M. W. Joynson	1985
Captain M. G. Bence-Trower	1987
Captain C. S. T. Page	1989
Captain W. H. C. Swinton	1991

REGIMENTAL SERGEANT MAJORS

1st Battalion

Warrant Officer Class 1 (RSM)
J. Hughes   1957

Warrant Officer Class 1 (RSM)
W. Rodger   1960

Warrant Officer Class 1 (RSM)
J. Forsyth   1963

Warrant Officer Class 1 (RSM)
J. Grant   1965

Warrant Officer Class 1 (RSM)
F. Smith   1968

Warrant Officer Class 1 (RSM)
D. Cameron   1971

Warrant Officer Class 1 (RSM)
G. I. Cooper   1972

Warrant Officer Class 1 (RSM)
J. Knight   1976

Warrant Officer Class 1 (RSM)
I. Beck   1978

Warrant Officer Class 1 (RSM)
J. Macfarlane, BEM   1981

Warrant Officer Class 1 (RSM)
G. Fowler   1984

Warrant Officer Class 1 (RSM)
I. Amos   1987

Warrant Officer Class 1 (RSM)
R. Walker   1988

Warrant Officer Class 1 (RSM)
P. Jackson   1991

Warrant Officer Class 1 (RSM)
J. G. Spence   1993

2nd Battalion

Warrant Officer Class 1 (RSM)
J. Braid   1954

Warrant Officer Class 1 (RSM)
F. Adams   1957

Warrant Officer Class 1 (RSM)
C. Graham   1963

Warrant Officer Class 1 (RSM)
E. Marchant   1967

2nd Battalion Company

Warrant Officer Class 2 (CSM)
J. Phillips   1971

2nd Battalion

Warrant Officer Class 1 (RSM)
J. Dargie   1972

Warrant Officer Class 1 (RSM)
T. Forrest   1973

Warrant Officer Class 1 (RSM)
J. M. Bunton, MBE   1976

Warrant Officer Class 1 (RSM)
R. Wilkie   1979

Warrant Officer Class 1 (RSM)
R. MacKenzie   1981

Warrant Officer Class 1 (RSM)
R. Clemison   1983

Warrant Officer Class 1 (RSM)
J. Harper   1987

Warrant Officer Class 1 (RSM)
D. Wood   1989

Warrant Officer Class 1 (RSM)
J. G. Spence   1992

F Company

Warrant Officer Class 2 (CSM) R. Convery   1993

COMMANDANTS OF THE GUARDS DEPOT

Lieutenant Colonel V. F. Erskine Crum, CIE MC   1957
Lieutenant Colonel D. W. Scott-Barrett, MBE MC   1963

Lieutenant Colonel I. A. Ferguson   1972
Lieutenant Colonel W. H. M. Ross   1982

ADJUTANTS OF THE GUARDS DEPOT
Captain A. J. R. Harrison   1957
Captain J. R. Arthur   1961
Captain W. H. M. Ross   1971

REGIMENTAL SERGEANT MAJORS OF THE GUARDS DEPOT
Warrant Officer Class 1 (RSM) W. Rodger   1958
Warrant Officer Class 1 (RSM) R. Jackson, MM   1992

ORDERS OF BATTLE 1956–1993

Seven Orders of Battle are included and show those officers and senior NCOs filling key appointments in the two battalions of the Regiment at moments of particular interest over the last forty years. While every effort has been made to ensure the completeness of these Orders of Battle, total accuracy cannot be guaranteed.

1st Battalion at Lydd during the period prior to the Suez landings in 1956.

2nd Battalion in East Africa 1963/64.

1st Battalion in Malaysia 1964.

1st Battalion on arrival in Belfast 1971.

2nd Battalion in Londonderry 1972.

2nd Battalion during the Falkland Islands War 1982.

1st Battalion on completion of the merger of battalions in 1993.

1st Battalion

1956

Lydd

Commanding Officer	Lieutenant Colonel T. F. R. Bulkeley, MBE
Second-in-Command	Major A. N. B. Ritchie
Adjutant	Captain The Lord Napier and Ettrick
Intelligence Officer	Lieutenant A. E. Hopkinson
Signal Officer	Captain H. C. D. Laing
Assistant Signal Officer	Captain C. P. A. Bertie
Quartermaster	Captain (QM) D. Fraser
Transport Officer	Captain M. C. Scott
Chaplain	The Reverend W. T. Y. Browne, RAChD
Paymaster	Major J. Kirkpatrick, RAPC
Regimental Sergeant Major	D. McN. Whyte
Drill Sergeant	W. Rodger
Drill Sergeant	K. Thompson
Pipe Major	J. Roe
Drum Major	A. Moon
Regimental Quartermaster Sergeant	A. Fleming
Orderly Room Quartermaster Sergeant	G. Hartley

	Headquarter Company	Right Flank	B Company	C Company	Left Flank	Support Company
Coy Comds	Maj N. D. P. Macdonald of the Isles	Maj J. Swinton	Maj T. N. Rivett-Carnac	Maj The Hon W. E. H. Lawson	Maj D. C. Prior	Maj A. I. D. Fletcher
2ICs	Capt O. B. Varney	Capt H. H. T. Dawson	Capt T. A. Boam	Lt M. R. Hodson	Capt D. M. Lumsden	
Pl Comds		2Lt M. I. V. Bowater	2Lt M. W. Delmar-Morgan	2Lt J. R. Arthur	2Lt P. D. A. Copeland	Lt J. A. Dunsmure *Machine Gun*
		2Lt S. J. E. Turner	2Lt S. H. Hubbard-Ford	Lt R. W. Mackworth-Praed	2Lt J. W. Blair	Capt E. J. W. Hulse *Anti-Tank*
		2Lt A. B. Robertson			2Lt R. G. S. Johnston	Lt G. H. L. Campbell *Mortar*
CSMs	A. Moseley	J. R. Connell	J. G. Cameron	C. Douglas	H. Norton	A. Croucher
CQMSs		N. Simpson	F. Brotherton	A. Hayter	M. White	A. Hamilton

244

2nd Battalion

1963/4

East Africa

Commanding Officer	Lieutenant Colonel G. P. M. Ramsay
Second-in-Command	Brevet Lieutenant Colonel P. J. H. Leng, MBE MC
Adjutant	Captain D. M. Naylor
Assistant Adjutant	Lieutenant M. I. E. Scott
Intelligence Officer	Lieutenant A. H. Clowes
Signal Officer	Captain J. M. Clavering
Quartermaster	Captain (QM) D. McN. Whyte
Transport Officer	Captain (QM) F. Adams
Medical Officer	Captain J. Bradshaw Smith, *RAMC*
Chaplain	The Reverend M. C. Cowper, *RAChD*
Paymaster	Major A. Cook, MBE MC, *RAPC*
Regimental Sergeant Major	C. Graham
Regimental Quartermaster Sergeant	J. Leslie
Orderly Room Quarteraster Sergeant	T. Newcombe
Drill Sergeant	J. Grant
Drill Sergeant	M. Fitzgerald
Pipe Major	R. Kilgour
Drum Major	D. Hickling

	Headquarter Company	*Right Flank*	*No 3 Company Irish Guards*	*G Company**	*Left Flank*
Coy Comds	Capt G. H. L. Campbell	Maj D. C. Prior	Maj R. A. Plummer	Maj T. A. Boam	Maj M. B. Scott
2ICs	Capt K. G. A. Lumsden *Recce*	Capt J. P. O. Gibb	Capt P. M. Thomas	Capt R. Ingham Clark	Capt F. T. P. Spencer
Pl Comds	Lt I. W. McLaughlan *WTO*	Lt A. G. A. Morrison	Lt The Viscount Cole	2Lt D. V. Harvey	2Lt The Hon M. W. Vestey
	Lt P. R. Hill	2Lt J. R. Drummond-Moray	2Lt C. S. S. Davies	2Lt J. L. Seddon-Brown	2Lt T. Benyon
		2Lt D. Bergin	2Lt B. E. Bellew		2Lt L. H. C. Maclean
		Lt M. G. L. Whiteley *Support*	Lt C. R. Brown *Support*	Lt T. M. Bell *Support*	Lt M. C. B. Smart *Support*
CSMs	F. Gourlay	F. Smith	G. Shannon	J. Smith	J. Louden
CQMSs	A. Clelland	J. Watson	G. Lynas	W. Morcom	D. Dalgarno

* Before disbandment

1st Battalion

1964

Malaysia

Commanding Officer	Lieutenant Colonel A. I. D. Fletcher
Second-in-Command	Major Sir Gregor MacGregor of MacGregor, Bt
Adjutant	Captain T. P. J. Boyd-Carpenter
Intelligence Officer	Captain T. M. Bell
Signal Officer	Captain J. M. Clavering

Quartermaster	Captain (QM) J. Hughes
Transport Officer	Captain (QM) W. Wilbur
Medical Officer	Major R. V. F. Williams, RAMC
Chaplain	The Reverend F. Lyall, RAChD
Paymaster	Major J. H. A. Bryden, RAPC
Pilots	Captain A. J. M. Drake, Coldm Gds*
	Captain S. L. Gordon-Duff
	Captain The Hon S. J. Coleridge, Gren Gds*

Regimental Sergeant Major	J. Forsyth
Regimental Quartermaster Sergeant	C. Butcher
Orderly Room Colour Sergeant	G. Hagen
Drill Sergeant	R. Connell
Drill Sergeant	R. Melville
Pipe Major	J. B. Roe
Drum Major	B. Abethell
Master Cook	P. Moseley

	Headquarter Company	Right Flank	B (Training) Company	No 9 Company Irish Guards	Left Flank
Coy Comds	Maj S. J. E. Turner	Maj B. A. Stewart-Wilson	Capt J. A. Dunsmure	Maj J. D. Morrogh-Bernard	Maj M. I. V. Bowater
2ICs					
Pl Comds	Capt A. P. H. Parsons *Recce*	Capt D. H. Saunders		Capt J. S. Lockwood	Capt J. R. L. Whiteley
	2Lt A. D. K. Forbes *Aslt Pnr*	2Lt A. de C. L. Leask		2Lt T. B. E. Eugster	2Lt W. F. D. Bull
		Lt A. G. Ross			
				2Lt C. N. R. Thomson-Moore	Lt A. I. C. Gordon
		Lt R. Jenner-Fust		2Lt J. M. Gordon-Watson	2Lt C. A. H. Gwyn
		2Lt J. F. Warren		Lt R. A. Wilson *Support*	
		Lt J. Arbuthnott, *Support*			Lt R. Fane-Gladwin *Support*
CSMs	R. Connell	S. Rae	D. F. Roberts	M. Aldridge	E. Gifford
CQMSs	F. Lawrie	N. Redpath	J. Smith	G. Irvine	D. Torrance

* Joined during the tour

246

1st Battalion

1971

Belfast

Commanding Officer	Lieutenant Colonel M. P. De Klee
Second-in-Command	Major H. M. Maxwell-Hyslop
Adjutant	Captain I. C. Mackay-Dick
Intelligence Officer	Captain J. H. G. Allen
Operations Officer	Captain A. P. H. Parsons
Signal Officer	Captain J. W. S. Lawrie

Quartermaster	Captain (QM) C. Graham
Transport Officer	Captain (QM) E. H. Marchant
Medical Officer	Captain C. R. Winfield, RAMC
Chaplain	The Reverend K. Crozer, RAChD
Paymaster	Major J. H. A. Bryden, RAPC

Regimental Sergeant Major	D. Cameron
Regimental Quartermaster Sergeant	F. Milne
Orderly Room Quartermaster Sergeant	A. Heybourn
Drill Sergeant	T. Forrest
Drill Sergeant	D. McMillan
Pipe Major	A. MacDonald
Drum Major	B. Abethell

	Headquarter Company	*Right Flank*	*B Company*	*G Company**	*Left Flank*
Coy Comds	Maj B. A. J. Bell	Maj P. D. Johnson	Maj M. C. B. Smart	Maj A. de C. L. Leask	Maj J. M. A. Nurton
2ICs		Capt P. T. A. Clapton		Capt R. E. P. Spencer	Capt N. E. A. G. Cameron
Pl Comds		2Lt P. E. C. Gascoigne	Lt H. M. Snow	Lt J. J. Cargill	Lt E. A. Woods
		Lt A. R. Wilson	Lt (QM) F. Smith	Lt J. A. S. Lancaster, *Recce*	Lt J. T. Holmes
		Lt J. N. Crookenden	2Lt J. N. A. Crichton-Stuart	Lt R. C. Gow	Lt R. E. Whyte
		2Lt The Hon R. N. Bethell		2Lt N. A. G. Laing	
CSMs	D. Murphy	H. Forrest	J. Knight	W. Jamieson	R. Clarkson
CQMSs		W. Fullerton	F. Moody	J. Beattie	R. Harris

* *C Company was re-designated G Company when 2SG went into suspended animation*

2nd Battalion

1972

Londonderry

Commanding Officer	Lieutenant Colonel T. A. Boam
Second-in-Command	Major D. M. Naylor, MBE
Adjutant	Captain J. L. Seddon-Brown
Operations Officer	Major M. I. E. Scott
Intelligence Officer	Captain S. H. Rose
Signal Officer	Captain R. P. G. Le Marchand
Public Relations Officer	Captain J. P. Kiszely

Quartermaster	Captain (QM) E. H. Marchant
Transport Officer	Captain (QM) D. F. Roberts
Families Officer	Lieutenant (SSC) C. Brown
Medical Officer	Captain P. M. Brown, RAMC
Chaplain	The Reverend W. O. Jones, RAChD
RC Chaplain	The Reverend J. Williams, RAChD
Paymaster	Captain A. J. Field, RAPC

Regimental Sergeant Major	J. Dargie
Regimental Quartermaster Sergeant	J. Duncan
Orderly Room Quartermaster Sergeant	D. Cuthill
Drill Sergeant	J. Phillips
Drill Sergeant	J. Knight
Pipe Major	L. Ingram
Drum Major	T. Keith

Headquarter Company

Coy Comds	Maj M. I. E. Scott
CSMs	F. J. Hope
CQMSs	W. Glennie

Right Flank

Coy Comds	Maj J. M. Clavering
2ICs	Maj J. J. D. Cox
Pl Comds	Lt J. A. H. Greenfield
	Lt A. N. G. Laing
	2Lt J. G. Treadwell
	2Lt H. B. Llewellyn
CSMs	J. France, BEM
CQMSs	S. Carnegie

G. Company

Coy Comds	Maj R. Jenner-Fust
2ICs	Capt A. M. H. Joscelyne
Pl Comds	Lt E. A. Woods
	Lt D. V. Erskine Crum
	2Lt N. Dawson
	Lt G. F. J. Scott
	2Lt T. Bevan
CSMs	W. Jamieson
CQMSs	A. Lazenby

Left Flank

Coy Comds	Maj R. D. Buchanan-Dunlop
2ICs	Capt N. M. L. Barne
Pl Comds	Lt A. G. B. I. Cheape, Recce
	Lt J. H. K. Trevaskis, Anti-Tank
	Lt S. A. C. Price
	2Lt A. J. Cator
CSMs	I. Beck
CQMSs	R. McIntyre

2nd Battalion

1982

Falkland Islands

Commanding Officer	Lieutenant Colonel M. I. E. Scott
Second-in-Command	Major I. C. Mackay-Dick, MBE
Adjutant	Captain M. A. Bullough
Intelligence Officer	Captain A. W. Foster
Assistant Intelligence Officer	Lieutenant A. A. Bruce
Operations Officer	Captain T. S. Spicer
Signal Officer	Captain W. P. B. Ellis

Quartermaster	Major (QM) C. Brown
Technical Quartermaster	Captain (QM) E. Lawrie
Transport Officer	Captain (SSC) R. Paterson
Medical Officer	Lieutenant Colonel A. J. Warsap, *RAMC*
Chaplain	The Reverend A. Smith, *RAChD*
Paymaster	Captain D. W. O'Keefe, *RAPC*
Families Officer	Captain (SSC) F. J. Moody

Regimental Sergeant Major	R. MacKenzie
Regimental Quartermaster Sergeant	J. McGonigle
Orderly Room Quartermaster Sergeant	D. Archibald
Drill Sergeant	D. Wight
Drill Sergeant	J. Singler
Pipe Major	J. Riddell
Drum Major	D. Davidson
CSMIM	B. Sulley

	Headquarter Company	*Right Flank*	*F. Company*	*G. Company*	*Left Flank*
Coy Comds	Maj The Hon R. N. Bethell, MBE	Maj S. A. C. Price		Maj I. E. Dalzel Job	Maj J. P Kiszely
2ICs		Capt I. A. Bryden		Capt J. H. O'H Pollock, *Irish Guards*	Capt The Hon G. C. W. Grimston
Pl Comds		2Lt The Viscount Dalrymple	Capt J. R. E. Campbell-Lamerton, *Anti-Tank*	Lt M. W. Joynson	Lt A. M. Mitchell
		2Lt M. W. V. Mathewson	Capt P J. L. Farrelly, *Mortar*	Lt C. J. Blount	2Lt J. D. Stuart
		2Lt R. A. D. Lawrence	Capt R. A. Scott, *Recce*	2Lt C. S. T. Page	2Lt A. H. J. Fraser
CSMs	L. Braby	I. Amos	W. Bunyan	E. McKay	W. Nicol
CQMS	C. Callaghan	M. Allender		D. Stirling	S. Hill

1st Battalion

1 December 1993

Commanding Officer — Lieutenant Colonel T. M. Fitzalan Howard
Second-in-Command — Major A. W. Foster
Adjutant — Captain J. M. A. Orwin
Assistant Adjutant — Captain H. R. S. Clarke
Intelligence Officer — Captain W. J. Inglis
Operations Officer — Captain P. R. W. Turner
Signal Officer — Captain The Hon M. G. J. Knollys

Quartermaster — Captain (QM) R. Walker, MBE
Technical Quartermaster — Captain (QM) D. Wood
Transport Officer — Captain (LE) P. J. Jackson
Medical Officer — Captain A. G. Wilson, *RAMC*
Chaplain — The Reverend J. Ross, *OCF*
Regimental Admin Officer — Captain A. J. O'Hare, *AGC (SPS)*

Regimental Sergeant Major — J. G. Spence
Regimental Quartermaster Sergeant — C. Downie
Orderly Room Quartermaster Sergeant — K. Taylor
Drill Sergeant — D. Pickering
Drill Sergeant — P. McNab
Pipe Major — G. Webster
Drum Major — P. Coventry

	Right Flank	*B. Company*	*C. Company*	*Left Flank*
Coy Comds	Maj P. J. L. Farrelly	Maj A. B. P. Bell	Maj M. G. C. MacGregor of MacGregor	Maj J. H. de Haldevang
2ICs	Lt J. C. A. Buck	Lt W. D. Glen	Capt R. J. Bray	Lt R. B. Wallace
Pl Comds	2Lt J. B. Biddle	Capt L. B. N. Baring, *Anti-Tank*	Lt C. F. N. Peach	2Lt H. C. D. Anderson
	2Lt S. Carrick-Buchanan	Capt J. M. P. Jarrett, *Mortar*	2Lt C. S. Messervy-Whiting	2Lt K. M. Borton
	2Lt A. J. R. Jeffery	Capt T. J. S. Lucas, *Recce*	2Lt A. D. P. Chubb	2Lt A. P. Speed
CSMs	I. Norman	M. Nelson	T. Steele	I. Hood
CQMSs	J. McCabe	D. Simpson	S. Crosby	A. Cameron

Headquarter Company

Coy Comds — Maj C. A. Stuart
CSMs — R. Gray
CQMSs — M. Drummond

F Company Scots Guards

Coy Comd — Maj M. G. Bence-Trower
2IC — Capt J. H. M. Gough
Pl Comds — Lt R. J. Ferguson / Lt S. P. Orwin / Lt D. J. Mayer
CSM — R. Convery
CQMS — N. Stenton

NOMINAL ROLL OF OFFICERS

Previous volumes of the history of the Scots Guards contain a Nominal Roll of all officers who served in the Regiment from 1642 to 1955. This Roll brings the list up to date as at 1 December 1993. The criteria adopted in deciding the detail to be recorded under 'Theatre' includes official postings outside Great Britain, attachments to Foreign Armies and attendance on long courses overseas and emergency operational tours of duty in Northern Ireland. The list does not include those occasions when battalions have detached companies or other sub-units to undertake tasks of short duration such as, for example, when companies of the 2nd Battalion were dispatched to various parts of East Africa between 1962 and 1964. It should also be noted that for those serving in the 1st Battalion at the time, Malaysia includes service in Sarawak and Sabah during 'Confrontation' with Indonesia between 1964 and 1966. It should be further noted that campaigns prior to 1939 have not been shown.

The column 'Highest rank' indicates that reached in the Regular Army. Again it should be noted that every effort has been made to ensure the correctness of the information shown although complete accuracy cannot be guaranteed.

Name	Highest rank	Service	Theatre
ACLAND, *Sir* John (Hugh Bevil)	Maj Gen	1948–82	BAOR, Cyprus, Egypt, Kenya, NI, Rhodesia
ACLAND, Peter John	Lt	1975–78	BAOR, NI
ADAMS, Fred	Maj (*QM*)	*In the ranks* 1940–63 1963–74	BAOR, Kenya, Malaya, WW2
AIREY, Steven	Capt (*SSC(LE)*)	*In the ranks* 1967–90 1990 to date	BAOR, Cyprus, Hong Kong, NI
AIRY, *Sir* Christopher (John)	Maj Gen	*transferred from GREN GDS* 1974–89	BAOR, NI
ALLEN, Jonathan Harvey Glynne	Capt	1966–78	BAOR, Belize, NI, Sharjah

Name	Highest rank	Service	Theatre
ALLENDER, David Alex	Capt (*SSC(LE)*)	*In the ranks* *1964–90* 1990–93	Aden, BAOR, Cyprus, Falkland Islands, NI, Sharjah
ALVES, Nicholas Jeremy Hartley	Capt	1980–87	Hong Kong, NI
AMOS, Ian	Capt (*SSC(LE)*)	*In the ranks* *1963–89* 1989 to date	BAOR, Cyprus, Falkland Islands, The Gulf, Malaysia, Muscat, NI, Sharjah
ANDERSON, Hugh Charles Boscawen	2nd Lt	1992 to date	
ANDREWES, Edward William Eden	2nd Lt	1957–59	
ANDREWS, Charles Lawrie	Lt	1991 to date	NI
ARBUTHNOT, John Christopher Wastle	Lt	1959–66	Malaysia
ARCHIBALD, David James	Capt (*SSC(LE)*)	*In the ranks* *1966–87* 1987–91	BAOR, Falkland Islands, NI, Sharjah
ARMSTRONG, Robert William Fortescue	Capt	1983–87	Hong Kong, NI
ARTHUR, John Reginald	Lt Col	1955–84	BAOR, Nigeria, NI, Sharjah
ASTOR, *The Hon* Philip Douglas Paul	2nd Lt	1978	BAOR
BACCHUS, Andrew Julian	Capt	*transferred from* *INT CORPS* *1969–78*	BAOR, Belize, Hong Kong, NI
BAIRD-SMITH, David Charles Dominic	2nd Lt	1957–58	
BALFOUR, Hew Edward Ogilvy	Capt	1973–79	BAOR, NI
BALLANTINE-DYKES, Thomas Lamplugh	Lt	1969–76	BAOR, Belize
BARCLAY, James David Innes	Lt	1955–56	BAOR
BARING, Lorne Benjamin Nigel	Capt	1990 to date	BAOR, NI
BARNE, Nicholas Michael Lancelot	Maj	1967–79	BAOR, NI
BARNE, William Miles	Capt	1978–82	Hong Kong, NI
BARRAH, Ian Mark	Capt	1985–92	Belize, Cyprus, NI
BARROW, Simon Hoare	Lt	1957–58	
BASSET, Bryan Ronald	Capt	1952–57	BAOR
BEAT, Duncan Richard	Maj/Acting Lt Col (*DoM*)	1974–82	
BECK, Ian	Lt Col (*QM*)	*In the ranks* *1960–81* 1981 to date	BAOR, Belize, Hong Kong, Kenya, NI
BELL, Andrew Bruce Peregrine	Maj	1984 to date	BAOR, Canada, Falkland Islands, The Gulf, NI
BELL, Bruce Alec Jeffery	Maj	1949–84	BAOR, Hong Kong, Malaya, NI
BELL, Timothy Michael	Capt	1960–70	Kenya, Malaysia, Muscat
BENCE-TROWER, Mark Grant	Maj	1984 to date	Cyprus, NI, Spain, Zimbabwe
BENITZ, Bryan Macintosh	Lt	1953–58	BAOR

Name	Highest rank	Service	Theatre
BENN, Timothy John	Lt	1956–57	
BENNIE, Charles Hamish Alistair Reid	Lt	1972–76	BAOR, NI
BENYON, Thomas Yates	Lt	1963–66	Kenya, Muscat
BERTIE, Charles Peregrine Albemarle	Capt	1950–57	Egypt
BETHELL, *The Hon* Richard Nicholas	Maj	1970–88	Belize, Falkland Islands, Muscat, NI, Zimbabwe
BEVAN, Hugo Peter Charles	Lt	1955–57	BAOR
BEVAN, Timothy John	Lt	1972–75	NI
BIDDLE, Justin Barrington	Lt	1993 to date	
BLACK, Charles Archibald Adam	Lt	1956–57	
BLAIR, John Woodman	Lt	1956–57	
BLAND, *Sir* Simon (Claude Michael)	Lt Col	1943–78	BAOR, Malaya, Pakistan, WW2
BLOUNT, Charles John	Capt	1981–86	Falkland Islands
BOAM, Thomas Anthony	Maj Gen	1952–87	BAOR, Hong Kong, Malaysia, Nigeria, NI, USA
BORTON, Kenneth Michael MacNeill	Lt	1993 to date	
BOWATER, Michael Ian Vansittart	Maj	1955–68	BAOR, Canada, Cyprus, Malaysia
BOWSER, Niall Murray	Capt	1978–82	BAOR, NI
BOYD, Ian Walter	Lt	1954–56	BAOR
BOYD-CARPENTER, *The Hon Sir* Thomas (Patrick John)	Lt Gen	1956 to date	BAOR, Malaysia, Muscat, NI
BRAID, John	Maj (*QM*)	*In the ranks 1939–59* 1959–67	BAOR, Egypt, Kenya, Malaya, WW2
BRAY, Rupert James	Capt	1989 to date	BAOR, NI
BRIDGEMAN, John Henry Orlando	2nd Lt	1957–59	BAOR
BROOKE, Piers Leighton	Lt	1960–63	BAOR
BROOKE, Richard David Christopher	2nd Lt	1957–59	
BROWN, Clarke	Maj (*QM*)	*In the ranks 1952–72* 1972–87	BAOR, Egypt, Falkland Islands, Kenya, NI
BRUCE OF CRIONAICH, Alastair Andrew	Lt	1980–83	Falkland Islands, NI
BRUCE, Robert Rehinder Boyack	Capt	1959–63	Australia, BAOR
BRYDEN, Ian Anderson	Capt	1978–82	BAOR, Falkland Islands, NI
BUCHANAN-DUNLOP, Robert Daubeny	Col	*transferred from CAMERONIANS* 1968–88	BAOR, Berlin, Canada, NI, Sharjah, USA
BUCK, Julian Charles Alexander	Capt	1990 to date	BAOR, The Gulf, NI
BULKELEY, Thomas Foster Rivers	Brig	1936–68	France, WW2
BULL, William Francis Dalglish	Lt	1963–68	Malaysia
BULLOUGH, John Louis	Lt	1989–92	The Gulf, NI
BULLOUGH, Mark Andrew	Capt	1974–83	Falkland Islands, NI

Name	Highest rank	Service	Theatre
BULMER, James Esmond	Lt	1954–56	
BUNTON, James Muir	Maj (*QM*)	*In the ranks* 1958–79 1979–93	BAOR, Belize, Hong Kong, Malaysia, NI, Sharjah
BURNETT, George Parry	Lt Col	1941–76	BAOR, Belgium, France, Kenya, Malaya, USA, WW2
BURNHAM, *Lord*, William Edward Harry Lawson	Lt Col	1941–68	BAOR, Egypt, USA, WW2
CAMERON, Angus Ewen	Lt Col	1936–56	Malaya, WW2
CAMERON, Duncan	Capt (*QM*)	*In the ranks* 1962–72 1972–76	Aden, BAOR, Kenya, NI
CAMERON, Nigel Ewen Archibald Gun	Lt Col	1965–93	BAOR, Hong Kong, Malaysia, NI, USA
CAMPBELL, George Herbert Lorne	Capt	1954–65	BAOR, Cameroon, Kenya
CAMPBELL, James Alexander Moffat Bain	Capt	1975–83	BAOR, Hong Kong, NI
CAMPBELL OF AIRDS BAY, Michael McNeil	Maj	1961–71	BAOR, Kenya, Sharjah
CAMPBELL-LAMERTON, Ian Anthony	Lt	1983–87	Cyprus
CAMPBELL-LAMERTON, Jeremy Robert Edward	Capt	1979–83	Falkland Islands, NI
CAMPBELL-LAMERTON, Michael Patrick	Capt	1982–88	Hong Kong
CANTLIE, Bruce St George	Lt	1956–57	BAOR
CANTLIE, Hugh	Maj	1952–62	Australia, BAOR
CANTLIE, Paul	Lt	1954–56	BAOR
CARGILL, John James	Lt Col	1970 to date	BAOR, Belize, Canada, Cyprus, The Gulf, NI
CARNEGIE, Sidney John	Capt (*SSC*)	*In the ranks* 1959–82 1982–91	BAOR, Hong Kong, Malaysia, NI
CARNEGIE-BROWN, Mark Mackenzie	Col	1957–85	BAOR, Borneo, Belize, Gibraltar, Kenya, Nigeria, USA, NI
CARRICK-BUCHANAN, Sandy	Lt	1992 to date	BAOR, NI
CARSON, Donald	Maj (*DoM*)	1984–88	
CATHCART, *Earl*, Alan	Maj Gen	1939–73	BAOR, Belgium, Berlin, WW2
CATOR, Albemarle John	Lt	1972–75	NI
CECIL, John Strongbow Amherst	Lt	1959–62	
CHAMBERLAYNE-MACDONALD, (*formerly* MACDONALD OF THE ISLES) Nigel Donald Peter	Maj	1946–61	Egypt, Malaya
CHEAPE, Angus Geoffrey Bruce Ismay	Lt	1969–74	BAOR, Hong Kong, NI
CHUBB, Alasdair David Pierce	Lt	1992 to date	BAOR, NI
CLAPTON, Peter Thomas Archibald	Maj	1965–78	BAOR, The Gulf, Malaysia, NI, Sharjah

Name	Highest rank	Service	Theatre
CLARKE, John Robertson Stephenson	Col	1939–59	WW2
CLARKE, Hugo Rory Stephenson	Capt	1990 to date	BAOR, The Gulf, NI
CLARKSON, Robert Titus	Capt (*SRC*)	*In the ranks* 1951–57 1962–77 1977–83	BAOR, Kenya, NI, Sharjah
CLAVERING, John Muir	Col	1960–88	BAOR, Hong Kong, Kenya, Malaysia, Muscat, NI, Uganda
CLEMISON, Ronald	Maj (*RegC(LE)*)	*In the ranks* 1964–87 1987 to date	BAOR, Belize, Cyprus, The Gulf, NI, Hong Kong
CLOWES, Andrew Henry	Capt	1961–67	Kenya
CLOWES, *Sir* Henry (Nelson)	Col	1931–58	WW2
COBBOLD, Patrick Mark	Lt	1953–56	Egypt
COCHRANE, Malcolm Ralph	2nd Lt	1957–59	
COKE, Richard Townshend	Lt·	1974–77	BAOR, Belize, NI
COKE, *Viscount*, Thomas Edward	Capt	1987–93	BAOR, NI
COLQUHOUN, Ernest Patrick	Lt	1956–57	BAOR
CONSTABLE-MAXWELL, Christopher Thomas Bernard Turville	Lt	1959–62	
COOPER, George Ingram	Lt Col (*QM*)	*In the ranks* 1956–76 1976–91	BAOR, Hong Kong, Malaysia, NI
COPELAND, Paul John Norman	Lt	1954–56	Egypt
COPELAND, Peter David Athole	Capt	1956–61	BAOR
COPELAND, Peter Mark	Capt	1989 to date	BAOR, The Gulf, NI
CORSON, Christopher Michael	Capt	1987–91	BAOR, NI
COTTRELL, Edward Alexander Campbell	Capt	1982–86	Hong Kong
COURTNEY, David Geoffrey Stuart	Lt	1959–63	BAOR
COX, Jeremy John Douglas	Lt Col	*transferred from CAMERONIANS* 1968–93	BAOR, France, NI, Sharjah, Western Sahara
CRABBE, Colin Brodie	Lt	1962–64	
CRAWFORD, George Archibald	Lt	1959–62	
CRICHTON-STUART, Henry Colum	Lt	1957–60	Rhodesia
CRICHTON-STUART, *Lord* James Charles	Lt	1954–56	
CRICHTON-STUART, Jerome Niall Anthony	Maj	1967 to date	Australia, BAOR, Hong Kong, NI
CRICHTON-STUART, Patrick James	Lt	1974–77	BAOR, Belize, NI
CROOKENDEN, James Napier	Capt	1969–74	NI, Sharjah
CROSSMAN, Anthony David	2nd Lt	1955–57	BAOR
CROWE, Julian Edward Michael	Maj	1973 to date	Australia, BAOR, Belize, Berlin, Canada, Cyprus, NI

Name	Highest rank	Service	Theatre
CUTHILL, David Alexander	Capt (*SSC*)	*In the ranks* *1960–80* 1980–82	BAOR, Kenya, NI
DALGARNO, Donald	Capt (*SSC*)	*In the ranks* *1956–72* 1972–77	BAOR, Egypt, Kenya, Sharjah
DALRYMPLE, Andrew David	Lt	1982–85	Hong Kong
DALRYMPLE, *The Hon* Colin James	Maj	1940–56	Egypt, WW2
DALRYMPLE, *Viscount*, John David James	Capt	1981–87	Cyprus, Falkland Islands, NI
DALZEL JOB, Iain Erling	Maj	1967 to date	BAOR, Belize, Cyprus, Falkland Islands, NI, Sharjah
DAVIDSON, Matthew Munro	Maj (*RegC(LE)*)	*In the ranks* *1964–86* 1986 to date	BAOR, Belize, Cyprus, Hong Kong,, NI
DAWSON, Nicholas	Lt	1970–75	British Honduras, NI
DAWSON, *Sir* (Hugh Halliday) Trevor Bt	Maj	1952–61	BAOR, Egypt
DE CHAIR, Colin Graham Ramsey	2nd Lt	1962–64	Kenya
DE HALDEVANG, Jan	Maj	1982 to date	BAOR, Cyprus, The Gulf, NI
DE KLEE, Murray Peter	Col	1945–82	BAOR, Cyprus, Egypt, Malaya, Malaysia, NI, Saudi Arabia, Sharjah, South Arabia
DE SALIS, *Count*, Charles John	Maj	1948–60	BAOR
DELMAR-MORGAN, Michael Water	Lt	1955–57	BAOR
DENHAM, John Bovill	Col	1944–79	BAOR, Malaya, WW2
DOBSON, Dominic Stephen Christopher Charles	Maj	1979–93	BAOR,Canada, Hong Kong, NI
DRUMMOND, James Edward MacGregor	Capt	1985–88	BAOR, NI
DRUMMOND, *The Hon* James Reginald	Lt	1957–58	
DRUMMOND MORAY, David Maurice Stirling Home	Capt	1965–73	British Honduras, Malaysia
DRUMMOND MORAY, John Robert Stirling Home	Capt	1963–68	Australia, Kenya
DRURY-LOWE, Patrick John Botelor	Capt	1950–58	Australia
DRURY-LOWE, Simon Jasper Packe	Lt	1956–59	BAOR
DRYSDALE, John Duncan	2nd Lt	1955–56	BAOR
DUFFIN, Charles John Riddel	Lt Col	1942–68	BAOR, Egypt, Malaya, WW2
DUFFIN, Simon Charles Hugh	Lt	1972–77	BAOR, NI
DUNBAR, Claude Iain Hurley	Maj Gen	1929–63	Berlin, Malaya, WW2

Name	Highest rank	Service	Theatre
DUNCAN, John	Capt (*SSC*)	*In the ranks* 1952–73 1973–79	BAOR, Kenya, NI
DUNCAN, John Donald Graham	Capt	1968–76	BAOR
DUNCAN-SMITH, George Iain	Capt	1975–81	BAOR, NI, Rhodesia
DUNSMURE, Alistair Mark	Lt	1958–59	
DUNSMURE, James Alexander	Col	1955–90	BAOR, Belize, Cyprus, Malaysia, NI
ECCLES-WILLIAMS, Mark Benedict	Lt	1979–81	NI
EDMONSTONE, Archibald Edward Charles	Capt	1982–87	Cyprus
ELDON, *Earl* of, John Joseph Nicholas Scott	Lt	1956–57	BAOR
ELLIOT BAXTER, Normile Edward Alexander George Wyndham	Capt	1949–56	BAOR, Egypt, Malaya
ELLIOTT, Christopher Frank	Lt	1958–60	BAOR
ELLIS, William Paul Basil	Capt	1980–83	Falkland Islands
ELMHIRST, Roger Thomas	Lt	1954–56	BAOR
ELWES, Henry William George	Lt	1954–56	BAOR
ERSKINE, Philip Neil	Maj	1953–71	BAOR, New Zealand
ERSKINE, Robin David	Capt	1970–79	BAOR, Belize, NI
ERSKINE CRUM, Douglas Vernon	Brig	1970 to date	BAOR, Belize, NI, Hong Kong, Sharjah
ERSKINE CRUM, Rupert Edward Charles	Capt	1988 to date	BAOR, The Gulf, NI
ERSKINE CRUM, Vernon Forbes	Lt Gen	1940–71	BAOR, India, NI, WW2
FAIRCLOUGH, Andrew John	Lt	1992 to date	BAOR, NI
FAIRHOLME, James Graham Nicholls	Capt	1986 to date	BAOR, NI
FALKLAND, *The Master of*, Lucius Alexander Plantagenet Cary	Capt	1985–91	Cyprus, The Gulf, NI
FANE-GLADWIN, Peter Francis	Col	1935–63	BAOR, Cyprus, Egypt, Malaya, Palestine, WW2
FANE-GLADWIN, Richard Archibald James	Lt	1959–65	Malaysia
FARRELLY, Peter John Lawrence	Maj	1978 to date	BAOR, Cyprus, Falkland Islands, NI
FELLOWES, *The Rt Hon Sir* Robert	Lt	1960–63	BAOR, Kenya
FERGUSON, Iain Alexander	Col	1952–82	BAOR, Kenya, Sharjah
FERGUSON, John Patrick	Lt	1980–83	Hong Kong, NI
FERGUSON, Rory James	Lt	1990 to date	NI
FITZALAN HOWARD, *Lord* Michael	Maj Gen	1938–71	BAOR, Malaya, WW2
FITZALAN HOWARD, Thomas Michael	Lt Col	1971 to date	BAOR, Hong Kong, NI
FITZHERBERT, *The Hon* Thomas Alistair	Capt	1976–82	NI

Name	Highest rank	Service	Theatre
FLETCHER, Archibald Ian Douglas	Col	1942–70	BAOR, Kenya, Malaya, Malaysia, WW2
FORBES OF ROTHIEMAY, Ygr, Anthony David Knox	Maj	1963–93	BAOR, Belize, Malaysia, NI, Norway
FORREST, Thomas Smith	Capt (SSC)	In the ranks 1956–76 1976–78	BAOR, Malaysia, NI
FORSYTH, James	Capt (QM)	In the ranks 1944–65 1965–71	BAOR, Malaya, Malaysia, WW2
FOSTER, Andrew William	Maj	1976 to date	BAOR, Belize, Falkland Islands, NI
FOSTER-BLACK, Trevor John William	Capt	1989–93	The Gulf, NI
FOWLER, Graham	Capt (QM)	In the ranks 1967–87 1987–89	BAOR, Hong Kong, NI, Nigeria, Sharjah
FRANCE, John William Anderson	Capt (SSC(LE))	In the ranks 1954–79 1979–84	BAOR, Belize, Kenya, NI
FRASER, Anthony Henry Joseph	Capt	1981–84	Cyprus, Falkland Islands
FRASER, Donald McGregor	Maj (QM)	In the ranks 1932–52 1952–63	Egypt, Malaya, WW2
FRASER, The Hon Kim Ian Maurie	Lt	1965–67	Malaysia
FRASER, The Hon Simon Augustine	Lt	1958–60	BAOR
GASCOIGNE, Patrick Edward Cecil	Lt Col	1971 to date	BAOR, Cyprus, Falkland Islands, Hong Kong, NI
GIBB, Colin	Lt	1957–59	BAOR
GIBB, John Philip Ogilvy	Maj	1955–66	BAOR, Kenya
GLEN, William Douglas	Lt	1990 to date	BAOR, NI
GLOUCESTER, HRH Henry William Frederick Albert, Duke of	Field Marshal	25th Colonel of the Regiment	1937–74
GORDON, Andrew Iain Campbell	Lt Col	1963–92	BAOR, Cyprus, Falkland Islands, Hong Kong, Malaysia, NI, Norway, Pakistan
GORDON-DUFF, Simon Lachlan	Maj	1961–68	Aden, Cyprus, Kenya, Malaysia
GOSSELIN, Timothy Patrick Arnold	Capt	1955–61	BAOR
GOUGH, Jonathan Harold Murray	Capt	1989 to date	BAOR, The Gulf, NI
GOW, David William Mearns	2nd Lt	1966–69	BAOR
GOW, Sir (James) Michael	Gen	1943–86	BAOR, Kenya, Malaya, WW2
GOW, Roderick Charles	Capt	1967–78	BAOR, Belgium, NI

Name	Highest rank	Service	Theatre
GRAHAM, Campbell	Maj (*QM*)	*In the ranks* *1946–67* 1967–82	BAOR, Kenya, NI, Sharjah
GRAHAM, John	Maj	1941–58	Egypt, Malaya, WW2
GRAHAM, Rory Stuart	Lt	1974–77	BAOR
GRANT, James Irvine	Maj (*QM*)	*In the ranks* *1943–68* 1968–80	BAOR, Kenya, Malaya, Malaysia, WW2
GRANT, William Marr Couper	2nd Lt	1979–80	
GRAY, Richard	Capt (*SSC(LE)*)	*In the ranks* *1966–90* 1990–93	BAOR, NI
GREENFIELD, James Anthony Hume	Maj	1971–92	BAOR, Belize, NI
GREENOCK, *Lord*, Charles Andrew Alan Cathcart	2nd Lt	1972–75	BAOR, NI
GREENWOOD, Alexander O'Connor	Lt Col (*QM*)	*In the ranks* *1926–42* 1942–61	BAOR, Malaya, WW2
GRIFFITHS, Guy Holford	Lt	1979–83	Hong Kong, NI
GRIMSTON, *The Hon* Gerald Charles Walter	Maj	1973–83	BAOR, Belize, Falkland Islands, Hong Kong, NI
GWYN, Charles Anthony Hugh	Capt	1963–71	BAOR, Malaysia, NI
HAMPSHIRE, Dominic James	Lt	1991 to date	BAOR, NI
HANCOCK, James Henry Thomas	Capt	1986 to date	BAOR, The Gulf, NI
HARDY, John Masterman	Capt	1978–83	Hong Kong, NI
HARPER, John Eadie	Capt (*SSC(LE)*)	*In the ranks* *1968–89* 1989–93	BAOR, Cyprus, NI
HARRISON, Antony James Robinson	Maj	1948–71	BAOR, Kenya, Malaya
HARVEY, David Vincent	Lt	1961–63	Kenya
HARVEY, Peter Francis	Capt	1962–71	BAOR, Hong Kong, Kenya, Muscat
HAYWARD, James Richard	Maj	1983 to date	BAOR, Hong Kong, NI
HENDERSON, Charles Richard	Lt	1979–82	NI
HENDERSON, James Stewart Barry	Lt	1955–56	
HERBERT, Rory Peter Boyd	Lt	1991 to date	BAOR, NI
HEYBOURN, Anthony Sinclair	Maj (*SRC*)	*In the ranks* *1953–75* 1975–83	BAOR, Gibraltar, Hong Kong, Malaysia, NI
HICKS, Brian Erwin	Maj (*DoM*)	1982–84	
HILL, Peter Richard	Capt	1960–65	BAOR, Kenya
HILL, Piers Charles William	Lt	1986–89	NI
HILLEARY, Alasdair Malcolm Douglas Macleod	Lt	1974–78	BAOR, NI
HILLEARY, Duncan Ruaraidh Douglas Macleod	Lt	1979–81	Hong Kong, NI
HOBBS, Andrew Casper James	Capt	1989 to date	NI
HOBDAY, Neil Peter Whyte	Capt	1979–84	Hong Kong, NI

Name	Highest rank	Service	Theatre
HODSON, *Sir* Michael (Robin Adderley), Bt	Capt	1953–60	BAOR
HOLLING, Kieran Benedict	Capt	*transferred from RE* 1990 to date	BAOR, Falkland Islands, The Gulf
HOLMES, John Taylor	Brig	1970 to date	BAOR, The Gulf, NI, Muscat, USA
HOPE, Francis Jefferson	Capt (*SSC*)	*In the ranks* 1956–78 1978–83	BAOR, Hong Kong, Kenya, NI
HOPE-GREGORY, Ian Rowdan	Maj	*transferred from 13/18 H* 1974–82	BAOR, Belize, Brunei, NI
HOPKINSON, Anthony Erik	Capt	1953–65	Cyprus, Jordan, Kenya
HORSMAN, Albert Christopher	Lt	1957–58	
HOWE, James Hakin	Maj (*DoM*)	1959–74	
HOYER-MILLAR, *The Hon* Alastair James Harold	Lt	1956–57	BAOR
HUBBARD-FORD, Simon Hugh	Capt	1956–61	BAOR
HUGHES, Joseph	Maj (*QM*)	*In the ranks* 1935–60 1960–71	BAOR, Egypt, Kenya, Malaysia, Palestine, WW2
HULSE, Edward Jeremy Westrow	Capt	1953–58	BAOR
HULSE, Richard Arthur Samuel	Lt	1955–56	BAOR
HUTCHISON, Timothy Michael Oliphant	Capt	1988 to date	BAOR, Bosnia, NI
HUTTON, Julian Kilpatrick	Lt	1984–87	NI
INGHAM-CLARK, Frederick Thomas	Capt	1983–87	Hong Kong, NI
INGHAM-CLARK, Roderick	Capt	1958–65	Kenya
INGLEBY-MACKENZIE, Roderick Alexander	Maj	1973 to date	BAOR, Cyprus, The Gulf, Hong Kong, NI
INGLIS, William James	Capt	1990 to date	NI
INGRAM, Linden Maurice	Capt (*SSC*)	*In the ranks* 1960–85 1985–93	BAOR, Malaysia, NI
INNES, Malcolm Alastair	Lt	1958–59	BAOR
INNES, William Anthony Wolseley	Capt	1955–63	BAOR
JACKSON, Philip Garnett	Capt (*SSC(LE)*)	*In the ranks* 1972–93 1993 to date	BAOR, Belize, Cyprus, Falkland Islands, NI
JAMIESON, Peter Lindsay Auldjo	Lt	1957–58	
JARRETT, Jonathan Michael Patrick	Capt	1987 to date	Belize, NI
JEFFREY, Andrew James Ronald	Lt	1992 to date	
JENNER-FUST, Richard	Maj	1962–73	BAOR, British Honduras, Malaysia, NI
JOHNSON, Peter David	Maj	1959–85	BAOR, Belize, Hong Kong, Kenya, NI
JOHNSTON, John Walford Philip	Lt	1959–61	BAOR

Name	Highest rank	Service	Theatre
JOHNSTON, Robert Gordon Scott	Lt	1956–57	
JOPP, Lincoln Peter Munro	Capt	1986 to date	BAOR, The Gulf, NI
JOSCELYNE, Andrew Michael Hubert	Col	1966–87 *transferred to* GREN GDS	BAOR, Belize, Cyprus, Falkland Islands, Muscat, NI, Sharjah
JOYNSON, Michael William	Capt	1978–89	Belize, Cyprus, Falkland Islands, NI
KELLY, James Richard	Maj	*transferred from* ROYAL MARINES 1985 to date	BAOR, Falkland Islands, The Gulf, NI
KELWAY-BAMBER, Euan Glen	Maj	1978–88	Hong Kong, BAOR, NI
KEMP, *The Hon* St John Durival	2nd Lt	1957–58	
KENT, *HRH* Edward George Nicholas Paul Patrick, *Duke of*	Field Marshal	26th Colonel of the Regiment	1974 to date
KESWICK, Henry Neville Lindley	Lt	1957–58	
KIRKWOOD, Guy Conner	Lt	1991 to date	BAOR, NI
KISZELY, John Panton	Brig	1968 to date	BAOR, Cyprus, Falkland Islands, NI
KNOLLYS, *The Hon* Christopher Edward	Capt	1987–91	NI
KNOLLYS, *The Hon* Michael James George	Capt	1988 to date	Belize, NI, Zimbabwe
KNOLLYS, Nicholas Francis	Capt	1969–79	BAOR, NI, Muscat, Sharjah
KNOLLYS, *The Hon* Patrick Nicholas Mark	Capt	1982–88	Cyprus
LADEN, Douglas Murray	Capt (*SSC(LE)*)	*In the ranks* 1964–87 1987 to date	BAOR, Hong Kong, Malaysia, NI, Sharjah
LAING, Alasdair North Grant	Lt	1969–74	BAOR, Hong Kong, NI
LAING, Hugh Charles Desmond	Maj	1952–73	BAOR, Hong Kong, Muscat, Sharjah, USA
LAING, Nicholas Alexander Grant	Capt	1971–77	BAOR, NI
LAING, Timothy James Arthur	Capt	1975–82	Belize, BAOR, NI
LAMBERT, Peter Tobin	Capt	1989 to date	BAOR, Belize, The Gulf, Iraq/Kuwait, NI
LAMBERT, Roger Mark Uvedale	2nd Lt	1977	
LAMMING, John Christopher Robert	Capt	1986–90	NI
LAMPSON, *The Hon* Victor Miles George Aldous	Capt	1961–67	Kenya
LANCASTER, Julian Arthur Seymour	Lt Col	1967 to date	BAOR, Cyprus, NI, Muscat, Sharjah, United Arab Emirates
LAURENCE, Alastair Howard	Maj	1957–68	Malaysia
LAW, Michael	Maj	1943–58	BAOR, Malaya, WW2
LAW, Robert	Capt	1974–85	Australia, BAOR, Belize
LAWRENCE, Christopher John Davidson	Capt	1974–80	BAOR, Belize, NI

Name	Highest rank	Service	Theatre
LAWRENCE, Robert Alasdair Davidson	Capt	1979–83	Falkland Islands, NI
LAWRIE, Ewan	Lt Col (*QM*)	*In the ranks* 1956–77 1977 to date	BAOR, Cyprus, Falkland Islands, Malaysia, NI
LAWRIE, Frank	Maj (*QM*)	*In the ranks* 1948–72 1972–84	BAOR, Malaysia, NI, Malaya, Sharjah
LAWRIE, Julian Walter Sloane	Maj	1965–92	BAOR, Cyprus, NI, Norway
LE MARCHAND, Rudolf Peter George	Capt	1967–78	BAOR, Hong Kong, NI, Muscat
LEASK, Anthony de Camborne Lowther	Brig	1963 to date	BAOR, Malaysia, NI, USA
LENG, *Sir* Peter (John Hall)	Gen	1944–64 *transferred to R ANGLIAN*	BAOR, Egypt, Kenya, WW2
LESLIE, David John	2nd Lt	1987–89	BAOR, NI
LEWTHWAITE, Rainald Gilfrid	Brig	1934–68	France, Palestine, WW2
LINDSAY, Ivan James	Lt	1982–85	Hong Kong
LINDSAY, Robert Hugh	Capt	1986 to date	BAOR, Bosnia, The Gulf, NI
LINDSAY, *The Hon* Thomas Richard	Lt	1956–57	BAOR
LLEWELLYN, Henry Bolitho	Lt	1972–77	BAOR, Belize, NI
LONSDALE, (*formerly* BERGIN), David Theodore, James	2nd Lt	1962–64	Kenya
LORIMER, Henry	Lt	1960–62	
LORIMER, Robert	Lt	1958–59	BAOR
LOVEDAY, Cyril John	Capt (*SSC(LE)*)	*In the ranks* 1960–86 1986–92	BAOR, Cyprus, Hong Kong, Malaysia, NI
LOUDEN, John	Capt (*SRC*)	*In the ranks* 1950–70 1971–78	BAOR, Kenya
LUCAS, Timothy James Stephen	Capt	1989 to date	NI
LUMSDEN, Keith Gordon Andrew	Capt	1956–65	BAOR, Kenya
LUMSDEN, Nicholas Andrew	Lt	1979–82	Hong Kong, NI
LYELL, *Lord*, Charles	Lt	1958–59	BAOR
MACFARLANE, James McCrindle	Capt (*SSC*)	*In the ranks* 1966–85 1985–92	BAOR, Hong Kong, NI
MACGREGOR OF MACGREGOR, Malcolm Gregor Charles	Maj	1979 to date	BAOR, Hong Kong, NI
MACGREGOR OF MACGREGOR, *Sir* Gregor, Bt	Brig	1944–80	BAOR, Greece, Malaya, Malaysia, Palestine, USA, WW2
MACKAY-DICK, Iain Charles	Maj Gen	1965 to date	BAOR, Cyprus, Falkland Islands, Malaysia, NI
MACKENZIE, Ronald James Charles	Capt (*QM*)	*In the ranks* 1965–84 1984–89	BAOR, Belize, Cyprus, Falkland Islands, Hong Kong, NI

Name	Highest rank	Service	Theatre
MACKINTOSH, Charlach Rob Douglas	Lt	1954–56	BAOR
MACKWORTH-PRAED, Ralph William	Lt	1955–57	BAOR
MACLAREN, Shaun Andrew Peter	Capt	1973–80	BAOR, NI
MACLEAN, *The Hon Sir* Lachlan Hector Charles, *Bt*	Maj	1962–73	Aden, Kenya, Sharjah
MACNAMEE, Richard Charles	Capt	1988 to date	BAOR, The Gulf, NI
MACPHERSON, Angus Cameron Stewart	Maj	1982 to date	BAOR, Cyprus, Gibraltar, NI
MADDEN, Christopher John Frank	Lt	1959–60	BAOR
MAILER-HOWAT, Patrick Lindsay Macalpine	Lt	1974–76	BAOR, NI
MAITLAND, Timothy David	Lt	1958–59	BAOR
MANASSEI, *Count*, John Paul	Lt	1957–58	
MANN, Simon Francis	Capt	1972–81	BAOR, NI
MARCHANT, Ernest Hedley	Capt (*QM*)	*In the ranks* 1950–71 1971–75	BAOR, Cyprus, Egypt, NI
MARR, Michael Alexander de Chollett	Capt	1985–91	Cyprus, Zimbabwe
MATHEWSON, Alastair Douglas	Maj	1983 to date	Belize, Cyprus, NI, Zimbabwe
MATHEWSON, Mark William Victor	Lt	1980–83	Falkland Islands
MAXWELL-HYSLOP, Hew Mark	Maj	1954–78	BAOR, Hong Kong, Kenya, NI
MAY, Marcus Geoffrey Robert	Lt	1978–81	NI
MAYER, Damian John	Lt	1992 to date	NI
MAYFIELD, Andrew Charles	Capt	1986–91	BAOR, NI
MAYFIELD, Richard	Lt Col	1949–74	BAOR, Egypt, Malaya, NI, Sharjah
McCOWEN, Donald William Henry	Lt	1956–57	BAOR
McEUEN, James Stewart	Capt	1989 to date	NI
McKAY, Iain Alastair	Maj	1958–75	Cameroon, Canada, France, Kenya
McLAUGHLAN, Ian Wellwood	Brig	1961–92	BAOR, Belize, Hong Kong, Kenya, NI
McLEOD, Robert James	Capt	1986–91	BAOR, NI
MELGUND, *Viscount*, Gilbert Timothy George Lariston Elliot	Lt	1972–76	BAOR, NI
MELVILLE, *Viscount*, Robert David Ross Dundas	Lt	1956–58	BAOR
MELVILLE, Robert Gow	Capt (*SSC*)	*In the ranks* 1947–69 1969–75	BAOR, Malaysia, Sharjah
MENZIES, Simon Stewart	Lt	1987–90	BAOR, NI

Name	Highest rank	Service	Theatre
MENZIES OF MENZIES, (*formerly* STEUART MENZIES) David Ronald Steuart	Lt	1954–61	Australia, Egypt
MESSERVY-WHITING, Charles Sinclair	Lt	1992 to date	BAOR, NI
MILLER, Rupert Harry	Lt	1978–82	BAOR, NI
MILLER-THOMAS, Brian Alexander	Lt	1953–56	Egypt
MILLOY, Alan	Capt (*SSC(LE)*)	*In the ranks 1966–88* 1988 to date	BAOR, Belize, Cyprus, The Gulf, NI
MILNER-BROWN, Anthony Lewis	Maj	1956–80	BAOR, Belize, Kenya, Malaysia, NI, Sharjah
MINTO, *Earl of*, Gilbert Edward George Lariston, *formerly Viscount* MELGUND	Lt	1946–56	Cyprus, Malaya
MITCHELL, Alasdair Macfarlane	Capt	1979–87	Cyprus, Falkland Islands, Hong Kong, NI
MITCHELL, Gordon Ross	Maj (*QM*)	*In the ranks 1941–62* 1962–77	BAOR, Borneo, Egypt, Palestine, Sharjah, WW2
MOIR, Malcolm Joseph Peckston	2nd Lt	1977	BAOR
MONCRIEFF, Charles St John Graham	Maj	1951–60	BAOR
MONCRIEFF, Christopher Stuart Steele	Capt	*transferred from QOH* 1984–87	Cyprus
MONK, James Stuart Richard	Lt	1963–66	Kenya
MOODY, Frederick James	Capt (*SSC*)	*In the ranks 1961–80* 1980–86	BAOR, Malaysia, Sharjah
MORRIS, Jonathon Jeremy Creighton	Capt	1961–69	BAOR, Malaysia
MORRIS, Timothy Creighton	Lt	1956–57	BAOR
MORRISON, Alastair George Angus	Maj	1963–80	Aden, BAOR, Belize, Kenya, Muscat, NI
MORRISON, Alexander Francis	Maj	1978–89	Hong Kong, NI
MORRITT, *The Hon Sir* (Robert) Andrew	2nd Lt	1956–58	BAOR
MULLENEUX, Simon James	Capt	1988–92	NI, Zimbabwe
MURPHY, Duncan Francis	Lt (*SSC*)	*In the ranks 1958–79* 1979–81	BAOR, Kenya, NI
NAPIER, James Alexander	Maj	1967–93	BAOR, Hong Kong, NI
NAPIER & ETTRICK, *Lord*, Francis Nigel	Maj	1950–60	BAOR, Malaya
NASON, Michael Carey	Capt	1955–63	BAOR
NAYLOR, David Murray	Maj Gen	1957–92	BAOR, India, Kenya, Muscat, NI
NAYLOR, Richard Christopher	Lt	1955–56	BAOR
NICKERSON, George Henry Fagan Stewart	Maj	1984 to date	BAOR, The Gulf, Muscat, NI

Name	Highest rank	Service	Theatre
NICKERSON, George Stewart	Maj	1943–80	BAOR, NI, West Africa, WW2
NICKERSON, Hugh William Fagan Stewart	Capt	1987–93	NI, Western Sahara
NICOL, Randall Lewis	Major	1967–79	BAOR, Belize, Berlin, British Honduras, NI, Sharjah
NICOL OF ARDMARNOCH, Donald Ninian Duncan	Maj	1958–86	BAOR, Kenya, Lesotho, Malaysia, NI
NUNNELEY, Charles Kenneth Roylance	Lt	1955–56	BAOR
NURTON, John Michael Anthony	Brig	1961 to date	BAOR, Malaysia, NI
OGILVY, James Robert Bruce	2nd Lt	1983	Hong Kong
O'HARA, Hugh Fowler	Capt (*SSC*)	*In the ranks 1963–83* 1983–85	BAOR, Malaysia, NI
ORWIN, Jeremy Mark Antony	Capt	1989 to date	BAOR, The Gulf, NI
ORWIN, Simon Peter	Lt	1991 to date	NI
OTTON, David Douglas	Lt	1979	
PAGE, Charles Spencer Thomas	Maj	1981 to date	BAOR, Cyprus, Falkland Islands, NI
PARSONS, Andrew Peter Harold	Col	1959 to date	BAOR, Belgium, Italy, Malaysia, NI, Zimbabwe
PASCOE, John Frederick Richard	Lt	1959–62	BAOR
PATERSON, Ronald	Capt (*SSC*)	*In the ranks 1961–81* 1981–86	BAOR, Belize, Cyprus, Falkland Islands, Malaysia, NI
PEACH, Charles Edward Neville	Capt	1992 to date	BAOR, NI
PETRE, Robert Bernard	Lt	1956–58	BAOR
PHILIPSON, Anthony Thirlwall	Maj	1940–71	Egypt, WW2
PHILLIPS, John George Crispin	2nd Lt	1957–58	
PORTER, Nigel David Sykes	Lt	1954–57	Egypt
POTTER, Robert Nicholas	Maj	1969–86	BAOR, Cyprus, Falkland Islands, NI, Sharjah
PRAIN, David Eustace Gurney	Lt	1956–57	BAOR
PRIAULX, Osmond William	Maj	1944–63	BAOR, Kenya, Malaya, WW2
PRICE, David Evan	Lt Col (*DoM*)	1987 to date	The Gulf
PRICE, Simon Anthony Carew	Maj	1970 to date	Australia, BAOR, Cyprus, Falkland Islands, The Gulf, NI
PRIOR, Douglas Christopher	Maj	1949–68	BAOR, Cyprus, Egypt, Jordan, Kenya
PRIOR, James Douglas	Lt	1985–87	BAOR, NI
PURVIS, John Robert	Lt	1957–58	
RAEBURN, *Sir* (William) Digby (Manifold)	Maj Gen	1936–70	BAOR, Norway, WW2
RAMSAY, Alexander John Patrick Maule	Maj	1968–81	BAOR, Belize, NI, Sharjah
RAMSAY, George Patrick Maule	Col	1942–67	BAOR, Egypt, Kenya, Malaya, WW2
RAMSAY, Neil Gordon	Maj	1948–58	BAOR, Egypt, Malaya

Name	Highest rank	Service	Theatre
RANKIN-HUNT, David Rankin	Lt	1979–81	NI
READMAN, Robert Anthony	Lt Col	1940–68	Belgium, Malaya, Norway, Palestine, Venezuela, WW2
REUVID, Jonathan Michael	2nd Lt	1959–60	BAOR
RHODES, Sam	Lt Col (*DoM*)	1938–59	WW2
RICE, Craig D'Arcy	Capt	1988 to date	BAOR, Belize, The Gulf, Iraq/Kuwait, NI
RITCHIE, Alastair Newton Bethune	Maj	1940–58	Malaya, Palestine, WW2
RIVETT-CARNAC, *The Rev Canon Sir* (Thomas) Nicholas, *Bt*	Maj	1945–56	BAOR, Palestine, Malaya
ROBERTS, Donald Fraser	Maj (*QM*)	*In the ranks* 1948–71 1971–82	BAOR, Belize, Egypt Malaya, Malaysia, NI
ROBERTS, Stephen John	Maj	1966–78	Australia, BAOR, NI
ROBERTS, Timothy Henry Raynes	2nd Lt	1985	Cyprus
ROBERTSON, Alastair Barry	Lt	1956–59	
ROBERTSON, Anthony Neil	Lt	1955–56	BAOR
ROMER, Malcolm Nigel	Lt Col	1936–60	Malaya, WW2
ROSE, Rhoderick Angus Campbell	Lt	1954–58	BAOR
ROSE, Simon Harvey	Capt	1965–75	BAOR, British Honduras, NI
ROSS, Antony Gordon	Brig	1962 to date	Australia, BAOR, Hong Kong, Malaysia, NI
ROSS, Thomas Bell	Capt (*QM*)	*In the ranks* 1954–74 1974–77	BAOR, Kenya, Malaysia, Malawi, Sharjah
ROSS, Walter Hugh Malcolm	Lt Col	1964–87	Aden, BAOR, Hong Kong, NI
SANDERSON, John Christopher	Capt	1955–60	BAOR
SAUNDERS, David Hugh	Maj	1959–76	Lebanon, Malaysia, Muscat
SCOTT, Gilbert Franklin James	Lt	1969–72	BAOR, British Honduras, NI
SCOTT, Michael Balfour	Lt Col	1953–78	BAOR, British Honduras, Kenya, Malaysia
SCOTT, Michael Ian Eldon	Maj Gen	1960 to date	BAOR, Cyprus, Falkland Islands, Kenya, NI, USA
SCOTT, Roderick Arthur	Capt	1978–82	BAOR, Falkland Islands, NI
SCOTT, *The Hon* Simon Peter	2nd Lt	1959–61	BAOR
SCOTT-BARRETT, *Sir* David (William)	Lt Gen	1942–79	BAOR, Berlin, Egypt, Malaya, WW2
SCOTT-BARRETT, Nicholas Huson	Capt	1971–78	BAOR, NI
SEDDON-BROWN, Jonathan Lovett	Col	1962 to date	BAOR, Cyprus, Italy, Kenya, Malaysia, Muscat, NI, Zimbabwe
SEYMOUR, Adrian John Conway	Col	1940–64	BAOR, Cyprus, Malaya, Palestine, WW2

Name	Highest rank	Service	Theatre
SHAND, Ian Russell	Lt (SSC(LE))	In the ranks 1971–91 1991–93	BAOR, Cyprus, Falkland Islands, NI
SHELLER, *The Hon Mr Justice*, Charles Simon Camac	2nd Lt	1955–56	BAOR
SHELTON-AGAR, Charles Wedderburn Shelton	Lt	1958–60	BAOR
SHUTTLEWORTH, Noel Charles	Maj	1953–63	BAOR, Canada, Kenya
SINCLAIR, Roderick John	2nd Lt	1964–66	
SMART, Michael Charles Boddington	Lt Col	1961–91	BAOR, Berlin, Holland, Italy, Kenya, NI, Norway, USA
SMELLIE, William James Buchanan	2nd Lt	1982	
SMITH, Francis	Capt (*QM*)	In the ranks 1951–71 1971–78	BAOR, Cyprus, Egypt, Kenya, NI, Sharjah
SMITH, Herbert	Maj (*QM*)	In the ranks 1920–47 1947–69	China, Egypt, WW2
SNOW, Henry Martin	Maj	1966–84	BAOR, Hong Kong, NI, Sharjah
SOLLARS, Geoffrey Peter	Capt (*SSC*)	In the ranks 1955–78 1978–83	BAOR, Kenya, NI
SPEED, Andrew Prescott	Lt	1993 to date	
SPENCER, Francis Thomas Philip	Capt	1959–65	BAOR, Kenya
SPENCER, Richard Eugène Peter	Capt	1965–75 *transferred to ALC*	BAOR, Malaysia, NI
SPICER, Timothy Simon	Lt Col	1976 to date	BAOR, Cyprus, Falkland Islands, NI
STEUART-FOTHERINGHAM, Walter Scrymgeour	Lt	1958–63	
STEWART, John Cochrane	Maj	1976 to date	BAOR, Cyprus, NI
STEWART-WILSON, *Sir* Blair (Aubyn)	Lt Col	1949–84	Austria, BAOR, Malaya, Malaysia, New Zealand
STIRLING OF KEIR, Archibald Hugh	Lt	1960–63	BAOR, Kenya
STISTED, Charles Duncan	Capt	1983–89	Belize, Cyprus
STRATHMORE & KINGHORNE, 17th *Earl* of, Fergus Michael Claude Bowes-Lyon	Capt	1949–61	BAOR, Malaya
STRATHMORE & KINGHORNE, 18th *Earl* of, (*formerly* LORD GLAMIS) Michael Fergus Bowes-Lyon	Capt	1980–84	Hong Kong, NI
STREET, Rupert Henry de Sinner	Lt	1989–92	BAOR, NI
STUART, Charles Andrew	Maj	1986 to date	BAOR, The Gulf, NI
STUART, James Douglas	Maj	1981 to date	BAOR, Falkland Islands, NI
STUART, William	Capt (*SSC*)	In the ranks 1960–79 1979–83	BAOR, Hong Kong, NI

Name	Highest rank	Service	Theatre
SWALLOW, Charles John	Lt	1957–59	
SWINTON, *Sir* John	Maj Gen	1944–79	Australia, BAOR, Cyprus, Malaya, WW2
SWINTON, William Henry Cospatrick	Capt	1985 to date	Cyprus, NI
TAYLOR, Giles Alick Parry	Capt	*transferred from R HAMPS* 1991 to date	NI
TENNANT, Mark Edward	Capt	1966–73	BAOR, Berlin, NI, Sharjah
TETLEY, Alexander	Capt	1987 to date	BAOR, Belize, Cambodia, NI
THOMPSON, David Howard	Maj	1985 to date	BAOR, The Gulf, NI
THOMSON, Robert Hair	Lt Col (*QM*)	*In the ranks 1938–56* 1956–70	BAOR, Egypt, Palestine, WW2
THOMSON, William Bennet	Capt	1952–59	BAOR, Egypt
THORNHILL, Simon	Maj	*transferred from WG* 1983 to date	Belize, Cyprus, NI
THOROLD, Michael Bernard	2nd Lt	1962–64	Kenya
TIARKS, Mark Gerhard Phipps	2nd Lt	1978–80	BAOR
TILLOTSON, Ronald	Capt (*QM*)	*In the ranks 1938–56* 1956–65	BAOR, Kenya, Malaya, WW2
TIMPSON, Nicholas George Lawrence	Lt	1960–63	Kenya
TRAPPES-LOMAX, David Edward	Maj	1950–63	Aden, Egypt, Malaya, Muscat
TREADWELL, John Gerald	Capt	1972–80	NI
TREVASKIS, Jeremy Hugh Kennedy	Capt	1969–79	NI, Belize, Muscat
TRIMBLE, David William	Lt	1958–60	
TURNER, Mark Nicholas Down	Maj	1979 to date	BAOR, The Gulf, Hong Kong, NI
TURNER, Philip Ronald William	Capt	1988 to date	NI
TURNER, Simon John Edward	Maj	1955–67	Cyprus, Malaysia
USHER, Robert	Capt	1977–83	BAOR, Hong Kong, NI
VAIL, Paul Dominic	Capt	1982–87	Hong Kong, NI
VARNEY, Guy Nicholas Buckingham	Capt	1985–88	Cyprus, NI
VARNEY, Mark Lindesay Buckingham	Maj	1979–88	BAOR, Cyprus, NI, Zimbabwe
VARNEY, Owen Buckingham	Capt	1951–57	Egypt
VEITCH, Barry	Maj (*QM*)	*In the ranks 1962–83* 1983 to date	BAOR, Cyprus, Lesotho, Malaysia, NI
VESTEY, *The Hon* Mark William	2nd Lt	1962–65	Kenya
VESTEY, *Lord*, Samuel George	Lt	1960–63	BAOR, Kenya
WALKER, Raymond	Capt (*SSC*)	*In the ranks 1966–91* 1991 to date	BAOR, Belize, The Gulf, Hong Kong, NI, Sharjah

Name	Highest rank	Service	Theatre
WALLACE, James George Chisholm	Capt	1974–81	BAOR, NI
WALLACE, Robert Ben Lobban	Lt	1991 to date	BAOR, NI
WALTER, David Finlayson Wylie-Hill	Maj	1954–64	BAOR, Egypt, Kenya
WARNER, Courtenay Forbes	Lt	1959–60	BAOR
WARREN, Jeremy Frederick	Maj	1963–87	BAOR, Hong Kong, Malaysia, NI
WATTS, Samuel Roy	Maj (*QM*)	*In the ranks 1930–53* 1953–65	BAOR, Cyprus, Egypt, WW2
WEBB, Michael Hinton	Lt Col	*Former service in South African Army* 1951–63	Egypt
WELD-FORESTER, Anthony Edward	Lt	1976–77	
WELSH, Mark Alexander Lindsay	Lt	1963–66	Kenya
WENCK, Paul Francis Peter	Maj	1987 to date	Belize, Cambodia, Iraq/Kuwait, NI
WHITELEY, John Robert Lee	Maj	1955–69	BAOR, Cyprus, Malaysia, USA
WHITELEY, Michael Geoffrey Lee	Lt Col	1961 to date	BAOR, Hong Kong, Kenya, Malaysia, Muscat, NI, Sharjah
WHYTE, Donald McNab	Maj (*QM*)	*In the ranks 1937–57* 1957–72	BAOR, Kenya, Malaya, WW2
WHYTE, Robin Edward	Maj	1970–80 1983 to date	BAOR, Cyprus, NI
WILBUR, William	Maj (*QM*)	*In the ranks 1939–59* 1959–69	BAOR, Malaya, Malaysia, WW2
WILKIE, Ronald John	Capt (*QM*)	*In the ranks 1963–81* 1981–87	BAOR, Cyprus, NI, Malaysia, Sharjah, Uganda
WILMOT, *Sir* Robert (Arthur), *Bt*	Capt	1958–66	BAOR
WILSON, Anthony Richard	Maj	1969–78	BAOR, NI, Sharjah
WILSON, David Charles Ashley	Capt	1984–89	
WOOD, Donald Joseph	Capt (*SSC(LE)*)	*In the ranks 1971–92* 1992 to date	BAOR, Belize, Cyprus, NI, Zimbabwe
WOODS, Edward Anthony	Maj	1968 to date	BAOR, Hong Kong, Muscat, NI, Sharjah
YOUNG, Norman Alan	Capt (*SSC*)	*In the ranks 1965–87* 1987 to date	BAOR, Belize, The Gulf, Hong Kong, NI
YOUNGER, Alexander William	Capt	1987–90	BAOR, NI

APPENDIX G

GENERAL OFFICERS OF THE REGIMENT 1956–1993

Major General Sir John **ACLAND**,
KCB CBE DL

GOC South West District
1978–81
Commander Commonwealth Monitoring Force,
Rhodesia, and Military Adviser to the
Governor
1979–80

Major General Sir Christopher **AIRY**,
KCVO CBE

Senior Army Member, Royal College of
Defence Studies
1984–85
GOC London District and Major General
Commanding The Household Division
1986–89

Major General T.A. **BOAM**, CB CBE

Head of British Defence Staff Washington and
Defence Attaché
1981–84
Commander British Forces Hong Kong and
Major General Brigade of Gurkhas
1985–87

Lieutenant General The Hon Sir
Thomas **BOYD-CARPENTER**,
KBE

Chief of Staff HQ BAOR
1988–89
Assistant Chief of the Defence Staff
(Programmes)
1990–92
Deputy Chief of the Defence Staff (Policy and
Personnel)
1992 to date

Major General Earl **CATHCART**, CB
DSO MC

GOC Yorkshire District
1969–70
GOC Berlin (British Sector)
1970–73

Major General C.I.H. **DUNBAR**, CB CBE DSO DL	GOC North West District 1959–62 GOC Berlin (British Sector) 1962
Lieutenant General V.F. **ERSKINE CRUM**, CIE MC	Commander 4th Division 1967–69 Chief Army Instructor, Imperial Defence College 1969–70 GOC and Director of Operations Northern Ireland 1971
Major General Lord Michael **FITZALAN HOWARD**, GCVO CB CBE MC	Commander Allied Command Europe Mobile Force (Land) 1964–66 Chief of Staff Southern Command 1967–68 GOC London District and Major General Commanding The Household Division 1968–71
Field Marshal His Royal Highness The **DUKE OF GLOUCESTER**, KG KT KP GCB GCMG GCVO	25th Colonel 1937–74
General Sir Michael **GOW**, GCB DL	GOC 4th Armoured Division 1973–75 Director Army Training 1975–78 GOC Scotland 1979–80 C in C BAOR and Commander Northern Army Group 1980–83 Commandant Royal College of Defence Studies 1984–86
Major General Sir George **JOHNSON**, KCVO CB CBE DSO	GOC London District and Major General Commanding The Household Division 1953–57
Field Marshal His Royal Highness The **DUKE OF KENT**, KG GCMG GCVO ADC(P)	26th Colonel 1974 to date

General Sir Peter **LENG**, GCB MBE MC (transferred to The Royal Anglian Regiment 1964)	Commander Land Forces Northern Ireland 1973–75 Director of Military Operations 1975–78 Commander 1st (British) Corps 1978–80 Master-General of the Ordnance 1981–83
Major General I.C. **MACKAY-DICK**, MBE	Commander 1st Armoured Division/Lower Saxony District 1992–93 Commander British Forces Falkland Islands 1993 to date
Major General D.M. **NAYLOR**, CB MBE DL	GOC North East District and Commander 2nd Infantry Division 1987–89 Director General Territorial Army and Organization 1989–92
Major General Sir Digby **RAEBURN**, KCVO CB DSO MBE	Director of Combat Development (Army) 1963–65 Chief of Staff Allied Forces Northern Europe 1965–68 Chief Army Instructor, Imperial Defence College 1968–70
Major General M.I.E. **SCOTT**, CBE DSO	GOC Scotland 1993 to date
Lieutenant General Sir David **SCOTT-BARRETT**, KBE MC	GOC Eastern District 1971–73 GOC Berlin (British Sector) 1973–75 GOC Scotland 1976–79
Major General Sir John **SWINTON**, KCVO OBE JP DL	GOC London District and Major General Commanding The Household Division 1976–79

Note. This appendix includes all senior officer appointments up the end of 1993. However, it is appropriate to record that in 1994 Major General I. C. Mackay-Dick was appointed to be GOC London District and Major General Commanding The Household Division, while in the same year Brigadier A. de C. L. Leask was promoted to the rank of major general and appointed Commander Land Forces Northern Island. It is also appropriate to record that in the autumn of 1994 Lieutenant Colonel A. J. Miller-Bakewell, The Blues and Royals, assumed command of the 1st Battalion vice Lieutenant Colonel T. M. Fitzalan Howard.

INDEX

Notes:
1. Ranks shown are the highest known to have been achieved by an individual.
2. Only those people whose names appear in the main text, and at Appendix A, are included here.
3. Infantry battalions are indexed in the form: Scots Guards, 1st Battalion, etc.; for cavalry regiments, see under Royal Armoured Corps.

280

281

282

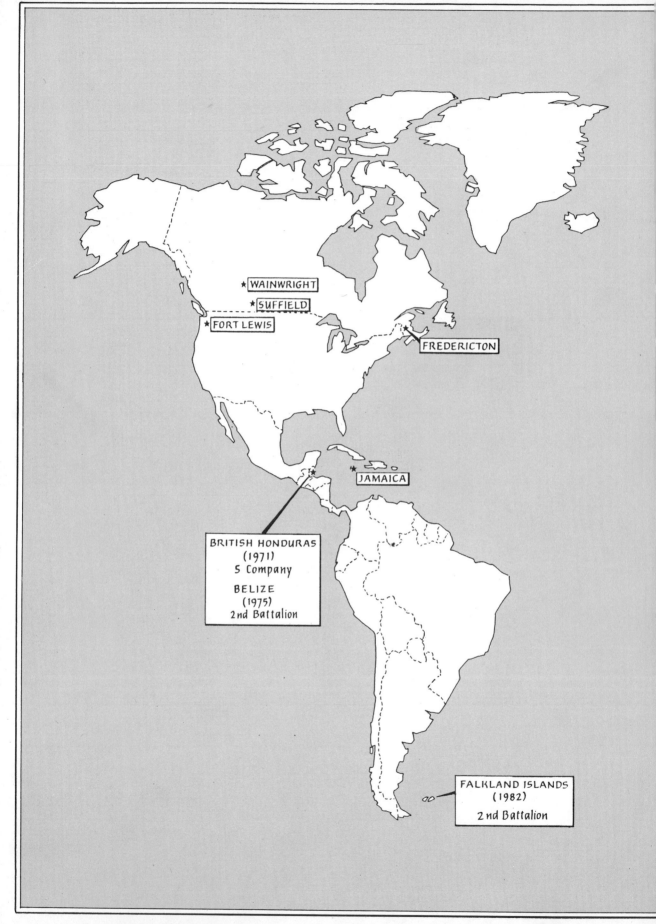